LIBRARY OF INTERNATIONAL STUDIES
VOLUME I

Revisionism

Revisionism

ESSAYS ON THE HISTORY
OF MARXIST IDEAS

EDITED BY LEOPOLD LABEDZ

FREDERICK A. PRAEGER, *Publisher*
NEW YORK

BOOKS THAT MATTER

FIRST PUBLISHED IN 1962

This book is copyright under the Berne Conven-
tion. Apart from any fair dealing for the purposes
of private study, research, criticism, or review, as
permitted under the Copyright Act, 1956, no por-
tion may be reproduced by any process without
written permission. Enquiries should be addressed
to the publisher.

Published in the United States of America in
1962 by Frederick A. Praeger Inc., Publisher,
64 University Place, New York 3, NY.

All rights reserved
© *George Allen & Unwin Ltd, 1962*

Library of Congress Catalog Card Number: 62-8394

This book is Number 102 in the series of
Praeger Publications in Russian History and World Communism

Published under the auspices of
the Congress for Cultural Freedom

PRINTED IN GREAT BRITAIN
in 10 point Times Roman type
BY SIMSON SHAND LTD
LONDON, HERTFORD AND HARLOW

CONTENTS

PART THREE: THE NEW REVISIONISM

PART FOUR: THE NEW LEFT

INTRODUCTION

It should be easy to define revisionism. It began with Eduard Bernstein's independent attempt to re-examine some of the original Marxian tenets, and the term should be used for subsequent efforts of this kind. Actually, the problem is rather more complex, and the use and abuse of the term has a long and involved history. In our own time it is applied not only to social-democratic reformists, or to disillusioned young communists, but also to leaders of the Communist establishment. Marshal Tito is officially branded a 'modern revisionist' in the Sino-Soviet bloc, the word is applied to Premier Khrushchev by the Albanian Communists, while Chairman Mao is esoterically referred to in Moscow as a 'revisionist dogmatist'.

We seem to have reached a point when Marx's spiritual heirs, legitimate or otherwise, can truly say: 'We are all revisionists now.'

This would be vehemently denied by each of the various guardians of orthodoxy, each seeing his own as the only true interpretation, while it is those who deviate from it who are the revisionists. Clearly, revisionism is to Marxist movements what heresy is to religious ones. Ideas which set into a canon sooner or later require revision. When revision comes from above, one dogma replaces another. It is then called 'a creative development of Marxism'. When it comes from independent thinkers, it is considered heresy. Heresy is the shadow of every orthodoxy, and Marxism is no exception.

The essays in this volume have been arranged with this perspective in mind.

Marxian Marxism was not only an ideology postulating change but a theory with scientific claims ('scientific socialism'), predicting future economic, social, and political developments, so it was inevitable that its forecasts should eventually be confronted with the actual course of events, which differed from the expectations universally held by Marxists on the basis of the theory. The first thing they had to discard was the belief that the proletarian revolution would occur in the economically developed countries. Originally it was axiomatic that, as Engels expressed it, 'anyone who says that a socialist revolution can be carried out in a country which has no proletariat or bourgeoisie proves by this statement that he has still to learn the ABC of socialism.' With the advantages of hindsight we know that the historical perspective envisaged in the Communist Manifesto was wrong: one hundred years later the 'proletarians' of the West have more to lose than their chains and it was Mao's peasant armies that were blazing the revolutionary trail to 'socialism'. All this hardly fitted Marx's anticipation in the celebrated passage from *Das Kapital*: 'Centralization of the means of production, and socialization of labour, at last reach such a point where they become incompatible with their capitalist integument. This integument is burst asunder. The knell of capitalist private property sounds. The expropriators are expropriated.' And from the country which served Marx as a model for his prophecy came a sad exclamation made by the general secretary of the British Communist Party, John Gollan, in the Political Report he gave at its 27th National Congress: 'Is Britain, the first country of the Industrial Revolution, to be the last in the social revolution?' Nothing could be further from Marx's own vision than such contemporary Communist declarations, coming as they do from countries representing the wrong extremes of the 'conditions of production' spectrum.

But even though the actual developments did not bear out Marxian predictions, the discrepancy between theory and reality could do only limited harm to Marxist ideology. On the logical plane its conception of a dialectical relation between theory and practice could (and later did) serve to rationalize the modifications of the theory. On the psychological plane, millenarist aspirations were more important for revolutionary ideology than any amount of rational analysis of social realities. However, when Bernstein began to have his doubts ('Peasants do not sink; the middle class does not disappear; crises do not grow ever larger; misery and serfdom do not increase') and inaugurated the Great Debate in the socialist movement, the original theory was still relevant to the political thinking of Marxists. They were still taking it seriously *qua* theory and not just as a liturgy and although it was already well on its way to petrifaction, it had not yet quite congealed into an institutional dogma. This came only later, when revolutionary Marxists took power in a country where, according to their own premises, they could not and should not do so.

Marx was unquestionably a social analyst of genius; but although his own favourite maxim was *de omnibus dubitandum* he left his followers an ambiguous legacy. He rejected their tendency to turn his teachings into scripture ('Ce qu'il y a de certain, c'est que moi je ne suis pas Marxiste'), but his authoritarian attitude to theory, his intolerance of opinions other than his own, and his reluctance to change them in the light of evidence, were not a model of what we now regard as the scientific approach. The normal scientific procedure is to keep open the possibility of a theory being wrong, and in this sense all scientific theories have a hypothetical character subject to revision in the light of evidence. Scientists are thus revisionists in principle. But such an attitude, which is a norm for a genuine scientist, was incompatible not only with Marxist historical teleology, but—what is more important—with its revolutionary eschatology in which the chiliastic element had a far stronger appeal to his followers than any theoretical reasoning. This was the real obstacle to an openly revisionist attitude towards Marxian theory. It is not surprising that a chiliastic ideology should tend to become an orthodoxy, or that, in a scientific age, it should wear scientific garb. It was not very likely that a scientific theory would 'seize the masses' to become a 'material force'; masses are not moved by scientific arguments.

However, whether as a theory or as an established orthodoxy, the doctrine had to maintain contact with reality, if only for reasons of political efficacy. The theoretical modifications required could take different forms, but whatever their character, open or concealed, they represent a continuous process in which the doctrine encounters changes it failed to anticipate and tries to adjust itself to them. The process of adjustment is neither smooth nor inevitable. It may be directed 'from above', but hampered by the petrifaction of orthodoxy; it may be demanded from below, but then those who press for it may easily transcend the framework of the doctrine. Those who were ready to acknowledge the non-revolutionary character of highly industrialized societies were in fact moving towards the abandonment of its theoretical premises. Those who wanted to preserve the revolutionary mainsprings of their ideology had to invert the original doctrine and look for new pastures in non-industrial societies.

Whether the revisions are concerned with the ends or the means, with the rationality of purpose or the technology of power, whether their inspiration is humanist or autocratic, in all cases they must lead to important changes not only in the theoretical assumptions of the original Marxian *Weltanschauung*, but in its historical and philosophical perspective as well. The revolutionary character of our epoch stems from the impact of the industrial West on the economically backward countries, rather than from the capitalist fetters clamped on the productive forces in economically advanced states. Revolutionary attitudes were not connected in any obvious causal way with the Marxian conflict between the forces of production and conditions of production. On the contrary, they were mainly found in countries where the forces of production were weak and capitalist relations undeveloped. In short, the revolutionary process resulted from the *absence* of the Marxian capitalist conditions required for the socialist revolution, rather than from their development. This fact, paradoxical from the Marxian premises, underlined the subsequent dilemmas: in the industrialized capitalist countries socialists could not remain revolutionary without being politically ineffective, and in the non-industrialized countries revolutionaries could not remain socialist in the original nineteenth century meaning of the term. In both cases revision of the doctrine was inevitable; the division of Marxism into 'orthodox' and 'revisionist' only tended to conceal the fact that its premises had ceased to be relevant for either.

Thus, revisionism appeared on the historical scene when the old orthodoxy was no longer feasible; strictly speaking, all Marxists have been revising the fundamentals of the doctrine ever since. In this sense, the Bernstein controversy is a watershed between the Marxian and the Marxist phases of the doctrine[1] and the Marxist phase was of necessity revisionist vis-à-vis the Marxian phase. But this meaning of the term 'revisionism' is not, of course, the one generally in use. It is the more restricted meaning of the term which has gained universal acceptance. This refers to attempts to 'rethink' the Marxian doctrine independently of its official guardians. In historical terms the distinction is perfectly clear; there were two major outbursts of open revisionism: the socialist one before the first world war and the communist one after the second. But in terms of the history of ideas the distinction is by no means so unambiguous. Revisionism might be frontally defeated but creep in through the back door, and the 'orthodox' Marxists also contributed to the development of 'revisionist' ideas. Therefore a simple contrast between straightforward revisionism, with openly declared aims, and the theoretical rationalizations of the orthodoxy, does not give an adequate picture of the complex problem of the revision of Marxian ideas and the evolution of Marxism. Nor can the writings of all the 'orthodox' Marxists be dismissed as mere ideological rationalizations. Some of them, while 'standing Marx on his head' were more than scholastic sophistries, and have provided insights into the problems of our time. This applies of course only to those Marxists who were ready to think for themselves and not to the 'ideological function-aries'. It is surprising how many ideas of the former were eventually incorporated into the ruling orthodoxy (while their authors were as a rule branded as heretics).

Identifying the origin of ideas is an extremely difficult, if not impossible task, but it is possible to trace their chronological filiation. Seen from this angle, some of the most important instances of the 'creative development of Marxism' were cases of adoption. The historian of ideas cannot fail to detect that Lenin's notion of the 'vanguard' and his organizational principles of the party were formulated in a strikingly similar form by Ogarev and Tkachev long before the appearance of *What Is To Be Done*, that it was Helphand-Parvus who was the first to propose a 'proletarian' dictatorship in economically undeveloped Russia, an idea boldly taken over by Trotsky in his 'permanent revolution', and, with some (Marxist) inhibitions, by Lenin in his 'uninterrupted revolution';[2] that the

[1] This distinction, introduced by Mr M. Rubel, refers to Marx's own views and those of his followers.

[2] When Trotsky called for a proletarian dictatorship as an immediate aim of Russian social democracy in a revolutionary situation, Lenin retorted sharply: 'That cannot be! It cannot be because a revolutionary dictatorship can endure for a time only if it rests on the enormous majority of the people.' At the time Lenin opposed Trotsky's idea and wrote: 'Anyone who attempts to achieve socialism by any other route without passing through the stage of political

notion of 'imperialism' as 'the higher stage of capitalism' was in fact put forward by Hobson, Hilferding and Rosa Luxemburg before Lenin; that it was Bukharin who elaborated the theory of 'socialism in one country', while it was Stalin who established it as official doctrine; that Sultan Galiev[3] and Manabendra Nath Roy were Mao's predecessors in formulating ideas on the colonial revolution. Whatever modifications these ideas may have undergone in becoming part and parcel of the new orthodoxies, there is little doubt that they should be attributed to earlier thinkers rather than to those to whom they are usually credited.

These differences can be seen clearly in the first part of the present symposium, which is devoted to an area of Marxist thought in which the problem of revision was particularly acute, i.e. the theory of revolution. In *Revolution Revised* a number of Marxist thinkers who grappled with this problem are revisited and their ideas analysed in their relation to the orthodoxy and their contemporary relevance. Although branded as heretics, there can be little doubt about their belonging to the Marxist tradition. Their contribution to its revision has been more often abused than acknowledged and is now officially forgotten in the Communist countries; nevertheless, their work deserves to be remembered, and its study may help to understand the vicissitudes of revolutionary theory in the twentieth century.

Like revisionism itself, the idea of revolution is by now far from unambiguous. In the nineteenth century, when Marx was using the word, it had clear connotations: it recalled the images of the barricades, of the movement of the people against authority, leading to a change in the established order. The French revolution was the

democracy, will inevitably arrive at the most absurd and reactionary conclusions, both economic and political' (Lenin, *Sochineniya*, Moscow, 1947, Vol. 9, p. 14). Later, Lenin developed his own scheme of 'uninterrupted revolution'. The official Stalinist exegesis made great play with the differences between the two, but the historian of ideas (as well as the practical politician) finds these differences scholastically exaggerated. The theoretical difference between the two notions was that Lenin postulated 'a democratic stage of the dictatorship of workers and peasants' before 'a socialist phase of proletarian dictatorship'. This fine distinction turned out to be of no practical relevance to Lenin after his April 1917 Theses. On the other hand, a careful comparison between the Parvus idea of a 'telescoped' revolution, whether in its Trotskyist or Leninist form, and Marx's own ideas on the subject expressed in his *Address to the League of Communists* (1850), shows a number of important differences, although they reflected Marx's own revolutionary impatience. After the failure of his 1848 hopes he still rationalized his belief in the imminence of the socialist revolution. Only a decade later did he provide a different timetable for it: 'No social order ever perishes before all the productive forces for which there is room in it have developed' (Introduction to the *Critique of Political Economy*). The young Marx provides the main source of quotations for revolutionary and philosophical revisionists, the old Engels for both the reformist social democrats and the orthodox Party philosophers.

[3] Cf. Alexandre Benningsen et Chantal Quelquejay, *Les mouvements nationaux chez les Musulmans de Russie*, La Haye, Mouton & Cie., 1960.

accepted model of a social revolution, and 1917 seemed to confirm the image. In fact the part played by the Bolsheviks in this revolution was their first step towards the modification of the nineteenth century concept of revolution, which until then and for some time thereafter still served them as a prototype for action. There were many reasons to discard this prototype. One was obvious and often mentioned— the development of weapons; but no less important was the evolution of new techniques for the conquest of power by a Party of 'the new type'. Thus not only was the nineteenth century image of the revolution discarded, the concept itself acquired a new meaning in the Communist vocabulary. It came to signify the conquest of power by the Party. It was not just a question of muskets and machine-guns, of the symbolic painting by Delacroix becoming obsolete through technological developments. It was in the first place the result of the Leninist organizational principle: the revolution ceased to be necessarily a mass movement from below to overthrow the oppressors, and became an organized operation in which the spontaneity of social action was no longer regarded as a necessary condition of social change. Lenin himself was suspicious of spontaneity (*stikhiya*), but he still shared the old vision of revolution as an elemental upheaval, which should be used tactically but which could not be imposed from above. He shared the nineteenth century revolutionary outlook hypostasizing the revolution; he visualized it as smashing the old order and its state machinery and replacing it by new unsullied forces released through the revolution. Hence, for instance, his abhorrence of the idea of participation in 'bourgeois governments' ('Millerandism') which he regarded as treason to revolution, a sentiment quite general at the time among revolutionaries. They looked upon the revolution not just as a social phenomenon, one among many mechanisms of social change, but as a symbol of hope, the gate opening to the millenium; compromise with the forces of the old order was taboo, there could be no dealings with the representatives of Evil.

After the Revolution the experience gained in the struggle for power brought some modifications of this attitude. The eschatology still remained, but far greater tactical flexibility was admitted in the methods of gaining power. The word revolution was now used to designate a most variegated set of practices. The symbol replaced reality. The Yugoslav Communists gained power by organizing guerrilla warfare, as did the Chinese Communists. Both refer to the revolution in their countries. Rumanian Communists also speak about the revolution in their country, which allegedly took place after the war. What happened was that Vyshinski, while Soviet troops occupied the country, slammed the door in the royal palace and forced the king to hand over authority to the 900 members of the Rumanian Communist party. And there were no revolutionary movements in the other countries of Eastern Europe at that time; the new order was organized by leaders imported, as Tito said, with pipes in their mouths, in Soviet planes. Everywhere there was radical political and social change, with regimes imposed by the Soviet Army bringing about revolutionary consequences without a revolution. The Stalinist 'revolution from above' was exported and imposed from outside. Another variant of the conquest of power was seen in Czechoslovakia in February 1948, where the Party achieved its goal by combined pressure from below and from above.[4] Joining the bourgeois government—Lenin's hated 'Millerandism'— had by then become an accepted method of subversion from inside ('pressure from above'). Its chances of success depended of course on the outside relation of forces, there is little doubt however that the evolution of Communist revolutionary theory after the second world war and the proclamation of the possibility of the so-called peaceful transition to socialism are connected with the greater tactical flexibility required in the conditions of a new balance of power.

The undeveloped countries have become the main breeding ground for the extension of Communist influence. This necessarily involved an ever more radical revision of revolutionary theory. That old prerequisite of socialist revolution, the degree of development of the productive forces, was discarded long ago. In undeveloped countries it was by definition non-existent. But revolutionary attitudes in these countries could be used in the struggle for power. The revision of the theory was therefore mainly concerned with tactical questions: the relation to the 'national bourgeoisie' and intelligentsia, to the nationalist movements and governments in the new states. However, such 'creative developments of Marxism' are becoming more and more esoteric and the new theories less and less explicit.[5]

It was not accidental that in the history of Marxist thought it was the active politicians who devoted most thought to the theory of revolution, trying to relate the original Marxian scheme to actual social conditions, and either discarding it as Bernstein did, or re-thinking it to take them into account in the undeveloped countries. The future historian may well conclude that both the reformists in

---

[4] The method is frankly described and its universal lessons for Communists elsewhere drawn by Jan Kozak in *How Parliament can play a revolutionary part in the transition to socialism and the role of the popular masses*, published in English translation in London (1961) with an introduction by Lord Morrison of Lambeth. Kozak concludes that the 'Czech experience has shown that the specific form of transition in no way affected the results of the socialist revolution, the dictatorship of the proletariat.'

[5] For a discussion on the concept of 'popular democracy' see H. Gordon Skilling, 'People's Democracy and the Socialist Revolution', *Soviet Studies*, January–April, 1961. There is as yet very little open discussion on the new concept of 'national democracy', a transitional stage in undeveloped countries.

the economically advanced areas and the revolutionaries in the backward ones threw some light on the processes of social change.
Western sociologists in particular, with their neglect of the problem
of revolution, might gain from devoting more attention not only to
the problem itself (which is unusually remote from the empirical
Anglo-Saxon tradition) but also to the study of these forgotten
Marxist thinkers, who, for all their doctrinal blinkers, often dealt
with real problems and were sometimes brilliantly perceptive about
them. Revolutions, like accidents, do not happen; they are caused.
More often than not they come as a result either of neglected reforms
or of reforms applied too late. There can be little doubt that the
'marginal men' of the revolutionary intelligentsia, the 'armed
intellectuals', had as a rule far better understanding of the revolutionary situation than the Western analysts.

However, the same revolutionary intellectuals who were devoting
their intellect to the revolution had eventually to pay the price for
the independence of their thought. Sooner or later, they were dismissed as heretics. They were caught on the horns of a dilemma:
either they had to cease to be intellectuals or they ended by being
disarmed. Trotsky, the 'unarmed prophet', is only one example
among many. The idea that the philosopher's task is not merely to
interpret the world but to change it is easier to state than to apply.
Kings are rarely good philosophers and philosophers are rarely
successful Party secretaries. What appears as *junctim* in the *Theses on
Feuerbach* leads in the modern world of the division of labour straight
into what Werner Sombart called *Die Zwei-Seelen-Theorie*, i.e. the
clash at the personal level between revolutionary zeal and the
demands of analytical detachment. The politicians, concerned with
revolutionary theory, were crushed by those divergent demands as
much as the less active philosophers who devoted their intellectual
abilities to the analysis of more fundamental aspects of Marxian
theory.

Of these problems the questions of truth and alienation, of
freedom and social change, of personality and history, are among the
most prominent. They also raised most doubts among those Marxists
who indulged in independent thinking and consequently generated
most revisionist heat in the philosophical discussions which have
taken place among Marxist philosophers.

The second part of the symposium, *Personality, Truth and History*,
is devoted to these problems and to the Marxist philosophers who
were most outstanding in examining them. Preoccupation with such
problems was in itself sufficient to qualify them as revisionists, even
though in some cases, such as Lukacs's for instance, there was a
consistent endeavour throughout his career to remain on the side of
orthodoxy. The philosophical revisionists are mainly preoccupied
with ontological problems, which in the post-war context gives them

an existentialist tinge, although their terminology is quite different from that of Heidegger or Sartre. Both Bloch and Kolakowski arrive at this position from quite different starting points. The ethical questions of individual responsibility inevitably lead some revisionists towards a neo-Kantian position, while their preference for the young Marx's philosophical themes sends them on a neo-Hegelian trail. In the epistemological field, as can be seen from the Kolakowski essay, Aristotle and Spinoza have a greater influence than Lenin's *Materialism and Empiriocriticism*.

There is no one label which can be used to pinpoint the revisionist philosophers' position. In fact they represent manifold philosophical tendencies and their eclecticism is a rather healthy reaction against monolithic philosophical system-building. In general, they are not too positivistically inclined, which is also a reaction against the naïve positivism of the nineteenth century underlying much of Marxist 'scientism' and its crude exposition by Engels. This does not apply of course to such 'forgotten philosophers' as Bogdanov and Deborin, who do not show a similar tendency in their independent philosophical endeavours. In fact, Bogdanov had an opposite purpose: to establish a Marxist philosophy on a positivistic basis, and to bring it more into line with the scientific developments of the twentieth century. But it stops short of Engels's replacement of philosophy by positive knowledge. Deborin, with his insistence on Hegelian dialectics tended in the opposite direction, of subordinating science to philosophy. Both[6] tried to emphasize different aspects of the Marxist heritage: one in order to stress the autonomy of science, the other—that of philosophy. But these (conflicting) endeavours clashed with the purposes of the Party, which aimed at subordinating both science and philosophy to its control rather than giving them an independent position. It is interesting, however, to notice the hidden influence of these philosophers in the subsequent evolution of Marxist doctrine. One can easily trace some of the ideas which later were incorporated into the orthodoxy to the writings of these philosophers (without of course any acknowledgement of the source). There is a striking parallel here to the influence on the development of revolutionary theory of such heretics as Trotsky and Bukharin. The heretics go, but some of their ideas remain.

In contrast to these philosophers, the motivation of the modern Communist revisionists is incomparably more libertarian in character. The roots of their opinions are neither in German teleology, nor in the Russian *Shigalevshchina*, but in another tradition which leads to revolt against both. Within the framework of the Marxist tradition it is found in such revisionist formulations as Rosa Luxemburg's 'Freedom only for the supporters of the government, only for the

[6] On the subject cf. also David Joravsky, *Soviet Marxism and Natural Science*, Routledge and Kegan Paul, London, 1961.

members of one party—however numerous they may be—that is not freedom. Freedom is always freedom for the man who thinks differently'; or in Djilas, writing in *Borba* in 1953 that 'Every restriction of freedom of thought or opinion, even if made for the sake of the most splendid ideology, must inevitably lead to the corruption of those responsible for it'; or in Kolakowski, asserting in *Nowa Kultura*: 'No one is exempt from the moral duty to fight against a system of government, a doctrine, or social conditions which he considers vile and inhuman, by resorting to the argument that he finds them historically necessary.' Such revisionist sentiments are a direct challenge to any autocracy. It is not surprising that the outburst of such sentiments which culminated in the events of 1956 was treated as such by the guardians of orthodoxy, the autocratic rulers of the Communist states. The campaign against revisionism, this time appearing inside the Communist movement, revealed a great deal about the evolution of Communist ideology.

The New Revisionism, the third part of the symposium, deals with the origins and significance of East European revisionism, as it emerged between the thaw after Stalin's death and its suppression in 1957. It tries to put this phenomenon into historical perspective, as well as to locate its place in the history of Marxist ideas.

A Western sympathizer described the task of 'modern revisionism' as 'the re-establishment of contact between theory and practice, the abandonment of myths for reality, and an open analysis of the contradictions within the collectivist system, instead of their concealment.'[7] The Soviet *Philosophical Encyclopedia* (Vol. I, p. 415) put it quite differently of course: 'The revisionists turned to the early writings of Marx, selecting from them isolated pre-Marxist statements borrowed from the German philosophical schools which were one of the sources of Marxism.' And according to the Soviet *Political Dictionary*, revisionism is 'a trend in the working class movement that, for the benefit of the bourgeoisie, wants to debase, to emasculate, to destroy Marxism by means of a revision, i.e. by way of re-examination, distortion, and negation of its basic tenets.' Until the emergence of revisionism in the Soviet bloc itself, the official Soviet view was that it had been utterly routed half a century before by Lenin and others. It was therefore a matter of some surprise that so many years after this decisive defeat the struggle against revisionism suddenly had once again become a central theme in Soviet political literature, and the magazine *Moskva* (No. 1, 1958) even declared: 'Either we destroy Revisionism or Revisionism will destroy us; there is no third way.'

Another Soviet spokesman wrote:[8]

---

[7] François Fejtö, *Etudes*, Paris, January 1960.

[8] F. Ya. Polyanski, in *Kritika Ekonomicheskikh Teorii Predshestvennikov Sovremennovo Revizionizma*, Moscow, 1960, p. 61.

'Contemporary revisionists, using the "theoretical baggage" of their predecessors, change only some of their dogmas and supplement them with a new phraseology. It is precisely for this reason that the unmasking of the predecessors of contemporary revisionism is an important task in the struggle against the new-fangled "critics" of Marxism-Leninism, its theory and practice. The position of the revisionists on the fundamental questions of the Marxist revolutionary movement, its philosophy, political economy, and also its practical activity, is hostile to the unity of the world revolutionary movement and shows convincingly that revisionists are the agents of imperialism in the workers' movement.'

An entire library of anti-revisionist books has been sponsored by a leading Moscow publishing house (Sotsekgiz), and practically every issue of the 'ideological' magazines in 1958/59 contained at least one article against what the Moscow conference of Communist bloc leaders (in November 1957) defined as the 'main danger'. Stranger still, the polemics were by no means directed mainly against Democratic Socialism, the Communists' traditional rival in the working-class movement; they were aimed primarily at individuals, and entire sections, of the Communist movement in both East and West.

According to the traditional Marxist-Leninist explanation, revisionism appeared on the scene as the ideology of the labour aristocracy, and of petty-bourgeois elements that had penetrated the labour movement in a period of relative economic prosperity. But this reasoning could not hold water in present conditions, for it was difficult to argue that countries such as Yugoslavia, Poland, or Hungary went through an era of prosperity in the middle fifties, or that the revisionist leaders there acted on behalf of a bourgeoisie that no longer existed. New explanations and new arguments were needed to combat the new deviation; it was not sufficient merely to declare that the heretics had strayed from Marxist-Leninist orthodoxy; this, by now, was common knowledge and did not cut much ice. For even the orthodox Leninists have had to re-examine Marxism in the light of the exigencies of the middle twentieth century, to make adjustments and revisions. Kautsky and Plekhanov were in an easier position when they criticized Bernstein around 1900; the socialist parties then were still everywhere in opposition, the general political situation had not basically changed since Marx's and Engels's deaths. To most, if not all questions of the day, there was an answer in the scriptures. But Communism in power in 1956 was in a very different position; it was not easy to find in Marx's writings support and encouragement for the establishment of a totalitarian state, for the recurrent purges that wiped out, inter alia, most Communist leaders. This was explained (until Stalin's death) as the creative continuation and development of Marxism. After the twentieth CPSU congress it was partly disparaged as a distortion ('dogmatism') of Marxism-Leninism. But, in contrast to revisionism, it was regarded as a venial sin, for it was believed to have a transient character which did not affect the basic tenets of the creed.

The growing preoccupation with revisionism revived interest in the historical revisionist debate. Unfortunately, these new studies contained little that was new, and the general approach was certainly not less subjective than it had been ten or twenty-five years before. The following paragraph from a book on the subject published by Leningrad University may stand as illustration:

'During the last years of his life Engels felt a greater and greater distrust of Bernstein and Kautsky. His letters in the nineties contained an ever sharper condemnation of the opportunist tendencies in their views and actions. Engels criticized Kautsky more than once for his isolation from the masses. In a letter to Adler on January 11, 1894, he pointed to the fact that Kautsky had lost contact with the real party movement. In this context one begins to understand why Engels did not appoint Kautsky executor of his, and Marx's, literary legacy.'[9]

Such historiography makes considerable demands on the ignorance of the reader; for even a glance at the exchange of letters between Engels, Kautsky, Bernstein, Bebel and Victor Adler shows exactly the opposite. It is true that Engels, for personal reasons, excluded Kautsky as literary executor. But he did appoint Bernstein. According to the reasoning of the Soviet author, it must follow that Engels was a 'reformist', for he preferred Bernstein, the future revisionist, to Kautsky, the guardian of Marxist orthodoxy.

The Soviet historian, for obvious reasons, has to prove that Kautsky had all along been a revisionist, a secret supporter of Bernstein. The left wing in German Social-Democracy fares somewhat better, but they too are not without blame: Mehring and Rosa Luxemburg are criticized for belittling the impact of revisionism, for failing to understand its social sources and significance, for regarding it merely as a 'literary trend'. Karl Liebknecht is upbraided for agnostic mistakes and 'general weakness in the field of philosophy'. 'Only the leader of Bolshevism, Lenin, put with all clarity the question about the class roots of revisionism and gave an unsurpassed characterization of it as bourgeois social reformism' (p. 71). This refusal to understand what the revisionism debate was really about—why revisionism prevailed in the West while 'orthodox' Marxism won through in the East—makes the study of this literature somewhat unrewarding.

[9] B. A. Chagin, *Borba Marksizma-Leninizma protiv filosovskovo revizion-izma v kontse 19ovo-nachale 20ovo vekov*. Leningrad, 1959, p. 34.

In the struggle against revisionism, the deviationists were found guilty on the following main counts (as well as on many minor ones):

1. They denied the Marxist theory of the pauperization of the proletariat.

2. They thought that contemporary capitalism could develop without crises that would become progressively more violent and eventually fatal.

3. They attributed undue importance to bourgeois ('formal') democracy.

4. They regarded Stalinism as a specific political-economic system rather than a minor transient aberration.

5. They criticized the principle of *partiinost* in Marxist-Leninist theory and Leninist philosophy in general.

6. They believed that a gradual transition into socialism was possible by means of reform rather than revolution.

7. Most of them were willing to make concessions in regard to the principle of the dictatorship of the proletariat.

8. They denied or belittled the economic role of the socialist state.

9. They disagreed with the Soviet concept of proletarian internationalism and in its place advanced the demand for a national communism or, at any rate, a larger degree of independence for Communist states and parties.

There are two basic differences between the way orthodox Marxists conducted their polemics against revisionism sixty years ago, and the more recent onslaught on Communist revisionism. Kautsky, Plekhanov, and the others did not waste time dealing with second or third-rate ideological opponents; they preferred to tackle Bernstein, who had provided the most consistent critique of orthodox Marxism. Soviet anti-revisionist literature is of a very different character; it is often directed against little-known Polish litterateurs or Yugoslav writers, against Hervé and Gates, Giolitti and Salzberg. Whatever their merits or demerits, these men have not made any major theoretical contribution to Marxism and its critique.

The other basic difference between the debate of 1900 and the more recent polemics lies in the very approach of orthodoxy then and now. Kautsky, Plekhanov, and the others seriously examined Bernstein's contentions in the economic, social, political, and philosophical fields, pointed to the weaknesses in his philosophical views, the mistakes in his statistics, the inconsistencies in some of his political proposals. It was, for a considerable time at least, a free discussion, and the front between revisionism and orthodoxy was neither clear nor unchanging during the two decades after the debate had started—there were many changes of view in both camps. But then German Social-Democracy could afford such freedom in a debate about the development of capitalist society while it was itself in opposition to that society and its institutions. Soviet Communism cannot afford a real debate, for too many vested interests are involved. The revisionists of the fifties emerged from the Communist camp, their critique has less to do with the development of capitalism since Marx—though that theme too is discussed—than with the development of *communist* society during the last forty years. But on that subject there can be no discussion. The decisive criterion in judging the revisionists' views had to be: does it undermine Soviet doctrines, institutions, and the regime as a whole, as understood by its leaders? The main criterion is not, and could not be, the question whether part or all of the critique of the revisionists is correct.

This does not mean that the Soviet leaders and their successors are not themselves constantly revising their own theories and policies. This official revisionism, however, has little to do with alienation and the young Marx; it is concerned solely with the exigencies of a society that has emerged since Marx and Lenin, and with circumstances that could not be foreseen by either of them.

The appearance of revisionism in Communist countries was not simply a symptom of the dissatisfaction of intellectuals prevented by the Party from using their eyes and brains. It was indicative of wider discontents which the intellectuals, bound by the doctrinal framework, articulated in a more or less mystified form. It reflected not only the conflicts between the Party bureaucracy and the intelligentsia, between the *apparatchiki* and the intellectuals, but general social tensions and national unrest. The latter was manifested mainly in the satellite countries, where it powerfully reinforced the revisionist fever. In the Soviet Union itself it was less pronounced and articulate; no Kolakowskis among the Soviet young intellectuals advanced such slogans as the one raised by the Polish pre-October students— 'Thinking has a colossal future.' But the attitudes conducive to revisionism were frequently displayed at the time in the Soviet Union as well.

Revisionism appeared inside the Soviet bloc in the short period between the 'thaw' and the 'freeze' and found public expression in 1956/57. By the time the counter-offensive against it had been fully developed in print, it had already ceased to be politically dangerous. It disappeared from the surface when the intellectual ferment which paved the way for the 1956 upheaval ended with the suppression of the Hungarian revolution and with the consolidation of the Gomulka regime in Poland.

The political reactions among the East European revisionists to the anti-revisionist reconsolidation varied. Some adapted themselves to the situation as best they could and began to develop theories of reconciliation, rather like some Russian Marxists after 1905/6. They lost all hope in the possibilities of political action 'from below'. Some retained a residual belief in the possibility of acting from inside the Party, others turned to individual pursuits, while some pinned their hope on the possibilities of long-term changes. Most of them have gone through both the revisionist and post-revisionist disillusion and, while retaining elements of Marxism in their thinking, have arrived at some sort of social-democratic position.

In contrast to revisionism in the East, neo-revisionist currents emerged in the West only after the events of 1956 in Poland and Hungary. It was between Khrushchev's 'secret' speech and these events that the revisionists inside the bloc became active; it was between these events and Khrushchev's ascendancy that contemporary Western Marxists began their heart-searching.

The last section of the book, *The New Left*, deals with the impact of the revisionist ferment in the Communist bloc on neo-Marxist groups outside it; it also provides a perspective to the problems and ideas with which they are grappling, since many of them already had been explored by earlier Marxist thinkers.

The term 'revisionism' applied to the 'New Left' may be misleading. Not all the groups constituting it come from a Marxist background. Indeed, in Great Britain, where the Marxist tradition was always weak, the writers of the 'New Left' designate as 'revisionists' those Labour Party theoreticians whom they regard as less fundamentalist than themselves. This usage of the term, although not universal, is more general in Great Britain.[10] But when the 'New Left' group was emerging, the Soviet 'ideological functionaries' unhesitatingly labelled it 'revisionist' and castigated it accordingly.[11] It is legitimate, therefore, considering its origin and the kind of problems and ideas it is concerned with, to look upon the 'New Left' as one of the tributaries of the revisionist mainstream.

It is very difficult to generalize about the 'New Left'. Its theoretical basis is even less crystallized than its political platform. At the most it is a vague tendency, which is moreover different in different countries. As a trend it became most self-conscious in Great Britain after the merger of a group of young students and teachers, disgruntled with the lack of radicalism in the official Labour Party, with a group of intellectuals who broke with the British Communist Party after the Hungarian revolution. According to their own testimony their ideas derived from very divergent sources: Marx and Dr F. R. Leavis, William Morris and D. H. Lawrence.

[10] Contrasting the book *The Long Revolution* by the 'New Left' author, Raymond Williams, with C. A. R. Crosland's *The Future of Socialism*, a reviewer wrote: 'On the one hand, on the Right as it is called, we have Crosland representing Revisionism; on the other—what it's called I need hardly say—we have Williams representing the New Left' (Richard Wollheim in *The Spectator*, March 10, 1961).

[11] Cf. for instance, 'English Revisionists of Marxism', *Oktyabr*, No. 8, 1958. More recently, the Soviet critics have become less outspoken, as the New Left writers were showing less political affinity with their revisionist counterparts east of the Elbe.

The old revisionism was defeated by the orthodox Marxists, but their victory was short-lived. The guardian of orthodoxy, Kautsky, was eventually himself called a renegade from the proletarian revolution by Lenin. The revolutionary myth, accepted by European social-democracy after 1848, could not withstand the reality of reformist society. Social-democracy clung for a while to its revolutionary shibboleths, but abandoned them in practice, and later also in theory.

Can the process of *embourgeoisement* have a similar effect on Soviet Communism? Is there a correspondence between Kautsky defending Marxist orthodoxy from Bernstein and Khrushchev defending Leninist orthodoxy from Mao?

Historical parallels can be misleading. Social democracy became reformist because it operated in conditions where reforms were possible through political democracy. The one-party system in the countries of the Soviet bloc provides a different background, and there is an equally marked difference in the internal structure of social-democratic and communist parties. The former, as one party among others, have abandoned their original revolutionary mythology; the abandonment of their myths by the latter would undermine the legitimacy of their rule and their title to the monopoly of power.

That does not rule out revisions and reforms from above, but it does in principle rule out their legitimate initiation outside the Party leadership. But while revisionism from below is condemned and suppressed, some of its ideas penetrate upwards and then the heterodoxy of independent thinking can in a suitably modified form be translated into the reformist orthodoxy of the Party bureaucracy.

Some such ideas do indeed find their way into the inner sanctum of the guardians of the faith. A case in point is the slow penetration of the elements of Western economic theory into the Soviet Union. Soviet political economy was first affected by the activities of the Polish revisionist economists who were familiar with Western economics and who, during the period of the thaw, engaged in a 'basic' discussion on the 'law of value'.[12] They were interested in transplanting into their own planning theory such Western economic ideas as input-output analysis and linear programming. These ideas also penetrated the Soviet citadel, via the Lange-Nemchinov axis and through other channels. In his essay Dr Zauberman describes this curious instance of 'revisionism through the back door'. Its implications are particularly interesting as the adoption of contemporary mathematical economics by Soviet economists directly touches upon what to many students (for instance, John Strachey in his old Left Book Club period) is the very core of the Marxist economic doctrine: its theory of value. Ironically enough, as Soviet society is officially

[12] Cf. *Ekonomisci dyskutuja o prawie wartosci*, Warsaw, 1956, and *Dyskusji o prawie wartosci ciag dalszy*, Warsaw, 1956.

moving from the stage of socialism ('to each according to his work') to the stage of full communism ('to each according to his needs'), economic choice becomes a more important element and marginalist thought suddenly becomes relevant for Soviet planning. What the effect will be of such revisionist infiltration on the labour theory of value and the doctrinal position in general, only the future will show, but there is little doubt that here is an area where theoretical revisionism both prompts and is prompted by the necessities of adjustment to economic change.

But although Communist reformism may be related to revisionism, it remains quite a different phenomenon from socialist reformism. It is not just a matter of increasing the welfare of the population, but of making the state more efficient in competition with 'capitalism', and it applies of course only to the Communist countries. For their rulers, reforms are not a process by which a monolithic gradually becomes a pluralistic society, and the totalitarian state, but not the state as such, withers away. When in fact changes are made, such as ending 'the cult of personality' or setting up *Sovnarkhozes* (Economic Councils) they are rarely referred to as reforms. The concept is applied mostly by outsiders, without a proper regard for Communist teleology;[13] inside, it is rather a question of the 'correct' policy of the Party or of the 'correction' of its errors. The use of the term 'reforms' implies that it is not necessarily a question determined by history in its Marxist interpretation.

For others the question is much wider: it transcends problems of terminology or even of the motivation of Communist reformism, important as it is to be clear about both. After all, for most people in this nuclear world of the twentieth century the overwhelming question is the reduction of the dangers resulting from ideological fanaticism, and the glorification of violence, revolutionary or otherwise, is obviously something humanity can ill-afford after the splitting of the atom. The question therefore is whether the changes occurring in the Communist world point to some sort of 'normalization' accompanied by a reduced role for ideology, even if only tacit and despite official assertions to the contrary. Is this the case? And what part can revisionism—from above or from below—play in it?

Changes within an ideological tradition do occur in history. The gentle universalism of primitive Christianity was followed by the fanatic ferocity of the Inquisition; on the other hand there can be

[13] A Polish visitor, the Catholic writer, Stefan Kisielewski, concluded a series of reports on Russia in the Cracow weekly, *Tygodnik Powszechny* (March 12, 1961), with the following words: 'The adversaries of the USSR in the West hope that it will become weakened through so-called revisionism. This word should be rather replaced by the term "reformism". If we are to define this Soviet "reformism" as a drive towards an improvement, elasticity, de-bureaucratization of economic management, then we have to state that it is only advantageous for the Soviet economy and does not weaken it, but strengthens it.'

tendencies in the opposite direction, mollifying ideological fanaticism and softening the political elite: 'going to Capua', 'embourgeoise-ment', Pareto's change from 'lions' to 'foxes', Ibn Khaldun's loss of *asabiyah*, Plato's cycle of dynastic decadence, Vico's remarks on the change in the nature of people ('first crude, then severe, then benign, then delicate, finally dissolute'), Macchiavelli's decline in *virtù*, Max Weber's *routinization of charisma*—all of these terms and reflexions point to some such mutation. Are we witnessing such a mutation in the Soviet Union? Is the 'end of ideology' in view on the other side of the Iron Curtain as well? The new Party programme hardly points that way;[14] and does not China look more like a country with Puritan or Wahabite characteristics?

Such questions find no answer at present, although they can be pertinently asked. The ideological tergiversations in the bloc, which must be analysed if we are to make a realistic guess, should be seen in the wider perspective of the history of ideas occurring and re-curring in Marxist thought ever since the first revisionist controversy. Just as the 'ideological stagnation' in the Communist world should not be confused with the 'end of ideology', so the gradual 'de-sophistication' of Marxist doctrinal disputes should not blind us to the continuity of certain issues emerging in these disputes.

It is of course not a question of Marx or of 'what he really meant'. By now it is clear that Marx can no more be treated seriously by Marxists, including revisionists, than Aristotle was by medieval theologians, alternately invoking him and the Bible as the ultimate authority. It is only when Marx the thinker is dissociated from Marx the prophet, and from the movement of which he is the patron saint, that it is at all possible to do him justice.[15] This is a different problem for the historian than the immediate question of the continuity of ideas within the Marxist tradition; and in this respect a new look at some of the forgotten Marxist writers is not uninstructive: any change in the ideology leading to political 'mutation' will obviously have to take up some of the ideas already elaborated in earlier revisionist discussions. Indeed, most of the ideas propounded by modern revisionists were already pretty clearly stated by their predecessors. Also the idea of the democratic evolution of post-Stalinist Communism, so popular among the 'New Left', is not without some historical precedents, as can be seen from Mr Croan's essay on Otto Bauer.

It is indeed true that the Communist world, like everything else, undergoes an evolution. We are witnessing an increase in diversity in the Communist bloc and within it there is a new distribution of power

[14] Cf. special issue of *Survey* (No. 38, October 1961) on 'The Future of Com-munist Society'.

[15] The best analysis of this kind is in *Marxism, An Historical and Critical Study* by George Lichtheim, Routledge and Kegan Paul, London, 1961.

between different Communist states. But internally the Party still remains at the pinnacle of power: 'Polycentric' Communism does not mean the diffusion of political power *within* the Communist states.

This and this alone could promise a more pluralistic society pressing for a greater degree of freedom. The diffusion of political power remains the decisive criterion of democratic development and its necessary condition. Without it open revisionism cannot reappear, the shackles of orthodoxy cannot be removed, and the problem of the freedom of thought in general cannot be posed.

The essays in this volume are intended to put this problem into a historical and contemporary perspective. Many of them were first published in the magazine *Survey*, one in the *Journal of Politics*, and they are reproduced here through the kind permission of their editors.

L.L.

PART ONE

REVOLUTION REVISED

democrats. Marx had left behind no completely unambiguous theory for the takeover of political power by the proletariat, and when Engels turned his attention to this subject in 1895 there was no question of his revising Marx; what he was trying to do was to fill in the general framework of Marx's utterances on this particular section of socialist theory with concrete references drawn from the social situation as it had changed in the years since 1848. How ambiguous Marx's utterances were can be judged from the fact that in his theory of revolution Lenin thought that his ideas were completely in harmony with Marx.

In his preface Engels starts from the situation in the middle of the century and admits that at that time he had been mistaken in his estimate of the chances of success for socialism: 'History showed that we were wrong, revealed that our views at that time were an illusion.' His words imply a clear renunciation of the French revolution as a model for the proletarian revolution, and already show the discrepancy between his thought and that of Lenin later. Engels thought that it was a characteristic of all previous revolutions that their vehicle was a minority; what distinguished the socialist revolution, on the other hand, was that it would have to be accomplished by a majority of the population. In 1848 that was not yet the case; the proletariat was a minority. But now, at the turn of the century, the position had changed.

How was this increase in the size of the proletariat manifested? Firstly, in the progress of industrialization, and secondly—and here Engels approaches close to revisionism—in the election figures. And the socialist parties had to concentrate on long-term persistent work in the parliamentary sphere; this lesson applied not only to Germany, but to all countries, including Russia. But German social-democracy was to be the pioneer in the new venture.

These ideas bear a very strong suggestion of Bernstein's thesis of the 'peaceful transition from capitalism to socialism' which lies at the heart of revisionist theory, even if Engels does not deny that at the end force and revolution will have to play their part, as the revisionists did later. But in so far as he postponed the day of the final struggle to a remote future and cautioned socialists to be circumspect in the meantime, he helped to make the transfer of the strategy and tactics of revisionism from the field of practical politics to the field of theory. In his address to the Stuttgart congress of the SPD Bernstein referred explicitly to Engels's preface to clear himself of the charge of heresy.

Other indications of a certain departure from rigid Marx-ortho-doxy can be seen in Engels' letters to Josef Bloch (who was later to publish the *Sozialistische Monatshefte*, the revisionist organ), dated September 12, 1890, to Conrad Schmidt, who later also adopted

revisionist policies, dated October 27, 1890, and to Heinz Starken-
burg, dated January 25, 1894.[3]

These letters are concerned with interpretations of historical
materialism, more precisely, with the relations between the economic
base and the political, juridical, and spiritual superstructure, and in
them Engels emphasizes the specific importance of the non-economic
factors in the historical process.

Bernstein fastened on to these letters. He used a passage from the
letter to Bloch as a motto for one section of the first chapter of his
Voraussetzungen in which he gives a full analysis of the three letters.
Of course, Bernstein's conclusions went far beyond anything that
Engels had said and in the end broke up the entire system of historical materialism. His first critical work, *Probleme des Sozialismus*
(the articles published between 1896 and 1898) questioned certain
particular predictions made by Marx; the decisive step away from
Marx followed in 1899 when he published his *Voraussetzungen des
Sozialismus und die Aufgaben der Sozialdemokratie*, and the line of
argument was continued in 1901 with his small work *Wie ist wissenschaftlicher Sozialismus möglich?*

Bernstein arrived at his critical attitude towards some particular
Marxist predictions not merely from an examination of the political
situation in Germany in the nineties, which was marked by the
electoral successes of the SPD—a phenomenon which, as we have
seen, was not without its influence on Engels—but equally from the
picture presented by economic conditions. The nineties were a period
of great prosperity; no significant crisis disturbed the steady growth
of the German national economy. The prospect held out in the Erfurt
programme, 'The army of superfluous workers will become ever
greater, the crises inherent in the nature of the capitalist mode of
production will become more extensive and devastating', was flatly
contradicted by the economic reality, for the workers too had their
share of the benefits of economic expansion. Bernstein, who once
said of himself that 'The decisive influences on my thinking as a
socialist were not of a doctrinaire kind, but facts, which forced me
to correct the ideas underlying my beliefs', and who because of his
familiarity with the English way of looking at things was more free
of prejudice in his observation of facts than other Marxists such as
Kautsky, was bound to be struck by this discrepancy between theory
and reality. At first, therefore, his criticism was directed primarily
against the prediction of the increasing impoverishment of the
proletariat with its closely related contention that capitalist crises
would grow more severe and lead rapidly to the collapse of the
capitalist system.

After a careful examination of the relevant statistics, Bernstein

---

[3] Published in *Dokumente des Sozialismus*, ed. by Bernstein, Stuttgart, 1903,
II, p. 65 ff.

came to the conclusion that capitalism itself had developed from within itself a number of stabilizing factors which made an early collapse of capitalist society highly improbable. As production increased, so did mass consumption, and the real income of the workers was raised. Bernstein discovered a trend that was making in the precisely opposite direction from impoverishment, and analogous arguments against increasingly acute crises.

One of the most important stabilizing factors, incompatible with the Marxist schema of the development of capitalist society, was in Bernstein's view the growing differentiation within society. Things were not developing towards that concentration into two sharply opposed classes foreseen by Marx, a growing army of proletarians on one side, and on the other a class of capitalists, ever smaller in numbers but greater in wealth; on the contrary, there was growing differentation within the classes. On a careful statistical basis Bernstein tried to show that the middle classes were successfully resisting the trend towards large-scale undertakings.

First of all, there was no trend towards concentration in the occupations providing services (Bernstein even at that time was aware of the importance of these branches of the economy), in trade, and above all in agriculture. Medium sized farms had even shown themselves to be superior to large farms. He observed the rise of a new middle class of officials and office workers, and noted that it was important for the industrial workers to win these new groups as allies. Moreover, Bernstein claimed to have proved that differentiation, and not concentration, could be observed not only in classes but also in the distribution of incomes. For him, finally, exploitation was to be measured not in economic but in ethical terms. 'Exploitation, where it refers to the relations between men, always means the morally objectionable use of one man by another, means—as the root of the word suggests—robbery in a disguised form.'[4]

This conclusion brings Bernstein to a decisive turning point. Criticism of particular Marxist predictions does not by any means imply the breakup of the system of historical materialism. In itself it may be regarded as no more than a changed attitude, arising from the force of facts, towards the tempo of the historical process, a process at the end of which, now as before, stands socialism. But Bernstein went beyond this 'minor revision' and so placed the very core of Marxism in question. The break was finally accomplished in an address he gave in Berlin in 1902, shortly after his return from England. He deliberately chose to put the question, how is scientific socialism

[4] E. Bernstein. *Wie ist wissenschaftlicher Sozialismus möglich?* (Berlin, 1901), p. 12. The words used in the original are *Ausbeutung*, exploitation, and *Beute*, booty or prey.

possible? in Kantian terms; he threw economic determinism overboard and transferred the justification of the struggle for socialism from the world of what is into the world of what ought to be. For him socialism had become both postulate and programme, not the scientific recognition of the laws of historical development. This address was the forerunner of all subsequent efforts to make the Kantian ethic serve as the reasoning underlying socialism.

What practical conclusions did Bernstein draw from his theoretical views for the policy of the SPD? In the first place, the road to political power for social-democracy lay through Parliament; this was nothing new, since the SPD had been following that road since 1890. What was new, what Bernstein called for, was the theoretical recognition of the road that had long been followed in practice. The decisive assumptions which for Marx were to lead to the proletarian revolution, the concentration of capital and the numerical growth of the working class, had not been realized and Bernstein doubted whether they ever would be. In these circumstances the cardinal task for social-democracy was to win and to improve political democracy. But this was not all that was required. There must in addition be federalism, local autonomy and self government, and self government he extends not only to the political but also to the economic domain. Consequently he regarded the establishment of consumer co-operatives as a means to promote socialism. His attitude to producer co-operatives was sceptical, although he admitted that they might be successful if established in conjunction with consumer co-operatives. He also advocated that socialists should take a larger interest in artisan, handicraft, and peasant co-operatives.

Trade unions, too, were one element in democracy and self government. In some passages of the *Voraussetzungen* there are even hints of the current practice of co-determination (Mitbestimmung). As far as foreign policy was concerned, Bernstein thought the SPD should pay greater attention to the national factor.

Today most of this appears to us platitudinous, and it had already been embodied in the policy of the SPD before 1914. But it had not been adopted in official theory. The refusal of the party leaders to abandon the traditional Marxist ideology explains the verdict of the Dresden party congress on revisionism. The opening paragraph of the resolution adopted there ran:

'The congress condemns emphatically the revisionist efforts to change our tactics, based on the class struggle, which have been tested and crowned with success, in such a way as to replace the capture of political power by defeating our enemies by a policy of accommodating ourselves to the existing order. The result of such revisionist tactics would be to make of the party one that is content with the reform of bourgeois society instead of one that is working for the quickest possible transformation of the existing bourgeois order into a socialist society.'

Bernstein did not allow himself to be put off by this resolution. In 1898, in self-conscious pride, he had written to the Stuttgart congress: 'The vote of an assembly, however high its standing, cannot of course turn me from the views I have gained from the examination of social phenomena.' But it was in no small measure as a result of the Dresden resolution that from then on social-democracy was regarded by many as hostile to the intelligentsia and intellectually intolerant, and that the SPD was far less successful than the Labour Party in winning intellectuals to its cause. As far as practice went, the SPD continued its revisionist policy, but almost always with an uncertain and tentative air, as in the question of a coalition with bourgeois parties, not least because the official con-demnation of revisionist theory made it impossible to bring theory and practice into harmony.

For Bebel and the other party leaders Marxism became, more and more, the ideology which helped to hold the different tendencies in the party together. It was believed that this was the only way of avoiding a split in the party and of keeping the allegiance of the masses, and at party congresses speakers frequently denied the practice of their daily work; when 1918 came they were scarcely if at all equipped to take over the government.

The fate of the SPD was shared by almost all parties of the Second International on the European continent. The dispute about revision-ism in Germany had its parallel in other parties about the right road to socialism, in part independently of the German presentation of the question, even though the debate arose from the same complex of problems, in part directly caused by it. But nowhere, before 1914, did revisionism succeed in becoming official party theory. Even the great *tribun du peuple* Jean Jaurès, whose life bore the impress of the idealist philosophy with which he started, and who, like Bernstein, advocated resolute attention to the tasks of the day, met with opposition in the French Socialist Party.

In Russia the revisionists suffered a tragic fate. There the disputes in the German party had particularly serious repercussions, for the Russian social-democrats had always followed the SPD closely, regarding it as the great exponent of the theory and practice of the political struggle. From about the turn of the century the revisionist quarrel took root in Russia; it is true that there it was set going not so much by the discrepancy between Marxist theory and the changed social reality—for capitalism had not progressed nearly so far in Russia as in Western Europe—as by the doubts entertained by many Russian intellectuals, Marxists until then, in the philosophical foundations of the Marxist system. The inclination of the Russian mind to speculation, much stronger than the German, may have been in part responsible. It was the neo-Kantianism then being taught in the German universities, particularly in Marburg, which attracted many Russian Marxists, including Nikolai Berdyaev, later to become a Christian philosopher, and the economist Peter Struve; it led them to a critical re-examination of the sociological and economic, as well as philosophical views of Marx. For a time revisionism gained the upper hand among the Petersburg revolutionary intelligentsia.

That revisionism was unable to maintain the lead in the long run was due above all to the fierce resistance of one man, no other than Lenin. While still in exile in eastern Siberia, he took up the battle in the sharpest terms with his former friends, and used in support of his argument the rejection by the leaders of German social-democracy of Bernstein's thesis. It was in fighting the Russian variety of revisionism that Lenin elaborated his own ideology. The greater rigidity and dogmatism which he introduced into Marxism can be partly explained by this conflict. That, in the course of the dispute, Lenin arrived at theoretical and practical conclusions which estranged him from the official policy of the German party can only be mentioned here in passing, since a fuller treatment would take us too far afield.

In any case, the outcome in Russia was a defeat for revisionism, and the Mensheviks, like the German social-democrats, continued to swing irresolutely between radical theory and pragmatic practice, while the Bolsheviks elevated Lenin's interpretation of Marxism to unassailable dogma. The triumph of the Bolsheviks in the October revolution and the creation of the Third International, did nothing to create a more favourable climate for revisionism in western and central Europe in the years after the war. On the contrary; the SPD was now in effect sharing in the government, but ideological competition from the communists prevented them from drawing the theoretical consequences from the real political situation. The discrepancy between programme-theory and daily activities, fatally obvious even before 1914, could not be eliminated by the SPD in the Weimar Republic. It is true that the Goerlitz programme of 1921, in drafting which Bernstein took a decisive hand, was revisionist in spirit, but after amalgamation with the USPD (independent socialists) it was replaced in 1925 by the programme adopted at the Heidelberg congress, which reverted to the Erfurt tradition; but this was as little able to bridge the gulf between theory and practice as the earlier one had been.

The efforts of the founder of revisionism and his collaborators appeared to have been in vain. When Bernstein died in 1932, his funeral was indeed made the occasion for a tremendous demonstration by the social-democratic workers of Berlin; but six weeks later the brownshirts marched through the Brandenburg Tor and German social-democracy faced the biggest defeat in its history. Under the impact of this defeat the German social-democrats began, even in the years of Hitler's dictatorship, to think afresh, and this was reflected in the official programme adopted in 1945 and in the platforms worked out in 1952 (Dortmund) and 1954 (Berlin). The abandonment of a dogma made sacred by tradition now found expression not only in practical socialist policy—there was nothing new in that—but also in its programme. The chief aim of the revisionists, to bring SPD theory and practice into harmony, was thus reasserted, even though in the meantime changes in society had made certain of Bernstein's particular contentions out of date.

The change is revealed most clearly in the basic programme adopted at the Bad Godesberg congress in November 1959. In contrast to all former programmes, which invariably began with an analysis of the dominant trends in social development, on which predictions about the future course of events were then hung, the Godesburg programme opens with a declaration of the enduring 'fundamental values of socialism', of freedom and justice. From these, and not from any insight into purportedly inescapable laws of historical development, socialist policy in its various spheres of activity is deduced. The harnessing of socialism to the realm of what should be, the turn towards a philosophic idealism, for which Bernstein was one of the first to call, has thus been officially embodied in the programme of German social-democracy.

II. Between Marx and Lenin: George Plekhanov

SAMUEL BARON

The life of G. V. Plekhanov (1856-1918), widely known as 'the father of Russian Marxism', spanned the eventful epoch from Russia's humiliating defeat in the Crimean War to the Bolshevik Revolution. The Crimean debacle, by highlighting the inadequacy of Russia's socio-economic system, called forth a series of innovations that took Russia across the great divide separating a traditional from a modern society. Hence Plekhanov confronted a different constellation of circumstances from that which had faced the radical intelligentsia in the age of Nicholas I. Sharing their abhorrence of Tsarist despotism, he dedicated his life, as they had done, to its destruction. But whereas they could find no point of support for achieving their ends in a serf-based society, he 'discovered' in a Russia undergoing capitalist development the social forces essential to the task. In contrast to his predecessors, who were inclined to liberal-democratic or 'utopian' socialist solutions, his experience of Russia's altered circumstances led him to advocate a Marxian programme.

In Plekhanov's person the best traditions of the Russian intelligentsia fused with the broader stream of European Marxism to produce both a vigorous political movement and a strikingly impressive intellectual output. Not without reason has he been regarded as the last in that line of great figures in the history of the Russian intelligentsia that began with Belinsky and Herzen. Russian writers of the most diverse political and philosophical orientations have agreed in characterizing him, in spite of his close identification with Marxism, as one of the most gifted, cultured, and influential men of his time. The liberal historian Kizevetter, for example, wrote of him: 'No disagreement with the socio-political views of G. V. Plekhanov can dim in anyone's eyes either the brilliant literary talent or the powerful and original mind and the many-sided erudition of this remarkable writer and great political figure.'[1] Moreover, he was one of the most sensitive and creative disciples of Marx. Not only did he produce incisive and persuasive analyses of contemporary Russian socio-political life, but he also pioneered in the extension of Marxian modes of investigation and thought into literary criticism, the history

[1] *Golos Minuvshevo*, No. 1, 1916, p. 325.

of Russian social thought, and other fields of knowledge. His qualities won for him the admiration of Engels and Kautsky, not to mention lesser lights, and a leading place in the councils of the Second International.

A lifelong champion of the urban proletariat, Plekhanov was born and reared in a remote country village in Central Russia. This militant adversary of Tsarist autocracy was the scion of a land-owning gentry family noted for its tradition of loyal service to the Russian state. Intending to make his career in the army, as had his father before him, Plekhanov enrolled in the Voronezh Military Academy at the age of ten. By that time his father had succeeded in installing in him those habits of discipline, industry, and self-reliance that he displayed all his life. From his mother he assimilated a love of learning, and a sense of altruism and devotion to justice. These latter qualities, confirmed and given sharper focus during his training at Voronezh, made him readily susceptible to the populist (*narodnik*) propaganda he encountered in the capital after his graduation. Contacts of that sort led him first to transfer from a Petersburg higher military school to the Mining Institute, and not long after to abandon completely his formal education. Determined to become a professional revolutionist, Plekhanov burned his bridges behind him in December 1876, by addressing an anti-government demonstration of workers and students on Kazan Square in the capital.

The next three years of Plekhanov's life were given to the populist organization 'Land and Liberty' (*Zemlia i Volia*) in which, because of his devotion to the cause, his skill as an agitator, and the range of his knowledge, he quickly rose to a position of leadership. Twice during this period he was arrested, but on each occasion he managed to secure a speedy release. Although the chief target of the populists was the peasantry, his agitational endeavours chanced to centre upon the capital's factory workers, a circumstance of considerable import-ance for his ideological evolution. As an editor of the organization's periodical publication, he demonstrated the originality of thought and felicity of expression that became the hallmarks of his writing. In 1879, Plekhanov's adamant stand in favour of populist orthodoxy as against the expansion of terrorist activities precipitated a schism in 'Land and Liberty'. He then became a leader of the ill-fated 'Black Repartition' (*Cherny Peredel*), which failed to compete successfully with the more dynamic terrorist group, 'The People's Will' (*Narodnaia Volia*).

Early in 1880, Plekhanov went abroad for what was intended to be a brief stay. He never returned to his native land until after the overthrow of the Imperial Government in 1917. He had already come to doubt certain of the foundation premises of populism, and hoped to find in the West the information that would buttress his position. Instead, his scholarly investigations and his experience of Western conditions gave him the perspective for a critique of populism and for a new insight into the nature of Russian reality. He became convinced that capitalism was already well-launched in Russia; that the populist dream of a peasant revolution leading directly to an anarcho-socialist order based on the village commune was a fantasy; that Russia's destiny lay not in any unique historical evolution but in following the course of development traversed by Western Europe. The doctrines of Marxism, accordingly, were no less applicable to Russia than to the West.

In 1883 Plekhanov and a few friends organized the 'Emancipation of Labour' group, dedicated to switching the Russian revolutionary movement on to Marxian tracks. In *Socialism and Political Struggle* (1883) and *Our Differences* (1885), he elaborated a Marxian analysis of Russian socio-economic life and from it deduced a revolutionary programme. In opposition to the populist programme, it called for an extended *political* struggle as the way to socialism, and it designated the industrial proletariat rather than the peasantry as the mass basis of the movement. In keeping with these views, Plekhanov advanced as the principal tasks of the infant group the spread of Marxian propaganda in Russia, and the drawing together of elements of a Russian workers' party. The first objective of the party must be the conquest of political liberty.

For a decade the tiny 'Emancipation of Labour' group, based in Geneva, seemed to make little progress in attracting support either among Russian students in Switzerland or in Russia itself. Their ideas did gradually gain ground, however, and in the first half of the nineties led such notable figures as Lenin, Martov, Struve, and Potresov to embrace Marxism. In the next few years, the era of 'legal Marxism', the permissive attitude of the government enabled the new evangel to win a much broader following. Plekhanov made a notable contribution to this breakthrough, particularly with his book *On the Development of the Monistic Conception of History* which, according to Lenin, 'reared a whole generation of Russian Marxists'. Meanwhile, in the nineties, the Russian labour movement had come to life and with the assistance of the social-democrats had carried off some well-disciplined and successful strikes. There then arose among the socialists a tendency ('economism') that counselled primary if not exclusive emphasis on economic rather than political struggle, an emphasis which, it was alleged, corresponded to the spontaneous development of proletarian consciousness. About the same time, Bernstein launched his revisionist theses upon the socialist world. Plekhanov discerned a kinship between these two 'heresies',and unleashed a whole series of scathing polemics against them.[2] Almost

[2] These writings are to be found in his *Sochineniia*, XI, XII.

the first to sound the tocsin against Revisionism, he proved himself a very paragon of Marxian orthodoxy in these battles.

In 1900, Plekhanov and his associates in 'Emancipation of Labour' (Axelrod and Vera Zasulich) joined with Lenin, Martov, and Potresov in the publication of the newspaper *Iskra*. Their collaboration had as its purpose the defence of Marxian orthodoxy and the organizational preparation groups into an all-Russian party. As they put together a draft programme for the party, sharp differences between Plekhanov and Lenin emerged, especially with respect to the agrarian programme. The publication of Lenin's *What is to be Done?* in 1902 had brought no protest from Plekhanov; nor did the organizational question divide the two, either in the programme discussions or at the 1903 party congress. Moreover, the congress that split the party into Bolshevik and Menshevik factions found Plekhanov siding with Lenin against Martov, Zasulich, and Axelrod. The strain of Jacobinism in him was in the ascendant for the moment, and probably he did not yet fully comprehend the implications of Lenin's organizational views. But shortly after the congress he rejoined his old friends, and in a series of critical articles brought under examination the assumptions and the dictatorial tendency in Lenin's position.

In the last two decades of his life, Plekhanov was increasingly absorbed in artistic, literary, and historical studies. He by no means retired from political life, however, a proposition under-scored by his vigorous reaction to the great events of the period—the two wars and the two revolutions that grew out of them. As an expression of his 'defeatist' attitude towards the Russo-Japanese War, he demonstratively shook hands with the Japanese delegate to the Congress of the International in 1904. In contrast, he adopted a 'defencist' position during the World War; in his view the victory of German militarism—which he believed had precipitated the conflict—would spell disaster for the progressive movement not only in Russia but in all of Europe.[3]

Apart from his stand on the two wars, there existed a high degree of correspondence between Plekhanov's general line in 1905 and in 1917. The year 1905 may be taken as the testing-time for the revolutionary prognosis Plekhanov worked out in the 1880's. The bourgeoisie, upon which he had counted heavily in the revolution against absolutism, did not live up to expectations. The peasantry, whose role Plekhanov always tended to under-estimate once he became a Marxist, proved itself a potent revolutionary force. Nevertheless, this experience did not cause him to modify his revolutionary theory in any fundamental respect.

After 1905, Plekhanov remained relatively free of close organizational ties. Combating both the 'revolutionary adventurism' of the

[3] His position is fully elaborated in *O Voine* (2nd ed.; Petrograd, n.d.)

Bolsheviks and the 'liquidationist' tendency among the Mensheviks, he sought in vain to bring about a reunification of the party on the line he advocated. In 1917, he greeted the March upheaval as the long-awaited first revolution. Returning to Russia soon after, he urged continuation of the war to victory in defence of the newly-won political liberty. Though the precedent of the French Revolution was always in his mind, Plekhanov forgot what Professor Namier has cogently remarked, that 'in 1792 war broke out in the third year of the revolution, while in 1917 revolution broke out in the third year of the war.'[4] The peasant-soldiers heeded his exhortations no more than did the workers and peasants his plea that it was folly in the midst of a life-and-death struggle with a foreign enemy to press class warfare. Theoretical considerations concerning historically attainable goals made no impression on a populace hungry for 'peace, land, and bread'. Plekhanov was impotent to stop the Bolshevik march to power. He could take little consolation from his certainty that the Russian people would have to pay dearly for the recklessness of the Bolsheviks. As if his cup of bitterness were not already full, in the last months of his life ignorant and over-zealous Red Guards harassed the ailing Plekhanov—who had given thirty-five years to the cause of the Russian proletariat—as 'an enemy of the people'.

Plekhanov may well have been one of the keenest observers of the social and political life of his time. Still, in retrospect, we can see that he committed extremely grave errors of judgment. Paradoxical though it may seem, if much of Plekhanov's power derived from his sensitive employment of Marxian ideas in analysis, his failures are traceable to the excessive rigour of his Marxian orthodoxy on programmatic and tactical matters. For in the two decades prior to the World War, that orthodoxy was becoming less and less appropriate to the changing societies of Europe. The clearest symptoms were the rise and triumph of Revisionism in the West and of Bolshevism in Russia. Plekhanov relentlessly combated the one and the other under the banner of orthodoxy and lost both battles.

In bringing Marxism to Russia, Plekhanov succeeded in illuminating certain aspects of its social life that had until then remained in the shade. He proved, what was indubitably the case, that capitalism had penetrated Russia, had dislodged it from its former stability, and had undermined the peasant commune upon which the populists rested their hopes. Eschewing that subjectivism in regard to means and ends which he identified as the earmark of populism and every other brand of utopianism, he sought instead to harmonize revolutionary goals and strategy with the objective historical process which in his view established the limits of rational social action. In

[4] 'History and Political Culture', in *The Varieties of History*, ed. F. Stern (New York, 1956), p. 377.

Russia, the level of economic development (ultimately the limiting factor), and hence the social structure and the mental disposition of the people, precluded the possibility of socialism for the time being. Accordingly, Plekhanov took upon himself the difficult task of devising a programme for a socialist movement in a country admittedly far from ready for socialism.

It may be inferred that his model for the future historical development of Russia was based upon the French Revolution of 1789 and the experience of the Social-Democratic Party of Imperial Germany. Reasoning by analogy, on the basis of the development of capitalism in Russia, he projected first a 'bourgeois' revolution for his country. The rise of capitalism brought into being the bourgeoisie and proletariat which, acting in concert, would overthrow absolutism as in the West, substituting for it a bourgeois-constitutional government and civil liberty. It is important to note that, in his opinion, 'the people' and not the bourgeoisie had struck the *decisive* blow against absolutism in the Western 'bourgeois' revolutions; and, as far as Russia was concerned, he declared again and again: 'political freedom will be won by the working class or not at all.'[5] In the bourgeois regime the proletariat, organized in the social-democratic party, was to acquire the political experience indispensable to its future governing role. Meanwhile, gathering strength as capitalism developed further, the proletariat ultimately would secure the political preponderance that would enable it to inaugurate the socialist order.

In all of this, Plekhanov tacitly admitted a fundamental similarity between the historical destiny of Russia and the West. But he was too perceptive not to realize that there also existed important differences. Anticipating Trotsky's and Lenin's 'law of uneven development', he introduced certain modifications that took account of these differences. Most significant was his attempt to establish an organic connection between the socialist revolution and the 'bourgeois' revolution which must precede it, and from which he believed it would be separated by a more or less extended interval. The connecting link he envisaged was proletarian class-consciousness; it should be awakened at the earliest possible moment and continuously increased in breadth and depth up to the achievement of socialism.

As he saw it, Russia's peculiarity consisted in the belated emergence of the movement against absolutism—a consequence of its economic backwardness. Owing to the diffusion of ideas from West to East, socialists were already active in Russia even before that movement was well under way. The socialists rather than the bourgeois liberals must summon the workers to the struggle for political liberty, thus

[5] He made this resounding claim at the founding congress of the Second International in 1889.

guaranteeing their participation as a *class-conscious* force, bent on advancing its own demands. Fighting alongside the bourgeoisie against absolutism, the workers nevertheless would be under no illusions about the relation of their interests to those of their temporary comrades-in-arms. They would view the revolution not as an end in itself but as the means of acquiring the rights which would permit them better to defend their interests against the bourgeoisie and more freely and effectively to pursue their ultimate goal of socialism.[6]

Plekhanov strove to introduce an amendment advantageous to the socialists into a Russian historical evolution he believed would be basically similar to that of the West. He could hardly have done otherwise once he decided upon a Marxian programme for a retarded country such as Russia. But he failed to appreciate that his modification threatened to disrupt the orderly Marxian sequence of economically-determined, historical stages. The locus of contradiction was his concept of class-consciousness. It comprised: (1) a realistic appraisal of the role and status of the class in existing society; (2) a correct diagnosis of its real interests and the tactics proper to their realization; and (3) the formulation of goals in full recognition of the limits imposed upon action by the existing level of historical, and especially economic, development. To expect any mass group to assimilate and to be guided by such a set of principles, to be capable of such a comprehensive sociological and historical sensitivity, required the kind of confidence which only a faith in historical inevitability could give.

The achievement of proletarian class-consciousness, insofar as it involved a grasp of the antagonism of interests between bourgeoisie and proletariat, lay well within the realm of the possible. But if that were achieved, then could such a class-conscious proletariat be expected to strike the decisive blow against absolutism, as Plekhanov thought, and then to agree to yield political predominance to that bourgeoisie it had learned to identify as its class enemy? Was a mass group, especially amid the passion and confusion of a revolution, likely to take as the controlling principle of its action an abstract historical scheme? Besides, might not the bourgeoisie shrink from collaboration in the struggle against absolutism with a proletariat which openly avowed its intention presently to destroy bourgeois society? Might not its own class consciousness counsel different policies than those its opponents, the social-democrats, prescribed for it?

Plekhanov did not realize that his proposed 'improvement' on the history of the West could not be implemented without, at the same time, causing a series of compensatory adjustments that would make

---

[6] The elements of this strategy were first set out in his *Socialism and Political Struggle* and *Our Differences*. These works are included in *Sochineniia*, II.

the outcome radically different than what had transpired in the West. Having anticipated the 'law of uneven development', he failed to deduce the corollary 'law of combined development' which projected as the consequence of unevenness, a different historical destiny for backward countries, including even the skipping of whole historical stages. Plekhanov recoiled from deducing any such 'law' because for him the sequence of economically-determined historical stages figured as the ultimate and inviolable framework of action; he could not conceive of a successful revolution which violated that 'law of history'.

What was initially an undetected theoretical inconsistency in Plekhanov's system became in 1905, and much more so in 1917, a critical political issue. In 1905, he saw the bourgeoisie retire from the revolutionary coalition before Tsarism had been struck a decisive blow. It declined to play the role for which he had cast it. On the other hand, among the workers the Bolsheviks won substantial support for a proletarian policy of alliance with the peasantry against Tsarism and, in effect, against the bourgeoisie as well. Yet Plekhanov refused to admit that the events of 1905 necessitated any fundamental change in the architecture of his revolutionary system. In 1917, although displeased with certain policies of the Provisional Government, he defended it ardently against Lenin's campaign for its overthrow. Again and again, he reminded all who would listen of Marx's dictum that no economic formation passes from the historical stage (i.e., capitalism from Russia) until it had exhausted its potential for development. Again and again, in his articles and speeches,[7] he recalled Engels's strictures against a premature seizure of power as the worst possible thing for the interests of the working class. Again and again, as in 1905, he labelled Lenin and his followers Blanquists and Tkachevists, 'alchemists of revolution', who sought to achieve a socialist revolution when the necessary conditions for it were wanting.

In 1917, Plekhanov and his ideas were defeated in the arena of political power. But years before, with remarkable prescience, he had set forth a series of judgments foretelling much of what happened in Russia after 1917. On the very threshold of his Marxian career, he gave warning of the possibility that a revolutionary committee might seize power and elect to retain it even though recognizing the divergence between the people's aims and its own socialist objectives. It might then attempt to organize national production along socialist lines, in the absence of both the objective conditions for and popular approval of socialization. In that case, 'it would have to seek salvation in the ideals of "patriarchal and authoritarian communism", introducing into those ideals only the

[7] They are collected in *God na Rodine* (Paris, 1921), 2 vols.

change that a socialist caste would manage the national production instead of the Peruvian "Sons of the Sun" and their officials.'[8] In this, as in the following passage, he decried policies that might lead to a restoration of 'oriental despotism', the term by which he designated the system of oppression Russia had borne for centuries.

Attacking Lenin's organizational plans in 1904, months before Trotsky's critique, which has been much more widely publicized in recent times, Plekhanov remarked:

'Imagine that the Central Committee recognized by us all possessed the still-debated right of "liquidation". Then this would happen. Since a congress is in the offing, the C.C. everywhere "liquidates" the elements with which it is dissatisfied, everywhere seats its own creatures and, filling all the committees with these creatures, without difficulty guarantees itself a fully submissive majority at the congress. The congress constituted of the creatures of the C.C. amiably cries "Hurrah!", approves all its successful and unsuccessful actions, and applauds all its plans and initiatives. Then, in reality, there would be in the party neither a majority nor a minority, because we would then have realized the ideal of the Persian Shah.'[9]

He went on to remind the social-democrats that theirs was 'the party of the conscious, growing and developing proletariat (i.e. a popular and democratically-organized party)', in contrast to the conception of the Bolsheviks who 'evidently confuse the dictatorship of the proletariat with a dictatorship over the proletariat'. Desiring the attainment among the masses of the highest possible degree of political awareness and sensitivity, he had in 1885 written lines that could be read as an indictment of contemporary Soviet society: 'And even if there came into being a state which—without giving you political rights—wanted to and could guarantee your material welfare, in that case [should you accept that situation], you would be nothing more than "*satiated slaves, well-fed working cattle*".'[10]

To those who saw in Lenin the offspring of Plekhanov, he objected that if the Bolshevik leader qualified for the description then he was at best an illegitimate son. At the very last, however, Plekhanov seems to have grasped the inner connection between his own revolutionary system and the Bolshevik Revolution. According to Leo Deutsch, a comrade who spent many hours with 'the Father of Russian Marxism' in his declining days, Plekhanov repeatedly put to him the question 'that deeply tormented him: "Did we not begin the propaganda of Marxism too early in backward, semi-Asiatic

[8] *Sochineniia*, II, p. 81.
[9] *Ibid.*, XIII, p. 90.
[10] *Ibid.*, II, pp. 365–6.

Russia?" [11] In the end, he appears to have understood that he could not be absolved from responsibility for what had happened, which in fact flowed logically from his insistence upon the vital link between the Russian bourgeois and socialist revolutions. As for Lenin and Trotsky, in the 1920's they inadvertently admitted their error in having forced the pace of history. Acknowledging in effect that Plekhanov's warnings had been valid, countless times they inveighed against Russia's 'peasant barbarism', which at every turn impeded and thwarted the advance towards that socialist society which was to have been the most rational, the freest, and the most abundant in human history.

I suggested earlier that Plekhanov's image of Russian historical development in the post-absolutist regime was strongly coloured by his knowledge of the Social-Democratic Party's experience (perhaps to 1890) in Imperial Germany. To be sure, he expected Tsarism to give way to a democratic political order rather than to the kind of pseudo-parliamentary system represented by Bismarck's Germany. If it had, the Russian socialists could have gone about their business in greater security and freedom than their German counterparts. But if a revisionist tendency arose and ultimately triumphed in German socialism, then the likelihood of the same occurring in Russian socialism would have been all the greater. Plekhanov fought resolutely for the suppression of revisionism in Western socialism, but to no avail. There is no reason to believe he would have been more successful in Russia if the bourgeois-democratic regime he anticipated had materialized. Once again, his inflated expectations regarding proletarian class-consciousness proved to be his Achilles heel.

Plekhanov envisaged under a Russian bourgeois-democratic regime a social-democratic party embracing the largest possible number of workers, engaging in political campaigns and parliamentary activities, fostering the growth of trade unions, and maintaining close contact between party and labour organizations. He frankly stated the desirability of social reforms, recalling for example Marx's enthusiasm about the winning of the ten-hour day for the British workers. He clearly recognized the possibility of securing favourable social legislation and other improvements for the proletariat under conditions of political democracy. Nevertheless, he staunchly denied that these circumstances necessarily militated against the maintenance and increase of proletarian class-consciousness, so long as society remained divided into classes.

His trenchant critique cast doubt on the contention of the revisionists that wealth was becoming more widely diffused, and economic depressions less frequent and less disruptive. On the other hand, he

[11] Quoted by E. Kuskova, 'Davno Minuvshee', *Novy Zhurnal*, LIV (1958), p. 139.

tended to minimize the importance of factory legislation and the progressive income tax in altering class relationships under capitalism. His central thesis was that, in proportion as capitalism develops, 'the position of the worker worsens relatively, even though his material situation improves in the absolute sense'. Even if, as a consequence of militant struggle, the proletarian worked shorter hours and received higher pay, he was exploited more heavily than before, Plekhanov insisted, since the gains he made were less than proportional to the increase in his productivity.

'The proletariat is in the position of a person who is swimming against a powerful current; if he submits without resistance to the force of the water, he would be carried *very* far back; but he does resist; he tries to move forward and therefore the current pushes him back *not so far* as it *might*; but *nevertheless* it did *move him back*, because all the same *it was much stronger*.'[12]

Considerations of this sort, he reasoned, provided the basis for the persistence and augmentation of proletarian class-consciousness. So long as the workers understood the situation, so long as they obtained every improvement through class struggle rather than class collaboration, so long as the socialists kept before them the ultimate goal of the labour movement, the requisite élan would not flag.

While holding this view, Plekhanov was not unaware of the existence of 'opportunism' in the German labour movement. 'Opportunism' signified the pursuit of immediate gains by any means including class collaboration, with the attendant implication that the ultimate aims of socialism were lost sight of or even deliberately written off. The rise of opportunism came in response to the new status labour was achieving in a socio-political context quite different from that in which Marx had written the *Communist Manifesto*. The sense of having progressed by more or less peaceful means led the working class to favour evolutionism over revolutionism as the path to continued advancement. For the worker it was of relatively little concern whether the improvement in his conditions was relative as well as absolute. Plekhanov's dramatic figure of the man swimming against the current could make little impression upon people who knew, from direct experience, that they had gained ground. Having gained it by certain tried and proven methods, they were reluctant to leave the known and successful for the unknown. The trade unions, with their bureaucratic organization and substantial funds and property, became the particular stronghold of opportunism and reformism.

As in the Russian case, empirical considerations took precedence for the proletariat over the abstract arguments of theoreticians for

[12] *Sochineniia*, XI, p. 220.

whom doctrinal dicta were binding. On occasion, Plekhanov exhibited a degree of tolerance for opportunism in the labour movement; but he never tired of castigating the revisionist intellectuals who, he declared, had betrayed Marxism. He was blind to the fact that their theories merely reflected a changed set of conditions and a changed mentality among the proletariat. He evaded the issue by asserting that basically nothing had changed. The leadership of the German party could not evade the issue because of the pressure of the trade unions, which bulked increasingly large in the party. To be sure, the orthodox faction appeared for a time to have retained the upper hand; but subsequent developments made clear that revisionism had in fact come to dominate German Social-Democracy.

Plekhanov's life ended in tragedy. The events of the first two decades of the twentieth century, the triumph of revisionism in the most advanced countries and the triumph of Bolshevism in backward Russia, sounded the death knell for that orthodox Marxism of which he was one of the two or three leading exponents in the Second International. When, in 1914, the Social-Democratic Party supported Imperial Germany's war policy, a whole set of his cherished convictions collapsed. His own 'defencist' position had the effect of isolating him from the main currents of popular sentiment when at long last Tsarism was overthrown in 1917. The October Revolution constituted an irreparable blow to that scheme of Russian historical development in which he had implicitly believed for almost four decades.

In Soviet Russia, particularly in the Stalinist era, Plekhanov and much of his work were either condemned or simply neglected. The apotheosis of Lenin and the attribution to him of virtually all the ideological and organizational attainments of Russian Marxism contributed even more effectively to the same end. Thanks to Lenin's endorsement of them as 'obligatory textbooks of communism',[13] Plekhanov's philosophical works have fared better in the Soviet Union than his other writings. It would hardly have accorded with the spirit of Stalin's Russia to pay homage to a man who saw in the Westernization of his country the highroad to progress; who viewed Lenin's revolutionary innovations and the Bolshevik seizure of power as a perversion rather than a fulfilment of Marxism; who insisted on the primacy of aesthetic quality over ideology in art; and who, in the last years of his life, adopted as his own Kant's dictum

[13] This is why his philosophical works, almost alone of the vast corpus of his writings, are available in English. Only now, over thirty years after the appearance of the first edition of his collected works, is a second edition being prepared in the USSR. The biographies of Plekhanov by V. Vaganian (Moscow, 1924) and S. Volfson (Minsk, 1924), were long ago relegated to oblivion in the USSR because, from the Soviet point of view, they did not judge their subject sufficiently harshly.

that the individual must always be considered as an end in himself, never as a means.

BIBLIOGRAPHICAL NOTE

Except for his writings on the World War (*O Voine* and his articles in *Prizyv*) and of 1917 (collected in the two volumes of *God na Rodine*), almost all of Plekhanov's works are included in his *Sochineniia*. Available in English, and providing an introduction to his philosophical and literary-artistic views respectively are *In Defence of Materialism* (London, 1947), and *Art and Social Life* (London, 1953). The first is an abbreviated title for his celebrated *On the Development of the Monistic Conception of History*. The long and stimulating introduction to his three-volume *History of Russian Social Thought* has been translated into French. Articles on Plekhanov by the present writer can be found in *The Russian Review*, January 1954; *American Slavic and East European Review*, December 1953, October 1955, April 1957; *Journal of the History of Ideas*, June 1958.

III. Freedom and Revolution: Rosa Luxemburg

F. L. CARSTEN

Among the rather unimaginative and pedestrian leaders of the German Social-Democratic Party of the early twentieth century— who were occupied with the task of achieving better living conditions for the workers and passing high-sounding resolutions against the evils of bourgeois society (which did not oblige anybody to take any action)—one was entirely different: a fiery woman of Jewish-Polish origin, small and slender, slightly lame from a childhood disease, an orator who could sway the masses, a professional revolutionary who seemed to belong to the Russian world from which she came rather than to modern Germany. Rosa Luxemburg was born on March 5, 1871, in the small Polish town of Zamosc near Lublin into a fairly prosperous Jewish middle-class family. Her span of life coincided almost exactly with that of the German Empire which Bismarck had founded at Versailles a few weeks before her birth; its collapse in November 1918 she outlived only by some weeks. Her family sympathized with the aspirations of the Polish national movement, and at the age of sixteen Rosa Luxemburg joined an underground revolutionary socialist group called *Proletariat* and participated in its clandestine activities among the workers of Warsaw. In 1889, when threatened with arrest and imprisonment, she was smuggled out of Poland by her comrades and went to Zürich, the centre of the Russian and Polish political émigrés. There she studied at the university and took part in the intense political and intellectual life of her fellow Socialists, in the heated discussion where the battles of the coming Russian revolution were fought out in advance.

Her political activities remained intimately connected with Poland. She was a co-founder of the Social-Democratic Party of the Kingdom of Poland and Lithuania in 1894 and a chief contributor to its paper published in Paris. She was opposed to the slogan of independence for Poland, which was advocated by another Polish Socialist party, the PPS; instead she advocated the overthrow of the Tsarist autocracy in alliance with the Russian working class as the primary task of the Polish revolutionary movement. She aimed at the establishment of a Russian democratic republic within which Poland would merely enjoy cultural autonomy. To Poland she returned during the revolution of 1905 to participate in the revolutionary struggle. There her party had become a mass party which issued papers and leaflets in several languages, organized trade unions and strikes, and co-operated closely with the Russian Social-Democratic Workers' Party. After a few months of great political activity, however, Rosa Luxemburg and her lifelong friend Leo Jogiches were arrested. She was kept in prison for four months, but was then released on account of her German nationality (she had contracted a *pro forma* marriage with a German comrade so as not to be hampered in her political work) and expelled from Poland, never to return.

It was in Germany that she made her home at the end of the nineteenth century; there she worked together with Karl Kautsky, the editor of the theoretical weekly of the German Social-Democrats, *Die Neue Zeit*, and the propounder and popularizer of Marxist theories. In the columns of this paper and at German Party congresses she crossed swords with Eduard Bernstein, who had just published his articles on 'Problems of Socialism', emphasizing the evolutionary transition from capitalism to socialism and 'revising' orthodox Marxism in a Fabian sense.[1] In the columns of *Die Neue Zeit* Rosa Luxemburg soon crossed swords with another redoubtable figure of the international socialist movement, V. I. Lenin, on the question of the organization of Russian Social-Democracy and the powers of the central committee of the Party, which showed that she was well aware of the dangers threatening the revolutionary movement from within. There too she commented vigorously on the Russian revolution of 1905 and discovered in it a new weapon of primary importance, the political mass strike, which she attempted to transfer to Germany. Her close association with Kautsky came to an end after some years during which she learned to distrust his Marxist jargon and to doubt the readiness of the Social-Democratic leaders to accompany their revolutionary words by similar deeds.

During the years preceding the outbreak of the First World War Rosa Luxemburg became the acknowledged theoretical leader of a left wing within the German Social-Democratic Party, whose ahderents claimed that they were the only true heirs of Marx's revolutionary ardour. She also published her most important theoretical work, *The Accumulation of Capital*,[2] in which she tried to demonstrate that capitalism could expand only so long as it had at its disposal non-capitalist, colonial markets: with their progressive absorption and their conversion to capitalism through the division

---

[1] See *Soviet Survey*, No. 32, April-June 1960, pp. 14ff. Rosa Luxemburg's attack on Bernstein was published in 1900 as a pamphlet with the title *Sozialreform oder Revolution?*

[2] English translation, London, 1951.

of the world among the imperialist powers the system was bound to reach its 'final phase':

'Imperialism is simultaneously a historical method of prolonging the existence of capitalism and the most certain means of putting an end to its existence in the shortest possible time. This does not imply that the final goal must be reached inevitably and mechanically. Yet already the tendency towards this final limit of capitalist development expresses itself in forms which will make the last phase of capitalism a period of catastrophes.'[3]

She maintained in conclusion that

'the more capital, through militarism, in the world at large as well as at home, liquidates the non-capitalist strata and depresses the living conditions of all working people, the more does the daily history of capital accumulation in the world become a continuous chain of political and social catastrophes and convulsions which, together with the periodic economic catastrophes in the form of crises, will make the continuation of capital accumulation impossible . . . even before capitalism has reached the natural, self-created barriers of its economic development.'[4]

In Rosa Luxemburg's opinion capitalism was doomed and its final crisis was inevitable: a point on which she differed from Lenin, whose *Imperialism, the Highest Stage of Capitalism*, written a few years later, contained certain analogies with her analysis of imperialism, but avoided any definite pronouncement on the 'inevitability' of capitalist collapse.[5]

It is not, however, on economic theories such as these that Rosa Luxemburg's fame as a socialist writer rests. This is, above all, due to her uncompromising stand against war and militarism. In February 1914 she was arrested and sentenced to twelve months imprisonment on a charge of inciting soldiers to mutiny because she had declared publicly: 'if they expect us to murder our French or other foreign brothers, then let us tell them: "No, under no circumstances!" ' At the outbreak of war in August 1914 the German Social-Democratic Party—like most other socialist parties—decided to support the fatherland and to grant the war credits demanded by the government; this decision was opposed only by a small minority in the

[3] Rosa Luxemburg, *Die Akkumulation des Kapitals, Gesammelte Werke*, VI, Berlin, 1923, p. 361.

[4] *Ibid.*, pp. 379–80.

[5] Hence Rosa Luxemburg has always been criticized by her 'Marxist' commentators: see, for example, the remarks of the Marx-Engels-Lenin-Institut beim Z.K. der SED in Rosa Luxemburg, *Ausgewählte Reden und Schriften*, I, Berlin, 1951, p. 408.

party caucus and by not a single deputy at the decisive vote in the Reichstag on August 4th. Rosa Luxemburg from the outside hotly attacked this policy and never forgave the party's leaders for their betrayal of the ideals to which they had once subscribed:

'With August 4, 1914, official German Social-Democracy and with it the International have miserably collapsed. Everything that we have preached to the people for fifty years, that we have proclaimed as our most sacred principles, that we have propounded innumerable times in speeches, pamphlets, newspapers, and leaflets, has suddenly become empty talk. The party of the international proletarian class struggle has suddenly been transformed as by an evil spell into a national liberal party; our strong organizations, of which we have been so proud, have proved to be totally powerless; and instead of the esteemed and feared deadly enemies of bourgeois society we are now the rightly despised tools of our mortal enemies, the imperialist bourgeoisie, without a will of our own. In other countries more or less the same breakdown of socialism has occurred, and the proud old cry: "Working men of all countries, unite!" has been changed on the battlefields into: "Working men of all countries, slit each other's throats!"

Never in world history has a political party become bankrupt so miserably, never has a proud ideal been betrayed so shamefully.[6]

She explained why German Social-Democracy was able to change its policy so quickly and successfully, without encountering any major opposition inside the party:

'It was precisely the powerful organization, the much-lauded discipline of German Social-Democracy, which proved their worth in that the whole organism of four millions allowed itself to be turned round within twenty-four hours at the behest of a handful of parliamentarians and let itself be joined to a structure, the storming of which had been its lifelong aim . . . Marx, Engels, and Lassalle, Liebknecht, Bebel, and Singer educated the German working class so that Hindenburg can lead it. The better the education, the organization, the famous discipline, the building-up of trade unions and party press is in Germany than it is in France, the more effective is the war effort of German Social-Democracy in comparison with that of the French.'[7]

Soon Rosa Luxemburg and her circle of friends, intellectuals like herself, began to organize opposition to the war and to issue clandestine anti-war leaflets, signed with the pen-name of Spartacus:

---

[6] Underground leaflet of the Spartacus League of April 1916: *ibid.*, II, Berlin, 1951, p. 534.

[7] *Die Internationale*, No. 1, 1915: *ibid.*, II, p. 521.

hence their group came to be known as *Spartakusbund* (Spartacus League). Thus they remained faithful to the resolution that had been voted for the first time by the Congress of the Socialist International at Stuttgart in 1907 at the suggestion of Rosa Luxemburg, Lenin and Martov:

'If the outbreak of war threatens, the workers and their parliamentary deputies in the countries in question are obliged to do everything to prevent the outbreak of war by suitable means. . . . If war should nevertheless break out, they are obliged to work for its speedy termination and to strive with all their might to use the economic and political crisis created by the war for the mobilization of the people and thus to hasten the overthrow of capitalist class rule.'[8]

Their underground activities soon landed most of the leaders of the Spartacus League in prison. Rosa Luxemburg was arrested in February 1915 and, with the exception of only a few months, spent the remaining years of the war in various German prisons—until she was freed by the revolution of November 1918. In prison she wrote her most eloquent denunciation of the war, in which she clearly established the responsibility of the German Imperial government because the Austrian ultimatum to Serbia had been issued with its consent, because it had assured Austria in advance of German support in case of war, and because it had given Austria 'an entirely free hand in its action against Serbia'. *The Crisis of Social-Democracy*, written under the pen-name of Junius, bitterly condemned the war and even more bitterly condemned the policy of the German Social-Democrats:

'This world war is a relapse into barbarism. The triumph of imperialism leads to the destruction of civilization—sporadically during a modern war, and finally if the period of world wars which has now started should continue without hindrance to the last sequence. We are today faced with the choice, exactly as Frederick Engels predicted forty years ago: either the triumph of imperialism and decline of all civilization, as in ancient Rome, depopulation, desolation, degeneration, one vast cemetery; or the victory of socialism, that is the conscious fight of the international working class against imperialism and its method: war. . . .

'Yes, the Social-Democrats are obliged to defend their country during a great historical crisis; and this constitutes a grave guilt on the part of the Social-Democratic Reichstag fraction, that it declared solemnly on August 4, 1914: "We do not desert the fatherland in the hour of danger"; but it denied its own words at the same moment,

[8] *Internationaler Sozialisten-Kongress Stuttgart 1907*, Berlin, 1907, p. 102: Thursday, August 22, 1907.

for it *has* forsaken the fatherland in the hour of its greatest peril. The first duty towards the fatherland in that hour was to show it the real background of this imperialist war; to tear away the tissue of patriotic and diplomatic lies which surrounded this attack on the fatherland; to proclaim loudly and clearly that for the German people victory or defeat in this war is equally disastrous; to resist with all force the muzzling of the fatherland by the state of siege . . . finally, to oppose the imperialist war aims of the preservation of Austria and Turkey—that is of reaction in Europe and in Germany— by the old truly national programme of the patriots and democrats of 1848, the programme of Marx, Engels, and Lassalle: by the slogan of the united, great German republic. That is the banner that should have been raised, a banner that would have been truly national, truly liberal and in conformity with the best traditions of Germany, as well as of the international class policy of the working class.'[9]

Rosa Luxemburg's voice became the symbol of opposition to the war, but it remained a cry in the wilderness. Although many Germans became war-weary on account of mounting casualties and increasing hunger, the Spartacus League never mustered more than a few hundred members, and the non-revolutionary, pacifist Independent Social-Democratic Party became the mass opposition party in the later years of the war. Although the Spartacists joined this party, its leaders were men far removed from Rosa Luxemburg's revolutionary idealism, men like her old enemies Eduard Bernstein and Karl Kautsky. Even after the revolution of 1918 it was the Independent Social-Democratic Party which became the mass party of the radicalized section of the German working class; while the newly founded German Communist Party, the successor of the Spartacus League, remained a small sect.

It was in prison, too, that news reached Rosa Luxemburg first of the February and then of the October revolution in Russia; her revolutionary ideals seemed at last to have reached the realm of reality, if not in Germany then at least in Russia. And it was in prison too that she wrote what must remain the most important testimony to her independence of spirit, a trenchant criticism of Lenin's policy after the October revolution. As early as 1904, at the same time and for the same reasons as George Plekhanov,[10] she had criticized Lenin for his advocacy of

'a ruthless centralism, the chief principles of which are on the one hand the sharp distinction and separation of the organized groups of the avowed and active revolutionaries from the surrounding, if un-organized, yet revolutionary active circles, and on the other hand the

---

[9] *Ausgewählte Reden und Schriften*, I, pp. 270, 372–3.
[10] See *Soviet Survey*, No. 32, April-June 1960, p. 99.

strict discipline and the direct, decisive intervention of the central authority in all activities of the local party groups. It is sufficient to remark that according to this conception the central committee is authorized to organize all local committees of the party, therefore also empowered to decide upon the personal composition of each Russian local organization, from Geneva and Liège to Tomsk and Irkutsk, to impose upon them its own local rules, to dissolve them altogether by decree and to create them anew, and thus finally to influence indirectly even the composition of the highest party organ, the party congress. Thus the central committee appears as the real active nucleus of the party and all other organizations merely as its executive tools.'[11]

Against Lenin's formula that the revolutionary Social-Democrat was nothing but 'a Jacobin who was inseparably linked with the organization of the class-conscious proletariat', Rosa Luxemburg emphasized that it was in a conspiratorial organization of the type created by Blanqui that tactics and activity were worked out in advance, according to a fixed plan, that its active members were but the executive organs of a higher will which was formed outside their sphere of action, and blindly subordinated to a central authority which possessed absolute powers. In her opinion, the conditions of Social-Democratic action were entirely different,

'not based on blind obedience, nor on the mechanical subordination of the party militants to a central authority; and it is equally out of the question to erect an absolute partition between the nucleus of the class-conscious proletariat which is already organized in firm party cadres, and the surrounding sections which are already engaged in the class struggle and are being drawn into the process of class education.'

According to her, Lenin's ideas amounted to

'a mechanical transfer of the organizational principles of the Blanquist movement of conspirators into the Social-Democratic movement of the masses of the workers.'

Social-Democracy was not 'linked' with the organization of the class-conscious workers, but was 'the proper movement of the working class', so that Social-Democratic centralism had to be of an entirely different quality from that of Blanqui. Local organizations had to have sufficient elbow-room so that they could deploy their initiative and make use of the existing opportunities to further the

[11] 'Organisationsfragen der russischen Sozialdemokratie', *Die Neue Zeit*, XXII, Stuttgart, 1904, pp. 486–7.

62   REVISIONISM

struggle; while the ultra-centralism advocated by Lenin was designed
to control, channel, and regiment the activity of the party.[12]

Thus Rosa Luxemburg realized at a very early stage the dangers
inherent in the Bolshevik type of organization; but this did not
prevent her from co-operating with Lenin during later years and
from welcoming the Russian revolution as 'the most tremendous fact
of the world war'. Her criticisms of Lenin's policy after the October
revolution were above all directed against his agrarian policy and
against the anti-democratic, dictatorial tendencies inherent in
Bolshevism. Lenin, at the time of the October revolution, had taken
over the agrarian programme of a non-Marxist party, the Social
Revolutionaries, which sanctioned the division of the expropriated
estates of the nobility among the peasants and created a strong class
of peasant proprietors. Rosa Luxemburg predicted that this policy
would

'create for socialism a new and powerful class of enemies in the
countryside, whose opposition will be much more dangerous and
tenacious than that of the noble landlords had ever been'

and that

'an enormously enlarged and strong mass of peasant proprietors will
defend their newly acquired property tooth and nail against all
socialist attacks. Now the question of a future socialization of
agriculture, and of production in Russia in general, has become an
issue and an object of a struggle between the urban workers and the
peasants.'[13]

How right she was the years of Stalin's forced collectivization were
to show; but she did not consider whether, in the conditions of
1917, Lenin, if he wanted to seize and to retain power, had any
alternative but to sanction occupation of the land by the peasants,
which was proceeding spontaneously and independently of his orders
or wishes. On this point she was more orthodox than Lenin.

Far more weighty was Rosa Luxemburg's criticism of the anti-
democratic policy of Lenin and Trotsky, of their suppression of free
political life, of their establishment of a dictatorship not of the
masses, but over the masses. She declared quite unequivocally that

'it is an obvious and indisputable fact that without a free and un-
censored press, without the untrammelled activity of associations and

[12] *Ibid.*, pp. 488–9, 491–2.
[13] Rosa Luxemburg, *Die Russische Revolution*, ed. Paul Levi, Berlin, 1922,
pp. 86–7.

meetings, the rule of the broad masses of the people is unthinkable.'[14]

And she prophesied correctly that

'with the suppression of political life in the whole country the vitality of the Soviets too is bound to deteriorate progressively. Without general elections, without complete freedom of the press and of meetings, without freedom of discussion, life in every public institution becomes a sham in which bureaucracy alone remains active. Nothing can escape the working of this law. Public life gradually disappears; a few dozen extremely energetic and highly idealistic party leaders direct and govern; among them in reality a dozen outstanding leaders rule, and the élite of the working class is summoned to a meeting from time to time to applaud the speeches of the leaders and to adopt unanimously resolutions put to them; *au fond* this is the rule of a clique—a dictatorship it is true, but not the dictatorship of the proletariat, but of handful of politicians, that is a dictatorship in the bourgeois sense.'[15]

Rosa Luxemburg had not become an adherent of 'bourgeois democracy', nor was she against dictatorship. She stood on the platform on which Marx had stood in 1848; dictatorship of the broad masses of the people was to her the same as revolutionary democracy, a dictatorship against the small minority of capitalists and landlords, but not against the people:

'Dictatorship, certainly! But dictatorship means the way in which democracy is used, not its abolition; it means energetic, resolute interference with the acquired rights and economic conditions of bourgeois society, without which there can be no question of a socialist revolution. But this dictatorship must be the work of the class, and not of a small, leading minority in the name of the class; i.e. it must originate from the continuous active participation of the masses, must be directly influenced by them, must be subordinate to the control of the whole people, and must be borne by the increasing political education of the masses.'[16]

These masses must participate actively in the political life and in the shaping of the new order, 'otherwise socialism will be decreed and imposed from above by a dozen intellectuals'.[17]

The masses, however, cannot acquire political education and experience without political freedom: it is here that Rosa Luxemburg

[14] *Ibid.*, p. 108.
[15] *Ibid.*, p. 113.
[16] *Ibid.*, pp. 116–17.
[17] *Ibid.*, p. 111.

realized the deep gulf which separated her libertarian socialism from totalitarian socialism:

'Freedom only for the supporters of the government, only for the members of one party—however numerous they may be—that is not freedom. Freedom is always freedom for the man who thinks differently.'[18]

It is proof of her political genius that she could write these words a few months after the inauguration of the Bolshevik dictatorship. The essay was not published in her lifetime, however, but only some years after her death by her pupil Paul Levi (who succeeded her in the leadership of the German Communist Party) after he had broken with Moscow.

The German revolution of November 1918 freed Rosa Luxemburg from prison. She spent the remaining few weeks of her life in feverish activity, exhorting the masses to revolutionary action, pouring scorn over the moderate Social-Democratic leaders who suddenly found themselves in power, writing numerous articles for the communist paper, *Die Rote Fahne*, which she edited together with Karl Lieb-knecht. In contrast with the majority of communists, she considered it necessary to participate in the elections to the German National Assembly which were to take place in January 1919; but she did so for reasons entirely at variance with those of the large mass of German socialists, who put their faith in the introduction of parliamentary democracy, and not in the continuation of violent revolution. She wanted to use parliament as a revolutionary platform, as a means of furthering the cause of revolution:

'Now we stand in the midst of the revolution, and the National Assembly is a counter-revolutionary fortress which has been erected against the revolutionary proletariat. It is thus essential to besiege and to reduce this fortress. To mobilize the masses *against* the National Assembly and to summon them to battle, for this the elections and the platform of the National Assembly must be used.

'It is necessary to participate in the elections, not in order to pass laws together with the bourgeoisie and its mercenaries, but to chase the bourgeoisie and its partisans out of the temple, to storm the fortress of the counter-revolution and above it to hoist victoriously the flag of the proletarian revolution. To do this a majority in the National Assembly would be required? That only those believe who render homage to parliamentary cretinism, who want to decide upon revolution and socialism through parliamentary majorities. It is not the parliamentary majority *inside* which decides the fate of the

[18] *Ibid.*, p. 109.

National Assembly itself, but the working masses outside in the factories and in the streets. . . .

'The elections and the platform of this counter-revolutionary parliament must become a means to educate, rally and mobilize the revolutionary masses, a step in the struggle for the establishment of the proletarian dictatorship.'[19]

Although the masses of the German workers proved more than reluctant to follow the communist lead, Rosa Luxemburg never lost her faith in them. The day before she was murdered by counter-revolutionary thugs, on January 15, 1919, she wrote in her last article, which contained an appraisal of the attempted seizure of power by the extreme left in Berlin, the so-called Spartacist rising:

'The masses are the decisive element, they are the rock on which will be built the final victory of the revolution. The masses have stood the test; they have made out of this "defeat" one link in the chain of historical defeats which constitute the pride and the power of international socialism. And this is why out of this "defeat" victory will be born. . . . Tomorrow already the revolution will arise again in shining armour and will frighten you with her trumpet-call: I was, I am, I shall be!'[20]

The course of the German revolution was to show how unjustified her faith in the masses and her revolutionary optimism had been, and when the masses in Germany moved they moved in a direction totally different from that which she had so confidently predicted.

A few weeks before Rosa Luxemburg was murdered, the German Communist Party was founded in Berlin. In its programme, published in December 1918, Rosa Luxemburg once more gave expression to the ideas which had inspired her criticism of Lenin's policy after the October revolution, to her clear refutation of the rule of a minority over the working class and of all putschist tactics (which so tragically came to a head in the Spartacist rising of January 1919):

'The proletarian revolution requires no terror to achieve its aims, it hates and despises murder. . . . It is no desperate attempt of a minority to fashion the world according to its own ideals, but the action of the many millions of the people, which is called upon to fulfil its historical mission and to transform historical necessity into reality. . . . The Spartacus League is not a party which wants to seize power over the working class or through the working class. . . .

[19] Article in *Die Rote Fahne* of December 23, 1918: *Ausgewählte Reden und Schriften*, II, pp. 652–3.
[20] Article in *Die Rote Fahne* of January 14, 1919: *ibid.*, p. 714.

C

The Spartacus League will never seize power unless it be through the clear, positive wish of the large majority of the working masses in Germany, never otherwise than on the basis of their conscious approval of the views, aims and political methods of the Spartacus League. . . . Its victory stands not at the beginning, but at the end of the revolution: it is identical with the victory of the many millions of socialist workers.'[21]

It was a tragedy, not only for itself, that the new party did not heed this advice of its founder; throughout its history it remained devoted to putschist tactics, and when it finally came to power it did so as a clique ruling over the workers and maintained in power by the bayonets of a foreign army.

In the new party programme Rosa Luxemburg also emphasized what in her opinion constituted the essential features of socialism:

'The essence of a socialist society consists in this, that the great working mass ceases to be a regimented mass, but lives and directs the whole political and economic life in conscious and free self-determination. . . .

'The proletarian masses must learn to become, instead of mere machines employed by the capitalists in the process of production, the thinking, free, and active directors of this process. They must acquire the sense of responsibility of active members of the community which is the sole owner of all social wealth. They must develop zeal without the employer's whip, highest productivity without capitalist drivers, discipline without a yoke, and order without regimentation. Highest idealism in the interest of the community, strictest self-discipline, a true civic spirit of the masses, these constitute the moral basis of a socialist society.'[22]

It is in ideas such as these, in her searching criticism of the conceptions of Lenin, in her emphasis on the moral and democratic basis of socialism that the lasting value of Rosa Luxemburg's thought can be found. Her theory of the inevitable collapse of capitalism, her blind faith in the masses and in revolution as such, her vast optimism as to the future of socialism have been disproved by events which she did not live to see. Yet enough remains to make her one of the outstanding exponents of modern socialist thought. It is no accident that she has been classified as a heretic in Eastern Europe and that the only recent edition of her writings omits all that is truly important among them. For Rosa Luxemburg, socialism and freedom were inseparable: those who have abolished freedom have no use for her ideas.

[21] *Was will der Spartakusbund?* ed. Kommunistische Partei Deutschlands (Spartakusbund), Berlin, 1919, pp. 17, 22–3.

[22] *Ibid.*, pp. 16–17.

IV. The Permanent Revolution: Lev Trotsky

HEINZ SCHURER

In the history of political ideas there are few that have been so pregnant with results as the theory of the permanent revolution, first tentatively suggested by the German-Russian socialist Parvus in 1905 and then elaborated in 1906 by Parvus's erstwhile disciple Trotsky. To the end of his life Trotsky would maintain that the events of 1917 in Russia had proved the theory right; recent students of the subject agree with him to the extent that the Bolshevik party when seizing power was inspired by conceptions first outlined by these two men.

The theory must be set against the mental climate in which it was born, marked particularly by the close interaction of German and Russian Marxism before 1914. The essence of the theory was a sensational suggestion which ran counter to all the models of the future then accepted by Marxist doctrine. It proposed that an economically under-developed country such as Russia might achieve the transition to socialism earlier than the economically advanced West. Was the idea merely a new, Marxist version of the old Slavo-phile and populist theme of the messianic mission of young, primitive, and healthy Russia showing the way to decadent Europe? On the contrary, the theory was the creation of the two most Westernized Russian Marxists who despised the 'intellectual kowtow before the Russian sheepskin'. Parvus, while of Russian origin, had made his name in German social-democracy as a champion of revolutionary Marxism against Bernstein's revisionist advocacy of a reformist policy making for democratic welfare capitalism.

The first distinct contribution Parvus made was his emphatic assertion of the imminence of the socialist revolution in the present age, not in some astronomically remote future. Passionately interested in the controversy between Marxism and revisionism then raging in Germany, Trotsky, then still in Russia, was deeply influenced by Parvus's attitude even before the turn of the century. With the German movement showing signs of losing some of its original fire, the idea gained ground that a stimulus might come to German socialism from Russia, a novel idea first put forward by the outstanding intellectual representative of German Marxism, Karl Kautsky. In 1902 he wrote that the centre of revolutionary activity might shift from Germany to Russia and the fresh breeze from the East might sweep away the philistine cob-webs which were beginning to enmesh the German party.[1] After the outbreak of the Russo-Japanese war, on the first day of the fateful year of 1905, the defeat of Russia looming ahead, Parvus would express Kautsky's sentiments in more certain terms:

'The Russian Revolution will shake the world. The Russian proletariat may well become the vanguard of the international socialist movement.'[2]

It was in the second half of 1904 that Trotsky came to stay with Parvus in Munich. Both men had taken up an anti-Lenin line during the famous split in the Russian Social-Democratic Party (RSDLP) in 1903. The quarrel had shifted towards different interpretations of the role of the Marxist literati in the Russian labour movement. Against Lenin, his antagonists, Parvus, Trotsky, and Rosa Luxemburg, supported by Kautsky, had emphasized the immense potentialities of spontaneous mass movements, contrasting the unorganized Russian working class, as the real hope of the future, with the emigré intelligentsia in Geneva everlastingly involved in hairsplitting theoretical squabbles.

Trotsky, then at loggerheads with both factions, had in his pocket the proofs of an unpublished pamphlet discussing the probable course of future events in Russia. He prophesied a political mass strike of the unorganized Russian workers as the opening chapter of the revolution. On January 22, 1905, the day of the massacre in front of the Winter Palace, Trotsky's prophecy appeared to come true. Rosa Luxemburg summed up the significant clash between the traditional and the new:

'At the head of the procession ikons were carried, but over the heads of the crowds hovered the spirit of Karl Marx.'

It was a classical statement of the belief of these Marxists that some Hegelian *Weltgeist* was working through the action of the masses. What happened next is best told in Trotsky's own words:

'The very next day after the bloody events in Petersburg, Parvus was overwhelmed with the thought of the exceptional role which the proletariat of backward Russia was called upon to play. Several days spent in Munich were filled with conversations which clarified a great deal to both of us and brought us personally close together.

[1] K. Kautsky, 'Slavyane i revolyutsiya'. *Iskra*, March 10, 1902, No. 18.
[2] *Iskra*, January 1, 1905.

The preface Parvus then wrote to my pamphlet has entered permanently into the history of the Russian revolution.'[3]

The conceptions put forward by Parvus thus arose out of the
immediate impact of the independent action of the unorganized
masses, masses not led by the RSDLP. This basic experience is an
integral aspect of the theory of the permanent revolution. In the
boldness of its perspectives, Parvus's preface went beyond anything
that had hitherto been dreamt of by Russian Marxists. Contrasting
the rise of the city in western Europe and the same process in Russia
and China, Parvus showed that the spearhead of the French and
German revolutions of the past, the mass of skilled urban craftsmen,
did not exist in Russia. Their place in the historically inevitable
struggle for democracy would be taken by the young Russian
proletariat. The peasantry, on the other hand, being an amorphous
social group, would never become an independent political force.
Thus the future revolutionary provisional government would by
necessity be a government of the workers' democracy. At this point
Parvus made a sharp distinction between workers' democracy and
the RSDLP; the RSDLP would have to choose between taking
responsibility for the provisional government and staying aloof from
the movement of the masses. The workers would regard this government as their own, whatever the attitude of the RSDLP. If the party
were at the head of the revolutionary movement of the Russian
proletariat, then this government would become a social-democratic
government.

'Such a social-democratic provisional government, however, will
not be able to establish socialism in Russia, but the very process of
destroying the autocracy will provide a favourable terrain for further
political effort.'[4]

Thus Parvus made it clear that in his opinion the work of Robespierre and St Just would be carried out by a workers' democracy
regardless of what attitude the squabbling RSDLP factions might
take.
   To assign such a tremendous role to the numerically small Russian
urban working class appeared a staggering idea to his contemporaries.
In April 1905 Lenin dismissed the new concept as harebrained,
arguing that a government established by the working class alone
had far too narrow a social basis. To last any time at all it would
have to be formed by an alliance of the proletariat with wide strata
of the urban lower middle classes and the masses of the poorer
peasants.[5] Rosa Luxemburg, so closely allied to Parvus politically, in

[3] L. Trotsky, *Stalin.* London, 1947, p. 430.
[4] Parvus's preface in N. Trotsky, *Do 9-ogo Yanvarya.* Geneva, 1905.
[5] V. I. Lenin, *Sochineniya.* 4th edition, vol. 8, pp. 262–3. Moscow, 1947.

her first article on the events of January 22nd, was much less bold.
The Bolshevik faction was then holding its congress in London, and
towards the end of his life Trotsky, looking back to those days,
wrote:

'The negative aspect of the centripetal tendencies of Bolshevism
first became apparent at this congress. The habits peculiar to a
political machine were being formed in the underground work. The
young revolutionary bureaucrat was already emerging as a type.'

When Parvus and Trotsky met again it was in Petersburg in October
1905, when the revolutionary wave was reaching its peak. In 1906
Trotsky was to write that the Russian working class had then displayed a strength that far surpassed the most sanguine expectations
of the Russian social-democracy. Contrary to the laws of probability,
it was the Mensheviks who thrived on the revolutionary atmosphere.
Out of the mass strike an embryonic institutional form of Parvus's
'workers democracy' had been born, the Soviet of Workers' Deputies.
It was a non-party organization, and for that very reason, the first
reaction of the Bolshevik faction had been to boycott it. Thus the
clash between the emigré intelligentsia and the rank and file came to
a head, as had been predicted by Parvus in January. In 1940 Trotsky
wrote:

'The Menshevik faction predominated in the Soviets, the rank and
file Mensheviks were carried away by the revolutionary developments; the leaders mused in perplexity over the sudden leftwards
swing of their own faction. The Petersburg committee of the Bolsheviks was frightened at first by such an innovation as a non-party
representation of the embattled masses.'[6]

Trotsky, who had been unable to fit into either of the emigré
factions, was the one national figure belonging to the social democracy which the struggles of 1905 had produced. This contrast between
his failure in the factional fight and his triumph in a spontaneous
revolutionary movement was bound to colour his outlook.

It was in this atmosphere that Trotsky and Parvus developed their
theory of the future of Russia in ever bolder terms. In their paper,
Nachalo, in November 1905 a line was advocated which went far
beyond Parvus's preface of January. Their prognosis was based quite
naturally on a further rise of the revolutionary temperature, on the
prospect of risings in the countryside reinforcing the urban workers.
Already a conflict had arisen between the employers and the workers
in Petersburg, the workers had started enforcing the eight hours day,
and the employers had answered with a lockout. In his essay on the

[6]L. Trotsky, *Stalin*, p. 64.

Revolution, written in 1908, Cherevanin, a right-wing Menshevik, deplored the action of the workers, as by their precipitate move they had split the common front against the autocracy.[7] Trotsky drew the opposite conclusion: the working class, having achieved democracy, would be forced to come into conflict with the employing classes, take over the factories, and run them on socialist lines. Since the urban working class would lead the struggle for democracy, the road to a permanent democratic order would only be established through proletarian dictatorship. However, that would be the task of an entire historical epoch, not an aim to be achieved overnight. Trotsky's telescoping of historical processes was completely at variance with the official party programme. The theory of the permanent revolution remained the idea of two outsiders. Of these Trotsky was the one to elaborate the concept in one of the most remarkable documents of twentieth century Marxism.[8]

In 1906, while in prison, Trotsky, building on the experiences of the past year, created his theoretical synthesis of the current doctrines of German left-wing Marxism and the lessons of 1905. He restated Parvus's thesis in great detail. Later he was to coin the term 'combined development' for the phenomenon of cultural borrowing by which the latest achievements of an advanced country are forced on to backward soil, making a Le Corbusier housing estate arise beside the nomad's tent. At one time he was to toy with the idea that Adlerian psychology, with its concept of the over-compensation of an inferiority complex, might provide an interesting parallel to the law of combined development. Out of the clash between old and new, intensified a hundred times by the violence of the contrast, would arise the powerful tensions in whose terms Trotsky viewed the Russian scene. At the beginning of 1905, under the impact of the events of January 22nd, Parvus had suggested that the Russian working class by itself would be able to establish democracy in the country. From the clash between the Petersburg workers and the employers over the enforcement of the eight hours day at the end of the same year, Trotsky had drawn the far bolder conclusion that the struggle for democracy and the struggle for socialism would occur not as two distinct issues separated by an interval, perhaps of centuries, but, in the conditions of a backward country, would be telescoped into one. In Russia, the democratic revolution when still only half completed would lead straightaway into the socialist revolution which would carry out the work of 1793. Democracy would be consolidated by socialism, not the other way round, and

[7] A. Tscherewanin, *Das Proletariat und die Russische Revolution*. Stuttgart, 1908.

[8] N. Trotsky, 'Itogi i perspektivy', in his *Nasha Revolyutsiya*, St Petersburg, 1906, pp. 224–86.

he underlined the need for the urban working class to make the utmost efforts to appear as a liberator to the rural masses, not as a new oppressor. Once the proletariat had gathered the peasantry behind the banner of the urban revolution, the army would inevitably go over to the victors.

In his essay Trotsky, having arrived at his conclusions from a consideration of the peculiar features of the Russian environment and from the experience of the first year of the Russian upheaval, set out to buttress his theory by extending its scope to the international sphere. The idea of such an East-West nexus had a respectable history. In 1855 Herzen had alluded to the King of Savoy's boast that Italy's reunification would be achieved by Italy alone, '*Italia farà da se*'. In a letter to Proudhon Herzen wrote:

'Russia, less haughty than Savoy, will not *farà da se*; she needs the solidarity and help of the peoples of Europe, but on the other hand freedom will not arrive in the West so long as Russia remains a soldier of the Tsar.'[9]

In 1905 there was a general expectation among Russian Marxists that the conflagration would spread from East to West, and in his forecast Trotsky tied the fate of Russia firmly to the fate of Europe, leaning heavily on the latest writings of Kautsky and Parvus. In 1904 Parvus, with his overpowering sense of the *Aktualität der Revolution* had said that international capitalism had turned into a closely interlocked system and thus not only the institution of private property, but the system of nation states had become fetters on further economic and cultural progress. The key to an unparalleled development of the productive forces was in the hands of the international working class, which would abolish private property and the nation state at the same time.[10] Kautsky, too, had emphasized the general ripeness of Europe for a transition to socialism. From this Trotsky inferred that the Russian question could only be viewed as a reflection of the basic question of the age. The general problems of the advanced capitalist world would be most acutely posed in a backward country where social and political tensions were particularly strong. Without the support of a victorious socialist revolution in the advanced West, the Russian permanent revolution would be doomed. However, it was equally inevitable that the Russian permanent revolution would spark off a revolution in the West. At the end of his life Trotsky put his theory in a nutshell:

'The complete victory of the democratic revolution in Russia is conceivable only in the form of the dictatorship of the proletariat

[9] E. H. Carr, *The Bolshevik Revolution 1917–23*, vol. 1. London, 1950, p. 57.
[10] Parvus, *Rossiya i Revolyutsiya*. St Petersburg, 1906.

leaning on the peasantry. The dictatorship of the proletariat which would inevitably place on the order of the day not only democratic, but socialist tasks as well, would at the same time give a powerful impetus to the international socialist revolution. Only the victory of the proletariat in the West could protect Russia from bourgeois restoration and assure her the possibility of rounding off the establishment of socialism.'[11]

Trotsky always thought that the countryside was to be ruled by the town, that the urban proletariat would give a lead to the peasantry. Once socialist measures were introduced in earnest, there would be an inevitable collision between the victorious working class and the rural masses. In isolation, the Russian proletariat were sure to be defeated in such a clash, unless the West European revolution came to its aid.

'The Russian socialist government will throw into the scales of the whole capitalist world the colossal weight given to it by the constellation of the Russian democratic revolution.'[12]

Were there any grounds for assuming such an impact of East on West? Again, Trotsky could draw on the experience of 1905, when there had been repercussions in Austria and Germany. It should be noted that, particularly in Germany, the excitement of the rank and file in the labour movement had greatly surpassed any determination on the part of the leaders; Bebel's recently published correspondence leaves no doubt that the leaders regarded their function as that of a brake.[13] From contemporary sources the pattern of spontaneous mass movement and restraining party leadership emerges with equal clarity. This fitted only too well into the general framework of ideas created in Trotsky's mind by the Russian experience.

It cannot be said that Trotsky was blind to the non-revolutionary aspects of German social-democracy.

'The European socialist parties—and in the first place the mightiest of them, the German—have developed their conservatism which grows stronger in proportion to the size of the masses affected, the efficiency of the organization, and the party discipline. Therefore it is possible that the social democracy may become an obstacle in the path of any open clash between the workers and the bourgeoisie.'[14]

However, this was no reason for pessimism.

[11] L. Trotsky, *Stalin*, p. 433.
[12] N. Trotsky, *Itogi i perspektivy*, p. 286.
[13] V. Adler, *Briefwechsel mit A. Bebel und K. Kautsky*. Wien, 1954.
[14] N. Trotsky, *Itogi i Perspektivy*, p. 285.

'The tremendous influence of the Russian revolution is shown by the fact that it kills party routine, destroys party conservatism, and the open struggle between the proletariat and capitalism becomes the order of the day. The fight for universal suffrage in Austria and Germany has become more intense under the impact of the Russian October strike. The revolution in the East infects the Western proletariat with revolutionary idealism and arouses the desire to "speak Russian" to the class enemy.'[15]

What impact did the Russian revolution in fact have on German social-democracy? No doubt the party had been pushed to the left. Hitherto the idea of the political mass strike, advocated fervently by Parvus for the last ten years, had found little sympathy in the party leadership. In 1905, fired by the Russia example, the party dropped its reluctance and accepted the idea. This fitted in well enough with Trotsky's conceptions. Yet at the time when Trotsky drafted his essay in 1906, the German party was beating a hasty retreat from this radical position under the pressure of the trade unions, which were horrified by the idea of a political mass strike. A man of Trotsky's cast of mind would not be dismayed by such a retreat. To him the great lesson of the tempestuous events of 1905 had been that the main force through which history was moving was the spontaneous action of the masses. Under its pressure, the warring factions, the Mensheviks and Bolsheviks, had been brought together, forgetting the disputes of the exile period. Parvus wrote about the role of the party leaders, 'We were but strings of an aeolian harp on which the wind of the revolution was playing.'[16] In his mind Trotsky drew a parallel between the Russia emigré *literati* and the German labour bureaucracy, both seen as potential obstacles in the path of history, and both inevitably to be pushed into the right direction by the pressure of events. The scorching lava of the 'embattled masses' would break through the crust of the German party's officialdom.

In 1930 Trotsky described his attitude towards the realignments within the RSDLP before 1917 as one inspired by revolutionary fatalism. In 1906 this philosophy, which after all went with a profound faith in the creative power of the masses and thus had a strong libertarian tinge, was expressed in the preface to the collection of essays in which the theory of the permanent revolution found its classical formulation. Trotsky went out of his way to emphasize that the permanent revolution would arise out of historic necessity.

'It is not an idea that we put forward as a premise to our tactics. The theory of the permanent revolution is a conclusion drawn from the inter-relationships of the revolution. We would be most wretched

---

[15] *Op. cit.*, p. 285.
[16] *Neue Zeit*, vol. 24, pt. 1, 1906, p. 113.

subjectivists if our tactics were nothing but a practical application of this abstract idea.'[17]

What happened in 1917 in terms of the theory? It had been born out of a novel interpretation of the contrasting elements of the Russian political landscape. Only at a later stage had the theory been developed and placed in an international setting. In 1917 the approach came from the opposite end. Lenin, who had hitherto never had any time for the theory, not even for its refutation, had arrived at the conclusion that world revolution would emerge out of world war. From this general conception the application to Russia was but one short step. If the capitalist world at war was pictured as a chain exposed to intense stress, the weakest link would snap. The socialist revolution in Russia would only be a prelude to the socialist revolution elsehwere. After February 1917 Lenin accepted the bold perspectives of the permanent revolution for Russia which would throw the lighted torch into the powder barrel of Western Europe. The spontaneous revolt of the masses in Western Europe would sweep away the conservative influence of the social-democratic parties. Lenin's new conception constituted a complete break with the traditions of Bolshevism. When on his return to Russia in April 1917 he presented his new prognosis, it had the effect of a bombshell on the Bolshevik leaders who had stayed in Russia during the war.

On the other hand, as far as Russia was concerned, Trotsky now definitely broke with the philosophy of revolutionary fatalism which had inspired his warnings against the 'wretched subjectivist' pitfall of making his abstract theory the basis for the tactics of the RSDLP. On this issue he completely swung round. There was no more talk of the pressure of events bringing Bolsheviks and Mensheviks together, no more talk of the logic of history working through the spontaneous action of the masses. The revolution became a process in which two of the greatest revolutionary leaders of all time, at the head of a formidable party, forced a new predetermined political pattern on their country. Fifteen years later Trotsky was to say that in all probability there would have been no October revolution if Lenin had not arrived in Petrograd in April 1917. Such an interpretation, which is generally accepted, places the accent plainly on the leaders and the organization. The idea which inspired the October rising was a combination of a brilliantly organized coup d'état in Russia with hopes for a spontaneous rise of the masses in the West. When persuading his fellow Bolsheviks to take the decisive plunge, Lenin made heavy play with the news of a mutiny in the German navy—a harbinger of even more formidable movements to come. In the moment of its apparent triumph the theory of the permanent revolution had been conquered by its surrender to a completely different

[17] N. Trotsky, *Nasha Revolyutsiya*, p. XVII.

conception. The basic premise on whose common acceptance Lenin and Trotsky had joined forces in 1917, their conviction of an imminent world revolution, proved unfounded. With its failure, as we can see now in retrospect, came Trotsky's eventual downfall.

Has the theory of the permanent revolution had its day? The answer would be no if the idea were reduced to some very general propositions such as that of the clash between the very old and the very new in the underdeveloped countries. The theory would still be relevant today if it was reduced to the suggestion that in conditions of a weakened traditional order a party of determined revolutionaries can seize political power, force a programme of industrialization on a backward country, and create a proletariat from above. Yet by whittling it down to these points most of the essence of the theory would be lost. The movements in Asia and Africa today which suggest the topical relevance of the idea are primarily inspired by nationalism. Trotsky's theory, when fully developed, was based on the strongest possible sense of internationalism. It envisaged the closest co-operation between a socialist Germany and a socialist Russia; when Trotsky wrote that democracy would be achieved in Russia through the dictatorship of the proletariat he had meant it perfectly sincerely. He had believed in the self-expression of the masses by means of institutions created from below as opposed to the rule of a party. In the new versions of Marxism produced by the Asian revolutions of our time, there is great emphasis on the role of the rural masses; in Trotsky's system there was the sharpest differentiation between town and countryside, with all his hopes placed on the town, linking this element of backward Russia with the whole culture of Western Europe. The theory of the permanent revolution belongs to a historical epoch which has gone for ever, the period of the Second International. The realities of today are very far removed from the dreams of the young man of genius who drafted his twentieth century version of the *Communist Manifesto* in a Petersburg prison cell in 1906.

v. Between Lenin and Stalin: Nikolai Bukharin

SIDNEY HEITMAN*

Among the outstanding figures in the history of Marxism, few occupy a more prominent place than Nikolai I. Bukharin. As one of the foremost theoreticians in the early history of the Bolshevik movement, he played a major role in the formation and development of Communist revolutionary thought. Although today his significant contributions to Bolshevik theory and practice are officially repudiated in the Communist world, their enduring impact has long survived his time in power.

A brief summary of the highlights of Bukharin's career in the Russian Communist movement reveals the source of his ideological influence.[1] Born in 1888, Bukharin was one of the youngest of the

* The writer is indebted to the Social Science Research Council and to the Ford Foundation for assistance which made possible the research on which this article is based.

[1] There is no comprehensive biography of Bukharin. The material in this essay is based on the research of the writer for his doctoral dissertation, 'Nikolai I. Bukharin's Theory of World Revolution' (Russian Institute of Columbia University). The only specialized works dealing primarily with Bukharin or some phase of his career and produced in the West are: Peter Knirsch, *Die Ökonomischen Anschauungen Nikolaj I. Bucharins* (Berlin: East European Institute of the Free University of Berlin, 1959); John E. Flaherty, 'The Political Career of Nicholas I. Bukharin' (unpublished doctoral dissertation, New York University, 1954); Daniel J. Nelson, 'The Views of N. Bukharin on the Future Communist Society' (unpublished master's thesis, Russian Institute of Columbia University, 1952); Sidney Heitman, 'Bukharin's Conception of the Transition to Communism in Soviet Russia: An Analysis of His Basic Views, 1923–1928' (unpublished Certificate Essay, Russian Institute of Columbia University, 1952). Two bibliographies of Bukharin's works have been published: Sidney Heitman, *An Annotated Bibliography of Nikolai I. Bukharin's Published Works* (Fort Collins, Colorado: privately printed, 1958), and Sidney Heitman and Peter Knirsch, *N. I. Bucharin*, Vol. I. in *Bibliographische Mitteilungen des Osteuropa-Instituts an der Freien Universität Berlin* (Berlin: East European Institute of the Free University of Berlin, 1959).

There are only two reliable and fairly detailed biographical sketches of Bukharin's life and work emanating from Soviet sources. One is an autobiographical article written in the early or middle 1920s and published in *Entsiklopedicheskii Slovar Russkovo Bibliographicheskovo Instituta Granat* (52 vols.; Moscow: Granat Russian Bibliographical Institute, 1910–34; XLI, Part I, pp. 51–6). The other is an article written by one of Bukharin's followers, D. P. Maretskii, and published in 1927 in *Bolshaia Sovetskaia Entsiklopediia* (1st ed.; 65 vols.; Moscow, 1926–31; VIII, pp. 271–83).

leading Bolsheviks. He joined the Social Democratic Party while still a student in Moscow University and worked for several years as a party organizer and propagandist among Moscow workers. After his third arrest for revolutionary activity, Bukharin escaped to Europe, where in 1912 he met Lenin and became one of his associates. After four years of exile in various European countries, where he continued his studies in economics and worked with left-wing socialist groups during the First World War, he emigrated to the United States in 1916. In New York he became co-editor with Leon Trotsky of a Russian language newspaper and helped to organize a group of radical socialists who later founded the American Communist Party.

Bukharin returned to Russia in April 1917 following the fall of the Tsarist government and worked closely with Lenin in planning and carrying out the November Revolution. In the summer of that year, Bukharin assumed the first of the many high positions he would come to hold when he became a member of the Central Committee of the Party and editor of *Pravda*. After a short break with Lenin in 1918 over the issue of a separate peace with Germany, Bukharin was made a member of the Politbureau in 1919. In the same year he played a major role in the founding of the Communist International and was elected to its Executive Committee. In 1926 he succeeded Zinoviev as its highest officer. Other important organizations in which he acquired leading positions at various times in his career include the Central Executive Committee of the Congress of Soviets, the Komsomol, the Central Council of Trade Unions, the Red International of Trade Unions, the Supreme Council of the National Economy, the Institute of Red Professors, the Communist Academy and the Academy of Sciences of the USSR, the Marx-Engels-Lenin Institute, and numerous other Soviet economic, cultural, scientific, and educational organizations.

At the same time, Bukharin also achieved outstanding prominence as one of the foremost Communist theoreticians. From the time he first joined Lenin in exile, Bukharin rose rapidly to first-rank importance among those who formulated and spread Bolshevik ideas. Possessed of a fertile mind, great erudition, and a prolific pen, he wrote hundreds of important books, pamphlets, and articles which influenced and expressed the Party's attitude towards a multitude of problems lying in such diverse areas as philosophy, economics, social and political theory, science, literature, art, and education. At the peak of his career in the nineteen-twenties, Bukharin was widely regarded as the leading theoretician and the foremost authority on Marxism in the Party, a distinction which had been acknowledged by Lenin himself.[2]

[2] In his so-called 'testament', Lenin is purported to have characterized Bukharin as 'the most valuable and biggest theoretician of the Party'. It should be

By virtue of his high posts, varied and widespread activities, and authority as a theoretician, Bukharin exercised greater influence in the Communist world during the middle and late nineteen-twenties than any other individual until that time except Lenin, and after Lenin's death in 1924 many Soviet and foreign observers came to regard him as the legitimate heir and successor to Lenin's political and ideological leadership of the international Communist movement. Bukharin's triumph was short-lived, however, for in 1928 Stalin launched his attack against the 'right-wing' of the Party, and in the following year Bukharin lost most of his important offices in the Party and the Comintern. Later he was compelled to repudiate his earlier contributions to the Communist movement and to pay degrading homage to Stalin. In 1937 he was arrested and charged with treason, and after a spectacular trial, he was executed on March 15, 1938. Since his death, Bukharin's name has been considered anathema in the Communist world. One of Bukharin's most significant accomplishments was his contribution to the evolution of Communist revolutionary thought. Bukharin's career spanned a period in the history of Bolshevism when its ideology was in a state of transition. In the decade preceding and following the Revolution of 1917, the Party still lacked a coherent body of revolutionary theory, considered essential to the success of its cause. Although the Bolshevik leaders subscribed generally to Marxism as the sole scientific doctrine capable of guiding the proletariat in its historically ordained mission to overturn capitalism and supplant it with communism, they also recognized the need to modify the doctrine and to accommodate it to the conditions of their day, while intent upon preserving its revolutionary content.

Foremost among the Party's revolutionary 'revisionists' was Bukharin, determined from the outset of his career as a Bolshevik leader to transform Marxian doctrine into an operative weapon in the struggle for world communism, in the light of his times and the needs of the Party. By 1928, his effort to provide a version of Marxism applicable to twentieth century conditions had taken shape in a comprehensive reformulation of the classical Marxian theory of proletarian revolution which represented a major landmark in the history of Marxian thought. One measure of the success of his efforts was the adoption in 1928 by the Communist International of his modified conception of the causes, processes, and goals of proletarian revolution as its official operative ideology.

Bukharin's revision of the classical Marxian scheme of proletarian revolution did not proceed in a systematic, orderly manner. Rather,

noted, however, that Lenin also added, 'But Bukharin's views can only with the very greatest doubt be regarded as fully Marxian, for there is something scholastic in him (as he has never learned and, I think, never fully understood the dialectic).' Leon Trotsky, *The Suppressed Testament of Lenin*, New York, 1935, p. 6.

it evolved gradually out of the complex interplay of ideas, personalities, and events of the early years of the Bolshevik movement and
was developed and expressed in scores of articles, books, and
speeches produced between 1912 and 1928. Among these numerous
works several merit special mention as outstanding landmarks in the
development of Bolshevik thought. These include:

Mirovoe Khoziaistvo i Imperializm,[3] written in 1914–15, in which
he first formulated his revision of Marx's doctrine of capitalist
development and laid down his theory of imperialism, as well as its
implications for the proletarian revolution—a year before Lenin
produced his own version of imperialism;

K Teorii Imperialisticheskovo Gosudarstva,[4] written in 1916, in
which Bukharin developed his theory of the state both before and
following a proletarian revolution—subjects left vague and ambiguous by Marx and Engels and also not treated by Lenin until a
year later;

Programma Kommunistov (1918),[5] a popular pamphlet outlining
the programme of the Communist Party in Russia, written shortly
after the November Revolution and distributed in millions of copies
to all parts of the country; it was subsequently translated into every
major western language and reprinted in many editions;

Azbuka Kommunizma (1919),[6] written jointly with E. Preobraz-
hensky, which became the standard textbook for an entire generation
of Party members in the nineteen-twenties;

Ekonomika Perekhodnovo Perioda (1920), the first detailed analysis
by any Marxist of the transition period between capitalism and
communism, which became a classic in its day;

Teoriia Istoricheskovo Materializma (1921), Bukharin's major
philosophical work, giving his distinctive interpretation of dialectical
and historical materialism; it gave rise to an historic controversy in
the Party over its implications for Soviet social and economic
theory;[7]

Imperializm i Nakoplenie Kapitala (1925), a restatement and
modification of the Marxian theory of the accumulation of capital,
which Marxists generally agreed stood in need of correction;

Kapitalisticheskaia Stabilizatsiia i Proletarskaia Revoliutsiia (1927),
originally a report delivered to the Executive Committee of the

---

[3] Moscow, 1918. An English translation was published in 1929 under the title,
Imperialism and World Economy.

[4] Published in *Revoliutsiia Prava* (Moscow, 1925), Part I, pp. 5–32.

[5] Petrograd: Petrograd Soviet of Workers' and Red Army Deputies.

[6] Translated into English as *The ABC of Communism*.

[7] See Raymond Bauer, *The New Man in Soviet Psychology* (Harvard University Press, 1952), for a brief discussion of this controversy and a more detailed
analysis of its consequences for the development of Soviet psychological theory
and practice.

Communist International[8] and subsequently published separately and widely distributed; it formulated the official Soviet and Comintern theory of the dynamics of proletarian world revolution during the current stage of 'capitalist stabilization';

a series of articles and pamphlets produced in the middle nineteen-twenties which spelled out the theory of 'socialism in one country' and the policy of gradualism in building socialism in Soviet Russia, and which were instrumental in defeating Trotsky and his supporters;[9]

the *Programme of the Communist International* (1928),[10] one of the basic documents in the history of communism, which intended to be, but failed to become, a modern, twentieth century version of the original *Communist Manifesto*.

In these and other works, Bukharin achieved a remarkable synthesis between classical Marxian social theory and Bolshevik revolutionary experience. While retaining in his modified conception of proletarian revolution the core of the original doctrine, he enlarged and elaborated it in a way that transformed it into a highly flexible, adaptable ideology that could be invoked under a wide variety of conditions unforeseen by Marx and Engels. Thus, Bukharin not only reaffirmed the essential claims of classical Marxism, but also converted it into a pragmatic instrument of social action.

The similarities and differences between Bukharin's revised version of the theory of proletarian revolution and the original doctrine of Marx and Engels may best be seen by summarizing the main provisions of Bukharin's thought as it finally crystallized by 1928. His point of departure was an expansion of the Marxian theory of capitalist development. Even before Lenin turned his own attention to this problem, Bukharin advanced the concept of a 'higher' stage of capitalist development beyond that of industrial capitalism, which Marx and Engels had been unable to foresee. In the normal

[8] See *Puti Mirovoi Revoliutsii. Sedmoi Rasshirennyi Plenum Ispolnitelnovo Komiteta Kommunisticheskovo Internatsionala. Stenograficheskii Otchet* (2 vols.; Moscow-Leningrad: 1927).

[9] 'Novoe Otkrovenie o Sovetskoi Ekonomike, ili Kak Mozhno Pogubit Rabochii-Krestianskii Blok; K Voprosu ob Ekonomicheskom Obosnovanii Trotskizma', in *K Voprosu o Trotskizme* (Moscow-Leningrad: 1925); *K Kritke Ekonomicheskoi Platformy Oppozitsii, op. cit.*; *Kak Ne Nuzhno Pisat Istoriiu Oktiabria*; *Po Povodu Knigi Tov. Trotskogo* '1917 g.,' *op. cit.*; *K Voprosu o Trotskizme*; *Teoriia Permanentnoi Revoliutsii, op. cit.*; 'O Kharaktere Nashei Revoliutsii i o Vozmozhnosti Pobedonosnovo Sotsialisticheskovo Stroitelstva v SSSR', in *V. Zashchitu Proletarskoi Diktatury*; *Sbornik* (Moscow-Leningrad: State Publishing House, 1928); *Put k Sotsializmu i Rabochii-Krestianskii Soiuz* (Moscow-Leningrad: 1927); 'O Novoi Ekonomicheskoi Politike i Nashikh Zadachakh,' *Bolshevik* (No. 7–8, 1924).

[10] *International Press Correspondence*, VIII, No. 92, December 31, 1928, pp. 1749–68. While the authorship of the Programme adopted in 1928 by the sixth world congress of the Communist International was officially attributed to the committee which prepared and submitted it for consideration, it was written by Bukharin, and amended in the programme commission.

course of evolution, Bukharin held, industrial capitalism, characterized by the domination of productive capital and free competition within individual states, leads to the rise of 'monopoly', or 'state capitalism', which is characterized by the 'organization' of production within single 'state trusts', by the rise of imperialism, and by the formation of a unified, global system of 'world capitalism'.

Bukharin argued that the progressive accumulation of capital and its centralization led in time to the transfer of ownership of the means of production to the hands of a few powerful bankers and financiers. As the contradictions of capitalism and competition inevitably result in a decline of the rate of profit, these finance capitalists, content at first simply to extract profit from competitive production, attempt to overcome the anarchy of production by means of monopolistic organization of the national economy. Partial organization leads to complete organization, and ultimately the capitalist state is employed to exercise centralized regulation and control of the entire economy from a single centre dominated by the finance capitalists. Thus, Bukharin held, industrial capitalism inevitably leads to 'organized state capitalism', in which the formerly anarchic productive economy becomes rationally ordered by the new 'Leviathan' state.

Although these measures succeed for a time in overcoming the consequences of the declining rate of profit, they do not eliminate the basic anarchy and contradictions of the capitalist system. The ceaseless growth of the organic composition of capital still compels the finance capitalists to seek new ways of earning profit. One solution of this problem is to intensify exploitation at home, which has limits set by the minimum needs of labour. Another is to seek foreign outlets for investment, where returns are greater than at home. Yet another is to market goods abroad, while a last measure is to employ and exploit foreign labour in underdeveloped areas of the world where lower wages yield huge 'super-profits'. Part of the profits of overseas expansion is shared with the labour elite at home, thereby winning it to the side of the capitalists, dividing the ranks of the workers, and repressing class struggle.

Although the contradictions of capitalism are thus overcome in the advanced capitalist states, the emergence of a world-wide capitalist economy as a result of the extension of capitalist relations simply transfers—'reproduces'—the contradictions to the 'higher' level of the world economy. There the contradictions are expressed at first in the form of peaceful economic competition among capitalist state trusts, which then extend political and military control over their economic zones of influence in order to exclude competitors, and in time the underdeveloped areas are converted into outright colonies. Continuing competition for empire leads inevitably to imperialist wars. At first they are limited in scope and intensity, but as the weaker states are conquered and annexed together with their empires by the larger ones, war becomes more frequent and destructive, encompassing finally the entire earth.

Just as ruinous competition during the earlier stage of capitalist development impels the capitalists to organize their national economies, so the emergence of a few huge super-powers as a result of imperialist war leads to efforts by the victorious finance capitalists to divide and exploit the entire world in an amicable, organized manner. At this point, where all of mankind is threatened with total subjection to finance capitalism, the contradictions of the system generate an insurmountable crisis and lead inevitably to its downfall. For when the world economy becomes susceptible to conscious, organized regulation from a single world centre, it becomes ripe also for its revolutionary transformation into a communist system. At this point, both the necessity and the feasibility of proletarian world revolution and communism are present. The inherently anarchic and contradictory character of capitalism prevents the finance capitalists from completing the process of organization of the world economy. Only the proletariat is capable of achieving this in a system of communism. Imperialist wars continue, and in the midst of one or between wars, the system of world capitalism reaches its end. The destruction of productive forces and the increasing misery caused by imperialism and war end in a crisis, in which world capitalism breaks down.

The first breach in the system may come in an advanced capitalist state, where intensified exploitation, political oppression by the state, and the suffering caused by war lead to a classic proletarian revolution. It may occur first in a semi-developed capitalist state, where exploitation of the proletariat by the capitalists and of the peasantry by both the capitalists and the remaining feudal landlords leads to a combination of proletarian revolution and peasant revolt. Or it may occur first in a colonial or an oppressed national minority area, where it takes the form of a revolt against imperialism by various classes. The determining factor in each instance is the relative strength of the forces of world capitalism and the forces of anti-capitalism and anti-imperialism. Breaches in the system occur first and successively thereafter wherever world capitalism is most vulnerable and the forces of revolution strongest.

Bukharin contended that although a 'weak link' in the chain of world capitalism may exist in an advanced capitalist state, in reality such links develop first in the colonial periphery. In the finance capitalist centres, the repression or elimination of anarchy, contradiction, and class struggle by the capitalist state effectively forestalls revolution for some time. In the colonial and semi-colonial areas, however, where the contradictions of world capitalism concentrate in the combined form of economic exploitation, national oppression and colonial tyranny, and where, consequently, misery, unrest, and hostility to capitalism are greatest, revolutions mature first. There also, Bukharin added, capitalism is weakest, for these areas lie far from the imperialist centres of the world and have not yet developed their own advanced forms of state capitalism. Thus the First World War, brought on by imperialist competition, led to the first breach in the world capitalist system at its most vulnerable spot—Russia, which was both an object of capitalist imperialism as well as a capitalist state itself. There the combination of proletarian revolution against capitalism, peasant revolt against capitalism and the vestiges of feudalism, and wars of liberation by national minorities severed the chain of capitalism at what was then its most vulnerable link.

An initial break in the system may be followed, as it was after 1921, by a period of recovery and reorganization of the forces of world capitalism. The system does not collapse as a whole or all at once. Revolutions against capitalism and imperialism rise and fall in uneven waves of crisis, breakdown, and recovery. Periods of recovery between crests of the revolutionary tide are only temporary, however, for after the first breach the system as a whole exists in a state of permanent crisis. Each successive break in the system compels the finance capitalists to restore the 'equilibrium' of the network on a diminished basis, which leads inevitably to an intensification of the basic contradictions of the system. Thus, although contemporary world capitalism had recovered after 1921 from the initial revolutionary crisis caused by the war and had succeeded in stabilizing itself, the recovery was only 'temporary' and 'partial', and new waves of revolution would inevitably follow.

Ultimately, Bukharin concluded, as additional areas of the world are successively detached from the capitalist network, the equilibrium of the system becomes completely undermined, and even the capitalist state trusts come down in ruin. Following a period of transition, during which the proletariat reorganizes the world into a system of universal communism, a new epoch dawns for mankind in which the way is opened for the unlimited and unprecedented flourishing of man and society.

Thus world capitalism leads inevitably to world communism by means of revolution. The process, however, in contrast to the classical Marxian view, proceeds in a complex manner and fills an entire historic epoch. In his words, quoting from the *Programme of the Communist International*:

'Between capitalist society and communist society lies a period of revolutionary transformation, during which the one is transformed into the other. . . . The transition from the world dictatorship of imperialism to the world dictatorship of the proletariat extends over a long period of proletarian struggles with defeats as well as victories;

a period of continuous general crisis in capitalist relationships and growth of social revolutions, that is, of proletarian civil wars against the bourgeoisie; a period of national wars and colonial rebellions, which, although not in themselves revolutionary proletarian socialist movements, are nonetheless objectively, insofar as they undermine the domination of imperialism, constituent parts of the world proletarian movement; a period in which capitalist and socialist economic and social systems exist side by side in "peaceful" relationships as well as in armed conflict; a period of formation of a union of soviet states; a period in which the ties between the soviet states and colonial peoples become ever closer.

'. . . Hence it follows that the international proletarian revolution cannot be conceived as a single event occurring simultaneously all over the world. At first socialism may be victorious in a few, or even in one single capitalist country. Every such proletarian victory, however, intensifies the general crisis of capitalism. Thus, the capitalist system as a whole reaches the point of its final collapse; the dictatorship of finance capital gives way to the dictatorship of the proletariat.'[11]

Bukharin's revision of the classical Marxian theory of the causes of proletarian revolution led necessarily to modifications of his conception of the revolutionary process itself. Since the prerequisite for the transformation of world capitalism into world communism is the creation first of a dictatorship of the proletariat throughout the world, and since the world dictatorship of the proletariat is established as the result of revolutions in countries at various levels of economic and social development, the general process by which the proletariat comes to power throughout the world and utilizes such power for the purpose of realizing communism is also varied and complex.

In semi-capitalist states and colonial areas, where revolutions mature first, the proletariat inevitably finds itself a minority of the population. If it is to overturn capitalism and sever the chain of imperialism, it needs allies in the struggle. The peasant masses in such countries, living under a combination of both capitalist and feudal exploitation, represent a potential reservoir of revolutionary power which can be mobilized if the revolution promises to benefit them. Accordingly, in order to secure the support of the peasantry and retain its support after a revolution, when the proletariat is small in numbers and requires allies in the struggle against counter-revolution and for socialism, it must advance revolutionary objectives that correspond with the interests of the peasants. This means, Bukharin maintained, that revolutions in semi-capitalist countries cannot

---

[11] *The Programme of the Communist International, op. cit.,* p. 1756. Minor changes have been made in the original wording and punctuation which do not change the meaning.

proceed directly towards a pure proletarian dictatorship or the immediate introduction of complete socialism. The political alliance that brings the proletariat to power must be maintained indefinitely in the form of a 'democratic dictatorship of the proletariat and peasantry', a political partnership in which the proletariat dominates while sharing power with the non-proletarian masses. Only after a period of economic development under the democratic dictatorship which broadens the socialized base of society and permits a transition to a true proletarian dictatorship does the revolution proceed towards pure socialist objectives. Hence the economic programmes in such countries must take into account the most pressing demands of the peasantry, which does not at first desire socialism, but rather an equitable distribution of land and liberation from the exploitation of feudalism and capitalism. Moreover, since the proletariat will be confronted in such countries with many vestiges of pre-capitalist economic forms, it will be unable for this reason also to proceed directly towards socialist construction in all areas of the economy. Rather, the proletariat may introduce socialist forms only in the large-scale enterprises inherited from the previous regime, while employing entirely different measures in the private, small-scale sector. There, it must strive by means of peaceful, evolutionary methods to eliminate private enterprise and supplant it with socialist enterprise, lest the political alliance that brings the proletariat to power and retains it in power be destroyed by class war. Accordingly, the proletariat must tolerate the indefinite existence of private production, attempting only by means of incentives, economic competition, propaganda, and example to eliminate the private sector of the economy and attract its members to the socialist forms of the future. Thus the transitional form of democratic dictatorship of the proletariat and peasantry must carry out transitional economic policy.

For all these reasons, Bukharin concluded, socialism in underdeveloped countries is established only slowly and gradually, governed in its pace of development and methods by the material legacy inherited from the previous regime, by the relative strength of the proletariat and other class forces, and by the extent and tenacity of small-scale, private enterprise. Any effort to accelerate or force the pace can lead only to a disruption of the inherent equilibrium of forces in transitional society and to a rift in the worker-peasant bloc.

In more advanced capitalist states, however, where the material base of society inherited from the bourgeois regime is broader, and where fewer pre-capitalist economic and social vestiges remain, the transition will be proportionately more rapid and direct. In such countries the revolution will take more nearly the form of a pure, classical proletarian revolution with only a minimum of 'bourgeois-democratic' tasks to complete and will move directly and rapidly towards socialism.

Finally, in areas where revolutions against imperialism break out but where capitalism has been only recently introduced, or not at all, and where, consequently, there is no proletariat and no base on which to construct socialism, the process of advancing towards communism will be far different. Such areas, he held, will be annexed directly into the growing proletarian-socialist sector of the world and advanced immediately towards socialism, thereby enabling them to 'skip the stage of capitalism'.

Summarizing his view of the process of revolution under the conditions of finance capitalism and imperialism, Bukharin stated, in the words of the Comintern Programme:

'The international proletarian revolution represents a combination of processes which vary in time and character: pure proletarian revolutions, revolutions of a bourgeois-democratic type which grow into proletarian revolutions, wars for national liberation, and colonial revolutions. The world dictatorship of the proletariat comes about only as the final result of this revolutionary process.

'The uneven development of capitalism, which becomes more accentuated in the period of imperialism, gives rise to various types of capitalism, to different shades of ripeness of capitalism in different countries, to a variety of specific conditions of the revolutionary process. These circumstances make it historically inevitable that the proletariat will comes to power in a variety of ways and degrees of rapidity and that a number of countries must pass through certain transitional stages leading to the dictatorship of the proletariat and must adopt varied forms of socialist construction.'[12]

From this brief summary of the major revisions introduced by Bukharin into the classical Marxian scheme of revolution it may be seen that his efforts to expand the original body of social and revolutionary theory and to incorporate within it both post-Marxian world developments and the experience of the Russian Revolution resulted, in effect, in the creation of a substantially new revolutionary doctrine that diverged considerably from the letter of the original. Whereas Marx and Engels had been concerned primarily with the problem of proletarian revolution in the most advanced capitalist states and had developed their theories with this in mind, Bukharin broadened the conception of proletarian revolution to encompass many other types of revolutionary movements in countries at various levels of economic and social development. Moreover, in modifying the classical Marxian scheme, Bukharin placed far greater emphasis than Marx or Engels had upon the role of conscious leadership by dispensing with the traditional Marxian prerequisites of a minimum level of economic development and the presence of a majority pro-

[12] *Ibid.*, p. 1761. Minor changes have been made in the original.

letariat, substituting instead the actions of the Communist Parties as primary determinants of revolution.

While departing in this way from the traditional Marxian conception of proletarian revolution, Bukharin permitted its application to a wider variety of specific conditions.

While the historic significance of Bukharin's revisions of classical Marxian revolutionary theory is obvious, two important questions relating to his thought logically arise—namely, the extent to which his views on revolution were original and the precise extent to which they influenced the development of Communist theory and practice. In considering these questions, it may be noted, first of all, that there is a close affinity between Bukharin's version of revolutionary Marxism, and ideas that have come to be known as 'Leninism' and 'Stalinism', implying a source of authorship other than Bukharin. While many similarities between Bukharin's views and those of Lenin and Stalin undoubtedly exist, it should be recalled that in the case of Lenin, Bukharin anticipated the former in at least two important instances—namely, the theory of imperialism and the theory of the state before and following a proletarian revolution— and in other instances directly influenced Lenin's own ideological development, as Lenin himself acknowledged. This in no way implies that Bukharin did not borrow heavily from the Leninist store of ideas as well, for he freely admitted this. At the same time, however, it is also true that in so doing, Bukharin did not simply take over Leninist ideas intact, but rather carried their implications and meaning further than Lenin had and ultimately achieved, as Lenin had not before his death, a system of thought that neatly integrated classical Marxism and the new Bolshevik concepts and which became the official outlook of the international Communist movement from the late nineteen-twenties onward.

With respect to the similarities between Bukharin's thought and that of Stalin's, it should be noted that, apart from a number of specific theoretical innovations introduced by Stalin before and after 1928 into the body of Bolshevik doctrine, his primary contribution to the development of Communist ideology was to harden the doctrine that had emerged by 1928 into a rigid dogma and to apply it to areas of Soviet life not yet fully affected by it in Bukharin's day. Stalin made two major ideological contributions before 1928, one on the nationality problem and the other on the theory of 'socialism in one country'. In the former instance, some Soviet specialists attribute all but the actual writing of Stalin's initial article on the nationality question in 1913 to Bukharin,[13] while the historical record clearly reveals that

---

[13] Abdurakhman Avtorkhanov, a supporter of Bukharin, states in his *Stalin and the Soviet Communist Party*; *A Study in the Technology of Power* (New York, 1959), for example, that Bukharin 'helped Stalin to compile his *Marxism and the National Question,* which first appeared under the title of *Social Democracy*

although Stalin first advanced the theory of 'socialism in one country' late in 1924, it was Bukharin, and not Stalin, who gave it its full theoretical expression and integrated it into the body of Bolshevik ideology. On the other hand, although Stalin added new doctrines after 1928 to the official body of Communist theory, in some instances these were merely reaffirmations or reformulations of ideas advanced earlier by Bukharin. An example of this is Stalin's theory of 'revolution from above' by which he justified his programmes of enforced industrialization and collectivization in the nineteen-thirties. The precedent for this theory, however, had been laid down as early as 1920 by Bukharin, when he characterized the dynamics of the transition period as an extraordinary process of 'reverse influence of the superstructure on the base', arising from the revolutionary, 'cataclysmic nature of the transitional process'.

It should be remembered, too, in estimating the influence of Bukharin's views on Stalin, that between Lenin's death in 1924 and Stalin's rise to unrivalled power after 1928, the ideology of the Party was still in a process of evolution. During this time, Stalin and Bukharin were political allies and held essentially similar views, but it was Bukharin, not Stalin, who dominated the Soviet scene in the ideological sphere. Accordingly, it is far more probable to assume that Bukharin provided the theoretical leadership of their political alliance, rather than the other way round. Later, although Stalin turned against Bukharin and repudiated some of his specific policies applicable to the late nineteen-twenties, he retained the essential core of Bukharin's thought without, however, crediting him any longer with its origin.

Summarizing the historical significance of Bukharin's role in the development of Bolshevik revolutionary doctrine, it may be seen that, among other things, Bukharin filled the ideological gap between the death of Lenin and the rise of Stalin. For although it is axiomatic in the Communist world to portray the evolution of Soviet ideology as a direct, continuous line of orthodox doctrinal descent running from Marx through Lenin to Stalin, there are important differences as well as similarities between Leninism and Stalinism. Both the differences and similarities, however, cannot be adequately understood without taking into account Bukharin's intervening influence between the years 1924 and 1928. It may well

and the Problem of Nationalities. . . . Bukharin found and translated for Stalin suitable quotations . . . and edited the entire book before it was accepted by Lenin for publication in 1913. . . .' (p. 23).

It should be noted, however, that while some writers sustain Avtorkhanov's contention, for example Bertram Wolfe in _Three Who Made a Revolution_ (New York, 1948, p. 582); others deny that Bukharin's views influenced Stalin in the writing of this article (see Isaac Deutscher, _Stalin; A Political Biography_, New York, 1947, p. 119, for example).

be for this reason, among others, that Stalin thought it necessary not only to break Bukharin's political authority as a prerequisite to his own unchallenged leadership of the Communist world, but also to destroy both him and his image in the Party as well.

VI. The Revolution in Asia: M. N. Roy

ROBERT C. NORTH

This was the summer of 1920, and revolutionaries from all over the world had begun to converge on Petrograd for the opening of the Second Congress of the Communist International. The famous old Smolny Institute, formerly a school for daughters of the nobility, now held the offices of various commissars, and it was there that leading Russian Bolsheviks welcomed the delegates. As soon as the ceremony was over, a great crowd marched in process to the Uritsky Theatre, where only delegates and spectators with special tickets were granted admittance. Despite precautions, the place was packed with people sitting on the floor and jamming every corner and passageway.

There, near the front, sat a tall, brown-skinned delegate, M. N. Roy, from India. Represented also were China, Korea, Turkey, Persia, the Dutch East Indies and more than thirty other states and dependencies. Throughout 1918 and 1919 Russian Communist leaders had expected post-war unrest in central Europe to explode into a general revolution, but in Germany, Hungary, and Austria newly-formed workers' and soldiers' soviets had met early defeat. By the opening of the Second Congress the Bolsheviks were looking hopefully towards possibilities for revolution in other quarters.

Lenin himself now mounted the rostrum to analyse the international situation. By 1914, he said, more than 600 million people had fallen subject to colonial rule, while another 400 million in Persia, Turkey, and China had been reduced to semi-colonial status. Indeed, the Great War, according to Lenin, had grown directly out of this division of the world among the imperialist powers, who had come to blows over which of the two great groups was to enjoy the right of robbing, exploiting, and crushing the rest of the world.

During subsequent sessions of the Congress, which were held in Moscow, the delegates discussed at considerable length the political strategy and tactics which Communists ought to follow in the encouragement of revolution in the colonial and dependent—as distinct from the western capitalist—nations. The outcome of these discussions was the adoption of the 'Theses on the National and Colonial Questions', which presented Lenin's views modified by proposals introduced by M. N. Roy in his 'Supplementary Theses'.

According to Lenin, the Communist International 'must be ready to establish temporary relationships and even alliances with the bourgeois democracy of the colonies and backward countries. It must not, however, amalgamate with it.' In contrast, while Roy agreed that 'it would be profitable to make use of the co-operation of the bourgeois national-revolutionary elements', he insisted that the Communist International and its constituent parties must struggle against any bourgeois control over the workers and peasants and must make every effort to develop the class consciousness of the working masses.

The difference between the two points of view was only a matter of emphasis, but it was sufficient to confuse the issue in Communist minds and to hamper the Comintern in seeking to exploit the revolutions of Asia.

At the time of the Second Congress M. N. Roy was barely thirty-three years old, but he had already served more than fifteen years as an anti-British revolutionary. He had been still in his teens when British intelligence agents first took note of his activities, and police from India and Southeast Asia all the way to China, Japan, and the United States were familiar with his movements. Prior to his arrival in Moscow, he had been operating in Berlin—and before that in Mexico City where Borodin, the Comintern agent, had won him over to Communism. Now the new convert stood face to face with Lenin and boldly challenged the views of Bolshevism's most seasoned strategist and theoretician. 'Two distinct movements which grow farther apart each day,' Roy declared, 'are to be found in the dependent countries. One is the bourgeois democratic movement, with a programme of political independence under the bourgeois order. The other is the mass struggle of the poor and ignorant peasants and workers for their liberation from the various forms of exploitation.'

In order to overthrow foreign capitalism, he argued, it would be profitable to make use of the co-operation of the bourgeois nationalist elements—but only in the initial stages and with circumspection. The foremost task was to form Communist parties in the dependent areas which would organize the peasants and workers and lead them to revolution and to the establishment of soviet republics.

Beyond this, Roy contended also that the revolutionary movement in Europe was absolutely dependent upon the course of the revolution in Asia. Super-profits extracted from the colonies were the mainstay of modern capitalism. 'Without control of the extensive markets and vast areas for exploitation in the colonies,' he told the Second Congress, 'the capitalist powers of Europe would not be able to exist even for a short time.'

Lenin took strong exception to parts of Roy's thesis. Drawing on his own experience, he reminded the delegates that the Russian Bolsheviks had supported liberal liberation movements against tsarism. Similarly, the Indian Communists were 'in duty bound' to support 'bourgeois liberation movements' without in any sense merging with them. Roy, moreover, had gone too far in declaring that the destiny of revolutionary forces in the West would depend decisively upon the strength of the mass revolutionary movement in Asia.

After considerable debate the Second Congress sought to resolve the argument by approving both theses. While collaborating with middle-class nationalists in the colonies and semi-colonies, Communist leaders were expected to make every effort to arouse and organize the working masses and to penetrate and gain leadership over existing revolutionary movements.

Over the ensuing half-dozen years, with headquarters first in Berlin and later in Paris, Roy developed his concepts for revolution in the colonies and semi-colonies around four central themes: (1) the absolute necessity for ensuring that leadership for each stage of the revolution should rest at all times with a Communist vanguard; (2) the usefulness of limited, tactical, and strictly controlled Communist co-operation with essentially hostile bourgeois democratic revolutionaries during early stages; (3) recognition of the wavering tendencies of the petty-bourgeoisie who, as an exploited class in the colonies and semi-colonies, shared with the peasantry and the proletariat certain interests which they did not at first perceive—but which, under Communist leadership, they could be brought to see; and (4) the necessity, during the initial revolutionary stages, of a Communist-led non-capitalist programme of development encompassing many 'petty-bourgeois capitalist reforms' such as the nationalization of transport and public utilities, the division of land among the peasants, and so forth.

In seeking to implement these concepts over the years, however, the Bengali revolutionary—through the lessons of experience and the irresistible pressure of his own reasoning—gradually worked his way out of Bolshevik doctrine and spent the latter part of his life searching for other explanations of Asia's crises and other solutions for Asia's problems.

Undoubtedly it was Roy's Indian background and his assessment of the independence movement in India that shaped his concepts of Asian class struggle. An important basis for his distrust of the bourgeoisie, for example, seems to have emerged from his perception of a significant shift in British policies—and his perception, also, of how the Indian bourgeoisie had responded to this shift.

Great Britain, unable to keep Indian markets supplied with

manufactured goods during World War I, had reversed its traditional policy of keeping India industrially backward, thus bringing the Indian bourgeoisie 'into its confidence', and presenting Indian capital with a free field of development. The British Government in 1916 had even gone to the length of appointing an Indian Industrial Commission in order to encourage industry in the country, and in consequence, by war's end, the Indian capitalist class had achieved such an economic security that the Government could no longer ignore bourgeois political demands, and in due course these were largely met by the Montague-Chelmsford Reforms. 'The object behind this remarkable change of policy on the part of British imperialism,' Roy asserted, 'was to split the revolutionary movement by making it clear to the bourgeoisie that it was no longer impossible for it to realize its ambitions under British rule.'

This turn of policy did not ensure that the bourgeoisie would be won over. On the contrary, 'The more the British Government makes concessions to the Indian bourgeoisie,' Roy maintained, 'the more ambitious the latter becomes. It knows quite well that it is necessary to make compromises with the Imperial capital, till the time comes when it will be in a position to contend openly for the right of monopoly of exploitation with the foreigner. But it also knows that British imperialism cannot be overthrown without the help of the masses.'

The bourgeoisie would deliberately deceive the masses, Roy believed, in order to capture their support and secure aggrandisement, and would seek to draw them into the National Congress. Still unaware of their own purposes, the masses would follow, for a time, but would not remain forever a reliable force behind the political manoeuvres of the bourgeoisie. 'The overthrow of the British rule will be achieved by the joint action of the bourgeoisie and the masses,' asserted Roy, thus revealing his position as only a hairsbreadth—a crucial hairsbreadth—from Lenin's, 'but how this joint action can be consummated still remains a question. It will be easier to solve this problem when the condition of the masses is analysed, in order to understand what a great gulf divides these two revolutionary factors.' In the long run the divorce of the masses from bourgeois leadership was inevitable; bourgeois nationalism would end in a compromise with Imperial supremacy, and the liberation of India would be left to the political movement of the workers and peasants—'consciously organized and fighting on the ground of class-struggle.'

Between 1922 and the convening of the Sixth Congress in 1928 Roy from time to time revised his assessments of bourgeois relationships with the British and with the Indian masses, but the main line of his argument did not change. Paradoxically, the logic of it eventually drove him from the Communist movement.

At the Fourth Congress of the Communist International in 1922, for example, Roy maintained that financial dislocations in Europe were forcing imperialism to look for new markets by which the equilibrium of world capitalism could be re-established. Western European capitalists hoped to achieve this new economic balance by promoting industrialization in countries like India and China.

In the beginning, Roy conceded, the various revolutionary upheavals in Asian countries had been a spontaneous reaction to intensified economic exploitation by Western imperialists. Now the national bourgeoisie, however, with increased industrialization and opportunities for profit, was withdrawing its support from national revolutionary movements and seeking imperialist protection. As a consequence, Roy declared,

'The national revolutionary movement in these countries . . . is not going to be successful under the leadership of the bourgeoisie . . . It is only under the leadership of a political party representing the workers and peasants that the national revolutionary struggle can come to final victory in these countries.'

The Fourth Congress supported Roy's analysis:

'The dominant classes in the colonies and the semi-colonial countries are unable and unwilling to lead the struggle against imperialism as this struggle is converted into a revolutionary mass movement.'

Yet the contradiction, so evident at the Second Congress, still plagued the Comintern. For the Fourth Congress, while upholding Roy's argument, was at the same time making plans for tactical co-operation in China with Sun Yat-sen's middle-class Kuomintang. How could these two antagonistic attitudes be reconciled? And how was a Communist tactician to foresee the precise moment when the essentially hostile national bourgeoisie would expend the last of its revolutionary potentialities and go over to the reaction?

Addressing the Fifth Congress in 1924, Roy asserted that in India, where national capitalism was growing rapidly, the national bourgeoisie had already been won over to support the Empire. 'Because the Indian bourgeoisie knows better than anybody else that the discontent of the masses is economic and not nationalist,' he said, 'the exploiting class in India demands protection from the exploited. Indian capitalism is running straight into the arms of British imperialism, and the same tendency will soon be seen in other countries.'

By 1926 Roy was convinced that bourgeois nationalism had ended in a complete compromise with imperialism in India. The deepening schism between the national bourgeoisie and the petty-bourgeoisie had split the Swaraj, or Home Rule Party, which previously had served as a bridge between the constitutionalism of the big bourgeoisie and the revolutionary inclinations of the petty-bourgeoisie. 'The split in the Swaraj Party,' he declared, 'means the burning of that bridge.' The last obstacle to an agreeable compromise between British imperialism and the Indian bourgeoisie had been successfully removed. The British policy of industrialization was allowing Indian capitalism to grow—within certain limits.

How then, in view of his distrust of the nationalist bourgeoisie, did Roy conceive that the revolutionary movement could be furthered in India?

In 1923, when he was operating in Berlin, Roy had written to comrades in India about forming a 'party of workers and peasants', and later he developed this scheme to encompass the establishment of a nationalist People's Party, which would attract members from a broader class base, but would contain a 'Communist Party inside it' Similarly, in a letter written towards the end of November 1926, the Foreign Bureau of the Indian Communist Party, of which Roy was a member, recommended the organization of an illegal Communist faction inside a legal Workers and Peasants Party. According to Roy's plan the Workers and Peasants Party would include left-wing elements of the petty-bourgeoisie—always, in Communist theory, a vacillating class—which had rejected nationalist bourgeois leadership; the object was 'gradually to develop the W. and P. P. into the real Communist Party by means of ideological education and political training connected with action'. The Workers and Peasants Party, in due course, would enter a more broadly based nationalist People's Party.

If Roy had remained in his European headquarters, or in Moscow, or if he had returned to India at this juncture, the whole course of events might have taken a different turn; but towards the end of 1926 he was sent by Stalin to China, where the Comintern was confronted by extraordinary difficulties in maintaining its alliance with the bourgeois nationalist Kuomintang.

Roy was to help straighten matters out. After reaching Vladivostok via the Trans-Siberian Railway, he boarded a special Soviet ship which by-passed Shanghai—where he was wanted by the British police—and took him directly to Canton. There an aeroplane had been assigned him for the trip to Hankow, where the Kuomintang government and Borodin's mission had their headquarters, but the motor had broken down and the journey had to be made overland by train and palanquin.

Roy had first seen China in 1916 when, on the advice of Sun Yat-sen, he had conferred with the German ambassador about the purchase of arms for an uprising in India. Now China itself was in the grip of armed revolution, and as the bearers carried him through one small village after another he saw peasant soldiers hanging from the trees, the consequence of their participation in the struggle.

By the time Roy and his party reached Hankow Chiang Kai-shek was already on his way over 'to the camp of the imperialists', and only the left wing—the *petty-bourgeois* left wing—of the Kuomintang remained in alliance with the Comintern.

At this juncture Roy's third central concept—his assumption that the petty-bourgeoisie, as an exploited class, could be brought to recognize their common interests with the peasantry and the proletariat—led him and the whole Chinese Communist movement into serious difficulties.

Borodin and other Comintern representatives in China, Roy felt, had grievously overestimated the big bourgeoisie associated with Chiang Kai-shek and had underestimated the petty-bourgeois intellectuals, small merchants, and professional people. The crucial task was to mould the left-wing Kuomintang government, now established in Wuhan, into a revolutionary democratic anti-imperialist regime based on a bloc of three classes—the petty-bourgeoisie, the peasantry, and the proletariat—under 'proletarian hegemony'.

It was Roy's belief that such a three-bloc revolutionary regime in China—by agrarian reform, and the nationalization of heavy industry, transport, and public utilities under Communist supervision—could initiate a phase of non-capitalist development which would telescope the dialectical process and prepare the way for the dictatorship of the proletariat and for socialism. During this period of non-capitalist development, he maintained, the state would continue to uphold private property to an extent sufficient to support the petty-bourgeoisie, the peasantry, and also certain 'capitalist methods' of organization and production, but would not permit capitalist exploitation of people. Thus the possibilities for limited capitalist development would be maintained for a time, and the class struggle would continue under the vigilant hegemony of the proletariat. The opposing bloc of foreign imperialists, Chinese militarists, Chinese big bourgeoisie and Chinese feudal remnants would provide the threat which would give the revolutionary coalition cohesive force and thus hold the 'block of three classes' together.

The chief obstacle to this policy was the fact that the Chinese Communist Party, having no army of its own, was dependent upon Kuomintang forces which had been armed and to a considerable degree trained by the Russians, but which remained under the command of 'unreliable' generals; most of the officers were regarded by the Communists as feudal militarists, or allies of the big bourgeoisie. The problem was how to achieve Communist control over these armies.

D

Borodin's inclination had been to preserve relations with the generals at almost any cost, and it was this policy which had induced him to cling to Chiang Kai-shek almost to the moment of the latter's *coup* against the Communists. Now Roy urged the proclamation of a radical agrarian programme and the encouragement of peasant revolution in the countryside as a means of winning the rank and file of the Kuomintang armies—most of them landless peasants— away from the 'militarists' and over to Communism. Only an agrarian revolution, he believed, would turn the trick, and that meant nationalization of the land, confiscation of large estates, and the promise of distribution among the poor peasantry.

It was Roy's estimate of the petty-bourgeoisie that turned out to be the fatal flaw in his reasoning. Perceiving that the members of this class were almost universally 'exploited' by the big bourgeoisie, and that many of the small merchants depended upon the peasantry for produce and markets, he assumed that the leaders of the Kuomintang left wing would be compelled to acquiesce in an agrarian revolution.

Events soon revealed, however, that these leaders were no more enthusiastic about peasant revolution or 'proletarian hegemony' than Chiang Kai-shek had been. Most of the Kuomintang political leaders and army officers were landholders and had no disposition towards insurrection in the countryside. Indeed, it was no small task to arouse enthusiasm for agrarian reform and the arming of poor peasants even among the leaders of the Chinese Communist Party at that time. Within the course of a few weeks—and long before the Communists had made any progress in weaning the rank-and-file soldiery from their officers—the Left Kuomintang government at Wuhan turned against the Chinese Communists and sent Roy, Borodin, and the Russian military advisers packing back to Moscow.

For the return journey the Comintern assigned Roy three large touring cars driven by GPU men and fitted with auxiliary springs and extra petrol tins lashed to the running boards. The cavalcade proceeded north-west across the Mongolian deserts to Urga and thence to the Soviet Union.

Roy had failed abysmally—as had the entire Communist leadership from Stalin down—but he did not leave China without grasping a number of realities which changed the whole subsequent course of his life.

The threat to Communist-led revolutions in Asia, he had written soon after his arrival in Canton, did not reside in the gunboats and artillery of the imperialists and their warlord allies. The greatest challenge to Communism arose from the new American tendency— not unlike the new policies he had observed the British formulating for India—to undercut the revolution with good works. The United States, pursuing a policy of 'liberal imperialism', could re-channel the whole Chinese revolution—a feat that the old-style imperialist could never accomplish.

The usual imperialist tendency, he argued, was to suppress the nationalist revolutionary movement by force and to bolster up the old regime of reactionaries and militarists. Such a policy, however, would only accelerate the development of the revolution. On the other hand, if industrialization could be accomplished in China and other colonial and semi-colonial countries by capital exported from the United States and other imperialist powers, it would 'mark a big step forward in the stabilization of world capitalism'. Already there were indications that the United States might follow such a policy of peaceful penetration and so kill with kindness the violent revolution, otherwise inevitable, that would bring victory for Communism in China. So clear was his perception of this possibility that in later years Roy could not comprehend what he considered to be the blindness and obtuseness of American policies towards the Chinese revolution.

Parallel developments, Roy thought, were taking place in India. In September 1927, shortly after his arrival in Moscow from China, he prepared a draft resolution on the Indian question. 'Imperialism,' he wrote, 'must proceed very cautiously in this new path which is as likely to lead it out of the post-war crisis as to destruction. The implication of the new policy is the gradual "de-colonization" of India, which will be allowed eventually to evolve out of the state of "dependency" to "Dominion Status". The Indian bourgeoisie, instead of being kept down as a potential rival, will be granted partnership in the economic development of the country under the hegemony of Imperialist finance. From a backward agricultural colonial possession, India will become a modern industrial country, a member of "the British Commonwealth of free nations". India is in a process of "de-colonization" insofar as the policy, forced upon Imperialism by the post-war crisis of capitalism, abolishes the old, antiquated forms and methods of colonial exploitation in favour of new forms and new methods.'

These new and highly unorthodox concepts did not go unnoticed in Moscow. Stalin and his colleagues, indeed, needed a scapegoat for their China debacle, and now Roy's theory of decolonization gave them one. There were opening attacks by Eugene Varga, and then, at the Sixth Congress of the Communist International, in mid-1928, Otto Kuusinen closed in. He began by quoting Roy at the Second Congress against Roy upon his return from China.

'Foreign imperialism, which has been forced on the Eastern peoples,' Roy had declared in 1920, 'has unquestionably impeded their social and economic development and has deprived them of the possibility of reaching the stage of development which has been reached in Europe and America. Owing to the imperialist policy which endeavours to retard industrial development in the colonies, the native proletariat has, in fact, begun only lately to exist.'

'But Comrade Roy holds different views now,' Kuusinen asserted, and he quoted the paragraph of the draft resolution on India that dealt with dominion status. 'Thus Comrade Roy sees that the decolonization policy of British imperialism would lead to the weaking and dissolution of the British Empire.'

In terms of the dialectics of history it was out of the question for the British Empire to dissolve except as the outcome of bitter struggle, and Kuusinen's charge was a serious one. Far more important, however, was the fact that Stalin had to place upon one scapegoat or another the responsibility for his humiliating failure in China. Where could he find a better candidate than this comrade who seemed to have denied the reactionary role of imperialism and the inevitability of struggle?

Expelled from the Comintern, Roy returned to India, where he spent six years in jail for his revolutionary activities. Deprived of ideological reading matter during his imprisonment, he turned to the physical and social sciences for clues to the patterns and motivations of political and social behaviour. In the years following his release he moved steadily from materialism to humanism and became a philosopher rather than a political leader.

For Roy the revolutionist, this compulsion constantly to search for the truth and constantly to adjust his convictions thereto was a tragic weakness. For Roy the philosopher, on the other hand, it was his greatest strength.

VII. From the Communist Manifesto to the Declaration of '81'

Z. A. B. ZEMAN

Marx and Engels wrote their famous *Manifest der Kommunisten* at a time when revolution was the order of the day. Soon after the printers finished with the pamphlet in January 1848, yet another eruption occurred in France, and it reverberated throughout Europe. The *Annual Register* for that year recorded that:

'a people so intelligent and inquisitive as the Germans were not likely to remain in an age like this contented spectators of a political freedom enjoyed by others, but denied to themselves, and they only waited for an opportunity to translate into action the theories and doctrines which had long been the favourite theme of some of their most popular writers. Such an opportunity was the outbreak of the French revolution in February in the present year, and the result was unexampled in history. Thrones, Dominations, Princedoms, Powers were then scattered like leaves before the storm. Never before had been witnessed such an upheaving of society throughout so vast an extent. Greater changes had for a time been wrought when the armies of Napoleon traversed Europe from Paris to Moscow, and every capital was entered by a victorious foe. But those attacks were from without; the nations bowed their heads like willows to the blast for a time, but when it had swept past they stood erect again, and, in the eloquent words of Mr Canning, after the deluge of conquest had subsided, the spires and turrets of ancient institutions reappeared. Now, however, the shock that was felt was from the throes of intestine convulsion: class was arrayed against class; the burghers against the army; and a war of opinion as well as of the sword has commenced, of which no man can venture to prophesy the result.'[1]

Although the slogans on the banners of the revolution pointed to the shape of things to come, the established governments succeeded in asserting their authority. In Vienna it was said that the *Wir*—the majestic plural of the Imperial Edicts—simply consisted of the initials of Windischgrätz, Jelačić and Radetzky, the men who succeeded in restoring order in the Habsburg dominions; in France,

[1] *Annual Register*, p. 356.

Italy, and Germany the deluge also subsided, and the revolutionaries themselves disappeared with the turbulent waters. In May 1849, soon after his thirty-first birthday, Marx was ordered to leave Prussian territory; after a short interlude in France, he made London his permanent home. Nevertheless, his experience of the storm which scattered temporal powers like leaves remained with Marx throughout his poverty-stricken, though tranquil, life: his main effort was directed towards the discovery of the laws behind this seemingly haphazard phenomenon.

Indeed, revolution was either the aim or the point of departure of all Marx's thought. Class struggle, the disharmony between the 'basis' and the 'superstructure' of his conception of society, the dialectics of progress—in short, all the essential elements of his philosophy—involve a revolutionary explosion somewhere along the line. It was the outstanding landmark of his historical landscape, one which no society could avoid passing.

Marx surveyed European history from a great height, wheeling like a sharp-eyed bird of prey, and hovering above the volcanic formations that dotted the countryside. The violent break with the past in France in 1789 served him as the prototype of the bourgeois revolution which had swept away the feudal order, and which would repeat itself elsewhere in similar conditions. The uprising of the weavers in Lyons in 1831 and again three years later, the Chartist movement in this country, and the rebellion of the Silesian weavers revealed to him the revolutionary potential of the working class. An industrial proletariat was accumulating in many areas of western Europe; soon, after a temporary alliance with the bourgeoisie, it would destroy the fabric of the society dominated by the middle-class, and emerge victorious at the end of the revolutionary process. There were no compromises possible: the 'epoch of the bourgeoisie' had simplified class antagonisms; by 1848, society was, for Marx, 'splitting up into two great hostile camps, into two great classes directly facing each other: Bourgeoisie and Proletariat'. (*Communist Manifesto*.) The clash between these two classes would lead on to another cataclysm, which would mean no less than the 'forcible overthrow of all existing social conditions'.[2]

Nevertheless, after 1848, the revolutionary tide in Europe began to ebb. The barricades were cleared away; some of the banners of the revolution lay discarded, while others passed into different hands. Until the day of Marx's death in 1883, no large-scale revolutionary event—apart from the Polish uprising of 1863 and the *communard* movement in Paris after the Franco-Prussian war—took place. In the meantime, however, his doctrines began to exercise an ever-growing influence among certain groups of European socialists. Whereas the working class movements in England and in France

[2] P. 91 in Moscow 1959 ed.

resisted its attractions, Marx's philosophical system came to dominate German socialism. It provided Leibknecht's Social Democrats
in Germany with an ideological basis, and it gave their party a sense
of direction. After the merger with the non-Marxist Lassalleans in
1875, the Social Democrats soon became the dominant component
in the new organization. Two years after the 'unity congress' in
Gotha in 1875, Social Democracy began to make an impression in
the industrial districts of North and South Germany; it did not
spread into Bavaria and other parts of the South, or to the Ruhr,
until the time of Bismarck's anti-socialist laws. Nevertheless, after
twelve years of persecution, the party emerged—in 1890—not only
unscathed, but considerably strengthened. It still was, as it had been,
a Marxist and a revolutionary party. But after the first, heroic period
of its existence, certain inconsistencies between the doctrine and the
demands of practical politics began to appear. Although some of its
leading members were inclined to treat it as a kind of overgrown
debating society, the Social-Democratic Party (SPD) was, first of all,
a political mass-organization. It was represented in the *Reichstag*, it
had to make its political programme acceptable to a large and
growing number of voters, it had to defend their immediate interests,
and it had to find its place in the German state. There were a number
of *Reichstag* deputies and other leading socialists in Germany who
concentrated, in the early 'nineties, on the political tasks in hand, and
who let their more theoretically minded comrades worry about the
relations between political practice and Marxist doctrines. They
realized that they could not put before the electorate a programme
that postponed all work for the amelioration of the workers' lot
until after the revolution. They were in fact political empiricists and
not doctrinaires; although they later fought many a bitter battle with
the Marxist fundamentalists, they never achieved a clear-cut victory.

The Erfurt party congress in 1891—the first after the repeal of the
anti-socialist laws—indicated in which direction the future con-
troversies lay. The first, general part of the programme it drew up
still treated the German social scene as a classical Marxist battle-
ground:

'The number of proletarians is increasing all the time, the army
of redundant workers is swelling, the differences between the ex-
ploiters and the exploited are becoming ever sharper, the class
struggle between the proletariat and the bourgeoisie is growing more
embittered; it divides modern society into two hostile camps, and it
is the common hall-mark of all industrial countries.'[3]

In the second section of the Erfurt programme, on the other hand,
concrete political and social demands were formulated. On the

[3] Schulthess, *Geschichtskalendar 1891*, p. 123.

political side, they included the demand for universal, direct, and secret suffrage, for more powers for the *Reichstag*, for equal rights for women, and for the secularization of education. In the sphere of social legislation, the Social Democrats went further than the Trades Law Amendment Act, the principal legislative achievement of the current session. The Socialists wanted an eight-hour day and thirty-six hours continuous rest in a week for industrial workers; stricter regulation of employers' relations with labour; a national health service, and a uniform system of insurance.

Such a programme, formulated by the representatives of a powerful mass organization, implied steady parliamentary work for reform within the existing framework of the state; although it may have seemed outrageous to conservative politicians, the demands it incorporated were by no means impracticable. Its second part pointed to evolution rather than revolution; its very division into two distinct sections contained the elements of the later controversy between the revisionists and the fundamentalist revolutionaries: the programme made no attempt to define the respective merits of parliamentary work and of revolution.

For the time being, however, the Social Democrats did not entirely discard revolution as a vehicle of social progress. At the Erfurt congress, Bebel's statement that 'capitalist society is working hard for its own downfall, and we only have to wait for the moment when power drops from its hands' was violently applauded by the hands that waited to pick up this power.[4] Although the German socialists still believed that a change of 'all existing social conditions' would occur, it was to be a long-term process, something quite different from the type of revolution—a 'forcible overthrow'—Marx had originally envisaged. The capitalist clockwork was still running down, of course, according to Marxist laws, and there was no point in trying prematurely to smash it up. The inevitable contradictions of capitalist society were working to the advantage of the Social Democrats: a glance at the election returns sufficed to confirm their hopes. Their party was well on the way to becoming the most powerful political organization in the country. It had incurred political responsibilities, its future looked indeed promising, and there was no good reason to expose it, by stressing its revolutionary character, to persecution by the state.

Nevertheless, while the idea of revolution began to fade in Germany, the party received an injection of revolutionary talent from unexpected quarters. The Tsarist regime was the *bête noire* of the German socialists; in Russia revolutionaries of every kind, including the few incipient groups of Marxist socialists, led a precarious underground existence. There were, in the late 'eighties and the early 'nineties, many students from Russia and Russian Poland at Swiss

[4] *Protokoll des Parteitags in Erfurt*, p. 172.

universities who dreamed revolution while pursuing their academic courses. They regarded Germany as the promised land of socialism; the success of the SPD exercised on them a strong attraction. A few of them actually joined its ranks, and they came to play a prominent part in the history of European revolution. The first arrival in Germany, a few weeks after the Erfurt congress, was Alexander Helphand, a Russian Jew from Odessa who had read economics at Basle university; he was soon followed by his friend Julian Marchlewski, who, incidentally, is now regarded as one of the founding fathers of the Polish communist party; a few years later, Helphand had the opportunity to introduce Rosa Luxemburg to German journalism.

These Marxists from eastern Europe later played a prominent part, inside German Social Democracy, in the original revisionist controversy: although the conflict between the 'fundamentalists' and the 'practical politicians' had been latent for several years, it came into the open only in 1896. In that year Eduard Bernstein made the opening moves in his campaign to bring Marxism, and the Social Democrat party, up to date in a series of five articles entitled 'Probleme des Socialismus Eigenes und Übersetztes'.[5] He dismissed as futile the hopes for an imminent break-up of the capitalist system, and questioned their basic premises: the increasing impoverishment of the masses, the concentration of capital, the inevitability of economic crisis. He asked whether, from the point of view of the socialist movement, the breakdown of the existing system was desirable, and he answered the question in the negative. Bernstein was one of the first theorists to face the dilemma of socialism in times of economic prosperity: he contrasted the axioms of Marxism with political and economic realities, and found the doctrine lacking.

At first, the German Social Democrats made no objections; even Kautsky, the 'Pope of Marxism', agreed with the theses that were first expounded in the paper he edited. Nevertheless, the appearance of Bernstein's articles coincided with Helphand's (now better known under his pen name of Parvus) term in office as the editor of the *Sächsische Arbeiterzeitung* between 1896 and 1898: he made his newspaper into a fortress of Marxist orthodoxy. From Dresden, with his east European friends Rosa Luxemburg and Julian Marchlewski, Helphand began a ruthless campaign in defence of Marxist dogma. Revolution was for him the treasure Marx had bequeathed to the socialist movement, and he abhorred the thought of frittering it away piecemeal in the small change of gradualism; he dismissed the foundations of Bernstein's argument as an attempt to solve social problems in a 'purely statistical manner'. His criticism, which was echoed in a number of socialist newspapers, moved Bernstein to

[5] *Neue Zeit*, 1896–1897, vol. 1.

reply: he diagnosed Helphand's sickness as 'social catastrophitis'. At this point, in March 1898, the tone of the controversy became harsher and more personal; the worthies of German Social Democracy found Helphand's tone excessively violent. The senior party theorists disagreed with most of his arguments; Bebel thought he was ignorant of German conditions; his former patron, Kautsky, found only a few belated words of sympathy for Helphand's convictions. They were, however, applauded by the Russian Social Democrats. From his exile in Switzerland, Plekhanov, the grand old man of Russian Marxism, cheered Helphand's resolute stand. Lenin wrote from Siberia to his mother to send him copies of Helphand's articles in the *Sächsische Arbeiterzeitung*; they made a profound impression on young Trotsky.

Nevertheless, sometime before the opening of the revisionist debate, the eclipse of the revolutionary idea was revealed in a different context. In March 1895 the party organ *Vorwärts* published excerpts from Friedrich Engels's introduction to *The Class Struggles in France, 1848-1850*, by Marx, in which Engels concluded, after examining the revolutions in France of 1948 and 1871, that the methods of struggle against the established order employed in 1848 had become outdated, and that advances in the technical and the military fields had strengthened the position of the ruling classes. The newspaper's own editorial announced that Engels had proved that the proletariat was no longer thinking in terms of 'returning to the old barricade-revolution, and that it possessed a much better revolutionary means in penetrating dying capitalist society with the socialist idea'.[6] Although Engels pointed out that in certain cases, as, for instance, a breach of the constitution, the contract between the prince and the people would fall into abeyance, and Social Democracy would then be free to choose its own means of defence, no one in the party was quite certain as to what these means should be.

In the summer of 1896, Helphand made an attempt to answer precisely this question.[7] Helphand regarded barricades as a meeting point of the malcontents, a kind of primitive means of organization; he also suggested that the workers should develop their own self-government, their own police and civil service. A powerful mass organization was in a position to disrupt the state apparatus completely. In a showdown with the state authorities, the old practice of downing tools, which used to precede the fight on the barricades, would come into play; it would, of course, have to be carefully planned and organized; it would develop into a 'mass strike'.

[6] *Vorwärts*, March 30, 1895.

[7] In a series of articles entitled 'Staatsrreich und politischer Massenstreik', *Neue Zeit*, 1895–96, vol. 2. They were published in 1897 in pamphlet form, under the title *Wohin führt die politische Massregelung der Sozialdemokratie? Kritik der politischen Reaktion in Deutschland*.

Demonstrations, proclamations, and posters, would have a corroding effect on the morale of the troops; the mass strike would not centre, as barricade fights used to, on the town. It would affect the whole country and cripple every means of communication; it would make government activity impossible.

Helphand advisedly avoided the term 'general strike': it was a syndicalist term and unlike the syndicalists, he did not regard the mass strike as a political panacea. He thought it would be employed only when the political rights of the working class were in danger. Nevertheless, Helphand's penetrating analysis marked an important advance in the ideology of revolution. The German Social Democrats were inclining towards a revolutionary fatalism; Helphand, the foreigner in their ranks, was one of the few who gave thought—at that time of deep peace and prosperity—to the technical side of revolution. He contrasted the growing might of the state with the increasing power of the workers' mass organizations, and he examined the possibility of a showdown. The shape of the St Petersburg Soviet of 1905 was discernible in his recommendation of workers' self-government; Trotsky's bold and prophetic pamphlet, written shortly before the Russian revolution of 1905,[8] was inspired by Helphand's articles on the mass strike.

While the German socialists found themselves, at the turn of the century, less and less able to muster any interest in revolution, it was difficult for their Russian comrades to conceive of a political activity which did not involve the 'forcible overthrow of all existing social conditions'. Although they often looked to German Social Democracy for guidance, they were faced with entirely different problems. They were trying to run a Marxist movement in an industrially backward country, where the working and middle classes were few in number when contrasted with the vast masses of the peasants. It was technically impossible, in Russian conditions, to run a mass movement on the German lines: although the Russian Marxists made repeated attempts to enter into contact with the working class, and to organize it for political action, their efforts often ended in failure. At best, they succeeded in carrying out a certain amount of clandestine agitation among the workers at individual factories; although there was a great deal of industrial unrest in Russia in the last years of the nineteenth century, it was mostly spontaneous. It may have been originally inspired by socialist propaganda, but the outbreak, the course, and the conclusion of an industrial disturbance usually eluded control by the Social Democratic groups. Their members faced the possibility of imprisonment, banishment, or self-imposed exile; by 1902, the young generation of Russian Marxists, among them Lenin, Martov, and Trotsky, had joined the old guard—Plekhanov, Axelrod, and Zasulich—in exile in western Europe.

[8] *Do Deviatovo Yanvarya*, Geneva, 1905.

Whereas the older people, after many years of absence, were out of touch with their home country, the more recent arrivals were firmly resolved to remain in contact.

The elaborate underground connections between the emigrés and their organizations in Russia were, however, maintained only with the greatest difficulty; soon even the younger refugees succumbed to the occupational hazards of exile. Without political responsibilities of any kind, armed with a variety of interpretations of Marxist dogma, they engaged in violent and endless debates. Nevertheless, from the point of view of the student of revolution, important developments were taking place among the Russian socialists.

First of all, Lenin began to evolve his theory of party organization. For a socialist, this was a matter of first-rate importance: the shaping of the party was closely connected with its future functions. This much had become clear, some eight years earlier, in 1894 and 1895, in the course of the 'agrarian' debate inside the German party. During this controversy it was conclusively shown that to widen the basis of a revolutionary party meant to decrease, and finally to obliterate its revolutionary character. This was the last thing Lenin wanted to happen. He envisaged the party as an organization of professional revolutionaries, who could 'lead' the working class. It would thus remain small and exclusive, under the tight control of its leader, and entirely impervious—in case an opportunity, like the introduction of a constitution, should present itself—to the temptation to temporize with the established order.

Early in 1904, shortly after Lenin began to mould a faction of the Russian Social Democrat party to his own image, Trotsky met Alexander Helphand for the first time. The Russian-Japanese war was then in full swing, and Helphand was writing, for *Iskra*, articles on 'War and Revolution'.[9] He maintained that the war would weaken the Tsarist régime, and for this reason deplored the strife inside the Russian party. Trotsky, having talked to Helphand on many occasions, and having read the proofs of his pamphlet *Do deviatovo Yanvarya*,[10] left for Russia a few weeks after the outbreak of the revolution in January; Helphand followed him in October. Their friendship bore some interesting revolutionary fruit. They organized the October strike, they played an important part in the St Petersburg Soviet, and they ran *Nachalo*, the best-selling revolutionary paper.

Together they developed a theory of revolution, and attempted to put it into practice. The Soviet, the strike, the newspaper—the practical side of their activities, and creditable achievements in themselves—all served a new conception, then being developed by the two friends: the theory of 'permanent revolution'. It is dealt with,

[9] They were reprinted in *Rossia i revoliutsiya*, published in St Petersburg in 1906.
[10] See above, p. 107.

in greater detail, in another place; here it should suffice to say that it consisted basically of a two-fold idea: the 'bourgeois' and the 'proletarian' revolutions would, in a backward country like Russia, merge into one; such a revolution would have to be followed and protected by a series of revolutionary upheavals in the West. It implied a far-reaching revision of Marxist thinking on the subject; it had some interesting antecedents. The first part of the idea was deeply rooted in Helphand's low estimate, dating from 1892, of the revolutionary capacity of the Russian middle class;[11] the second, the international, feature of permanent revolution was inherent in Helphand's activities in Munich during the first five years of the century. He attempted, with some success, to bring together the Russian and the German socialists, maintaining that, as the Germans ran a mass organization and the Russians were inspired by revolutionary spirit, they had a lot to learn from each other.

The revolution of 1905 failed: once again, the state proved its resilience, and neither socialism nor democracy achieved a decisive victory. Although the tremors that followed the eruption travelled westward, they did not reach further than central Europe. Trotsky, Helphand, and other members of the Soviet were arrested and banished to Siberia; other revolutionaries who had come back to Russia to participate in the upheaval returned to their places of exile. By now, however, the original Marxist view of revolution had undergone a considerable change. It still remained, for the Russian Marxists, the necessary vehicle of progress. But it was accepted that it would first occur in an underdeveloped country; the 'bourgeois' and the 'proletarian' revolutions were envisaged as taking place concurrently; it was thought that the proletariat of the highly industrialized countries of the West would follow suit. Among the Russians, however, the theory and practice of revolution lost some of the determinist quality it had acquired in Germany. The various components of a showdown with the established authority—agitation, strikes, mutinies in the army and the navy—were restored to their rightful place. In 1905, they did not prove effective enough when confronted with the might of the state. The possibility that a foreign war might help the revolutionaries break out of the impasse—as it in fact did in 1917—was not considered. Although the possibility of the Russo-Japanese war weakening the Tsarist system had been hinted at, Marxist thinking on the connection between war and revolution remained curiously barren. The French revolution, 1848, the sporadic outbreaks of social unrest throughout the nineteenth century, had all occurred independently of international conflicts; the Paris commune and the 1905 revolution in Russia, however, represented the writing on the wall which, because of the ultimate failure of these movements, the Marxist observers found difficult to

[11] Four articles in the *Vorwärts* of June 1892, entitled 'Die Lage in Russland'.

decipher. They were unable, in theory no less than in practice, to grasp the opportunities offered by a defeat of the government in a military venture abroad.

On the outbreak of the Great War the Russian exiles were as unprepared for revolution as they had been ten years earlier. At the same time their faith in the international loyalty of the working classes came in for a severe buffeting. They had lost sight of the strength of the national idea, and they were bitterly disappointed by the demise of the Second International; in their calculations, they underestimated the revolutionary charge of nationalism.

But although there were no signs to support Lenin's hopeful wish that the 'imperialist war' would soon be transformed into a series of 'civil' engagements, it was working to the advantage of the revolutionaries. On Russia the strain of the struggle told earlier than on other members of the two formidable coalitions that faced each other across the endless battle lines; after nearly three years of exhausting warfare the Tsarist regime gave way to the establishment of a constitutional republican government in March 1917. The revolutionary cabinet in Russia inherited the obligations of the old regime, together with a considerably weakened state apparatus, including an army on the verge of defeat and demoralization. Its decision to carry on the war meant courting disaster.

In March 1917, the exiles learned of the events in their home country from newspaper reports. In Zürich, Lenin immediately set out to find a way of returning to Russia. He faced a difficult problem. The Entente governments could not have been expected to let him and his friends agitate against the continuation of the war in Russia; after a few hectic days, help came from unexpected quarters. Alexander Helphand, the much maligned expert on revolution, came to the rescue of the revolutionaries. He was now a naturalized Prussian subject, one of the richest men in Germany (he had, after the failure of the 1905 revolution, turned his attention to money-making activities), whose advice was valued by the Social Democrats as much as by the German Foreign Ministry. After the outbreak of the war, he came out on the side of the socialists who supported their national government, and thus earned a good measure of opprobrium from his former Russian comrades. But they were unaware of his attitude to the war. Parvus maintained that the impact of Prussian guns on the Russian proletariat would be fatal for the Tsarist autocracy, and that the revolution in Russia would be followed by a revolutionary movement in Germany. He had succeeded in convincing the stiff-collar civil servants in the *Wilhemstrasse* that the revolution in Russia was a worthy cause deserving support and even financial sacrifice. He had founded a 'scientific' institute in Copenhagen, and the Russian exiles he had succeeded in recruiting for this venture in Switzerland crossed Germany, early in 1916, on their way to the Danish capital. Lenin's 'sealed train' journey in April 1917 was merely a variation on the previous experiment.

While he was impatiently waiting for the arrangement of his passage through Germany, Lenin's approach to the problem of revolution began to change. Before March he had been accustomed, like many other Marxists, to taking a leisurely, panoramic view of the event; now, a microscopic technique had to be employed. Tactical questions had to be considered, and the actual decision to take over power had to be made. Even before his return to Russia, in his 'Letters from Afar' for *Pravda*, Lenin insisted on the need for complete flexibility in revolutionary action. He abhorred the idea that it should be, at this point, forced into the 'Procrustean bed of narrowly conceived theory'.[12] Determination to act, skilful deployment of forces against the weakening enemy, seizure of the means of communication, destruction of the existing organs of the state, the formation of a 'people's militia', such were the main tenets of Lenin's tactics. He knew that the 'success of both the Russian and the world revolution depends on two or three days of fighting'.[13]

At the time of the Bolshevik uprising in November the Russia of 1914 no longer existed: Lenin and his government controlled only a fraction of its former territory. For the time being, this nucleus had to be protected against internal and external enemies. Felix Dzerzhinski took care of the former; a judicious mixture of diplomacy and propaganda was employed to deal with the latter. German armed forces were in occupation of a large part of European Russia, and the conclusion of peace with the Central Powers was the immediate task of Soviet diplomacy. But Trotsky skilfully exploited the negotiations at Brest-Litovsk as a platform for propaganda directed at the working classes in the West. The international element in the theory of permanent revolution was now to become operative; the new masters in Petrograd hopefully scanned the horizon for signs of unrest among the German, Austro-Hungarian, French or British workers. The strikes in Germany and in the Habsburg monarchy early in 1918 were, however, put down by the military; the belligerent Powers were now getting ready for the final and decisive engagement on the western front. Here, the strength of Europe was concentrated: at the most dramatic point of the war, the revolution in Russia was an experimental side-show.

In the meanwhile, Marxism had been raised to the rank of official doctrine in Soviet Russia, and pronouncements on questions of dogma could now be backed by the authority of the state. For some time, the Bolshevik leaders continued to regard the foreign scene through the prism of world revolution, a relentless struggle between the forces of capitalism and socialism. But this proved neither a

[12] *Sochineniya*, 3rd ed., vol. 23, p. 321.
[13] *Idem*, vol. 26, p. 153.

profitable nor a politic occupation, and, more important, domestic problems claimed the undivided attention of the Russian rulers. Stalin perceived the problem: the practice of socialism in one country replaced Lenin's and Trotsky's theory of world revolution. In the years before World War II, Stalin was not greatly interested in the progress of socialism abroad. He certainly showed no skill in furthering it; it was not for him—as it had been for Lenin in the heroic era of the revolution—an essential premise of survival. Nevertheless, Stalin was ready to exploit the situation obtaining in central and eastern Europe as a result of the war. Between 1944 and 1948, communist regimes were established in no fewer than eight east European countries. This was the first major victory of 'Marxist' revolution since 1917, a victory in which the Red Army was the decisive factor: Stalin's tactics in eastern Europe were even less hampered by theoretical considerations than those of Lenin in 1917.

Indeed, since Stalin became the dictator of the proletariat, Marxist thinking on the subject of revolution has not kept pace with political developments. The last contribution of importance to the theory of revolutionary tactics was made by Lenin; the author of the concept of permanent revolution made an attempt to clarify its general outlines. At present, official Marxist theorists are making the best use they can of a rather obsolete equipment, and it is unlikely that another Lenin or Trotsky will rise from their ranks. With every successful revolution—in Russia, eastern Europe, and China— Marxist theory and communist practice came into sharper contrast: Marxist socialism was being more successful outside the classical territory for its application. The emergence of entirely new factors on the international scene, the decline in the appeal of Marxism in the highly industrialized countries on the one hand and, on the other, the success of revolution in China, all have added to the confusion of Marxist thinkers.

In the present situation, the traditional attitudes towards revolution still occur in a variety of permutations. There is agreement as to the desirability of world revolution, among communists; when they take a long-term view of its unfolding, Mao Tse-tung as much as Mr Khrushchev comes under the spell of Marx's determinism. For them, capitalism is still working for its own destruction and the revolutionary mechanism is unwinding as it did when Bebel spoke at the Erfurt congress. Sharp differences exist, however, between the Chinese and the Russian leaders as to the manner of achieving their goal. The Chinese revolutionaries are now taking a more vigorous line than their Russian comrades. They are less hampered by considerations of diplomacy; they find it easier to export blue-prints for revolution than credits and goods. Whereas Mr Khrushchev is well aware of the need to 'develop creatively' Lenin's more belligerent texts, the Chinese are using precisely these as their starting point.

In the Chinese view, proletarian revolution remains a violent event, when the 'old militarist bureaucratic state machine' must be smashed and replaced by its revolutionary equivalent. They have often hinted at certain 'muddle-headed people' who confuse 'socialist transformation by peaceful means' with the act of 'seizing political power'. In a revolutionary situation, the army is clearly the most important single factor for the Chinese: they insist that no successful revolution has ever occurred without the disintegration of the army of the old order. They have realized, on the other hand, that the new 'proletarian' army may be used to extend the frontiers of the revolution: they have praised Stalin's manner of employing the Red Army in eastern Europe. But there are some violent upheavals that are not, in Peking eyes, worthy of the name of revolution. Whereas the Russians approve of weakening the 'imperialist camp' by national bourgeois revolutions, the Chinese are suspicious of them, and they are inclined to wonder whether support for them is not a waste of communist revolutionary efforts. Similarly, they are more selective than the Russians as far as 'united fronts' are concerned. Here, in the view of the Chinese leaders, communists are running the risk of 'right opportunism' unless they maintain freedom of action inside such alliances; that is, primarily, the freedom to expand 'people's armed forces' or to run partisan warfare, as required. The Russian attitude to these questions is diametrically opposed to the Chinese. The Russians will not waste their time in smashing the old state machine when they can rely on subversion and infiltration into the existing apparatus of the state.

The Chinese theorists forcefully reaffirmed their position early in November 1960:[14] their delegation to the Moscow meeting of communist parties certainly carried a militant brief. After lengthy discussions behind closed doors, a 'Statement of the Meeting of the Communist and Workers' Parties' was published. It purports to be the same kind of document as the original Manifesto of Marx and Engels: it surveys the contemporary social, political, and international scene, and it slides easily into broad generalizations. But its language is no longer fresh, and its general observations lack the acuteness of those made in the first Communist Manifesto. That was a forceful and passionate revolutionary appeal: the Moscow statement on the subject of revolutions is overcast by shadows.

Although the latest communist manifesto referred to the 'crisis of capitalism', it no longer envisaged a clear path for the establishment of socialist systems. The *terra firma* of Marx's thinking on the connections between the development of industry and the advent of proletarian revolution, a thought on which Lenin and Trotsky built

[14] Especially in a leading article in *Hsinhua*, on November 2, 1960, entitled 'A Basic Summing-up of Experience gained in the Victory of the Chinese People's Revolution'.

their hopes, in 1918, of a revolutionary explosion in the West, has disappeared from under the feet of Marxist theorists. They are now looking hopefully towards the industrially backward peoples of Asia and Africa, territories where Marx would have felt a complete stranger. Nevertheless, here the 'imperialists' have run into difficulties which will make it possible for the 'peoples of the colonial countries to win their independence both through armed struggle and through non-military methods'. No attempt was made to clarify the communist attitude towards participation in 'national bourgeois' governments. 'Co-operation' with middle-class parties had been roundly condemned by Lenin: it proved, however, a remarkably successful technique of revolution in eastern Europe after the end of World War II. The Soviet rulers command a useful store of experience on the subject, but they are clearly reluctant to reveal the contents of their Trojan horse. At the same time, the question of participation in multi-party governments as well as of their support by the communist establishment has been one of the disputed issues between Moscow and Peking, and it was glossed over in the 'Statement'. Indeed, the differences between the Russian and the Chinese views of revolution are unlikely to have been settled in Moscow. They transcend the framework of Marxist theory: revolution can now be simply regarded in terms of achieving political power in the state.

PART TWO

PERSONALITY, TRUTH, AND HISTORY

VIII. Philosophy and Society: Alexander Bogdanov

S. V. UTECHIN

Alexander Alexandrovich Bogdanov (real name Malinovskii) (1873–1928) is unknown to the general public and is scarcely known even to philosophers and political scientists, though in recent years Bertram Wolfe (in *Three Who Made a Revolution*) and especially Leonard Schapiro (in *The Communist Party of the Soviet Union*) have restored to him his due position in the history of the Party— that of 'one of the founders of Bolshevism and its recognized leader alongside Lenin in 1904–7', in the words of his obituary in *Pod znamenem marksizma*, the chief philosophical journal in the USSR at that time. He is very little known now because, first, he practically never attempted to extend his influence and activities outside the Russian context, and second, Stalinist historiography transformed him, in common with most other opponents of Lenin, into an 'unperson' (except as a target for occasional abuse).[1] Yet his influence upon contemporary thinking in Russia in matters of ideology, and his role in the history of Marxist theory, were at least as important as his activities as a Party politician. In the preface to the 1923 English edition of Bogdanov's *Short Course of Economic Science*, the translator (J. Fineberg) wrote '. . . it serves today as a textbook in hundreds if not thousands of Party schools and study circles now functioning in Soviet Russia.' As for his theoretical significance, it would probably be no exaggeration to say that Bogdanov's was the boldest and most comprehensive attempt ever made by anyone considering himself a Marxist to reconcile Marxism with modern thought.[2]

Bogdanov had a very high opinion of Marx's role as a philosopher. 'No doctrine,' he wrote, 'no system among those which existed before Marx was "philosophy" in such a strict and full meaning of

[1] This treatment of Bogdanov is now changing: the note on him in *Filosofskaya Entsiklopediya* (vol. 1, p. 177) is quite informative.

[2] The fullest presentation in English of Bogdanov's ideas is in J. F. Hecker, *Russian Sociology* (2nd ed.), London, 1934, pp. 270–87. There are also brief accounts in T. G. Masaryk, *The Spirit of Russia*, London-New York, 1919, vol. II, pp. 344–6; G. A. Wetter, *Dialectical Materialism*, London, 1952, pp. 92–100; V. V. Zenkovsky, *A History of Russian Philosophy*, London, 1953, vol. II, pp. 741–4.

this word as is historical materialism. None had reached such a unity of views on cognition and life, none had opened up such endless opportunities for actively harmonizing cognition and life. In the teaching of Marx, philosophy for the first time found itself, its place within nature and society, instead of above and beyond them.'[3] 'Only such a cognitive act can be called "philosophic" which creates or transforms *general forms of cognition*. This definition is fully applicable to the teaching of Marx, who has transformed not only social science, but also the forms of cognition of social life. *All* cognition lies within the sphere of this reforming action; all cognitive forms—and the most general of them first of all—acquire under its impact new meaning and significance.'[4] Two ideas of Marx in particular are credited by Bogdanov with this effect—that the philosopher's task was not merely to interpret the world but to change it, and that social consciousness was determined by social existence. He considers them to be basic to Marx's thought, and they serve as cornerstones of Bogdanov's own system. They are, for Bogdanov, inseparably bound together as two aspects of one notion: 'Cognition as adaptation to the work and struggle in society (*prisposoblenie k sotsial 'no- trudovoi borbe*), cognition as a tool which by processing the life experience creates the conditions for the success of the further struggle against nature, and philosophy as a special organizing centre of cognition—all this through Marx's teaching has found its place in real life. Having fused themselves with life and consciously subordinated to it, as organs to a whole, cognition and philosophy for the first time became capable of really embracing all life, really mastering it.'[5] But Bogdanov was far from idolatry. He subjected Marxian teaching to the same kind of examination as any other theory that he considered important, and where he found it wanting in exposition or substance he said so with the complete assurance of an independent thinker.

Bogdanov is particularly critical of dialectical materialism. As regards materialism, he considers this term altogether inappropriate for Marx's views: 'Although Marx called his doctrine "materialism", its central concept is not "matter", but practice, activity, live labour.'[6] It was true that there were expressions of sympathy towards materialism in the philosophical works of Engels and such phrases as 'the unity of the world consists in its materiality'. Yet 'if we compare two world views, one of which [pre-Marxian materialism—S.V.U.] has a contemplative attitude towards things and claims to comprehend their absolute essence, while the other is fundamentally

---

[3] 'Revolution and Philosophy', reprinted in *iz psikhologii obshchestva*, 2nd ed., St Petersburg, 1906, p. 275.

[4] *Ibid.*, p. 274.

[5] *Ibid.*, p. 277.

[6] *Filosofiya zhivovo opyta*, 3rd ed., Petrograd-Moscow, 1923, p. 238.

active and denies cognition of absolute essence, then it will become clear that to denote them by the same name of "materialism" is a misunderstanding', one more example of a familiar phenomenon in the history of thought—the retention of an old term after its content has been radically changed.[7]

Bogdanov's own epistemological position, which he calls empirio-monism, was developed under the strong influence of the empirio-criticism of Mach, Avenarius, and Petzoldt, regarded by Bogdanov as the highest achievement of contemplative philosophy. At the end of the first collection of articles published under the title *Empiriomonism*, Bogdanov thus summarized the task he had undertaken: 'to find the way by which it would be possible to reduce all interruptions in our experience to the principle of continuity.'[8] And the main conclusion, which has ever since been the chief target of attack by the adherents of orthodox dialectical materialism, was this: 'Among the main interruptions of experience the first and the most familiar to modern consciousness is the chasm dividing "mind" and "matter". Modern positivism [i.e. Empirio-criticism—S.V.U.] has shown the identity of the *elements* into which the content of both these fields of experience falls; the interruption was thus reduced to two types, differing in principle, of the connection of elements—physical and psychic. Our analysis has led us to the conclusion that these two types of connection do not at all differ in principle, that they are two consecutive phases of the organization of experience: *the psychic is experience organized individually, the physical is experience organized socially.* The second type is one of the results of the development of the first.'[9]

There is no need here to go into the arguments produced by dialectical materialists—they are well known. They all, from the reasoned expositions of L. Akselrod and Deborin through Plekhanov to the invective of Lenin, culminate in the contention that Bogdanov's position is essentially identical with Berkeley's solipsism.[10] Bogdanov himself rather lightly brushed aside this contention as coming from a 'crude lack of understanding' and the identification of all experience with sensory experience.[11] But it must be said in fairness that the transition from individual to collective experience in Bogdanov's scheme is not entirely convincing.

[7] *Ibid.*, pp. 255–6.
[8] *Empiriomonizm*, Book 1, 2nd ed., Moscow, 1905, p. 184.
[9] *Ibid.*
[10] L. Akselrod (Ortodoks), 'Novaya raznovidnost revizionizma', *Filosofskie ocherki*, 3rd ed., Moscow-Petrograd (1923?), pp. 173–86; A. Deborin, *Vvedenie v filosofyu dialekticheskovo materializma*, Moscow, 1922, pp. 357–64; G. V. Plekhanov, 'Materialismus militans', *Protiv filosofskovo revizionizma*, Moscow, 1935, pp. 339–449; V. I. Lenin, *Materialism and Empirio-Criticism. Critical Comments on a Reactionary Philosophy*, Moscow, 1947.
[11] *Filosofiya zhivovo opyta*, p. 180.

As for dialectics, Bogdanov disagrees with the substance of Marx's and Engels's views, which he considered confused and arbitrary. '. . . the basic concept of dialectic with Marx, as with Hegel, did not achieve full clarity and completeness; and thanks to this the . . . application of the dialectical method becomes imprecise and vague, arbitrariness creeps into its scheme, and not only the limits of the dialectic remain indetermined, but sometimes its very meaning is grossly distorted.'[12] Quoting a passage from *Anti-Dühring* on dialectic contradictions, Bogdanov comments: '—Engels . . . uncovered only the contradiction between two *concepts* . . . and not a contradiction between real forces or tendencies. But a contradiction of two concepts is only an ideal contradiction, existing only in thought; to reduce a physical fact to it . . . means to go over to the point of view of idealism, to return to the dialectic of Hegel—'[13] The treatment of the other main 'laws' of dialectics is equally unsatisfactory. 'Having lost sight of . . . the live, real sense of dialectic, Engels and Marx also lost the possibility of explaining the transition of quantity into quality.'[14] As for the 'negation of the negation', Engels uncritically accepts Hegel's 'triad' which Bogdanov finds fruitless and arbitrary. Bogdanov rejects the term 'development' as imprecise and substitutes for it the notion of an 'organizing process', defining the dialectic as 'an organizing process going on by the way of struggle between opposite tendencies'.[15] But the emphasis is not on the struggle. 'If this process has any beginning, then it is clear that *before* its beginning there was *as yet* no struggle of two opposing forces . . . and in this respect there existed some sort of an *equilibrium*. If the process ends anywhere, then there is no doubt that there is no longer a struggle between these two forces and in relation to them a certain *new equilibrium* has established itself.'[16] Thus even where dialectical processes take place, and they are not universal according to Bogdanov, the struggle is seen as a transitory phenomenon.

The doctrine of historical materialism Bogdanov found on the whole far more satisfactory (the term 'materialism' has, according to him, a purely symbolic meaning here).[17] He contends that no facts were known which contradicted it and no other theory of history was remotely able to compete with it. Yet the rapid development of all branches of science and learning since the doctrine had first been formulated made it possible to place new demands upon it. Bogdanov's complaints about Marx's formulation of historical material-

---

[12] *Ibid.*, p. 242.
[13] *Ibid.*, pp. 243–4.
[14] *Ibid.*, p. 248.
[15] *Ibid.*, p. 242.
[16] *Ibid.*, p. 252.
[17] *Ibid.*, p. 255.

ism are threefold.[18] First that it is somewhat incomplete: 'It does not make clear what is the direct significance in life of a whole large field of social phenomena—does not explain why ideology is needed by society, what social purpose it serves . . . and to what degree it is necessary; . . . the question is also omitted to what extent ideology is essentially homogeneous or heterogeneous in relation to "the economy".' Secondly, some of the basic concepts of historical materialism as formulated by Marx are rather imprecise and ambiguous, in particular the concept of the 'economic structure' of society (because it includes 'property relations', although law in general is regarded as part of the superstructure or ideology) and that of the productive forces (because it includes both the material means of production and the mental faculties of the producers). Finally, the old formula does not determine the logical connection between the theory of historical materialism and the doctrine of development in other spheres of life.

In the process of revising and supplementing, which we cannot follow here in detail, Bogdanov suggests definitions and makes propositions which go beyond his initially stated complaints and considerably alter the traditionally accepted substance of historical materialism. The most important of these departures are:

'Social existence and social consciousness in the exact meaning of these words are identical.'[19]

'. . . Society as a whole is a system of co-operation in the widest sense of the word.'[20]

'. . . ideology is a mechanism of adjustment [*prisposoblenie*] to work and to the social struggle for existence.[21] Custom, law, morality are a special series of adaptation-mechanisms directed towards achieving the most harmonious mutual relations between people in the social-labour process.'[22]

'. . . progress means an increase in the fulness and harmony of conscious human life . . .'[23]

With these general notions on society,[24] Bogdanov views history[25] as a process primarily motivated by the struggle against nature and the resulting technical and scientific advance, with various

[18] 'The Development of Life in Nature and in Society', reprinted in *Iz psikhologii obshchestva*, pp. 40–1.

[19] *Ibid.*, p. 57.

[20] *Ibid.*, p. 59.

[21] *Ibid.*, p. 83.

[22] *Ibid.*, p. 83.

[23] *Ibid.*, p. 35.

[24] For their criticism from the positions of Marxist orthodoxy see I. Vainshtein, *Organizatsionnaya teoriya i dialekticheskii materializm*, Moscow-Leningrad, 1927, chapters 6–9, and S. Gonikman, 'Teoriya obshchestva i teoriya klassov Bogdanova', *Pod znamenem marksizma*, 1929, No. 12, pp. 43–62.

[25] In his textbooks of economic science and in *Nauka ob obshchestvennom soznanii*, Moscow, 1914, 3rd ed., Petrograd-Moscow, 1923.

organizing adjustments being as a rule developed accordingly to facilitate and ensure further progress. Bogdanov did not ignore instances of retrogression, attributing them to the failure of one or another ideological form. He distinguishes three main stages in historical development, each with an integrated system of economy, ideological forms, and types of thought. The first is the stage of authoritarian society with a natural self-sufficient economy, authoritarian institutions, and religion as an authoritarian form of thought. The second stage is that of exchange economy with individualist norms of behaviour and speculative thought, with a variety of philosophic schools and a multiplication of the branches of science and learning. It is at this stage that individual human personality, whose emergence had marked the transition from the authoritarian society, acquires considerable autonomy. This autonomy, however, which at first contributes to progress, later becomes an obstacle to further progress as the strife of individual interests contradicts the unifying tendencies of the machine age. The victory of these tendencies will inaugurate the third main stage in history—that of collective self-sufficient economy and 'the fusion of personal lives into one colossal whole, harmonious in the relations of its parts, systematically grouping all elements for one common struggle—the struggle against the endless spontaneity of nature. . . . An enormous mass of creative activity, spontaneous and conscious, is necessary in order to solve this task. It demands the forces not of man but of mankind—and only in working at this task does mankind as such emerge.'[26] All ideological forms, including philosophy and the sciences, merge at this stage into one 'universal organizational science' necessary for the great task of harmonizing the efforts of mankind. Bogdanov undertook to lay the theoretical foundations of this future all-embracing science, which he called Tectology.[27]

The transition to the future collectivist society involves the problem of revolution, and we shall briefly consider Bogdanov's theory of revolution. According to him '. . . even fairly considerable differences between the elements of a whole do not yet mean that contradictions are necessary; contradictions arise . . . only when these elements are not only different but also *develop in different directions*. However, in this case too the possibility of eliminating contradictions through organizing adjustments does not completely disappear. . . . There is only one case when differences between elements of a social whole must turn into an insoluble contradiction, and that is when the groups of society develop in *opposite directions*: one in a pro-

[26] 'In the Field of Sight', *ibid.*, p. 5.
[27] A. Bogdanov, *Tektologiya, vseobshchaya organizatsionnaya nauka*, Berlin-Petersburg-Moscow, 1922. It is interesting to see to what extent Bogdanov's 'tectological' ideas have now been taken up in cybernetics; cf. N. Wiener, *The Human Use of Human Beings*, London, 1954.

gressive direction towards expanding the struggle against external nature and perfecting the means of productive work, the other in a regressive direction towards parasitism and the consumption of products of the labour of others.'[28] In such a situation a revolution occurs and the progressive class takes over the direction of society, provided it has developed the necessary organizational abilities (e.g. the bourgeoisie in the French revolution)—otherwise the elimination of the parasitic class in the revolution will lead to retrogression and a general decline of society similar to that which marked the transition from antiquity to the Middle Ages.

There was at first some uncertainty in Bogdanov's writings on whether or not the new forms can be created in the process of revolution itself. In 1902 he wrote: 'In no case can they [revolutions] be moments of direct creation of new techniques and new ideology: both must be ready in the productively developed class.' Returning to the example of the French revolution he continued: 'All implements of the new society were already prepared in the framework of the old; only the life activity of the new forms was chained by the dominance of the old and could not freely unfold until this dominance was removed.'[29] But in 1906, in the middle of the first Russian revolution, he wrote: 'Revolution is social criticism and social creation simultaneously reaching the highest intensity. . . . Its critical work—the removal of general contradictions of social existence and consciousness—and its creative work—the creation of new forms of collective life—have one and the same meaning, one and the same aim.'[30] However, the outcome of the 1905 revolution convinced Bogdanov of the correctness of his earlier view, which he firmly held for the rest of his life. This is the root of Bogdanov's idea of Proletarian Culture, which in his view should be essentially identical with the future socialist culture. A practical programme for the development of this new culture was set forth in *Cultural Tasks of Our Time*, published in 1910.[31] The two central tasks were the creation of a 'Proletarian Encyclopaedia' which should play a role analogous to that played by the great French *Encyclopédie*, and the establishment of a Workers' University as a comprehensive educational and scientific institution outside the existing educational system and academic bodies and destined in the end to supersede them. The chief task of these undertakings, and thus the main content of proletarian culture, would be the elaboration and implementation of Bogdanov's 'tectological' views.

[28] 'The Development of Life in Nature and Society', *ibid.*, p. 105.
[29] *Ibid.*, p. 107.
[30] The article 'Revolution and Philosophy', *ibid.*, p. 271.
[31] Cf. a revised version in the article 'Proletarian University', in A. Bogdanov and V. Polyanskii, *Nauka i proletariat*, Saratov, 1920. See also A. Bogdanov *Elementy proletarskoi kul'tury v razvitii rabochego klassa*, Moscow, 1920.

Seen against this theoretical background, the Russian revolution of 1905 had the task of removing the survivals of the authoritarian period, and failed because neither the bourgeoisie nor yet the proletariat had the necessary organizational abilities to take over. The revolution of 1917 had to complete the task by securing a democratic order of society, eliminating in the process retrogressive features, such as authoritarianism, which was considerably strengthened by the war. Even during the first revolution Bogdanov had insisted on the importance of correct theory: '. . . only the greatest precision and clarity of the basic points of view can guarantee our young party from programmatic and tactical mistakes, infinitely more harmful and dangerous in an epoch of revolution than in peacetime. The wider and more complicated the practice, the more important is the role of the theory which illuminates and controls it.'[32] During the 1917 revolution, when he developed a considerable publicistic activity, and particularly after the seizure of power by the Bolsheviks, Bogdanov constantly gave warning against utopianism and 'maximalism', against expecting the realization of socialism 'tomorrow', against the view that socialism 'first conquers and then is implemented'.[33] '. . . So long as the working class does not control its organizational tools, but, on the contrary, is controlled by them . . . it obviously cannot and *must not* attempt to solve directly the organizational task of the world, to implement socialism. It would be an adventure without the slightest chance of success, an attempt to build a world palace without knowing the laws of architecture. It would be a new bloody lesson, probably more cruel than the one we are experiencing now [i.e. the World War—S.V.U.].'[34]

Under a democratic republic it was possible to use the parliamentary method for settling the contradictions of interests, for counting the forces, for finding out what concessions are necessary, for the peaceful subordination of that side which turned out to be the weaker but expects to become stronger in the future. Under Lenin's 'republic of Soviets' this way out was closed and there was a great risk of a civil war involving 'colossal squandering of the best forces of the nation'. Lenin's plan, a product of the authoritarian way of thinking, was completely incompatible with a scientific conception of the state and of class relations.[35] The task of the proletariat in Russia, as in other countries, was 'to continue the former struggle and organization, consciously and consistently to gather, develop, and systematize the emerging germs of the new culture—the elements of socialism in the present.' The gradual 'creative realization of the socialist class order' would in the end lead the proletariat 'to that

[32] Introduction to the 2nd edition of *Iz psikhologii obshchestva*, p. 1.
[33] A. Bogdanov, *Voprosy sotsializma*, Moscow, 1918, *passim*.
[34] 'Programme of Culture', *ibid.*, pp. 68–9.
[35] 'The State as a Commune', *ibid.*, p. 97.

victory which will transform this order into one embracing the whole of humanity. Socialist development will find its consummation in the socialist revolution.'[36]

The common denominator of the whole of Bogdanov's thought and the goal of all his actions was, I think, the idea of *harmony*. This explains his urge for a monistic interpretation of experience, his emphasis on equilibrium as the more fundamental state in both nature and society than the essentially transitory state of struggle, his views on progress, history, and revolution, his 'tectological' approach to reality (with a strong Fëdorovist[37] strain—the idea of overcoming nature's entropic effect on the human body), and his version of the socialist ideal. This explains the apparent contradictions between his enthusiasm for Marx's philosophy and his desire to reconcile it with the subsequent achievements of philosophy and science, his initial acceptance and later rejection of Lenin's organizational views, between his stand against the Duma in 1906–7 and his preference for parliamentary democracy in 1917.

There is a surprising gap in Bogdanov's comprehensive system—surprising because he dwelt at such length on the problems of energy, activity, organization, and authority, and because he was for several years a practical revolutionary leader—there is no analysis of the phenomenon of political power. It is doubtful whether Bogdanov was aware of it and of the problems it involves, being in this respect an antipode of Lenin. For three decades, from the first years of the century until the beginning of the 1930s, Bogdanov's ideas were a most potent factor in shaping the outlook of the radical intelligentsia and of the more educated workers in Russia, and he could count among his followers people of such intellectual and political standing as Lunacharskii, Gorkii and Bukharin. But despite the great influence of his ideas among Russian Marxists, Bogdanovism has remained a revisionist trend instead of becoming the official ideology.

[36] 'The Ideal and the Way', *ibid.*, pp. 102, 103.
[37] On N. F. Fëdorov and his ideas, see N. Lossky, *History of Russian Philosophy*, 1951; V. V. Zenkovsky, *A History of Russian Philosophy*, vol. II, 1953; S. V. Utechin, 'Bolsheviks and their Allies after 1917: the Ideological Pattern,' *Soviet Studies*, vol. X, No. 2, October 1958; R. Hare, *Portraits of Russian Personalities between Reform and Revolution*, 1959.

IX. The Forgotten Philosopher: Abram Deborin

RENÉ AHLBERG

Abram Moiseyevich Deborin, born in Kovno in Lithuania, the child of poor Jewish parents, belongs unjustly to the forgotten philosophers. He became known in the twenties as the exponent of an individual brand of Marxism, orientated in method towards Hegel, and his own work is intimately bound up with the development of Soviet philosophy. Until the condemnation of his dialectical philosophy in 1931 he was considered the leading Soviet philosopher and was often mentioned in the same breath as Lenin. And Lenin himself included Deborin's first book *Introduction to the philosophy of dialectical materialism* (written in 1908 and published in 1916 by Plekhanov), among those works which he considered worth thorough study. His *Philosophical Remains* (published by the Marx-Engels-Lenin Institute in Moscow in 1932) contains extracts and marginalia —not always friendly—which reveal his interest in this first Russian exposition of Marxist philosophy.

Today Deborin and his philosophical work are almost completely forgotten. Although he was elected to the Presidium of the Academy of Sciences of the USSR in 1935—that is, after his philosophy had been condemned—and remained there as secretary of the Department for History and Philosophy, the traces of his own activities have been almost completely eliminated from all Soviet philosophical publications. The new Soviet Encyclopedia devotes only a few unkind lines to this philosopher, who is today living in retirement in Moscow.

The sources for his biography are therefore very scanty and dry up completely after his condemnation. His life until 1931 is documented in works of reference; his life since then can only be inferred from occasional references to his membership of scientific institutions and from the very few of his writings published. As there is no accurate information about his life, any account must depend on what is said in a few reference books and on unconfirmed remarks in the literature on the subject.

Deborin left a government Jewish school in Kovno in 1897 and learnt the trade of locksmith. It was in Kovno, too, probably, that he first came into contact with a revolutionary movement. It is probable that at the end of 1899, because of revolutionary activities, he moved to the more remote Kherson in order to escape the clutches of the police. There is evidence of his revolutionary activity there. Like most of the young intellectuals who were later to become prominent in the revolution, he joined an illegal revolutionary circle and in this group of eagerly debating revolutionaries he laid the foundations of his political and philosophical convictions. But he was soon expelled from Kherson also and returned to his native town.

In Kovno he was overtaken by the fate of all Russian revolutionaries. He was arrested for treasonable activities and, after a conditional release, placed under police supervision. A year later he escaped from this by fleeing to Switzerland. In Berne, where he spent several years, he joined the Lenin wing of the Russian social democrats. At the same time he completed his education at the University in Berne, where he studied history and philosophy. His contributions to the Stuttgart social-democratic periodical *Die Neue Zeit*, which fall into this period, in style and content already show all the characteristic features of his later thought.

In his first articles—which incidentally were written in German—the influence of the Hegelian dialectic is unmistakable. The effect of the encounter with Hegel was so profound that at times he falls victim to the mania of many young Hegel enthusiasts and seems determined to force all political events into the Hegelian categories.

His astonishingly wide reading, apparent even in his first writings, later also gave direction to his philosophy. His extensive knowledge of pre-Marxist philosophy led him to attempt on the one hand to place Marxism in the historical development of philosophical ideas since Spinoza and, on the other hand—in accordance with the Hegelian triad—to interpret it as the great synthesis of the materialist philosophy of the eighteenth century with the dialectical elements of German idealism. Marx's achievement in doing this he regarded as the fusion, accomplished for the first time, of the concepts of 'matter' and 'dialectic' into a unified dynamic philosophy.

A far-ranging preoccupation with the history of philosophy very soon led Deborin to the conviction that Marxism could become an historical force only if—again completely in the Hegelian manner—it absorbed all the progressive elements of pre-Marxist philosophy. According to this interpretation the essence of Marxism could only fulfil itself by preserving all the lasting cognitions of the human spirit. Full of this idea, Deborin did not tire of exploring French, English, and especially German philosophy for materialist and dialectical elements.

It is therefore not surprising that the central theme of his first work, written in exile, is the dialectic. He began to prepare a history of the dialectic, tracing it from Spinoza through Kant, Fichte and Hegel to

Marx, which is as characteristic of his work as his later attempt at systematization in the realm of the natural sciences.

Given this interpretation of Marxism, it was only logical that Deborin, in spite of all his respect for Lenin's political and organizing genius, should not attribute any special importance to his philosophy. The Bolshevik version of a 'Leninist *stage*' of philosophy found no place in his far-ranging speculations. Among Russian Marxists he felt a bond only with that kindred spirit G. V. Plekhanov. To support his ideas he always refers to Plekhanov alone and makes him his chief witness. Lenin, on the other hand, appears in Deborin's work only as the great theoretician of the Revolution.

This philosophical development—in addition to political differences—helps to explain why Deborin parted company with the Bolsheviks in 1907 and joined the Mensheviks. The suggestion that his break with the Lenin wing arose as a result of far-reaching differences of opinion is supported by the fact that after the October Revolution he continued to remain in the ranks of the Menshevik Party and joined the Bolshevik Party only very much later— in 1928.

In 1908 Deborin returned to Russia. In the years that followed he led the restless, roving life of all Russian professional revolutionaries, which took him to, among other places, Warsaw, St Petersburg, and Poltava. The accounts of the influence of the October Revolution on his political convictions contradict one another. Some sources claim that he made a complete break with Menshevism—Deborin himself also put it this way—while others maintain that he continued to be a member of the Menshevik Party. The only undisputed fact is that, after a short political interlude as chairman of the Poltava city Soviet in 1917, he retired from active political life and devoted himself to teaching.

He taught at the Sverdlov University in Moscow and among the many honours bestowed on him were membership of the Institute of Red Professors, the Marx-Engels Institute, and the Communist Academy. In addition to his teaching activities he devoted himself to publishing the most important works of materialist philosophy. He edited for the 'Library of Materialists' and the 'Library of Atheism' the works of Holbach, Helvetius, La Mettrie, Toland, Diderot, and Hobbes. The complete edition of Hegel that he had planned— suspended in 1930—was intended, together with the works of Feuerbach, which he had already edited, to make the two most important forerunners of Marxist philosophy accessible to the Russian reader.

Deborin was torn from these teaching and editing activities in the mid-twenties by a philosophical discussion which resulted from his interpretation of Marxism and drew him again into political controversy.

In the first half of the twenties the principles of Marxist philosophy had by no means been fully elaborated. After the liberating experience of the Revolution the most dissimilar materialist currents had formed an essentially emotional alliance. All these philosophical movements were drawn towards one another by the feeling that they were called upon to provide spiritual guidance for the revolutionary materialist society. Each of the sects worked more or less in the conviction that the new world which had to be built would correspond to its ideals; and none took too seriously the contradictory utterances of the others. Before the great practical task theoretical differences faded into insignificance.

This apparent unanimity in the early phase of the Revolution was shaken for the first time in 1922 by the appearance of a programmatic article by O. Minin, a fairly primitive materialist who demanded the liquidation of philosophy in the Soviet Union. He started by saying that Soviet philosophy was a bourgeois survival and must be replaced by the positive sciences. This article was followed in quick succession by a number of articles and pamphlets written by materialist-minded natural scientists, who were unanimous in their demand that the remnants of philosophy should be replaced by the positive sciences.

These vociferous demands naturally brought opponents on to the scene. 'Vulgar' Materialism, as this crude version was called, was spreading so fast and gaining so much influence, particularly among students, that even Bukharin, then the party's chief ideologist, was forced to deal with this phenomenon. In 1923 he intervened in the controversy and sharply condemned Vulgar Materialism.

At Bukharin's side there was Deborin, who contributed a series of brilliant articles attacking Vulgar Materialism. His opposition, however, was expressed less in criticism of its theoretical premises than in the elaboration of a philosophically orientated programme, which by its scope alone made Vulgar Materialism appear intellectually provincial.

The theoretical resources of the Vulgar Materialists were insufficient for a serious controversy. The movement—which apart from O. Minin, centred particularly on the biologist Emmanuel S. Enchmen, who preached a peculiar form of philosophy, which he tried to reduce to biology—was soon replaced by a number of persons who had to be taken seriously. Among them—to name only the most influential—were Ivan Ivanovich Skvortsov-Stepanov (1870–1928), Arkadi Klement Timiriazev (1880–1955), the son of the famous Russian physiologist, and Liubov Isaakovna Akselrod (1868–1946). The new movement differed both from its Vulgar Materialist precursors and from the mechanical materialism of the eighteenth century. To distinguish themselves from their predecessors, its members called themselves *mechanistic* materialists.

E

The mechanistic group carried on the traditions of Vulgar Materialism in a very different form. It disputed the right of philosophy to exist in a socialist society with the following argument: just as, after the establishment of the dictatorship of the proletariat, Russian society had conquered all the irrational and blind forces whose victim it had been during the bourgeois capitalist phase of its history, and had established a rational, controlled, and planned social order, so it must free itself from all 'philosophical rubbish' in the realms of science and culture to make way for the positive sciences. Only by abandoning all philosophical fictions, the Mechanists believed, would the transition from the old bourgeois society to a new scientific epoch of history be completed.

They were thus trying to establish a scientific *Weltanschauung*, which was to be derived from summarizing and elucidating the findings of the positive sciences. In explaining all material and spiritual phenomena they adopted a strict determinism and strongly denied the right to existence of a philosophy distinct from the individual sciences. Analysis was the method by which they hoped to penetrate to the ultimate mysteries of being, and since, for them, the laws of the microcosm applied also to the macrocosm, they believed that by penetrating into the smallest particles they would be able to solve general problems of nature and society. A universalist method, such as the dialectic, seemed to them to be simply scholasticism.

In the summer of 1925 the Mechanists began openly attacking 'bourgeois survivals' in the Soviet Union. The occasion was furnished by Ryazanov's edition of Engels's *Dialectics of Nature*, which was published in 1925. Stepanov published a commentary on this book in which he maintained that Engels had proved that in socialist society only exact science remained. The dialectic of which Engels spoke was nothing but a familiar theory of evolution.

But Deborin, against whom Stepanov's article was directed, could with good reason cite Engels in his defence; after all, it was precisely in this book that Engels had tried to make the dialectic the necessary methodological foundation of the natural sciences. The controversy between Deborin and Stepanov therefore began over the question of the place Engels attributed to the dialectic in the natural sciences and to philosophy in a socialist society.

Engels's unfinished work, which exists only as a fragment, grotesquely enough provided both parties with a justification of their position. The contradictions and numerous intellectual ambiguous passages produced a situation in which both sides fought for years on end over the meaning of individual sentences and phrases. When Deborin appeared to be getting the upper hand the Mechanists began to divide Engels's intellectual development into two phases. They asserted that a part of the notes dated from a period when Engels was still caught up in bourgeois philosophical prejudices: Deborin could be referring only to these immature and pre-scientific passages. In the second stage of his development Engels had understood his mistakes and had tried to eliminate philosophy and dialectics from the natural sciences.

From this point of view the quarrel between Deborin and the Mechanists can be be regarded as a controversy over the views of Engels. Marx was allowed almost no say at all. His ideas were unambiguously expressed and hardly referred to the question under dispute. But Engels, in whose work materialist and idealist traditions were only very loosely interwoven, and who had died while trying to expand the historical materialism of his friend Marx into a comprehensive dialectical materialism, had left behind a great quarry from which Deborinists and Machinists could help themselves to powerful arguments. The fact that Deborin and his views finally prevailed did not remove the stumbling-block. The ambivalence of this work of Engels later provided the natural scientists of the Soviet Union with effective quotations to defend themselves against the attempt to fetter research by dogmatic philosophy.

To the mechanistic interpretation of Engels which in its extreme form was tantamount to the abolition of philosophy and dialectics as subjects to be studied and taught in the Soviet Union, Deborin opposed his idea of the inseparable link between the philosophy of dialectical materialism and a socialist order of society. According to this the guarantee for a scientifically planned society lay entirely in a scientifically worked out philosophy, whose function it was to prepare rules and norms by which society, state, and politics could be directed. The denial of Marxist philosophy as the supreme court of appeal would inevitably emasculate Soviet society.

Deborin emphasized that, historically, philosophy had always been one of the most important elements of state and society, and that therefore socialist society too must, for good or ill, remain bound up with Marxist philosophy. Without a clear theoretical concept of the future ordering of society there could be no purposeful quest for it in practical politics. Without responsible and scientific control of social and political development by philosophy, everything remained at the mercy of arbitrary, spontaneous impulses. With similar arguments he attacked the demand for the absolute autonomy of the positive sciences. The call for a self-sufficient science was to him synonymous with the renunciation of Marxist philosophy. For he was convinced that the natural sciences too were irrevocably bound by certain philosophical assumptions. They revealed their hidden workings only when the results were interpreted. As philosophy and science were inescapably coupled the connection would have to be admitted, explicitly recognized, and utilized to control the results; and as the sciences could not free themselves completely from philosophical implications it was the task of the scientific philosophy of Marxism to act as incorruptible conscience and to fight unscientific undercurrents in the sciences.

He opposed particularly violently the attempt to eliminate the dialectic as methodological basis in the natural sciences. Closely following Hegel, he considered the dialectical method to be logic, ontology, and theory of cognition in one. To suppress it in the individual sciences meant for him to give up a uniform and complete order of being. And since, for him, the dialectic represented an ontological principle governing all realms of life, its elimination from the natural sciences would lead to methodological confusion in which the results of research in the individual sciences would inevitably be frittered away and could no longer be integrated into a self-contained whole.

For five years (1925–29) the controversy between the Deborinists and the Mechanists revolved around these questions. Much ink was spilt on both sides, but neither party retreated. The Deborinists, who included Y. E. Sten, N. A. Karev, B. N. Gessen, V. F. Asmus, I. K. Luppol, I. I. Agol, M. L. Levin, I. I. Podvolotski, S. Levit, F. Telezhnikov, S. Novikov and many others, during these years became widely known as the 'dialectical school'. They agreed among themselves on the things they published; quoted each other, and for the rest followed their leader without question.

Their main organizational support, apart from scientific institutes and universities—where according to contemporary reports they held almost all the key positions—came from the Society of Militant Materialists, founded in 1924. In 1928 this society amalgamated with a splinter group under the name of Society of Militant Materialists and Dialecticians. In 1929 the Society, directed by Deborin, already had an organizational network which covered almost the whole of Russia. Its object, as Deborin put it, was 'to organize the systematic investigation of the Hegelian dialectic from the standpoint of Marxism'. With this aim in view the Society initiated a Hegelian renaissance in the Soviet Union, which very soon degenerated into a Hegel cult.

The publicity organ of the Deborinists was the periodical *Under the Banner of Marxism* (1922–44), which was translated into several languages and whose chief editor from 1926 to 1930 was Deborin. It had a direct influence on the course of the controversy as almost all disputed questions were discussed in it. Although until 1930 the journal followed the Deborinist line, it did not close its columns to its philosophical opponents. It was run in such a way that the most divergent points of view could find relatively free expression in it.

Although Deborin was appointed editor-in-chief only in 1926, his influence is apparent in all leading articles of the preceding years.

With a few exceptions, all his writings after the Revolution appeared in this journal and they alone gave it the unmistakable stamp which soon made it into a concept in the intellectual life of the Soviet Union. Deborin wrote that, in spite of the enormous load of work on his shoulders, Lenin, during the brief space of life left to him, concerned himself untiringly with all the questions connected with the journal and was able, by suggestions and proposals, to fill the editorial board with his spirit, so that fundamentally the periodical was his creation.

An examination of Deborin's philosophical attitude, as outlined above, shows that it contains ideas which, in the twenties, must have been extremely welcome to the Bolshevik Party. In the realm of politics his theory of the dialectical leaps in development has a close affinity to the ideas of the Party, which found in it the philosophical confirmation of its hopes for international revolution. The mechanistic theory of evolution could hardly have met with approval during the twenties.

Moreover, one only had to pursue Deborin's theory of the inevitable connection between philosophy, society and science through to its logical conclusion, with the Party's tasks in mind, to find in it a cleverly disguised device for using philosophy to control society and science unobtrusively and effectively. The theoretical leadership of society and science which he demanded for the philosophers encouraged the idea of the Party's practical leadership in those fields. Not only did he draw up the ideal blueprint of control; but he also took the first practical steps in that direction. In opposing all spontaneous impulses, for which he demanded prior philosophical sanction, he initiated their practical control. Unintentionally he thus prepared the method of social and political control from above, of which the Party was later to make clever use.

Moreover, the primacy of the dialectical method, which he finally succeeded in establishing against the opposition of the natural scientists, offered the opportunity, which could not be ignored, of suppressing all undesirable developments in the individual sciences. Here too he paved the way for the Party's later social and political practices.

It is not surprising therefore that the Deborinists were given effective support in their fight against the Mechanists. Later on this philosophical struggle provided an opportunity to link the Mechanists with the right-wing deviators of those years (Bukharin, Rykov, Tomsky) and thus to seal the philosophical verdict by a political one.

When the second All-Union Conference of Marxist-Leninist research institutes opened in the Communist Academy in Moscow on April 8, 1929, the Mechanists found themselves at a disadvantage. As the majority of the 229 delegates belonged in any case to the

Deborinist faction, the support of the Party was not needed to damn mechanistic materialism as an 'obvious deviation from the position of Marxist-Leninist philosophy'.

In his report to the conference Deborin once again summarized the points at issue. The crux of the controversy he continued to see in the Mechanists' refusal to recognize the use of the dialectic as compulsory in the natural sciences. With undiminished violence he accused Timiriazev and his followers of still not understanding that the crisis in modern natural science was caused by a crisis in fundamental methodological principles: 'We maintained,' he said to the conference, 'that the law of the unity of opposites must be made the basis of theoretical physics. Our opponents thereupon accused us of idealism, scholasticism, and every other deadly sin. Comrade Timiriazev has called me the "liquidator of the natural sciences". Who, if not Comrade Timiriazev, should guard the natural sciences against our plots?'

As before, he attacked the Mechanist charge that he had forced the dialectical method on the natural sciences and had therefore dictated laws to nature instead of inducing them from it. 'Comrade Timiriazev's ideas about Marxism are as confused as his ideas about Hegel's dialectic,' he said to the Mechanists. 'Like all Mechanists, he completely fails to understand the reciprocal connection between theory and practice. He believes in empiricism, proceeding at a snail's pace, and "Khvostism",[1] and denies the role of the dialectic as a tool of research. . . .'.

With the condemnation of the Mechanists, who included, in addition to Timiriazev and Akselrod, A. Varyash, V. L. Sarabyanov, Perov, Geylikman, Z. A. Tseitlin and others, Deborin reached the peak of his influence on Soviet philosophy. In his journal he noted with satisfaction that communist society had pronounced the final verdict. This verdict, passed by the most distinguished scientists in the country, must satisfy everybody.

His philosophical victory and his personal triumph over the Mechanists were effectively complemented by an increase in institutional power. His position as editor-in-chief of *Under the Banner of Marxism*, in those years the only philosophical journal, was confirmed by the conference. In addition he directed the Institute of Philosophy of the Communist Academy, was a member of the Presidium of that Academy, deputy director of the Marx-Engels Institute, and, after 1929, also an ordinary member of the Academy of Sciences of the USSR. Furthermore, he was responsible for the philosophical section of the first Soviet Encyclopedia, which had started appearing in 1926 under the overall editorship of his friend O. Y. Shmidt; this enabled him to exercise a direct influence on the shape of the Encyclopedia, which played an extremely important

[1] Lenin's term to denote lagging in the 'tail' of events.

part in forming political opinion in the Soviet Union. Until 1930 all the philosophical articles appearing in the Encyclopedia bear the stamp of his editorship. The Deborinists also controlled the philosophical department of the State Publishing House, which enabled them to examine all important theoretical publications. Another advantageous result of the second All-Union conference was the reform of Timiriazev's Scientific Research Institute in Moscow, until then under the control of the Mechanists, the directorship of which was given to the Deborinist I. I. Agol.

A survey of the development of Soviet philosophy up to 1929 shows that the Deborinists were not only victorious in all disputed questions, but also managed to secure a large organizational network.

The greater philosophical self-confidence of the Deborinists, which had been the result of the second All-Union Conference, and the claim to leadership, which they made soon afterwards, soon spoiled their relations with the Party. In 1929, however, the Party was still busy with other tasks. In the year of 'the great turn on all fronts of socialist construction' it was first of all necessary to break the opposition inside the Party to the policy of forced industrialization and collectivization. N. I. Bukharin, a member of the Politbureau, Rykov, then Soviet Prime Minister, and Tomsky, at the head of the trade unions, had come out against Stalin's policy of intensifying the class struggle. What could be more obvious in such a situation than to establish a connection between the 'rightist deviation' in politics and the 'rightist deviation' in philosophy? The spectacle of five years of controversy must have drawn the attention of even the least interested observer to the differences of opinion on the 'philosophical front'. After all, the Mechanists had been condemned as an evolutionary and positivist movement, which in political terminology meant 'rightist deviation'. The arguments used in the philosophical controversy offered themselves as a political weapon in the fight against all opposition to Stalin's general line of 1929.

It was no coincidence that the elimination of the Mechanists took place at the same time as the elimination of the Bukharin, Rykov, Tomsky group. Bukharin was accused of Mechanism in philosophy and in April 1929 lost his position as president of the Communist International. In November 1929 he was expelled from the Politbureau.

This being the state of affairs, it was clear that the alliance between the party ideologists and the Deborinists could only be of short duration. In 1930 the 'philosophical front' presented a completely different picture.

The controversy between the Deborinists and the Mechanists concerned the philosophical foundations of Marxism, in which a subtler way of presenting arguments could only have a disturbing and hampering effect. So long as the foundations of Soviet philosophy were not clearly defined, a third ideological position could hardly be established without impeding or even preventing the process of clarification which was just beginning.

After Deborin's success at the conference things changed. There was now only one philosophical line, of which the Party could expect that, after winning a brilliant philosophical victory, it would show the same intellectual brilliance in the execution of real tasks. But the hopes which the Party had put in Deborin remained unfulfilled. In the new situation it became clear that Deborin's dialectical philosophy had rather aristocratic characteristics and that its representatives were not prepared to give immediate sanction to the Party's practical measures. They continued to look upon Soviet philosophy, which they represented and wanted to purge of all non-Marxist elements and preserve in complete purity, as the highest and ultimate criterion of truth of social and political development. They continued to regard all concrete phenomena of Soviet society—in so far as they paid any attention to them at all—only from the point of view of Marxist theory and the Hegelian dialectic.

After the condemnation of the Mechanists the truce in Soviet philosophy lasted just a year, or more accurately until the joint session of the Institute of Philosophy of the Communist Academy and the Moscow Organization of the Society of Militant Materialists and Dialecticians held from April 20 to 24, 1930. Deborin gave the main speech and presided over the discussion which followed.

At the beginning of the conference Deborin still had good reason to believe that his philosophical ideas, which he had successfully defended against the Mechanists, would continue to have the approval of the Party; but by the end of the conference this had become more than doubtful. During the discussion it emerged that an anti-Deborin regrouping was taking place among Soviet philosophers. Deborin's report on 'Results and talks on the philosophical front' was attacked and criticized with surprising violence by a small group.

Characteristically, the new group did not criticize any concrete point of the analysis given in the report, but made a general attack on the Deborinists' claim to be the leaders of philosophy. This was a completely new attitude; it was not directed against this or that point of dialectical philosophy, it did not seize on any theoretical problem, but, while accepting Deborin's theoretical arguments, nevertheless aimed at the removal of the Deborinists. Immediately after the discussion Deborin commented that it was less a question of theoretical opposition to his philosophy than of the appearance of a new group, which defied exact definition, which apparently wanted to obtain control of the philosophical field, a group which, as he put it, was 'thirsting for power'.

In his final speech to the conference Deborin dealt with the arguments of his new opponents and announced that he would resist any attempt to discredit the philosophical leadership and to wrest it from his followers. 'Some comrades have said: your general line is correct, we don't want to break up the philosophical leadership; but on the other hand they have pursued a line which was aimed precisely at suppressing and discrediting the philosophical leadership. We shall fight against this. Why shall we fight? Naturally not because we cling to the leadership in philosophy, but because what the splinter group has said shows evidence of unhealthy symptoms.' Thus began the struggle between the Deborinists and the party ideologists for the control of Soviet philosophy.

In April 1930 the new group was not yet able to set its way against the Deborinists. Although Deborin had met a new and incomparably more dangerous opponent, the resolution 'concerning the results and new tasks on the philosophical front', which he introduced, was adopted by an overwhelming majority of the conference (there was only one vote against it).

The decisive turning point occurred some months later, the occasion being a semi-official article, published in *Pravda* on June 7, 1930, written by three, then still unknown, party ideologists: Mark Borisovich Mitin (born 1901), Pavel Fedorovich Yudin (born 1899), and Vasili Nikiforovich Raltsevich. They came from the Institute of Red Professors and therefore had an influential institution behind them. Mitin and Yudin were the heads of the Institute party organization. They thus represented a new type in the philosophical controversy, which until then had been fought by scholars.

The party ideologists justified their criticism of Soviet philosophy by reference to the approach of the Sixteenth Party Congress and the great practical tasks which it would present to the theoreticians. 'Reality is confronting theory with tremendous problems,' they wrote. 'It is necessary to start at once with the preparation and theoretical generalization of these problems on the basis of Marxist-Leninist methodology. Instead we notice that theory is lagging considerably behind.' This accusation was obviously directed at Deborin and his school.

They heaped reproach after reproach on official Soviet philosophy, accusing it of a lack of party-mindedness and of political neutrality, and imputing to it extreme formalism and the malicious separation of philosophy from the practical problems of the country. Their attack culminated in the demand that new tasks be formulated for philosophy, envisaging a fight on two fronts.

The philosophical equivalent of 'rightist deviation' in politics had been found in mechanistic materialism. Now—under the banner of a fight on two philosophical fronts—the party ideologists tried to establish the philosophical equivalent of 'leftist deviation', that is, of Trotskyism. Only if it could be proved that the leftist deviation represented a whole system which had penetrated into the official philosophy and of which there must therefore necessarily be a social equivalent, could the Party claim that its ruthless procedure against the Trotskyists was fully justified.

What was more obvious for this purpose after the equation of Mechanism with 'rightist deviation' had proved so successful than to say that Deborinism was the philosophical basis of Trotskyism? If Deborinism could be identified with Trotskyism, Deborin and his 'dialectical school' would be unmasked as forming an anti-state and anti-party movement and the philosophical foundations of Trotskyism would be laid bare.

Though cautiously phrased, the article did indeed accuse Deborin of Trotskyism. 'Fully aware of the great importance which the fight against Mechanism has played in strengthening Marxist-Leninist theory, we cannot, as some comrades are trying to do, pass over the shortcomings and mistakes which have occurred in communist philosophy in the past period of development. One of the major inadequacies has proved to be that in its development Marxist-Leninist philosophy has failed to unmask the theoretical foundations of Trotskyism.' As the development of 'Marxist-Leninist philosophy' had until then been in Deborin's hands, the implication was obvious.

Retrospectively, it can be seen that after the publication of the semi-official article of June 7, 1930 the Deborinists were pushed on the defensive. Subjectively, however, they did not feel themselves to be on the defensive at all. On the contrary, they published a strong criticism of the new ideas. The May number of their periodical *Under the Banner of Marxism* contained a counter-declaration, signed by the most prominent representatives of dialectical philosophy. Their answer to the criticism in *Pravda* was produced with surprising self-confidence and was still written completely in the tone of 'philosophical leaders'.

In the introduction they said: '*Pravda* of June 7th of this year contained an article by Comrades M. Mitin, V. Raltsevich and P. Yudin, entitled "Concerning the new tasks of Marxist-Leninist philosophy". But this article presents a correct appreciation neither of the present situation in the realm of Marxist-Leninist philosophy, nor of the tasks which confront us. As the article touches upon extremely important topical questions, we believe it necessary to examine these in greater detail.' The Deborinists pointed out that everything which was correct in the article of the three party ideologists was simply a restatement of their own philosophical views. 'But,' they continued, 'where the authors of the article express their own views they depart from the correct Marxist-Leninist position.'

While the party ideologists had defined Mechanism and Trotskyism as the two fronts on which Soviet philosophy must fight, the Deborinists now added 'formalism and eclecticism' as a new front, putting the article of the party ideologists into this category.

It is surprising that in their defence the Deborinists said nothing about the Trotskyism of which they had been obliquely accused. This is the more surprising as they examined all the other accusations in detail and pulled them to pieces with the skill they had already demonstrated many times before.

Either they were so involved in their traditional ways of putting problems that, conscious of their services in the fight against Mechanism, they dismissed as unimportant the accusation of not having done their duty of political supervision in one instance, or they were aware of an unfortunate omission in this question which they tried to pass over in silence. Another explanation might be that there was really an unadmitted elective affinity between Deborin's philosophy and Trotsky's political theories. The far-ranging learning, the delight in rhetorical glitter and stylistic form, the internationalist orientation and receptivity, even if critical, for the ideas for Western Europe, which characterized both Deborinists and Trotskyists, makes it possible to compare them on the basis of an intellectual, psychological elective affinity. But beyond this there is no proof of the existence of any close political or philosophical connection, as claimed by the Party.

Whatever the truth, the fact that the Party very soon gave official support to the article of June 7th decided the outcome of the controversy. Moreover, making the attitude of the article its own provided the Party with a specific point of view on all philosophical questions. It could now fall back on a philosophy whose creed was the unconditional support of the Party's practical measures with philosophical arguments.

However strongly the Deborinists defended themselves, and however good and convincing their arguments, they lost influence steadily. In the September 1930 issue of their journal they were made to publish a resolution directed against themselves. It appeared on the last page without comment, and marks the end of the phase during which the journal was directed in the spirit of Deborin's dialectical philosophy. The September number was the last to be produced by the old editors. The next number appeared, but only after Deborin's dismissal in January 1931, under the new direction of V. V. Adoratski, M. B. Mitin, and P. F. Yudin.

The elimination of Deborin's dialectical philosophy from Soviet intellectual life was accomplished in two resolutions which followed each other in quick succession: first, the resolution of the party cell of the Institute of Red Professors, of December 29, 1930, taken as a result of Stalin's personal initiative, which subjected Deborin's views to devastating criticism; and second, the decision of the Central Committee of the CPSU of January 25, 1931, which condemned the philosophical line of *Under the Banner of Marxism* and ordered a change of editorial board.

At the height of the conflict between Deborin and the three party ideologists, Stalin intervened in the controversy. On December 9, 1930 he appeared in the office of the party cell of the Institute of Red Professors and, during the meeting, coined the expression 'Menshevizing idealism' to describe Deborin's view.

Stalin's phrase about 'Menshevizing idealism' was in fact meaningless. But as it linked Deborin's views with two movements which Soviet terminology branded as counter-revolutionary and reactionary, it could be used against an opponent who could not be accused of any concrete misdemeanours. In this capacity the concept 'Menshevizing idealism' has continued to exist in Soviet terminology up to the present day.

It only remains to be said that the resolution of January 25, 1931 liquidated one of the most interesting phenomena in Soviet philosophy. Pilloried by the Party, Deborin and his school were submerged by a flood of suspicions and insults. Under pressure from the Party, and debarred from all active occupations, the Deborinists either took to self-criticism and turned into fierce critics of their former convictions—like I. K. Luppol (who vanished in the thirties) or V. F. Asmus (who is still writing today)—or else they remained firm in spite of the drive against them; in that case they had to endure trial for 'counter-revolutionary activities'—like B. N. Gessen and Y. E. Sten. Or else they retired completely from public life—voluntarily or under pressure—and became silent for ever.

Deborin had a twofold fate. It was noticeable that during the last months of the controversy he kept back and after the May declaration published nothing in his own defence. It is said that on January 1, 1931 he made a complete confession of his guilt before the Society of Militant Materialists and Dialecticians. It may be that when his followers were censured, this early self-criticism saved him from anything worse than losing control of *Under the Banner of Marxism*. He was allowed to keep all his other public positions. Some years later he was even elected to the Presidium of the Academy of Sciences and remained there until the end of the second world war.

As he admitted later (1933) in a long, self-critical speech at the Institute of Philosophy, Deborin had not finally abandoned his philosophical convictions in 1931. 'Our fundamental mistake,' he said, 'lay in separating theory and practice. I must admit that for a long time I did not understand that accusation, because, after all, I was constantly speaking of practice as the criterion of truth. I was speaking about it and writing about it. Only later did I understand that this was not all that was at stake. The essence of the matter was that we failed to establish a connection between our theoretical and methodological investigations and the concrete tasks of socialist construction, that we separated theory from life. This led to a state where some of the Menshevizing idealists developed to a certain degree into "inner emigrants" and later into political opportunists.'

Turning to his former followers, he demanded from them 'complete and unconditional surrender'. This, he thought, was the only possible decision for an honest communist.

Even though he bought his personal security and part of his public position with his 'unconditional surrender', the few of his articles which appeared after 1933 are devoid of any independent thought. They do not differ in any way from dozens of similarly nondescript productions. After disowning his philosophy he had really nothing else to say. He appears uncertain and indulges in false radicalism. His articles 'Karl Marx and the Present' (1933), and 'Lenin and the Present' (1934), are nondescript treatises in party jargon. After 1934 he turned almost completely away from philosophical subjects—for example in the articles 'N. A. Dobroliubov' (1936), 'I. P. Pavlov and Materialism' (1936), and 'Bourgeois or socialist humanism' (1937)—or he repeated the Party's political slogans—for example in the articles 'The warmongers' campaign against national sovereignty' (1951), and 'The Agency of American Imperialism' (1953). Whenever during the last years he ventured into the realm of philosophy he wrote about such out of the way subjects as 'Materialism and the dialectic in ancient Indian philosophy' (1956). His latest article 'Leibnitz as a Social Thinker' appeared in *Voprosy Filosofii* (No. 3, 1961).

The dialectical philosophy which Deborin and his disciples developed during the twenties has remained unique in the Soviet Union on account of its philosophical originality and intellectual range. Since then no worthwhile attempt has been made to work out an *independent Soviet philosophy*, unaffected by the political interests of the Communist Party, or to revive the traditions of the early days. After 1931 dialectical materialism became canonized and was turned into rigid dogma. Since then all work on philosophical questions has remained within the narrow limits of a general line which even lays down the choice of words.

x. Relativism and Class Consciousness: Georg Lukacs

MORRIS WATNICK*

Those who see much of the pathos of history lodged in its ironies could hardly find a better personification of that dialectic than in the career of the Hungarian philosopher-critic, Georg Lukacs—nor one so symptomatic of the perplexities of intellectual commitment in the Communist world.

Born in 1885 of a very prosperous family—his father was director of the Kreditanstalt of Budapest, then the largest bank in Hungary—Lukacs hardly knew late adolescence when he began to show that tense intellectuality, omnivorous erudition, and remarkable sensibility of spirit that were to be so apparent in much of what he later wrote and practised. After preliminary studies in Budapest, he moved to Berlin and, later still, to Heidelberg, sampling the best the German universities had to offer in the social sciences and humanities and, in turn, impressing his teachers, Simmel and Max Weber in particular, with his prodigious intellectual gifts.

As a student Lukacs took his intellectual bearings from the neo-Kantians, then the dominant school of thought in Germany. If we are to judge by his early aesthetic writings, however, he was least influenced by the consensus of neo-Kantian doctrine in matters of epistemology. He could not quite accept the view, for example, that our knowledge of the empirical world is, in the final analysis, merely a product of the immanent categories of understanding; nor, on the other hand, was he satisfied that ultimate reality or its attributes are beyond the reach of the human mind. In the moral and aesthetic sphere at least, it is apparent that he believed certain ultimates or 'real essences' to be cognisable through intuition. Far from being the subjective idealist of his later 'self-criticism', he was evidently most influenced by the semi-phenomenological position of Emil Lask at Heidelberg, an influence that later facilitated his shift to the objective idealism of Hegel.

* The author is grateful to the Russian Research Centre at Harvard University for making it possible to undertake research on the problem of class consciousness from which this study is derived. He also wishes to thank Mr Irwin Weil, Dr Alexander Eckstein, and Dr Zoltan Mihaly, all of Harvard University, for translating materials from the Russian, Hungarian, and Slovak.

Otherwise Lukacs was a fairly consistent neo-Kantian and nowhere more strikingly so than with regard to human, moral, and aesthetic problems and in the methodological approach to them. Like all others of that school, he rejected the pretentious Hegelian claim that philosophy is the all-inclusive summation of human knowledge. The empirical world, he insisted with other neo-Kantians, was properly the domain of specialized branches of knowledge and skill, e.g. that of the artist and writer in their efforts to capture its immediacies; all that philosophy can legitimately do is formulate the canons of validity by which to evaluate the performance of these specialized activities in the arts and sciences. And going a step further, it is also clear from his writings of the period that Lukacs shared the approach favoured by most neo-Kantians who concerned themselves with the social sciences. The rational methods by which natural science 'explains' the external world, he thought, had little to offer in aesthetics; to cope with its problems of meaning, purpose, and 'destiny', the critic needed the inner perception of understanding. And again—though here other neo-Kantians would have demurred—the understanding he sought was not the understanding of reason; taking his cue from the vitalism and intuitionism of Dilthey and Simmel, he urged that the human subject can achieve such understanding, particularly the understanding of his self, only through flashes of intuition given to those who live and struggle for it.

In leaving the shelter of the neo-Kantian system, Lukacs was not alone. Its structure of compartmentalized sciences and relativized values began to crumble with the first shock of war, making way for a renewed quest for a more 'total' system of ultimate truth. Many found it, for example, in the phenomenology of Husserl; Lukacs, on the other hand, was among those who re-discovered Hegel.

Just why Lukacs's Marxism should have induced him to join the newly organized Hungarian Communist Party is not clear, particularly since he had considerable misgivings about Bela Kun's leadership and policies. His own autobiographical memoir, written many years later partly as an *apologia pro vita sua*, speaks obscurely of his growing awareness of 'the imperialist character of the war' and of the impression made on him by the writings of the Hungarian syndicalist, Erwin Szabo. More probably, the deciding factor was the wave of revolutionary fervour set in motion by the Russian revolution. Be that as it may, we have his own word for it that when he joined the party in December 1918, it was without any semblance of Leninist indoctrination; of Lenin's wartime writings he knew next to nothing, and, to make matters worse, he had shown a special partiality for Rosa Luxemburg in what little reading he had done of pertinent contemporary literature.[1] In short, Lukacs had all the

[1] G. Lukacs, 'Mein Weg zu Marx', *op. cit.*, p. 228.

makings of a 'deviationist' from the very moment that he became a Communist.

At first, this did not matter. All the newly formed Communist parties of Western and Central Europe were made up of left socialists, crypto-syndicalists, and neophytes of every description, and the Hungarian party was no exception. Besides, Bela Kun could make good use of influential intellectuals in the critical days ahead. Lukacs was therefore admitted to the party, along with others of similar persuasion (among them Landler, Rudas, Revai, Forgarasi, Keraly, and Gabor), and even made Commissar of Education and Culture in the brief period of Communist dictatorship that followed in 1919. After the Kun regime was overthrown, he escaped to Vienna, where he was to spend the next ten years, a political victim within the Communist movement of his own reputation as one of the most challenging Marxists of our age. In fact, it was the publication in 1923 of his *Geschichte und Klassenbewusstsein*, the book responsible for that distinction, which stigmatized him as one of the most formidable of 'deviationists' in the movement and sealed his defeat as a rival of Bela Kun for the leadership of the Hungarian Communist Party.

The feud between the Lukacs faction in Vienna and the Kun-Rakosi group in Moscow erupted in full force the moment they found themselves in exile, with the outcome at first far from certain. In 1920, for example, Lenin took Lukacs and Kun alike to task for holding the 'left sectarian' views he had so recently castigated in others.[2] Still, the very presence of Kun and his faction in Moscow and their deft adaptations to every shift in line gave them a distinct advantage in the contest for Comintern endorsement. What finally decided the issue in Kun's favour, however, was the inopportune publication of Lukacs's book in 1923, just as the Comintern began a drive to 'bolshevize' its 'national sections', i.e. purge or 'discipline' opposition groups, particularly in western and central Europe.

Unorthodox as it doubtless was, Lukacs's book instantly became a symbol of everything the policy of 'bolshevization' was intended to stamp out. To tolerate 'deviations' of a purely doctrinal kind was to invite defiance of Comintern decisions on matters of more immediate political concern, particularly if they encouraged the impression that there was a basic difference between 'West European Communism' and 'Russian Bolshevism'. What began, then, as a matter of Comintern *realpolitik* quickly became a paroxysm of militant orthodoxy as well, venting itself on anyone who did not stand foursquare on the Leninist version of Marxism. Lukacs's book

[2] For Lenin's remarks, see *Sochineniya*, 3rd ed., vol. XXV, pp. 291-3. The views attacked by Lenin were published in *Kommunismus*, a journal then edited by Lukacs in Vienna.

was as if made to order for that purpose but Lukacs was not the sole offender; he was closely followed by Karl Korsch in Germany, whose *Marxismus und Philosophie*[3] shared many of Lukacs's views, and by Antonio Graziadei in Italy, who dared to challenge the relevance of the labour theory of value to the economics of exploitation.[4]

Doctrinal disputes among Communists have seldom shown much regard for the amenities but the campaign against Lukacs nevertheless established something of a record for calculated ferocity. To find a parallel to the barrage of dogmatic casuistry and personal vilification visited on him in the months following the publication of his book, one would have to recall the fanaticism of theological disputes long forgotten. The stock criticisms of the book—what they came to can be postponed for later discussion—were echoed and re-echoed in the pages of virtually every important Communist publication, until 'Lukacsism' became a term of abuse in party vocabulary. The longest and most vitriolic diatribe was indited by Ladislaus Rudas,[5] a close associate of his before he fell into disfavour and his life-long opponent thereafter. Kun, needless to say, made most of the occasion to rush into print with a denunciation of 'attempts undertaken in German literature to revise dialectical materialism or, to put it more accurately, to emasculate (it) by expunging materialism'.[6] In Germany, *Die Rote Fahne* (May 20 and 27, 1923) even went so far as to cite these 'revisions' as a warning to Communists against the dangers of studying Hegel—the very reverse, incidentally, of what Lenin had once urged. In the Soviet Union, the battle against Lukacs on the 'philosophical front' was joined by the party's leading philosophers, among them A. M. Deborin, I. Luppol, G. Bammel, and I. Weinstein, all intent on 'exposing' Lukacs's book as a 'deviation' from the tenets of Marxism-Leninism.[7]

The uproar over Lukacs reached its climax at the fifth congress of the Comintern in 1924. Bukharin confined his remarks to a brief reference deploring the 'relapses into the old Hegelianism',[8] leaving

[3] Originally published in *Grünberg's Archiv für die Geschichte des Sozialismus und der Arbeiterbewegung*, Bd. XI (1923), pp. 52–121, and later, as a separate study under the same title, Leipzig, 1930.

[4] A. Graziadei, *Preis und Mehrpreis in der kapitalistischen Gesellschaft*, German tr., Berlin, 1923.

[5] L. Rudas, 'Orthodoxer Marxismus?' *Arbeiterliteratur* (Vienna), September 1924, pp. 493–517; and 'Die Klassenbewusstseinstheorie von Lukacs', *ibid.*, October 1924, pp. 669–97, and December 1924, pp. 1064–89.

[6] B. Kun, 'Die Propaganda des Leninismus', *Die Kommunistische Internationale*, April 1924, p. 19.

[7] *Pod Znamenem Marksizma*, March, June-July, and October-November 1924; *Pravda*, July 25, 1924; *Pechat i Revoliutsia*, 1924, vol. 6, pp. 23–33.

[8] *Fifth Congress of the Communist International: Abridged Report* (published by the Communist Party of Great Britain, n.d.), p. 132.

it to the less scrupulous Zinoviev to blurt out the full political meaning of the episode:

'If we ... are going to pay more than lip service to Leninism ... we must not let this extreme left tendency grow up into a theoretical revisionism ... spreading and becoming an international phenomenon. Comrade Graziadei ... published a book ... attacking Marxism. This theoretical revisionism cannot be allowed to pass with impunity. Neither will we tolerate our Hungarian comrade Lukacs, doing the same in the domain of philosophy and sociology. ... We have a similar tendency in the German party. Comrade Graziadei is a professor; Korsch is also a professor. (Interruption: "Lukacs is also a professor!") If we get a few more of these professors spinning out their Marxist theories, we shall be lost. We cannot tolerate ... theoretical revisionism of this kind in our Communist International.'[9]

To all intents and purposes, this was enough to put an end to Lukacs's political career, almost for good; ousted from the central committee of the Hungarian party and from his editorship of *Kommunismus* in Vienna, it was not until the recent Hungarian uprising more than thirty years later that he could again play an active if brief part in politics.

Intellectually, however, the real pathos of Lukacs's survival as a Communist first began with his political *dénouement*. It is quite doubtful, to say the least, whether the orthodox case against his book in 1923–24 modified his views in any essential respect. Certainly, one could discern many of the arguments of *Geschichte und Klassenbewusstsein* in much that he was to write during the next thirty years, even if they were disingenuously brought into line with the structure of orthodox doctrine to make them less obtrusive.[10] If anything he has been least diffident of all about his continuing commitment to the Hegelian dimension of Marxist thought—the very 'deviation' for which he was castigated most severely of all in 1923–24.[11] Yet, for all his talents as a polemicist, he could not bring

[9] *Ibid.*, p. 17.

[10] A favourite target of Lukacs's critics in 1924, to take one example, was his assignment of an active rôle to human consciousness well beyond the 'reflection' doctrine found in Lenin's *Materialism and Empirio-Criticism*. In all his subsequent works of literary criticism, however, consciousness retains its dialectical, transforming rôle. For an example of how Lukacs approaches the problem in his more recent work, see his *Beiträge zur Geschichte der Asthetik* (Berlin, 1956), pp. 57–9. But in arguing for a less 'mechanistic' doctrine of consciousness than the one held by his critics in 1923–24, Lukacs could later invoke the support of Lenin's more sophisticated wartime studies in philosophy, which were not made public until 1929.

[11] Lukacs's most ambitious recent attempt to rehabilitate the Hegelian derivation of original Marxism is his *Der junge Hegel* (Zürich, 1948).

himself to defend his book, either then or at any time since. In this self-imposed silence, Lukacs did not succumb to any failure of nerve; the only way to account for his behaviour is to assume that, because of an overriding sense of party discipline, he preferred to act out the rôle to which the logic of his book implicitly committed him in any case—a logic that hypostasized the party as the institutionalized will and expression of proletarian class consciousness and thereby endowed it with a superior view of 'total' reality. In other words, the book contains a built-in veto, as it were, on its own defence against party criticism, thus giving Lukacs's silence at the time a melancholy consistency all its own.

What mitigated the commitment for close to a decade was that it did not require anything more than silence. Neither in Vienna, where he lived until 1929, nor in Berlin the year following, did Lukacs once recant his 'deviation' in public. This was in striking contrast to his zeal as a party stalwart in other respects; he could match expletives against Trotsky, for example, with the most seasoned professionals in Moscow.[12] It was only on his return to Berlin, after working in Moscow for a year (1930–31) on the staff of the Marx-Engels Institute, that his mood became increasingly apologetic, until it finally produced a sequel to the events of 1923–24 far more disconcerting than his silence during the intervening decade.

The biographic memoir he wrote just before Hitler came to power was still the subdued plea of one extenuating his past rather than an indictment, and might even be read, in part, as a subtle re-affirmation of views he professed to disavow.[13] As such, it was a mild foretaste of what was to come a year later when Lukacs had taken refuge in the Soviet Union. Addressing the philosophical section of the Communist Academy, he performed one of the most abject acts of self-degradation on record, repudiating not only his book but his entire intellectual past as well, and, in doing so, spared no words to convince his audience of his complete orthodoxy:

'The mistakes into which I fell in my book, *History and Class Consciousness*, are completely in line with these deviations [i.e. those attacked in Lenin's *Materialism and Empirio-Criticism*—M.W.]. . . . I began as a student of Simmel and Max Weber (I was then under the influence of the German philosophical tendencies, the *Geisteswissenschaften*) and developed, philosophically speaking, from subjective idealism to objectivism, fron Kant to Hegel. At the same time, the philosophy of syndicalism (Sorel) had a great influence on my development; it strengthened my inclinations towards romantic

---

[12] See his review of Max Eastman's '*Marx, Lenin and the Science of Revolution*', *Die Internationale* (Berlin), March 1927, pp. 189–190.
[13] See his 'Mein Weg zu Marx', *op. cit.*, pp. 225–31.

anti-capitalism. In the crisis of my entire world-outlook, brought on by the World War and the Russian Revolution of 1917, these syndicalist leanings were strengthened still more by my having been under the personal influence of the most important proponent of syndicalism in Hungary, Erwin Szabo. Thus, I entered the Communist Party of Hungary in 1918 with a world-outlook that was distinctly syndicalist and idealist. Despite the experience of the Hungarian revolution, I found myself immersed in the ultra-left syndicalist opposition to the line of the Comintern (1920–21). . . .

'The book I published in 1923 . . . was a philosophical summation of these tendencies. . . . This could be shown in detail in all the problems treated in my book, beginning with philosophical problems and culminating in the definition of class consciousness and the theory of crises. In the course of my practical party work and in familiarizing myself with the works of Lenin and Stalin, these idealist props of my world-outlook lost more and more of their security. Although I did not permit a republication of my book (which was sold out by that time), nevertheless I first came to full appreciation of these philosophical problems during my visit to the Soviet Union in 1930–31, especially through the philosophical discussion in progress at that time. Practical work in the Communist Party of Germany, direct ideological struggle . . . against the Social Fascists and Fascist ideology have all the more strengthened my conviction that in the intellectual sphere, *the front of idealism is the front of Fascist counter-revolution and its accomplices, the Social Fascists*. Every concession to idealism, however insignificant, spells *danger* to the proletarian revolution. Thus, I understood not only the *theoretical falsity* but also the *practical danger* of the book I wrote twelve years ago and fought unremittingly in the German mass movement against this and every other idealist tendency. My exile from Fascist Germany can only change the locale . . . of this struggle; its intensity will but increase with its absorption of Leninism. . . . With the help of the Comintern, of the All-Union Communist Party and of its leader, Comrade Stalin, the sections of the Comintern will struggle . . . for that iron ideological implacability and refusal to compromise with all deviations from Marxism-Leninism which the All-Union Communist Party . . . achieved long ago . . . Lenin's *Materialism and Empirio-Criticism* has been and remains the banner under which this struggle is carried forward on the intellectual front.'[14]

To many who heard him at the time, Lukacs's outburst of self-

[14] G. Lukacs, 'Znacheniye "Materializma i Empiriokrititsizma" dlya bolshevizatsii kommunisticheskikh partii' ('The Significance of *Materialism and Empirio-Criticism* for the Bolshevization of Communist Parties'), *Pod Znamenem Marksizma*, vol. 4, July-August 1934, pp. 143–8. The excerpts given in the text above are from pp. 143 and 147–8.

recrimination must have come as a painful reminder of recent developments in the Soviet intellectual world. His was the latest in a long succession of recantations by leading philosophers in the Soviet Union since 1931, and, because it came from a foreigner already notorious for his unrepentant 'deviationism', it was all the more symptomatic of how thoroughly Stalin had eradicated all traces of independent philosophical thought from Soviet Marxism. That they could once count themselves among Lukacs's severest critics was not a secondary consideration.

In this respect, Lukacs enjoyed a considerable psychological advantage over his Soviet philosopher-audience—the advantage of one who had accepted the prospect of a personal recantation as a foregone necessity when he chose the Soviet Union as his place of refuge in 1933. Lukacs, to repeat, had spent a year in the Soviet Union during the critical months (1930–31) when Stalin moved to substitute a coded state dogma for contending schools of Marxist thought. He could remember the resolution of January 25, 1931, in which the central committee of the party condemned both the 'mechanists' and the 'emergentists', then the principal schools of Marxist philosophy, as crypto-political 'deviations'. Nor could he have forgotten the spectacle of one Soviet philosopher after another recanting his 'errors', or, as he preferred to describe it in his own recantation, 'the philosophical discussion in progress at the time'.[15]

Presumably, then, Lukacs knew what was in store for him when he returned to the Soviet Union in 1933 and discounted it accordingly. But discounted on what terms? One answer—necessarily speculative as any answer to such a question must be—is that he had already partly discounted it in the price of self-censorship he had had to pay in the preceding decade for his commitment to the Communist cause. Having acquiesced in the consequences of 'bolshevization', he could find it all the easier to come to terms with the requirements of Stalinization—sufficiently, at least, to face the ordeal of a public recantation.

Still, Lukacs's behaviour has always been too much the corollary of a highly articulated political and philosophical ethos to be entirely or even largely the product of a self-propelling psychological chain-reaction. His acquiescence in the ban on his book may have prepared him pyschologically for the indignity of a public 'self-criticism', but it does not explain why he made it the occasion for traducing his intellectual past so indiscriminately when a briefer, *pro forma* recantation would have served the purpose just as well; nor does it account for the next two decades of unfailing panegyrics to Stalinism that made him the despair of his most devoted admirers, particularly

[15] For an account of the regimentation of Soviet philosophy, see I. M. Bochenski, *Der Sowjetrussische Dialektische Materialismus* (Bern, 1950), pp. 48–53.

those who were aware of their tongue-in-cheek character. Fear may have been one of the reasons, to be sure—particularly during the period of the purges—but what of the recantation that preceded his flight to the Soviet Union? And how, again, could fear alone have produced so violent a reaction to his own past? The easy explanation that his political conduct was a case of sheer opportunism, pure and simple, is the least satisfactory of all; for all his feints and accommodations, there has been enough selfless purpose in his career to belie that description.

But if it was neither opportunism nor fear, how then account for the Stalinism of a man who was never really a Stalinist at heart or, at least, never in the sense that he favoured actual Stalinist policies? Perhaps the most helpful clue we have is the impression given by his very recantation of 1934; it is truly the *mea culpa* of a man labouring under a sense of guilt of his own intellectual past and intent on exorcizing the memory of it, particularly the part that reminded him of Dilthey, Simmel, and Weber. Significantly, these names had inspired no such feeling of guilt in 1924, all the jibes of his orthodox critics notwithstanding. What made them so unpardonable ten years later was not any change in the attitude of official ideologues in Moscow, but the shock produced by Hitler's rise to power in Germany—a shock violent enough to induce a Manichean debauch in Lukacs about the very past he knew so much better. Where others would point to the elusive practical ambiguities of many an intellectual tradition—witness Marxism itself as an example—he now insisted that, 'Every concession to idealism, however insignificant, spells danger to the proletarian revolution,' or, as he was to put it more generally two decades later, 'There is no such thing as an "innocent" world outlook.'[16]

Accordingly, if Lukacs were taken literally, the *Geisteswissenschaften* of his youth now became the seed-bed of Hitlerism merely by virtue of the fact that his teachers had conducted their methodology on the intuitive understanding of human action and social goals. And since he was so much part of that intellectual world, he too shared the guilt of his teachers for the spell later cast by the Nazi mystique of irrationalism, intuitionism, etc.

Against any such explanation of his behaviour, it may be argued, of course, that since his Marxism was still greatly influenced by the ideas of his teachers, it must have occurred to him at the very least that his own case and that of countless others vitiated his entire line of argument. But even if this were so, it would have no bearing on his sense of guilt; what is being suggested here is that Lukacs was not

[16] G. Lukacs, *Die Zerstörung der Vernunft: der Weg des Irrationalismus von Schelling zu Hitler* (Berlin, 1955), p. 6. It might be added that this volume is largely an elaborate gloss on his recantation of 1934.

really repudiating the influence of the *Geisteswissenschaften* on his own thought, but only their source, not the brain child but its paternity. In other words, his guilt feeling was of the ambivalent kind (as guilt feelings frequently are), caused by the shock of recalling that he shared the same teachers with many of the spokesmen for Nazism, and by a frantic compulsion, therefore, to disavow them.

The same shock, moreover, which precipitated the repudiation of his own past, taken in conjunction with his hope for the future, would also help to account for his attitude towards Stalinism. Apart from all else, the impact of the shock was so great because the triumph of Nazism represented a rupture in the unity and continuity of European culture, one of the most urgent and sustained concerns of Lukacs's thought. Since the capitalist West, in his view, already found itself in a quagmire of cultural decadence, the Soviet Union stood as the sole remaining hope for nourishing and transmitting that culture to the future.

To anyone who took all this for granted, as Lukacs did in the face of much that he was to observe to the contrary, it was almost second nature to accept Stalinism as merely a passing historical episode and to rationalize any compromises with it as a price that had to be paid for a Soviet culture that would one day act as the West's better half.[17] That the price might come high for himself and for the society in which he was to live until the end of the war, was purely an instrumental consideration in his humanistic calculus; the 'essential life' in the 'hierarchy of lives', to recall his anti-naturalistic cast of mind, could only be achieved at the tragic sacrifice of life 'on the empirical plane'.

Superficially, all this might suggest that Lukacs's Stalinism was as though patterned on the model of Rubashov's capitulation. Actually, the resemblance is more apparent than real. Rubashov was an 'ideal type', drawn to articulate the grim logical implications of Communist doctrine for those who reason from its premises alone. Rubashov's capitulation therefore had to be a single act of *ex post* reflection after all real alternatives of action had been eliminated. What makes Lukacs's subservience to Stalinism so much more tragic was that it came by successive stages, in each of which he could still choose between alternative courses of action. In his case, therefore, it was not the disembodied logic of the doctrine alone that dictated

---

[17] His faith in the redemptive value of Soviet culture was to be shaken considerably by what he could see of it at first hand, but its underlying assumption—the thesis that Russian culture is an integral part of the larger European tradition—was one he still defended against those in the West who questioned it immediately after the war. See the text of his speech and his replies to Jaspers, de Rougemont, and others, Rencontres Internationales de Genève, *L'Esprit Européen* (Neuchatel, 1946), pp. 165–94. Ironically, he did not have to wait long to see the Soviet regime bending every effort to sever all cultural ties with the West, as if to bring about the very cleavage he denied.

the choices, but a doctrine mediated in experience through successive responses which failed to give human and social costs their due, even as means to an end.

The fate of his book was a small part of the cost he slighted. The attacks of 1923–24 were enough to put a quietus to all further discussions and, apart from an occasional disparaging reference, Communist literature has in effect suppressed the book by a conspiracy of silence, broken only recently by renewed attacks on Lukacs for his rôle in the Hungarian uprising. And again, much as though the compulsion to forget the past could not be satisfied, Lukacs has been the foremost accessory to the suppression of his own book. Sometimes one finds him ignoring the book entirely, even if his argument suffers from the omission;[18] more often, however, he has given himself to a regimen of recurrent self-flagellation. In 1938, to cite one of many such instances, he once again denounced his book as 'reactionary by virtue of its idealism, its faulty interpretation of the theory of reflection, its denial of the dialectic in nature.'[19] And most recently, when Merleau-Ponty reviewed the philosophical issues raised by the book in 1923, his study was enough to provoke Lukacs to a heated protest against what he called the 'treachery and falsification' of Merleau-Ponty's attempt to resuscitate a book 'forgotten for good reason'.[20] This last episode epitomizes the status of *Geschichte und Klassenbewusstsein* today; virtually proscribed to orthodox Communists, it has survived largely because it is best remembered by others as a major work of Marxism purged from the collective memory of the Communist movement and—to the added discomfiture of its author—as a precursor of the sociology of knowledge.

What is one to make of Lukacs's *Geschichte und Klassenbewusstsein* (History and Class Consciousness) today? And better still, to what purpose? Lukacs's pique aside, why indeed ruminate on a version of Marxism long repudiated with such finality by its own author and by the very movement for which it was intended? Surely, the ambivalence of a mind beset by the logic of its own commitment is hardly unique to Lukacs, much less a reason for pondering its argument

[18] Karl Mannheim's early development owed more to Lukacs than is generally appreciated, many of his basic categories of analysis being taken from Lukacs's treatment of the problem of ideology. Lukacs thus defeats his own purpose when he tries, as he did in one of his most recent books, to suppress his own rôle as the connecting link between Weber and Mannheim. See his *Zerstörung der Vernunft*, pp. 474–506.

[19] G. Lukacs, *Essays über Realismus* (Berlin, 1948), p. 158.

[20] M. Merleau-Ponty, *Les Aventures de la Dialectique* (Paris, 1955), Ch. II. Lukacs's letter of protest is reprinted in the French Communist reply to Merleau-Ponty's book, *Mésaventures de L'Anti-Marxisme* (Paris, 1956), pp. 158–9.

anew or for confronting it with the actualities of Communist power today. If so, why not simply write it off as a closed chapter in the early history of internal Communist politics, and nothing more?

Easy as it is to take this view—and, for the most part, it carries a ready plausibility in the English-speaking world—it is one that seriously misjudges the pervasive influence of the book on the most varied schools of current European thought and, what is perhaps more to the point, its enduring pertinence to the messianic dynamism of the Communist appeal.

To takes its influence first, *Geschichte und Klassenbewusstsein* had too much of the virtue of its defects as a *Parteischrift* to suffer oblivion. What saved it from becoming a mere item of antiquarian interest or, at most, the occasion for a psychological case study, were the very 'deviations' that have singled out Lukacs for over a generation, and in most cases *malgré lui*, as one of the few Marxists of Communist affiliation still worth studying for his own sake.

A good case in point is the new philosophical dimension his book added to the understanding of Marx's economic reasoning. Not that the conventional approach to the subject thereby lost its vogue; on the contrary, most economists in the English-speaking world, whether pro or con, continue to think of Marx's economics in their own positivistic terms and, given the assumptions of an autonomous science, can even argue cogently for their selective approach. What they cannot do—not since the publication of Lukacs's book, that is —without throwing the origin and meaning of Marx's economic doctrine out of focus, is to hold with Schumpeter that it was strictly the product of the classical Ricardian tradition and entirely *Hegel-frei*.[21] For it was Lukacs who not only rediscovered Marx's general intellectual debt to Hegel (something most Marxists had themselves slighted for over a generation), but who also succeeded in recasting his economic ideas as an elaborate 'philosophical anthropology'— or what English idiom would call a humanist social philosophy— permeated throughout by Hegelian categories of thought.

For all that, it would be claiming too much for Lukacs to suggest that he 'discovered' Hegel in Marx *de novo*. Others had preceded him in this, but without being as perceptive about the specific links between the two. Lukacs owed his greater success to his own intellectual needs. The process of conversion is seldom, if ever, a clean break with the past, and when Lukacs turned to Marxism during the first World War, he did so not only as a Hegelian but also, and more compellingly, as one who had to find in both systems a new and common framework for his pre-Marxist aesthetic humanism, with all its disdain for the 'alienated' existence of modern man.

As it happened, he could find that disdain transmuted in Marx's

---

[21] J. A. Schumpeter, *History of Economic Analysis* (New York, 1954), pp. 392, 414, 438.

category of 'alienated labour', and, late comer that he was to Hegel's philosophy when he turned to Marxism, it was all the easier for him to see the 'alienation of labour' as a sociological derivative of the self-alienation of the Absolute Idea. As such, it had none of the grim finality which the vision of 'alienated' man had conveyed in his pre-Marxist days. On the contrary, it now contained the certainty of its own eventual disappearance; like the Absolute Idea in its existential, i.e. 'alienated' form, it too would transcend itself through the evolving class consciousness of its historical subject and chief victim, the industrial proletariat, until finally an act of revolution made it possible for man to come into his own as his truly human self.

Read this way, all of Marx's thought, down to the very fine print of its economic analysis, became the work of a moral philosopher articulating the future of man's existence in the accents of a secular eschatology. Nothing could have been less welcome to the general run of Marxists, least of all to those who had opted for Leninism and the positivistic scientific norms that went with it. Those so inclined might have shrugged it off indulgently as Lukacs's personal Marxism, but they could always consult the available texts to assure themselves that it was not Marx's. And since Lukacs had little more to go on when he wrote his book (1919-23) than the truncated version of Marx's early writings published before the war, plus his own Hegelian turn of mind, the exegetes had no difficulty in documenting their case against his 'deviationism'.

It was not until a decade later (1932) when Marx's early philosophical studies in economics were published for the first time[22] that Lukacs had the satisfaction of learning how accurately he had read Marx's meaning. Not that publication of the manuscript could do anything to rehabilitate his work among orthodox Communists or even spare him the ordeal of a recantation two years later; what decided the case against him and kept it that way was the structure of orthodox Leninist doctrine as it stood in 1923 and as it was subsequently perpetuated in the official dogma of the Soviet state—largely, then, the metaphysic of naïve realism with its 'transcript' theory of consciousness, taken over from Lenin's *Materialism and Empirio-Criticism* and thus devoid of the pronounced Hegelianism of his later period. For reasons not hard to surmise, moreover, the 'alienation of labour' has seldom been a subject of conspicuous interest to Soviet Marxism, *in res* or in theory. Small wonder, then, that Lukacs

[22] Oekonomisch-philosophische Manuskripte', *Marx-Engels: Historisch-kritische Gesamtausgabe* (ed. V. Adoratski), Abt. I, Bd. III (Berlin, 1932), pp. 33ff. The best proof that the later Marx was as much under Hegel's influence when he wrote *Capital* as he was in his younger days was supplied by the draft notes of his economic analysis. Cf. K. Marx, *Grundrisse der Kritik der politischen Oekonomie* (Moscow, 1939).

had to bide his time for as long as he remained in the Soviet Union before returning to the theme to settle scores with his orthodox critics.[23] Here again, however, as in so many other cases, Lukacs became a prophet without honour in his own movement; it was his original 'deviationism' of 1923 which anticipated where it did not actually inspire, the drastic reappraisal of *Capital* and of Marx's general place in the tradition of western thought at the hands of a long line of later European scholars.[24]

Furthermore, it was Lukacs's book which supplied much of the impetus for the development of a sociology of knowledge, particularly the form it took in the work of Mannheim, an associate of his in the closing years of the war. Mannheim's mind was a hybrid of many divergent influences—notably, the neo-Kantianism of Weber and Rickert, the intuitionism of Dilthey, and the phenomenology of Husserl and Scheler—but, ironically enough, considering the results, it so happened that Lukacs was the one to furnish him with two of his principal methodological tools.

The idea that a system of thought might be conceived as an ideal type and then imputed to a social group, likewise thought of as an ideal type, was an inspiration Lukacs borrowed from his teacher, Max Weber, and by grafting it on to Marx's sociology of classes, he was able to derive a doctrine of proletarian class consciousness distinctly his own. Nevertheless, Mannheim found the reasoning

[23] It would be doing Lukacs an injustice to regard his *Der junge Hegel* merely as a polemic. Completed in 1938 but not published until a decade later, after Lukacs had left the Soviet Union, it quickly established itself as a work of major importance in its own right. Nevertheless, orthodox Leninists were bound to regard it as a rejoinder to their earlier attacks; for that, in part, is precisely what Lukacs intended, confident that he could now enlist the support not only of the younger Marx, but of the younger Hegel as well. Thus, denounced a generation before for having read too much of Hegel into Marx, he could now turn the tables on his orthodox critics by citing the *Realphilosophie* (also published for the first time in 1932) as evidence that Hegel's earlier philosophy might also be read, to some extent, as the work of an embryonic Marxist. Cf. *Der junge Hegel* (Berlin, 1954), pp. 369ff. This, of course, is not to suggest that Lukacs contrived a case to suit his polemical purpose; the parallelism between the younger Hegel's trend of thought on the alienation of labour and that of the younger Marx is indeed striking enough to have impressed other scholars long before Lukacs's study appeared. Nevertheless, even in making the most of it to confound his orthodox critics in the Communist camp, Lukacs cut a tragically subservient figure. Rather than argue the case on its own merits, he tried to make it more palatable by appealing *ad nauseam* to the authority of Lenin's post-1914 Hegelianism, even to the point of falsifying the record where his own work was involved. But all to no avail, judging by the orthodox Communist reaction. Cf. O. R. Gropp, 'Die marxistische dialektische Methode und ihr Gegensatz zur idealistischen Dialektik Hegels', *Deutsche Zeitschrift für Philosophie*, 1954, 1, pp. 69–112.

[24] The best survey of the voluminous literature in this field is offered in two studies by E. Thier and I. Fetscher in *Marxismusstudien* (Schriften der Studiengemeinschaft der Evangelischen Akademien), Tübingen, 1954, pp. 1ff. and pp. 173ff.

suggestive enough to take it over (minus its Marxian *tendenz*) and even couple it with still another lead from the same source. For it was Lukacs's highly instrumental Marxism, more than anything else, which suggested to Mannheim that *all* social and political doctrines which pass for knowledge might better be regarded as 'existentially determined' doctrines, i.e. as elaborate rationalizations of group interests—mainly the interests of classes—which must 'distort' the actualities of social life if they are to serve those interests effectively.

Clearly, a sociology of knowledge constructed on such lines could well turn out to be a sociology of illusions, with nothing to show for its trouble but the intellectual paralysis of total scepticism. For, if all thinking—barring that of the mathematician and scientist[25]—is bound to be tendentious thinking by virtue of its social origin, how can one conceivably distinguish between authentic knowledge and mere ideology? And even assuming that such a distinction were possible, would it not in turn entail the use of criteria no less tainted by the same source? Actually, these and other perplexities of the same order were largely of Mannheim's own making to begin with; they might have been avoided by a more careful analysis of the scope and purpose of empirical knowledge—the only kind that concerned him as a sociologist—and of the range of 'interests' which motivate the quest for such knowledge.

Failing that, the assumption that interest-charged thinking must be deceptive was bound to lead into an impasse from which Mannheim could see but one way out: a sociological form of epistemological relativism (or 'relationism', as he preferred to call it) which despaired of ever achieving any such thing as objectively valid knowledge *sine ira et studio* (save in neutral fields like science, of course) and settled for something considerably less. All ideologies, Marxism included, Mannheim consoled himself, have their share of truth along with their errors, the proportion varying with the social 'vantage point' from which each is propounded. Accordingly, if 'absolute' truth is unattainable, it might still be approximated through a synthesis of the most promising 'perspectives'.

By his influence on Mannheim, Lukacs thus precipitated something more than he cared to bargain for—a sociological case for relativism that backfired on his own Marxism. From its exempt position as the avatar of reason in history, Marxism was suddenly reduced in Mannheim's system to the status of another ideology, having no more inherent claim to objective validity than any of its

---

[25] In exempting the physical sciences and mathematics, Mannheim was inconsistent. Given the assumptions of his analysis, there is no reason for considering these fields of thought supra-ideological.

rivals.[26] And yet, Mannheim's relativism *per se* was the one thing above all which Lukacs could not blame for demoting Marxism without laying himself open to censure on the same grounds. For the fact is that his Marxism was itself nothing if not ultra-relativistic—no less radically so, at any rate, than Mannheim's sociology of knowledge. How, then, was it possible for that Marxism—considered in strictly theoretical terms and apart from all other considerations—to confirm its own validity as a creed to the master, and yet do no more than 'expose' itself as an ideology to the pupil?

The answer, as one might suppose, was not so much a matter of sociological relativism as of the philosophical presuppositions from which it proceeded in each case. Thus, for all his other ambiguities in this respect, there is little doubt that Mannheim rejected any notion of truth predicated on the assumption of an order of supra-empirical reality; all that concerned him, at least in his capacity as a sociologist, was the reality of 'life-situations' as they confronted men and societies. Since that and that alone is the reality which people see from different 'vantage points' in the social structure, their ideologies can be 'relatively' true only with respect to that reality. To be consistent, Mannheim would have had to assume that objectively valid knowledge about that reality is possible—else what would there be for ideologies to falsify?—and nothing, perhaps, did more to vitiate his entire line of approach than his own insistence that all truth is relative. But this aside, the imperfect 'relative' truth to which Mannheim subscribed was a truth made up solely of 'the data presented by the real factual thinking that we carry on in this world . . .'[27]—not of a hierarchy of truths, in other words, but of one-dimensional truths, all of the empirical type. By and large, then, Mannheim's sociological relativism bore the distinct marks of its neo-Kantian origin in two crucial respects: it refused to consider the problem of the truth-value of ideologies on anything by empirical terms, and, in doing so, it also insisted on regarding all ideologies as data, i.e. as something to be studied 'from without'.

Of all this there was hardly a trace in Lukacs's Hegelianized Marxism. What we find, instead is a built-in relativism, with the doctrine serving as its own referent and thus certifying its own superiority as a doctrine to all systems of bourgeois or pre-bourgeois thought. All that was needed for that purpose, from the standpoint of normal adequacy, was a philosophical justification for grading, or perhaps one should say 'weighting', the truth-value of different ideologies, and this Lukacs supplied by introducing what amounts to

[26] K. Mannheim, *Ideology and Utopia* (New York, 1949), pp. 110ff. That Mannheim did not take Marxism at its own claims does not mean that he thought little of it. On the contrary, he was inclined, if anything, to show it more partiality than other ideologies. *Ibid.*, pp. 66ff.

[27] *Ibid.*, p. 268.

a sociological version of the concept of 'two truths', derived from the Hegelian distinction between the actual and the real or rational world. This done, his argument could proceed to its conclusion with all the compulsive logic characteristic of any closed intellectual system.

Reduced to its essentials, the argument took two forms, one mainly philosophical, the other sociological.[28] The first of these, intended to vindicate the superiority of Marxism as a doctrine, i.e. as an account of the object of knowledge, runs the familiar Hegelian course. An ideology is of an inferior order of truth, according to Lukacs, if it is concerned only with the apparent truth of the actual or empirical world. Such an ideology takes the world as it is and tries to make it intelligible to man's understanding by reducing it to a pattern of scientific law or to a reasonable facsimile thereof. What emerges from such an approach is a world of the here and now, a pre-eminently logical world of fixed and enduring entities and arrangements and one which man's understanding can take piecemeal and on its own limited terms. Limited to its proper domain—the physical world—such an approach need not falsify reality; on the contrary, it may even promote man's understanding of and control over nature on a scale never before matched. Nothing, for example, could have been more congenial to the progress of physical science, given its positivistic temper, its specialized fields of subject matter and its need for quantification, than the intellectual setting provided by an ideology of this type.

And yet, when all this has been granted, argued Lukacs, the very conception of truth which makes such an ideology an inexhaustible source of man's knowledge of the physical world also blinds his vision to the realities of his own existence in the social world. It does this by inculcating the illusion, or what Marx called the 'false consciousness', that existing social arrangements are governed by immutable laws, very much like those which prevail in the processes of the physical world and, like them, beyond the power of man to change. To anyone so indoctrinated—and this, *ceteris paribus*, may comprise all classes of the population—all social processes take on a illusory or 'reified' appearance in the sense that they come to be regarded as having an 'objective', external reality of their own, as though they were something other than the activities of members of the same society in their relations with one another. This, according to Lukacs, is the clue to man's split personality as a member of modern society; what he thinks he does in that capacity (his con-

[28] Being largely a collection of essays published between 1919 and 1922, Lukacs's book lacks a clearly articulated structure. The account given here is therefore an attempt to assemble the main threads of his argument as they recur in different parts of his book.

sciousness) bears no relation to what he actually does (his existence).[29] If anything, the accomplishments of science tend to nourish the very social irrationality already fostered by the reified structure of its parent ideology. By isolating the facts of the empirical world for specialized study, for example, the social sciences have to disregard the organic unity which alone gives them meaning and, by treating them as hard and fast data, they convert what are essentially potentialities into finalities.

But to Lukacs, as to any Hegelian, the actual world of data is but an imperfect realization of the real or rational world—a world in which man's essential rationality will have superseded the reified existence he leads today. The truth of that rational world and of the process by which history evolves towards its realization is given not by the empirical understanding, but by speculative reason. An ideology based merely on the faculty of understanding cannot, therefore, discover the structure of totality which pervades the categories of the actual social world, much less appreciate the inner dialectic which drives it forward to its dénouement in the rational world. These are the province of reason alone, and if reason indicates that 'becoming appears as the truth of being, process as the truth of things, then this means that the developmental tendencies of history partake of a higher reality than the "facts" of mere experience.'[30] Clearly, then, what Lukacs's argument came to on the philosophical level was nothing less than the claim that Marxism is objectively more valid than any rival ideology on the ground that it alone incorporates the 'higher' truth of the dialectic of history.[31] But if all

[29] Though Lukacs regarded reification as the fatal weakness of 'bourgeois' thought, it is no less conspicuous in its Marxist guide in Lenin's pre-1914 view of the relationship between 'social being' and 'social consciousness', a view clearly traceable via Plekhanov, Kautsky, and Engels to nineteenth century materialism. In fact, this was one of the many reasons why orthodox Leninists were so outraged by the implications of Lukacs's Hegelianism.

[30] *Geschichte und Klassenbewusstsein*, p. 198.

[31] Whether this amounts to a case for the *absolute* validity of Marxism, as some critics have suggested, is open to doubt. The very concept of a dialectic in history has to 'relativize' the absolute, so to speak, to account for history as a process. The truth of Marxism would therefore have to be considered as part of the continuing interaction between the Notion and its particular and singular manifestations. Even in its pristine Hegelian version, then, dialectical thought would have to rule out such a claim for any doctrine. This applies *a fortiori* to the dialectic as conceived by Lukacs or, for that matter, by the early Marx. Both regarded it as the correct formulation of, as well as the actual course of, man's development throughout the 'pre-history' of his existence in class-structured societies. Hence their conclusion that much of the substance of their doctrine, particularly historical materialism, would be invalidated once reason fulfilled itself in the establishment of a classless society. Nevertheless, even if Lukacs stopped short of 'absolutizing' Marxism, his claim for its superior truth-value lacked nothing by way of doctrinaire presumption.

this is taken at face value, what remains of Marxism as a self-professed relativist doctrine? In claiming a superior *objective* truth for it, did not Lukacs, in effect, put it beyond the pale of proletarian class interests and of the subjectively infected outlook that goes with them? How then, could he still insist that Marxism is uniquely a proletarian doctrine?

Conundrum that this was , Lukacs nevertheless managed to eat his relativist cake and still have it. Obviously, this could not be done by describing Marxism as the natural response of workers to their lot under capitalism; quite apart from the inherent absurdity of such a view, any relativism based on an argument from psychology would only belie the doctrine's claim to objective validity. In fact, to avoid running any such risk, all empirical referents of this type, standing outside the terms of the doctrine itself, had to be excluded, leaving the doctrine enclosed within its own logic, as it were. The problem, then, was to find in Marxism itself, not in the ' "facts" of mere experience', a sociological framework for the two types of truth which would invest them with a social function without destroying their independent heuristic status. And given Marx's analysis of social trends in a capitalist society, the solution Lukacs needed could be derived easily enough, merely by a process of bi-lateral imputation. The social structure of modern capitalism tends increasingly to polarize around two antagonistic vantage points or class positions. In the ensuing struggle, each of these requires its own intellectual outlook and system of values as a matter of sheer strategic or objective necessity, whether its occupants realize it or not. With this as a starting point, the rest followed as a matter of course; Lukacs had only to pair off each of the two truths and its respective ideological elaboration with what he considered to be its correlative class position, and the outcome could be extrapolated, in so far as it depended on intellectual advantage, on the comparative truth-value of these ideologies.

Accordingly, what qualifies an empirically-oriented system of thought as the ideology of the bourgeoisie is not its appeal to this or that bourgeois, but its instrumental value to the class as a whole. The exceptional property owner may indeed take a dim view of the future but, if the bourgeoisie as a class is to maintain itself in power, most of its members must be persuaded no less than the workers they employ that the existing order is a permanent one. Nothing can serve that purpose better, in Lukacs's view, than a 'reified' structure of thought based on the limited truth of understanding; negatively, it serves to divert attention from the fatal weaknesses of the capitalist system as a whole, and positively it acts as a psychological prop for that system, by identifying what is merely a passing phase of man's historic existence with the eternal order of nature. This, needless to add, is nothing but self-deception on both counts but, undaunted by the paradox of his argument, Lukacs concluded that self-deception is precisely what is required of all or most members of the bourgeoisie if their class is to remain in power. 'The obstacle . . . which makes the class consciousness of the bourgeoisie a "false" consciousness,' he wrote, 'is objective; it is the situation of the class itself. It is an objective consequence of the economic structure of society, not something arbitrary, subjective or psychological.'[32]

Again reasoning by imputation, Lukacs could reach the opposite conclusion about the proletariat. Its position as a class requires that it break with existing social arrangements, even if workers themselves may not see it that way. As Marx had put it long before Lukacs: 'It is not a matter of what this or that proletarian, or even the entire proletariat, envisages as the goal at any particular time. It is a question of what the proletariat is and of what it will have to do historically, judged by the condition of its existence.'[33] Because that 'condition of existence' requires a revloutionary break with the existing economic system, it offers the only vantage point in the social structure from which the system as a whole and its 'laws of motion' can be observed in their proper perspective. But to do this, to see the system for what it is and without 'ideological distortions' of any kind, requires a type of class consciousness which is identical with the truth of the 'high reality' incorporated in Marxism itself—a truth that can transcend the illusions of 'reification' and envisage the rational society without classes beyond as the only alternative to man's self-alienation under capitalism. And by the same token, it is that truth which makes the proletariat as a class the instrument of reason in history. Carried to its logical conclusion, then, Lukacs's feat of self-validating scholasticism came to this, that Marxism= historic reason=proletarian class consciousness.

Not that Lukacs regarded the triumph of reason as a foregone conclusion in any deterministic sense; the outcome would depend on whether actual workers can come to appreciate the opportunity history offered them as a class. But even if they were to fail in this, Marxism would still remain, on Lukacs's terms, a uniquely proletarian doctrine. In this sense, it was decidedly a relativized Marxism, so much so that it could even specify the conditions which would invalidate its own categories of analysis. Having identified it with proletarian class consciousness, Lukacs had to rule it out as a

[32] *Geschichte und Klassenbewusstsein*, p. 65. In other woids, when Lukacs speaks of the 'false consciousness' of the bourgeoisie as being 'objective', he means merely that it is a necessary condition for perpetuating the power of the bourgeoisie as a class, not that it makes realistic thought 'objectively impossible' for the individual bourgeois. This latter misreading is not uncommon, a recent example being the otherwise valuable study of W. Stark, *The Sociology of Knowledge* (Glencoe, 1958), pp. 308ff.

[33] 'Die heilige Familie', *Gesamtausgabe*, Abt. I, Bd. III, p. 207.

F

doctrine for eternity; historical materialism, its instrument of analysis, for example, requires drastic modification before it can be applied to the study of pre-capitalist societies, and it might even outlive its purpose entirely, once the goal of a rational society were achieved.

To suppose, then, that Lukacs's relativism was of a kind with Mannheim's, as Stalinist spokesmen made a habit of doing while damning them both, is to identify two distinctly different approaches to the problem of the social determination of thought, however much one may have borrowed from the other. Where Mannheim scrutinized all systems of thought for their 'ideological' sins against the same type of truth, Lukacs singled out Marxism as the sole exception, endowed with the virtue of a 'higher' order of truth. But even with the issue so clearly drawn, Lukacs could not meet the challenge on his own ground. To have done so after the interdiction of his own book might have made him the target of renewed attacks in Communist circles. All he could do, on occasion, to make up for his silence was to fall back on the standard Leninist retort to relativism of any kind, viz., that while man's knowledge advances by a sequence of relative approximations, truth itself is 'objective' and 'absolute'. Whether or not Mannheim's relativism or anyone else's could be exorcized by this recourse to Lenin's *ipse dixit*, there was small comfort in it for anyone still left wondering what it had to do with the superior truth-value Lukacs had claimed for Marxism.

During the post-war period, the emergence of existentialism as a major school of thought in Western Europe saw Lukacs cast in still another of his many involuntary rôles, and again it was acted out with the tragi-comic effect of one reciting lines foreign to his own idiom. Certainly the result could not be charged to Lukacs's apathy or want of effort; quite the contrary, no one of his persuasion had more direct intellectual reason to be concerned about the existentialist challenge. Add to this the fact that Lukacs's prestige made him the one Communist spokesman certain to be given an attentive hearing in the west—nowhere more so, perhaps, than among the existentialists themselves—and the jaded response to his anti-existentialist tract[34] becomes proof all the more of how pathetically miscast he was for the part.

As one might have gathered from his own remarks many years later, when he could finally bring himself to repudiate Stalinist orthodoxy, the fault lay not with the audience nor with the actor—except in the sense that he lent himself to such a part—but with the script itself. The existentialist case, as that of any other rival doctrine, had to be confronted on its own ground, he acknowledged, not in

[34] *Existentialismus oder Marxismus?*, Berlin, 1951.

the arena of Leninist-Stalinist dogmatics.[35] But meeting the existentialists on their own ground was precisely what Lukacs dared not risk for the very good reason that they shared large tracts of it with the Marxism of *Geschichte und Klassenbewusstsein*.

What came from his pen as if by force of habit, then, could hardly be taken as anything more than a psychological commentary on its author—another *pis aller*, in short, compounded of the abusive *Vulgarmarxismus* and ultra-Leninist scientism which recur periodically in Lukacs's work whenever his 'deviationist' self might assert itself. Nor does one have to be addicted either to Lukacs's pre-Leninist Hegelianism or to the nebulosities of Sartre or Heidegger to see his attack on existentialism in anything but that light; it was too clearly a case of Lukacs at war with himself to pass for much else. To take but one of many telling examples, what was one to make of Lukacs's strictures against Heidegger's concept of 'existence' with its insistence that the world is meaningful only in so far as it is a function of man's subjectivity? All this, ventured Lukacs in approved Leninist fashion, is nothing but 'the chief epistemological thesis of subjective idealism that there is no object without a subject . . . and of an irrational, mystical variety of subjective idealism, at that. . . .'[36] Quite apart from the distortion of Lukacs's rendering of the concept, the fact remains that, whatever else he made of it, Heidegger's 'Dasein' is essentially what one finds underlying much of the argument of *Geschichte und Klassenbewusstsein*. It was also what Marx had in mind when he criticized Feuerbach's materialism for conceiving of 'the object, reality . . . only in the form of the object . . . not as human sense activity . . . not subjectively.' For all his professions of Leninist orthodoxy dating back to 1934, the more insistently Lukacs laboured the unqualified pan-objectivism of Leninist ontology in his polemic against existentialism, the less plausible it rang as an expression of his own Marxism.

All this is not to suggest that existentialists know Lukacs only in the rôle of an adversary, more concerned with his own *Parteilichkeit* than with the drift of their argument. For, by another of those strange ironies in which his career abounds, it so happens that his *Geschichte und Klassenbewusstsein* was the one book by a modern Marxist in which existentialists, particularly those in France, could find the likeness of their own philosophical temper reflected.[37] One

[35] An abbreviated English translation of his remarks may be found in *Soviet Survey*, Nov. 1956, pp. 15–19. Full text, see *Aufbau* (Berlin), Sept. 1956, pp. 76ff.

[36] *Existentialismus oder Marxismus?*, p. 170–1.

[37] This is true most notably of M. Merleau-Ponty. See his 'Marxisme et Philosophie' and 'Autour de Marx' in *Sens et Non-Sens* (Paris, 1948), and his more recent book, *Les Aventures de la Dialectique* (Paris, 1955), esp. Ch. II. For an exhaustive survey of the more recent literature bearing on Lukacs's influence on existentialist thought, see H. Dahm, 'Ist die sowjetrussische Dialektik latenter Existentialismus?' *Ost-Probleme*, October 26, 1956, pp. 1486ff.

of his more enthusiastic partisans has gone so far as to claim that Lukacs's *Die Seele und die Formen* and his *Geschichte und Klassenbewusstsein* make him the true founder of modern existentialism. Indeed, many existentialists, going on the strength of the affinities between their own doctrine and Lukacs's work, have even ventured to reinterpret the Marxism of Lukacs, and of the early Marx from which it is derived, as being itself a form of social existentialism.

The merits of such a claim would require an analysis going well beyond the scope of the present discussion. As with all attempts to recast one doctrine in terms of another, so in this case, much depends on the relative importance assigned to their different elements. But without an act of intellectual excision, one suspects that a Hegelianized Marxism such as Lukacs's would still remain a Marxism which defies the pure subjectivity of existentialist transcendence and counts, instead, on a dialectic of history, operating through the action of a social class, to lift humanity to a life of 'authentic existence'. It might well turn out, then, that any attempt to cast that Marxism in an existentialist mould would only result in something more Marxist than existentialist.

Be that as it may, there is no overlooking the startling affinity between the style of Lukacs's thinking, both before and after his conversion to Marxism, and the approach which recurs through all the variations of the existentialist theme: both emphatically reject the 'unauthentic' or 'ordinary' life of 'alienated' man; both discount truth of the positivist type as man's guide to 'authentic' or 'rational' existence; and in both, it is the experience of choice, commitment and action, particularly during moments of crisis, that transforms man into an authentic subject of his own existence.

If so, it is also on the 'existential' plane of choice and commitment that the dialectic of history would have to be enacted, not through the 'laws of motion' of the economic system. The predicament of political choice is, however, seldom, if ever, resolved by direct recourse to first principles alone, not even by one so sensitively attuned to them as Lukacs. In 1956, for example, it made for a vast difference in his political behaviour that his own anti-Stalinism could converge with the momentum of a nationwide uprising, and could also take its cue from the proceedings of the Twentieth Congress of the CPSU, rather than spend itself in frustrated silence, as it had in the years before. To anyone who scans all the four decades of his career as a communist, its long silences of submission no less than its brief eruptions of defiance, the record is enough to indicate a pattern of motivation far more tangled and tragic than that suggested by the heroic presentment of recent Lukacs enthusiasts. Their impression to the contrary notwithstanding, Lukacs *qua* communist is not a personification of his book; the sources of his political conduct are his own, embedded in the deepest recesses of his personality, and thus, in the nature of the case, something which cannot be reduced to the intellectual dimensions of a doctrine.

XI. The Philosopher of Hope: Ernst Bloch

JÜRGEN RÜHLE

We have no confidence, we have only hope. Ernst Bloch

Commenting on the publication in West Germany of Ernst Bloch's Das Prinzip Hoffnung, *a Hamburg critic noted that, even if everybody but this East German philosopher had been silent for the last few years, 'this document of marvellous poetry was enough to show that there was still great German literature, that it had lost nothing of its richness'. He added that Bloch (like Heidegger) was read in Montevideo, Kobe, and Melbourne. It is difficult to think of a more formidable exaggeration. Bloch is practically unknown outside Germany; as for his awkward and often slightly ridiculous style, the less said the better. Bloch's writings, especially in his later years, are a curious mixture of profound insight, confused and irrelevant deviations from his theme, and lip service to Stalinist ideology. Of C. G. Jung, Ernst Bloch observes somewhere in his* magnum opus *that the archaic element in his work makes an alien and unsuitable impression, as though the customs of Timbuktu had been grafted on to the traditions of Zürich. With even greater justification it would be said that the Stalinist element in Bloch appears like an importation from Timbuktu to Pankow—or to Ludwigshafen, where Bloch was born. For all that, it is a matter for regret that Bloch is not better known outside Germany; with all his oddities and intellectual perversities, he is probably the one original living communist thinker anywhere in the world. That he was head and shoulders above the exponents of official party ideology in East Germany need hardly be emphasized. The present biographical essay may serve as an introduction to Bloch's work during the last two decades. Among his earlier books* Vom Geist der Utopie (1918), Thomas Muenzer als Theologe der Revolution (1922), *and* Erbschaft der Zeit (1923), *deserve to be mentioned.*

The emeritus professor at the Karl Marx University of Leipzig, who began his career in 1918 with his *Vom Geist der Utopie*, is now 76 years old. A man with a luxuriant mass of greyish white hair, an impressively furrowed forehead, and an earnest face marked with the cares and hopes of a lifetime. His eyes are hidden behind thick glasses. His movements and general attitude have a nobility which gives meaning to every step and every word.

Although he never intended to be one, he is a German professor of the good old type, with the characteristic intellectual energy, retiring nature, and occasional absentmindedness: 'German thunder,' Heine said, 'is very German indeed: not very subtle, it approaches with a slow rumble.'

Bloch's philosophy is based on a human experience which he calls the darkness of the lived in moment.

'. . . in the final analysis the darkest moment of all is the present moment in which we are actually living now. The present moment is the centre of our experience and open to question; the moment we have just lived through is the most immediate moment and therefore least of all in a state to be experienced. Only when the present moment has just gone, or when and as long as it is being awaited is it not only lived in but also experienced. When the present moment is actually in existence it is shrouded in darkness. Only that which is just about to come or which has just passed has the distance, the lack of absolute immediacy which is necessary before the growing unconsciousness of a particular moment can come fully alive. The present moment in which we are, burrows within itself and does not feel itself. Hence the content of that which has just been experienced cannot be perceived.'[1]

On many occasions Bloch has encircled the mystery which reigns in this darkness of the present moment. He speaks of the 'That-ground', of the 'node of the world', of the 'womb of matter' and so on; but he regards the mystery as ultimately impenetrable and indefinable. He is willing to leave it at that.

It seems to him that the only definite fact is that there is ferment and activity in the life of man and the world. There is within us an urge, a striving, and a need to break away from the emptiness of the moment; we feel that non-being is a kind of non-having: the world is kept in motion by a *horror vacui*. Bloch argues, against Freud, that it is impossible to make such a specific instinct as the sexual libido the common denominator of the world; he speaks in more general terms of hunger, by which he evidently means not only the physical rumbling of the stomach, but need in general, dissatisfaction with the present state of things. By hunger he means everything inside us that longs to eat, drink, overwhelm, live fully and be fulfilled. Even in the pre-human and extra-human world Bloch has discovered this same urge to escape from the imperfection and unfulfilment of a shadow existence, from what the shoemaker-philosopher Jacob

[1] *Das Prinzip Hoffnung*, vol. I, p. 312.

Boehme called the 'Agony of Matter'. According to Bloch, this impulse from darkness into light is the origin of history and the power behind the evolving process of the world. The world process is tending towards an ultimate goal which Bloch calls the supreme good, Totum and Ultimum, Identity, Success, the breaking in of the What into the ground of the That. Again, Bloch refuses to give precise expression to this ultimate goal, since it has not yet emerged clearly enough and is still wholly a presentiment. It is the meaning of life, the conscience of history, blessedness and the Promised Land, the Utopian content which is implicit in the 'Linger on, thou art so beautiful' of the Faust plan. Bloch had given most concrete expression to what he has in mind in the words of Marx, 'the naturalization of man and the humanization of nature', or, in other words, 'socialized humanity in alliance with humanized nature will turn the world into a real home.' All our willing and yearning and hope is directed to this ultimate end which gives content and meaning to the world. There is a presentiment of the Ultimate, of the Ineffable in our wish-fulfilment dreams and in the ciphers of reality and archetypes which mysteriously rule our life and thought, in the fictional figures of super humanity such as Don Quixote, Don Giovanni, Odysseus and Faust, in the golden ground of music, in the eschatological promises of religion, in the shining world of Nature. A mysterious paradisian landscape emerges from the dawn of the future, a new heaven and a new earth to which everything tends but where no one ever was. Two sentences of Goethe's span the arch of the world as conceived by Bloch: 'In the beginning was the Deed' and 'The indescribable here is achieved'.

To a Western observer Bloch's philosophy, with its Old Testament fervour, its optimistic belief in progress, and its concept of political salvation, seems strangely exotic; the principle of Hope which Bloch advocates is out of fashion with us, at any rate with our augurs and philosophers. This may explain, though it does not excuse, the unfortunate fact that for many years Western Germany has ignored one of our most stimulating and important thinkers. One has also to take into account Bloch's peculiar and anything but happy merging of speculative philosophy and current politics. In the midst of profound general ideas he will suddenly refer to the cultural barbarism of America and to Soviet peace policy. C. G. Jung he dismisses as a 'frothy fascist psycho-analyst': A. Huxley as an 'individualistic fascist and criminal'. Stalin haunts Bloch's writings as a paragon of wisdom, just as Hegel was once haunted by the world-spirit on horseback—Napoleon.

On the other hand, however, there is an obvious difference between this philosophy and the ideology of the Communist Party; compared with this ideology, which Bloch himself has mischievously called a 'narrow-gauge theory', his work displays an overpowering wealth and audacity of thought, an intimate and masterly knowledge of the history of civilization, and an abundance of genuine wisdom, which compel our admiration quite independently of the philosophical and political contents of his work.

Bloch's main work, *Das Prinzip Hoffnung* (The Principle of Hope),[2] is a veritable encyclopedia of human aspirations and longings. Beginning with common or garden daydreams and the intoxicating hubbub of the fairground and the delirium of the opium-addict, he goes on to describe all the utopias and ideals which man has rigged up for himself from time immemorial in politics, learning, art, and philosophy. His survey of the whole realm of human hope culminates in the revelations which have come to humanity in its supreme moments.

In his later work, *Differentiations in the Concept of Progress*,[3] Bloch gave the outlines of a Marxist philosophy of nature and cosmology; in his memorable lecture on Hegel in November 1956, he suggested that Dialectical Materialism should be extended by a Marxist anthropology and a Marxist ethic and even a philosophy of religion based on Feuerbach.

It is not surprising that the SED has always been rather afraid of this 'worker on the philosophical front'. But it tolerated him as a distinguished ally, just as it tolerated Brecht (although neither was a member of the SED). Party professor Kurt Hager, the secretary of the Central Committee responsible for ideology, speaking of progressive philosophy, distinguished, with nicety of feeling, between 'adherents of dialectical materialism and such thinkers as Ernst Bloch'.[4] After long hesitation the Party decided, in the thaw of 1955, to bestow on Bloch the National Prize and the silver Order of Merit of the Fatherland: on this occasion it was acknowledged that his works, even if not precisely on the party line, 'combine a profoundly penetrating analysis and interpretation of the world with a progressive outlook'.[5] Bloch himself felt quite friendly towards the SED regime: in spite of many differences on matters of detail he hoped that Communism would lead to the realization of his dreams.

The revolutionary spark in Bloch's philosophy is the dialectic. He speaks somewhere of the warm stream and the cold stream in Marxism, the warm and the cold Red. The warm stream is the impulse to freedom, the thinking in terms of process, the revolutionary impulse of the dialectic; the cold stream is the realistic analysis

[2] Aufbauverlag, East Berlin, 3 vols., 1954, 1955, 1959.
[3] Sitzungsberichte der Deutschen Akademie der Wissenschaften zu Berlin, 1956.
[4] *Neues Deutschland* (East Berlin), July 8, 1955.
[5] *Ibid.*, October 15, 1955.

of situations, the thinking in terms of visible systems, the sobering insight into what is feasible and useful. The one is an expression of Marxism's hopes for the future, its goal of human redemption, its deeply human impulses, whilst the other is an expression of its adaptation to the tasks of the immediate present, political strategy and tactics—power politics. The warm stream represents the inspiration of a great idea; the cold stream the hard realities of the actual world: the dove on the rooftop as opposed to the sparrow in the hand. Although Bloch admits that the two kinds of red supplement one another, he himself obviously believes in the warm kind: for him Marxism is a doctrine of warmth. He does not find it difficult to make derogatory remarks about the cold Red; he says, for example, that whereas the warm Red is a faith, the cold Red is an acid, and it acts as a brake on the flight of the spirit. One is tempted to draw the conclusion which Bloch himself only hints at in this context: that Bloch's philosophy is an expression of the warm stream in Marxism and Stalinist dialectical materialism an expression of the cold stream. The difference is apparent if one compares the historical ancestors (apart from Marx) whom they claim for their respective ideas. 'The good new is never completely new,' Bloch writes in the Preface of his main work.

'Even Christians know, with amazement or a sleeping conscience, that all the Utopian aspirations of the great movements of human liberation, derive from Exodus and the Messianic parts of the Bible. And the conjunction of having and non-having which constitutes hope and yearning and the homing instinct has always been active in the great philosophies. It is active not only in the Platonic Eros, but also in the far-reaching concept of Aristotelian matter as the potentiality of being, and in the Leibnizian concept of tendency. Hope is directly active in the Kantian postulates of the moral consciousness, and it is active through the agency of the world spirit, in Hegel's historical dialectic.'[6]

This genealogy consists without exception of idealist thinkers, and this is not surprising, since the idea of dialectic as the dynamic impulse of history, was seized on mainly by thinkers who have risen above dull reality and hastened on ahead of it. How is it possible, however, to reconcile this genealogy with Zhdanov's declaration at the notorious philosophers' congress of 1947, that dialectical materialism has evolved entirely from the materialist philosophy of the past, in opposition to idealism, which has always looked after the interests of the selfish upper classes? If Zhdanov is right, Bloch's intellectual ancestors stand on the other side of the barricade. Of course, with the exception of Marx—but it seems likely that

[6] *Das Prinzip Hoffnung*, vol. I, p. 17.

Bloch and the Stalinists also differ in their views on Marxism.

Behind the practical political difference there is also a theoretical difference: the question whether the Soviet order of society already represents the realm of freedom of which Marx dreamt.

There are, Bloch says, many stages in the humanization of man still to be passed through, when work has been made free; it will not have been achieved for all time on the first day of the classless society. At the conference on the problem of freedom held in 1956 he declared quite openly that freedom in the so-called socialist states is by no means identical with the ultimate goal which they pursue and that in these states some of the bourgeois freedoms gained in the past no longer exist or have still to return.[7] And in his book *The Principle of Hope* he has confessed with the typical ponderousness which Heine attributed to all German philosophers:

'Revolutions realize humanity's oldest hopes: for that very reason they imply and require the increasingly concrete achievement of the ideal of freedom and the never completed journey towards its realization. Only if Utopia itself (that is, a kind of reality that has never been so far) were to take possession of the dynamic content of the Here and Now, would the Hope which is the ground of its existence be totally incorporated in reality. Until that day comes, the world of daydreams will continue; no instalment payment can make man forget it. A mere presentiment must not be made so absolute that remembrance of the ultimate goal is dimmed ... a remembrance expressed supremely in the words of the psalmist: If I forget thee, O Jerusalem, let my right hand forget her cunning.'

Bloch's philosophy marches out towards great horizons, revealing the 'quite titanic role of human action or freedom' of which Hommes has spoken. Without the possibility of choice, Bloch says, there can be no progress; and if the whole process of the world has been determined in advance, anything new can occur at most in the human consciousness, not in reality. If the whole of the future has been pre-determined, wonder and doubt can have as little place in the world as a desire for reform and change. All man can do is follow the iron logic of history or let it run its course—if everything has been pre-determined, man is not an engine driver but a mere passenger, who is simply allowed to buy a ticket to socialism at the Communist party's booking office. According to Bloch, however, man makes his own history; he is certainly dependent on tendencies and opportunities which are embedded in the budding entelechy of

[7] 'Freiheit, ihre Schichtung, und ihr Verhältnis zur Wahrheit.' Protokoll der Konferenz der Sektion Philosophie der Deutschen Akademie der Wissenschaften zu Berlin, 1956.

the womb of matter but 'the decision has not yet been taken and the thing itself has not yet emerged'. There are negative and positive potentialities, all existence is encompassed with the nothingness, to which the world is moving as it is also moving to the All, to a state of ultimate bliss and fulfilment. Failure and emptiness beckon from the horizon as well as happiness and fulfilment. The dreamed of heaven gleams against the dark background of hell: life is still swallowed up in death and it is still far from certain whether life or death will triumph in the end. We have no confidence, Bloch says, we have only Hope.

This conception of the openness and undecidedness of history is possibly the most exciting feature of Bloch's thought: it throws the rattling machinery of dialectical materialism entirely overboard and gives new scope to the freedom of the will and the power of decision. 'Freedom of the will,' Bloch said at the conference on Freedom which we have already mentioned, 'comes from a willing that is brought to fruition by a progressive series of choices, decisions and actions. Choice is the starting point of freedom. . . .'

This means that no one possesses the key to paradise, not even the Marxists or the party that claims to be always right. Man himself decides whether the world is to be more human or more devilish, whether the sky is to clear or grow dark and gloomy. National socialism and Stalinism (the 'cult of the personality') were not conjured up by some cunning trick in the workings of the laws of history but by our own failure, by our own unmindfulness of humanity. The wrathful protest of the people on June 17, 1953 and October 23, 1956 was not a barren bough on the tree of knowledge, no mere blunder in the irresistible advance towards Communism, but a *mene tekel* at the crossroads of history.

With this view of history, man himself moves into the centre of philosophy. Man, says Bloch, is not a slave, neither is he a master; he is not a serf, neither is he a feudal lord; not a proletarian and, just as certainly, not a capitalist. Man is the being for whom the future still holds much in store. He is constantly being transformed in and through his work. He comes again and again to frontiers and passes over them. The future of history lies in his bravery, not in some mythos of the proletariat. Man is the hinge on which the door to freedom swings. The SED expert on Bloch, his former pupil and later rival in Leipzig, Rugard Otto Gropp, rightly set at the head of his criticism the following statement: 'In his view of the world Ernst Bloch proceeds from man. It is this that gives his philosophy its fundamental character and differentiates it straightaway from dialectical materialism.'

Bloch's philosophy does in fact provide the basis for humanist socialism, i.e., a socialism of man, a socialism of humanity. Ten years before the Polish and Hungarian October risings he wrote:

'The root of history is the working man; once he has seized hold of himself and established himself in a real democracy without alienation and renunciation, something will come into the world in which no one so far has ever been: a true home.'[8]

The sinister and dangerous factor in Bloch's philosophy, from the standpoint of dialectical materialism, emerges very clearly from a myth of which there is an account in *The Principle of Hope*; the myth of the dual Helen. According to a fragment of Euripides, only a phantom of Helen was carried off to Troy; the real Helen survived the time of the disorders bravely and chastely in Egyptian exile. Her consort Menelaus finds her there to his great surprise when he returns home from Troy and at the same time the Trojan Helen, who has been carried on the ship, dissolves into a column of fire—the princely lady returns home an honest woman in her own flesh; everyone congratulates Menelaus on possessing such an honourable wife. 'However,' Bloch says, 'what happens in the real depths of the affair is this: the Trojan or phantom Helen has the advantage over the Egyptian Helen in that she has inhabited a dream for ten years and has indeed fulfilled the dream. This is not entirely counteracted by the later actual fulfilment; the radiant residue of the dream remains, there remains a wisp of fiery air, Fata Morgana has an independent existence. The object of the real fulfilment was not present in the adventures, as opposed to the dream-object; the fulfilled reality represents a very late acquaintance. Only the Trojan, not the Egyptian Helen, travelled with the army, absorbed the yearning of the ten utopian years, the bitterness and the hate-love of the cuckold, the many nights far from home, the rough camp life, and the anticipation of victory. The weights are easily exchanged: in this aporia the remarkable siren of the air in Troy, with whom is bound up a world of guilt, suffering, but above all of hope, remains almost the sole reality, and reality almost becomes a phantom. Quite apart from the coquettish glamour of the Trojan Helen, the Egyptian Helen lacks the utopian glamour of the Trojan Helen, she did not share the yearning of the voyage, the adventures of battle, the goal of achievement; and so the Egyptian reality as such seems to be on a smaller scale.'[9]

Ernst Bloch's philosophy is a communism of revolutionary illusions, illumined by the fiery glow of Utopia. Such a communism is infinitely superior to Stalinism, in spite of the latter's power and might: it is the incarnation of the hopes and sacrifices of many utopian years; his cause has nothing to link it with the reality of the labour camp and the execution cellar. That is what makes Party Professor Gropp so angry and scornful:

[8] *Freiheit und Ordnung*, New York, 1946.
[9] *Das Prinzip Hoffnung*, vol. I, pp. 201ff.

'By virtue of its mystical, teleologically inverted character, which seems to teem with problems, and also thanks to its journalistic style, the philosophy of Ernst Bloch exerts an attraction on certain strata of the intelligentsia and on students who have become divorced from practical affairs and have no political experience. They find here a philosophy the acceptance of which demands no open break with Marxism, because it calls itself Marxist, whilst allowing its adherents to detach themselves from Marxism. Bloch's philosophy appeals to a petit-bourgeois frame of mind which is inclined to socialism but evades the difficulties which socialist action involves in the conflict of the new and the old, and against the wiles of imperialism. Bloch's philosophy supplies an ideological foundation for presumptuousness vis-à-vis Marxism and for its ideological undermining.'[10]:

That Bloch himself is aware of this problem if not in relation to Communism, and that he is a convinced adherent of a Utopian mission is clear from the section in his main work which is entitled 'The Encounter of the Utopian Function with Ideology'. Since ideologies always stem from ruling classes, he writes, 'they justify the existing social order, inasmuch as they deny its economic roots and conceal the exploitation on which it is based.'

Utopia, therefore, only draws the spark, not the ashes, out of the fire of history:

'It is only in this way that Utopia extracts the things that belong to it from the ideologies and explains the progressive elements which continue to act historically in the great works of ideology itself. The spirit of Utopia is present in the ultimate essence of every great creative utterance, in the Strassburg Minster and the Divine Comedy, in Beethoven's prophetic music and in the latencies of the B Minor Mass. It is in the despair which is in a *Unum necessarium* even when it is lost in the Hymn to Joy. Kyrie and Credo are absorbed in the concept of Utopia, as that of hope understood, in quite a different way even when they have lost the reflex of a merely time-bound ideology, in fact just then. The exact imagination of the not-yet-conscious supplements critical enlightenment by revealing the gold which has not been attacked by nitric acid and the good that remains valid and emerges when class illusions and class ideologies have been destroyed. The only loss that culture suffers from the end of class ideologies, in which it was a purely decorative element, is the decoration itself, the artificially perfect harmonization. The function of Utopia is to rescue human culture from the idleness of mere contemplation; it opens up a view, on summits that have really been

[10] R. O. Gropp: 'Mystische Hoffnungsphilosophie ist unvereinbar mit Marxismus', *Forum* (East Berlin), No. 6, 1957.

attained, of the true content of human hope and undissembled by
ideology.'[11]

In the *Principle of Hope* Bloch denies that this is to be understood
in reference to communism, but who could prevent the young men
who streamed into his lecture room and read his books thinking of
it in reference to communism? Not only Eastern but Western
ideologists are habitually attacking Bloch for the unreal, fragmentary, and poetically hazy nature of his ideas. He himself would give a
very simple answer: 'Seeing through things is not the only test of a
sharp eye. Not regarding everything as being crystal-clear is equally
the sign of penetrating vision.'
One should read the statements of the couple of dozen SED
philosophers who have meanwhile tried, at the behest of the party,
to pin down the errors and obscurities in Bloch's theories.[12] Apart
from the misunderstandings, simplifications and misrepresentations
that have crept in, the attempt to provide an answer to everything,
to build a philosophy exclusively on scientifically exact foundations,
results in an inextricable jumble of contradictory ideas which
fundamentally has no meaning at all. Bloch has intentionally left
many issues undecided because in his view the 'thing itself' has not
yet emerged. Will it ever emerge? Bloch insists that his ultimate goal,
heaven on earth, is attainable, that one day the inward will become
outward and the outward inward. The ancient yearning for happiness will be fulfilled. This, however, is a theoretical conception and I
doubt if he believes in it in the depths of his heart. He once wrote:
'The absolute co-incidence (of the real and the ideal) has rarely,
probably never, occurred. In dreams, in the semi-waking state,
things were or seemed to be better.' Bloch's goal for humanity hovers
above the earth like a pole star, guiding and mathematically deter-
minable but infinitely remote. It cannot be extinguished by the
transient dark clouds of dictatorship.

For many years, owing to his delicate relationship with the SED,
Bloch's philosophy was confined to the esoteric circle of his Leipzig
pupils. It was only when the thaw set in that Bloch came before the
public eye. In 1953 there appeared the *Deutsche Zeitschrift für
Philosophie* (German Journal of Philosophy), edited by Bloch and
Wolfgang Harich, with two other professors, to which he contributed in every number. In 1954 and 1955 there appeared the first
two volumes of *Das Prinzip Hoffnung*. In 1956 he delivered three
great lectures on the renewal of Marxism, entitled 'Differentiations
in the Concept of Progress', 'Freedom and Truth', and 'Hegel and
the Power of the System'. At this period his lecture room in Leipzig,

[11] Vol. I, p. 174.
[12] Ernst Bloch's *Revision des Marxismus* (East Berlin), 1957.

the largest in the Karl Marx University, was always overcrowded. Leading exponents of the Party ideology came under his spell, including the Central Committee Secretary Hager. With the whole weight of his personality and philosophy Ernst Bloch stepped into the breach made by the Twentieth CPSU Congress. Like his friend Georg Lukacs in Budapest, he did not attack Communism in general but only its perversion. He wanted to make it stronger, more convincing, more human—quite a revolution in itself! 'Now at last,' he cried, to the tumultuous cheers of his audience, 'chess must be played, instead of draughts.'

When the *German Journal of Philosophy* began to appear in 1953, the year of the workers' revolt, and was immediately attacked by the Party, the *Berliner Zeitung*—at that time a mouthpiece of the opposition in the Soviet Zone—closed its notice of the Journal as follows (December 1, 1953):

'The *Deutsche Zeitschrift für Philosophie* is a professional journal which seems to be inspired by a valiant spirit, versatility, and high standards of scholarship. Its ideological significance must not be underestimated—if it continues true to its motto from the writings of Engels's "The more persistently and impartially science proceeds, the more it will find itself in accord with the interests and aspirations of the workers".'

A few years later, this goal had been attained. In 1956–57 the SED regime, which in 1953 had been able to confine itself to suppressing the workers, found itself compelled to proceed against the philosophers with the same brutality. The State Security Service occupied the editorial offices of the *Journal*, seized the current manuscripts, and arrested the editorial staff. Of the well-known young philosophers in East Germany, Wolfgang Harich was sentenced to ten years penal servitude, Günther Zehm to four years, Manfred Hertwig, editorial secretary of the *Journal*, to two years. Bloch's pupils, Richard Lorenz and Gerhard Zwerenz fled from Leipzig to the Federal Republic. Ernst Bloch himself was discharged and forbidden to publish or travel; at the last moment his arrest, which had already been ordered by Melsheimer, the Public Prosecutor, was called off for political reasons.

In the official findings on the case, as recorded in a letter from the SED directorate of the University of Leipzig, which was instigated by Ulbricht, Bloch was accused of 'leading youth astray'. What an honour for a philosopher: it is literally the same charge that was made against Socrates.

The steps taken by the police followed on an all-round campaign for a purge, personal and ideological, in the philosophy of East Germany. The editorial board of the *Deutsche Zeitschrift für Philosophie* was filled with Stalinists, and the process of correction went so far that all references to works by Bloch and Harich in the index to the periodical for 1956 were removed, an incident which recalled Orwell's 'memory-hole'. Philosophical and social-science institutes were combed through for revisionists; the lecture programme and the publishing plans in the philosophy faculty were reorganized. The dispute with Bloch became the subject of discussions among the top party leaders, particularly at the thirtieth session of the SED Central Committee in January 1957, and at the thirty-third in the following October. Conferences to discuss theory were arranged in order to bring philosophy once more on to the party line: on Bloch's philosophy (April 1957), on theoretical and practical questions of socialist morality (April 1957), on the Marxist-Leninist theory of the state (April 1958), and on dialectical materialism (May 1958). The argument was carried on in the press, particularly in the SED central organ *Neues Deutschland*, the Communist student magazine *Forum*, and in the 'purged' *Deutsche Zeitschrift für Philosophie*.

Despite this massive drumfire, Bloch uttered no word of self-criticism. At the thirty-third CC meeting Hager said of Bloch that 'it really is time to confront him with the demand that he break his silence, and state his position about the criticism and above all about the anti-state activities of his students. I think that is the only way to get the lines clear.'

Bloch let another six months pass before making a laconic and diplomatic profession of loyalty: 'At a time when the Bundestag is voting for atomic arms, while the Soviet Union declares its readiness to cease all atomic tests in its territory, I learn with great anger that the warmongers in West Germany, and not only there, are again trying to use my name to try to further their political ends. I emphatically dissociate myself from this. No philosophical controversy affects my allegiance to socialism, to peace, to German unity. And it is the German Democratic Republic on whose ground I stand, with whose humanist aspirations I agree, at the heart of which lies the abolition of the exploitation of man by man. Criticism can be honest only if it is exercised here on the soil of the Republic, and follows an unmistakably socialist road, and no other.'[13]

Obviously this declaration met neither of Hager's demands. Bloch did not define his attitude to the party's criticism of his philosophy, nor did he dissociate himself from his students. If you read the declaration slowly, sentence by sentence, it seemed to consist entirely of implicit reservations. Bloch swore allegiance to socialism, to peace, to German unity, to the abolition of exploitation—but any democratic socialist in the West could subscribe to the same goals. Of the DDR he said, Solomon-wise, that he stands on its soil and agrees with its humanist aspirations. And for good measure he added that he had a critical attitude towards this republic. The only thing

[13] *Neues Deutschland*, April 20, 1958.

in the statement favouring the regime was his assurance that he wanted to stay in the DDR.

Bloch was now deprived of his post at Leipzig, prevented from teaching, and forbidden to have any personal contact with his former students, but the SED pretended to be satisfied with this equivocal fragment of a loyalty oath and called off the campaign against him. In the autumn of 1958 he and his wife (who had been expelled from the SED early in 1957) were honoured as 'fighters against fascism' and at the end of October he was once more allowed to travel to the West to take part in the Congress of the Hegel Society in Frankfurt am Main. Exit visas were granted also on subsequent occasions.

Bloch seemed as little impressed by this clemency as he had been by earlier reprisals. When the Communist philosophers from the Soviet zone demonstratively walked out of the Hegel congress as a protest against the criticisms of Marx by Adorno, the Frankfurt sociologist, he remained seated. His name was missing from the signatures to the congratulatory address sent by the professors of the East Berlin Academy of Sciences to the government on the tenth anniversary of the DDR in October 1959.

At the end of the year, to the general surprise, the third volume of *Das Prinzip Hoffnung* was published in the Soviet zone; it had been held up by the censor for nearly three years. It was published without any of the changes which the SED had so long and so stubbornly demanded, and which Bloch had equally stubbornly refused to make. This astonishing surrender by the dictatorship must have been prompted by the forthcoming appearance of the complete text of the work in the West (it was published in Frankfurt am Main in 1959). By permitting a small edition to be published in the zone, Ulbricht avoided the kind of scandal which the Soviet authorities have let themselves in for by their inflexible attitude towards Pasternak.

However, this did not make much difference in the end. In September 1961, while on a visit to Tübingen, Professor Bloch applied for political asylum in the Federal Republic.

XII. Karl Marx and the Classical Definition of Truth

LESZEK KOLAKOWSKI

Given below in translation are extracts from two articles: the first, under the title 'Karl Marx and the Classical Definition of Truth', by L. Kolakowski, appeared in Studia Filozoficzne *(1959, 2), and was an expanded version of a lecture given in the University of Tübingen in December 1958. Kolakowski is Professor of Philosophy in the University of Warsaw; the second article is a reply to the first, and was written by Adam Schaff, also a Professor of Philosophy in the University of Warsaw and a member of the Central Committee of the Polish Communist Party; it appeared in* Nowe Drogi *(1959, 13) under the title 'Studies of the Young Marx: Marginalia to Kolakowski's article'. Since the articles were too long to reproduce in full, we have given extracts, and where necessary summarized the passages not given in translation; these are printed in italics.*

The end of the nineteenth century gave birth to two different though as a rule not clearly distinguished theories which attempted to represent man's practical activity as one of the primary categories of epistemological reflection. One of them—which we may call Marxism with a positivist orientation, and which is expounded in the philosophical writings of Engels—appeals to the *success* of human action as the criterion by which it is possible and right to *verify* the knowledge taken to be true when any activity was initiated. The other, which found its classical though extremely careless and imprecise expression in the works of William James, introduces the concept of practical *utility* as an element in the *definition* of truth, understanding utility not as an instrument to establish a truth in human knowledge independent of man himself, but as that which itself *creates* truth. Truth therefore is relative, varying according to its application in everyday life.

Let me stress a few points which show the contradiction between the two doctrines. One of them treats truth as a relation between judgment or opinion and the reality to which they refer, a relation which is independent of the knowledge which man has of it. Man's practical activity most certainly does not create truth, but only determines its realization.

The role of practical human activity as a criterion, as a method of verification, consists in the practical application of our knowledge in the hope of obtaining a specific result; success confirms the truth of our knowledge, failure compels us to abandon or modify it, but these procedures do not in the least affect the fact that a judgment is either false or true. If, for example, we are today uncertain whether there are rational beings living in the solar system elsewhere than on our planet, it is none the less certain that the statement: 'there are other rational beings besides those on earth' is, here and now, either true or false; for judgments have the property of being true or false independently of whether we know that property or are capable of proving its existence. From this point of view the classical definition of truth remains fully in force, taking into account that a statement is true or false in itself on the necessary and sufficient condition that the circumstances and processes are as it says in the reality which it is describing, and irrespective of whether anyone has succeeded or indeed ever will succeed in establishing this congruity by the criterion of practice or by any other. In this sense the relativity of knowledge can be accepted without difficulty; this concept is used with reference to the progress of human knowledge, inasmuch as human knowledge will never succeed in formulating scientific generalizations in a manner which precisely defines their validity or applicability.

This doctrine, universally accepted in Marxist circles, was popularized in Lenin's *Materialism and Empiriocriticism*—but it was also generalized; for Lenin considered it possible to apply the doctrine not only to judgments, but also to sense impressions which, he said, 'copy', 'photograph', 'reflect', etc. the objects of the external world. These expressions, it is true, were not favourably received by positivists; their content was too heavily charged with troublesome ambiguities. It seems to me, however, that with certain stipulations they can be accommodated, without detriment to Lenin's thought, within the framework of that classical definition of truth to which the Marxist tradition, since Engels, has appealed. It is obvious in any case that both authors mentioned understood the development of man's conceptual apparatus as an effort aimed at a continually more exact copying of the external world which is considered as a pre-existing model; that according to them human cognition, though incapable of absolutely and finally mastering its object, approaches it in a constant and progressive evolution, and that its unlimited improvement tends to make it more and more *like* reality; that it imitates more and more faithfully all the time the properties and relations of the world, which are themselves independent of this effort and exist in themselves outside human thought.

In the other theory mentioned, man's practical activity was raised to the level of an epistemological category in such a way that its functions are not confined to the verification of the congruity of human knowledge with a previously existing model, but are extended to the definition of the very concept of truth, falsehood, and nonsense. *Kolakowski notes that he is concerning himself here only with the central distinctive concept of Pragmatism in its first modern version.*

In this version of Pragmatism—not the only one, as we know—the truth of a judgment is defined as a function of the practical advantage which its acceptance or rejection gives a man. . . . According to this doctrine the truth or falsity of an assertion is made to depend on the individual and the sum of the needs which determine his aspirations at a given moment. To be true means to satisfy the criterion of utility. Truth is not a relation independent of its confirmation: it comes into being at the moment of its confirmation. This can be regarded as a variant of idealism, insofar as that doctrine holds no judgment is meaningful unless there is given a certain consciousness in relation to which the judgment is or is not valid.

In contrast to the theory described above as Marxism with a positivist orientation, the Pragmatist concept can obviously not be reconciled with the classical definition of truth. According to the first theory human cognition, limited as it is in its main lines by man's biological and social needs, nonetheless strives in a gradual and infinite approximation towards an absolute copy of a reality existing beforehand and always primary in relation to cognition, although subject to changes; cognition is equally a means of satisfying human needs and at the same time an instrument which allows us to describe the world as it is 'in itself'. According to the other doctrine, cognition is a form of biological reaction facilitating the optimum adaptation of particular organisms to their medium. The classical Pragmatist conception of cognition is in reality purely biological; you can say meaningfully that the reaction of an organism to the stimuli of its medium is or is not adequate, that is to say useful or harmful for the preservation of the organism. Such evaluations are applied also to cognition; it can be qualified from the same point of view and assessed as true or false according to its results. But to ask whether a judgment is true or false in the ordinary sense, i.e. whether its content corresponds to the world 'in itself', would be as fruitless an operation as to ask whether a patellar reflex is true or false. It is not known what 'resemblance' between the content of cognition and objects is supposed to mean. But it is easy to understand the question whether the sum of biological reactions called cognition effectively helps the organism to orient itself in its medium, whether it satisfies the needs or instincts of the organism. . . .

Kolakowski describes Engels's doctrine as a manifestation of typically nineteenth century optimistic scientism, and early Pragmatism as a philosophy of individual success which 'nourished' American minds at the time of rapid economic development. He notes an almost literal repetition of Jamesian formulas in Henry Ford's writings. This is followed by an analysis of Marx's 1844 Manuscripts, *and his concept of humanized nature. To make his hypothetical reconstruction of Marx's theory of knowledge more precise, Kolakowski distinguishes it from other systems with which it has a real or apparent affinity. He does not wish to discuss whether Spinoza's attempt to achieve an integral understanding of the world influenced nascent Marxism via Hegel, but stresses the importance of the striking resemblance between early Marxism and certain of Spinoza's ideas.*

He finds in Spinoza's view of the world what he has hypothetically indicated as the basis of the young Marx's epistemology; the idea that nature made up of particular parts and categories is an 'artificial' creation, arising from man's practical needs and his effort to master nature. The analogy holds, however, only up to this point. Spinoza believed that the conditioning of the intellect by its everyday practical activity made it incapable of authentic knowledge of reality, but that there existed a higher cognitive instrument—the power of intuition—free from the distortions which theoretical reason could not escape. Spinoza's intuition, in one version at least, like Kant's practical reason, made possible the penetration of reality 'in itself', which is concealed by the distorting images of imagination and the empirical sciences. Marx rejects this enigmatic world, consigning it to the category of questions which are not susceptible of meaningful formulation. For Marx the creation of an object 'for use' is identical with the act of destroying the object 'in itself'.

If the rejection of illusory images of knowledge which copies nature 'in itself' separates the epistemology of Marx from ideas of positivistic or scientistic inspiration, the rejection of knowledge which could assimilate reality by intuitive integration weakens possible analogies with Bergsonian thought. In this system, which it would be superfluous to expound here, we find the same Spinozan tendency to overcome the limitations and distortions inevitably imposed on us by discursive knowledge; to deprive discursive knowledge, precisely in view of its practical origin, of the validity at which the disinterested contemplation of truth aims. But Marx rejects the contrast between a world made in the image of man and a world pre-existing 'in itself', which you may try to grasp by the hopeless effort to transcend yourself as a human being. For the same reason, from Marx's viewpoint, it would be wrong to stigmatize discursive knowledge as 'distorted', since distortion, even if the word is relieved of its pejorative aura, could be confirmed only if we possessed a model with which the distorted image could be compared; an impossible operation since the world, as it is given to human kind, cannot be transcended. We have no right to suppose that pre-existing reality carries in itself qualities of human reality, nor have we any tools to explore the nature and kind of the distortions which it undergoes when it abandons its transcendentality to reveal itself to our eyes. Without denying its existence, or declaring it to be unknowable, we reject it as a possible object of investigation. . . .

If it would be true, from Marx's point of view, to say consciousness is things thought of, his idea can be even more correctly generalized in the statement that things are consciousness reified. The first assertion concerns only the origin of consciousness in the contacts of the human species with the resistance of its medium considered generally as a totality or a pre-existing 'chaos'; the second takes into account the world of things already formed and differentiated amongst themselves; the first of the two worlds is the primal *universum* 'in itself', the Spinozan substance, while the second consists of objects with various qualities organized into categories, into groups preserved in human thought and language.

The existence of this 'chaos' is, however, by no means unimportant to epistemology; it is this precisely which defines the contrast between the Marxian and the Pragmatist theories of truth. Truth understood as a relation of 'resemblance' between human judgments and an absolutely independent reality is not indeed acceptable in the Marxian image of the world, but at least it does not consist exclusively in a relationship of biological correspondence, i.e. a relation between the judgment and its practical utility to the individual who makes it. On this basis we are forced to admit that reality is not only produced entirely *ex nihilo* for each particular individual, but also that this creation must be remade for the individual at every moment; for it is possible and probable that a judgment accepted as true at one moment on the strength of the criterion of utility will become a moment later useless, devoid of sense or harmful, and therefore false. Pragmatist relativism—of which these formulations, though extreme, are none the less an unavoidable consequence if we take the 'classical' statements of James seriously and literally—cannot be reconciled with Marx's thought, and this for two main reasons. The first is the impossibility of creation *ex nihilo*; the second, the conception of human consciousness as a social instrument which cannot be reduced to the behaviour of particular organisms. Therefore reality is not the sum of the phenomena whose existence some individual finds it advantageous to affirm at a certain moment, or which constitute the momentary response of his consciousness to the promptings of his vital needs. There exists a reality common to all people, which remains constantly in its original state, a reality where the phenomenon of creation certainly takes place, but where a certain constant is also preserved, corresponding to what may be called human nature or the sum of human characteristics, biological needs, and social relationships which can properly be considered invariable. The concept of human nature retains its validity to the extent that the concept of a reality which is permanent as an epistemological category (a reality accessible to man, and so the only reality worth taking into account), is justified. The Aristotelean concept of truth applies also to this reality. The congruity of judgment and reality is no longer a relation of 'resemblance' between that judgment and the world 'in itself'; it applies to that world on which man has already imposed 'substantial forms'.

Kolakowski expands this 'not altogether classical' variant of the classical theory of truth, concluding that the replacement of God by man in Feuerbach leads Marx to the discovery of the world as a human product. Kolakowski then turns to the important consequences of this embryonic Marxian epistemology—which he thinks worthy of further development—in the field of the criticism of historical knowledge.

It is impossible to imagine that the human character of the world can ever be transcended in the cognition of man, who gave it this form. But the opinion is sometimes held that we are capable of liberating ourselves from everything in our image of the world which is imposed on us by changing historical conditions, or that an objective view of the world is possible within the limits determined by unchanging 'human nature'. This question has been much discussed with reference to man's knowledge of historical truth.

It seems possible here to adopt the standpoint from which Marx views the question of cognition in general, and regard historical knowledge as a function of tasks imposed on the investigator by his epoch. He analyses historical material and chooses his conceptual tools according to criteria of validity supplied by his own time and his particular milieu. In the history of ideas different interpretations of the same set of facts can give, each of them, a satisfactory explanation of all the phenomena observed. The historian of ideas often attributes to a thinker answers to questions which he had certainly never asked, but which the historian regards as valid from the standpoint of his own epoch. There is nothing surprising in this, and nothing from which we can free ourselves if the historical sciences are to exist. The historian of ideas is interested in understanding and interpreting known facts at least as much as in discovering facts previously hidden, and conflicting interpretations of the same facts can be defended, so that there is little hope that an absolutely definitive interpretation can ever be established once and for all. Technical criteria help us to choose between interpretations only to a limited extent. They make it possible to eliminate fantastic and grotesque interpretations but do not abolish the wide range of conflicting and tenable interpretations. It is rather unlikely that any new Platonic texts will be discovered, but certain that Plato's thought will never cease to be interpreted in the most various ways, and that no final version will ever establish itself permanently. It is the same with all historical work which makes advances without relying on new data. This situation is understandable if we take into account that we ask the thinkers of the past questions which our own situation imposes on us and which they did not ask themselves, because the sum of concepts which we use to investigate a problem took shape in our epoch. . . .

In relation to its material the science of the history of ideas is thus in a situation similar to that of the human species in relation to the world: it does not create its material *ex nihilo*, but imposes on it a definite system, and exercises a choice amongst factors which it is inclined unconsciously to assess as differentiated in one way or another according to importance. This is a statement of fact, not the expression of a deliberate intention to understand history as a projection of the present into the past; for the deliberate application of such a rule can lead to shocking distortions, and provides dangerous excuses for arbitrariness in the selection of facts and the neglect of data which do not fit in with an *a priori* hypothesis. The variable system of which I speak is a function of conditions never determined by the investigator according to his own preference.

Kolakowski goes on to argue that there is a limit to this similarity between scientific historical creation and the creative action of the human race as a whole upon its material 'substance'. The historian's use of a particular conceptual apparatus is conditioned by differences not only between historical epochs, but also between the world views which different social classes and groups create in one and the same epoch. When distinct representations of the same set of facts co-exist, and when each of them stands up to technical scrutiny, the choice between them is determined by a more general choice—the choice of a particular world-view, which forms an integral part of historical interpretation. In different world-views there are always and inevitably unverifiable elements, so that at a certain stage of analysis it is difficult to describe further decisions as choices between truth and falsehood. There is not much sense in hoping that total objectivity can be introduced once and for all into historical knowledge. This does not mean that we should not enlarge as much as possible the rational element in our philosophical structures, nor that there is no other way of qualifying statements which cannot be called true or false in the ordinary sense. It becomes a matter of choosing not between logical values but between values tout court. There are some grounds for the assertion, associated especially with the positivists, that value judgments cannot be deducted from descriptive judgments, but from the Marxian viewpoint it is inadequate.

It follows from our previous observations that from Marx's point of view the choice of values or rather—since it is not a question of deliberate and voluntary acts—of preferences determined by practical considerations, forms an indispensable part of human cognition. To put it differently, the things of which our world is made up are chosen since they are created (in the meaning which we have here given to that word). It might seem then that the acceptance of certain values is implicit in every act of cognition, which could give grounds for supposing that the previously mentioned difference between the two possible forms of intellectual assimilation is baseless. This is not really so, if we take into account that the evaluations or rather the practical principles inextricably bound up with human cognition, understood generally, must not only be unconscious if they are to exercise their influence, but have taken on the form of a constant *habitus* peculiar to man as such, and so historically invariable. Hence there is no need to remember them or take account of them at all in intellectual work. These principles, common to the whole human species, have made our external world what it is, constant in its basic divisions; the values and preferences which we have put into this world are now latent in it, and the world has lost, in our eyes, the stamp we have given it and its constant human coefficient; the stamp is born and dies with man: there is no reason for man to retain a separate consciousness of it. This world can be regarded as a given thing, since no other exists and since everything we have added to it or fashioned in it has undergone, as far as we are concerned, a process of fossilization into reality quasi- 'in itself'. It is different in the case of those principles and practical preferences which change in the course of human history, the variations of which are clearly visible to man, and which divide the species into classes, peoples, professions, sexes, generations, character types, specific life situations—in short, everything which somehow influences the sum of the values which each of us is inclined to put above others. It is obvious that this world of values is not automatically created by the world of things, which is common to almost everyone and in which habits common to the whole species are implicit; the description of this first world, or rather these many different worlds (of value judgments) cannot be deduced from the description of the other (from judgments about facts, if we accept this clumsy term). In this sense the Positivist objection is justified.

To explain the inadequacy of the statement that the world of factual judgments and the world of value judgments are heterogeneous Kolakowski invokes the argument previously used in connection with the problem of historical knowledge. All knowledge contains elements which cannot be reduced to factual judgments. In all knowledge, besides those elements which can be examined and verified by the application of technical rules, there are elements imposed by a general world-view, where practical preferences and principles resolve the inevitable questions to which there is no way of obtaining a scientifically grounded answer. In sociology, the history of ideas, the history of culture, etc., it is impossible to get along without choices determined by values—which does not mean that these choices are quite arbitrary. This observation does not make it possible to raise value judgments to the level of theoretical judgments, but it brings their logical position close to that of the humane sciences.

This attempted exposition of what I believe to be the basis of Marx's epistemology leads to a simple conclusion: Marxism at its inception formulated an embryonic project for a theory of knowledge which, later on in the evolution of the school of thought identified by Marx's name, was replaced by the radically different conception of Engels, and more particularly of Lenin. (I say more particularly because of the extreme formulations which Lenin used to describe his theory of reflection and of a consciousness which copies and imitates reality.) Let us dispense with analysis of the reasons which contributed to this peculiar development. There are certainly more than one (in the case of Engels we can hardly omit the simple influence of Positivist scientism, which was widespread in his day, and in Lenin's case the influence of the Russian materialist tradition; but this is only part of the explanation).

When we study Marx's manuscripts we also find obvious connections, which he himself made, between his conception of knowledge, his 'denaturalization' of the world, and the idea of the abolition of human alienation by a communist society. And although there is nowadays nothing easier than to point out how very utopian was Marx's conviction that 'communism as the positive abolition of private property' is identical with the abolition of human alienation in general, we may believe that his epistemological point of departure has not for that reason become philosophically unproductive. We know of other, analogous ideas—entangled in different contexts and so taking on different meanings—which appeared quite independently of the Marxist tradition in the work of many philosophers.

It is in any case probable that a certain method for the analysis of human knowledge, both for everyday experience and for the arts and sciences, could be worked out on the basis of this fundamental idea of Marx: man the cognitive creature is only a part of the whole man; this part is continually involved in the process of progressive autonomization, in spite of which it can only be understood as a function of the continuous dialogue between human needs and their objects; this dialogue, which is called work, creates both the human species and its external world, which for this reason is accessible to man only in its humanized form. In this sense it can be said that nowhere in the whole universe could man find a well so deep that he would not see his own face at the bottom of it.

XIII. Studies of the Young Marx: A Rejoinder

ADAM SCHAFF

The study of the young Marx has in recent years acquired a political importance. Because it is increasingly difficult to deny outright the role and significance of Marx, attacks on Marxism more and more frequently take the form of an alleged defence of 'true' Marxism against a 'corrupt' version. The young Marx, creator of 'authentic' Marxism, is opposed to the mature Marx, author of 'corrupt' Marxism. People who oppose the young Marx to Engels are doing exactly the same thing, because it is known that every step which Engels took in the realm of theory was not only known to Marx but expressly approved by him.

This opposition between the young and the mature Marx, by no means new in the history of Marxology, has now become a favourite method with revisionists, who process Marx in their own likeness. This distortion is possible to some extent because the study of the young Marx has so far been neglected.

There are two main reasons for the importance of and the current interest in the study of the young Marx.

A fuller knowledge of the young Marx's intellectual evolution is necessary for the deeper understanding of the origins and development of Marxism. Marx's works from this period only recently became accessible to the reader, and the basic study of that period, that of A. Cornu, is historical rather than interpretative. That it is so far the only work of this type is explained by the conditions of a period when false political considerations militated against the discussion of early Marxian humanism.

This brings us to the second reason for the topicality and attraction of Young-Marxian problems in the peculiar conditions of the current ideological struggle in Poland. The young Marx, as is easily understandable against the background of his age and his personal development, wrestled with the problem of the human individual and his relationship to society and nature (the world). He followed a natural path from bourgeois radical to revolutionary communist views, to which he then remained unswervingly true. But the problems of his youth, on the face of it similar in many respects to those which baffle the present-day existentialists, and the way in which the young Marx wrestled with them, were bound to attract people who came up against such problems because of the shocks which the workers' movement has experienced, and could find no answer to them outside existentialism. It is not surprising that such people, especially the young ones, enthusiastically 'discovered' the young Marx and his specific problems. It is not surprising that in circumstances of psychological shock and ideological chaos, they began to interpret the 'newly discovered' Marx in their own way, although in fact, because of textual difficulties and complicated connections between Marx and the Young Hegelians, unknown to our readers, they simply did not understand him.

Marx the existentialist, Marx the voluntarist, Marx the pragmatist—these are only a few of the freaks which have been presented, and sometimes still are, as a portrait of the young Marx. The conclusion to be drawn is that we must set about a more thorough study of him.

The question is: how should such a study be carried out?

Marx once explained one of the basic theses of his philosophy of history in this way: the anatomy of man is the key to understanding the anatomy of the monkey. In other words, higher levels of development make it easier for us to understand lower levels.

Acting on this principle, there is only one way to analyse the early Marxian period: in the context of Marx's development, in the light of his evolution, which becomes visible from the heights of his maturity. Early Marxian humanism shows its true visage in the *Critique of the Gotha Programme*; his conceptions of freedom, the problem of the relation of the individual to society, find their interpretation in the *Communist Manifesto* and the theory of class struggle there expounded, etc.

What then should we say of attempts to detach the young Marx from the mature Marx, or to set them against each other?

Such a procedure is possible in the case of an individual who abandons fully developed views for others quite different. This is not the case with Marx. Neither his youthful idealism, nor his changes of opinion in the years 1843–47, can be looked at as though they were a stable and fully formed system of views.

Such enemies of Marxism as Calvez and Bigot do not stop at contrasting the young Marx's views with the mature system of scientific socialism. To a historian of ideas this is nonsense, but at least they go the whole hog. But the revisionists usually leave Marx himself in peace, and contrast him with Engels, who is regarded as mainly responsible for the corruption of Marxism in the spirit of positivism according to some, or of dogmatism and schematism according to others. . . .

From the moment that Marx started work on *Capital* there was an agreed division of labour between them, and Engels's share included polemics in the philosophical field. Their correspondence shows that every step which either of the partners took was submitted to the other and criticized or approved. Marx not only had no objections to Engels's published philosophical views but unreservedly associated himself with them, in later years just as in the Young Hegelian period. . . .

Seen in this light, Kolakowski's article looks rather pathetic. If he is opposing Marx to Engels, this is mere nonsense, and shows that he is insufficiently acquainted with the history of Marxism. If he is opposing the young Marx to the mature Engels, this means opposing the young Marx to the mature Marx, which is no less nonsensical from the point of view of the historian of ideas.

The article has two themes. First, there are the deductions about the theory of truth, supposedly implicit in the epistemological views of the young Marx, reconstructed, or rather constructed, by the author on the basis of quotations from the *Manuscripts*. Then there are the arguments about the supposed contrast between Marx on the one hand, and Engels and Lenin on the other, in their views on the theory of truth, and hence in a number of other basic epistemological and ontological questions. This second theme, though it takes up much less space than the first, is the central polemical question. If the article did not raise it I should not rise to the first theme. Not because I do not see, or do not take seriously, Kolakowski's errors. But because, when we have representatives of bourgeois, Catholic, and revisionist thought amongst us, Marxists cannot waste their time replying to every nonsensical utterance in an esoteric article which a hundred people in Poland will read and twenty understand. Especially as the reply only awakens interest in the original article, and makes a sensation of it. But the political implications of the subject demand a polemical reply to Kolakowski's statements on the alleged antithesis between the views of Marx and Engels.

Kolakowski puts forward two theses:

(1) that the epistemological views allegedly reconstructed on the basis of statements in the *Manuscripts* are Marx's real epistemology:

(2) that Marx's epistemological views are opposed to those of Engels and Lenin.

I consider both these theses utterly false. But to simplify things, let us suppose to begin with that the first of them is correct. What follows?

In 1844, when Marx wrote his *Manuscripts*, he was twenty-six. Let us suppose that he did then express the epistemological views which Kolakowski, quite groundlessly, attributes to him. After 1844 Marx lived almost forty years longer, and these were the years of his mature creative work. True, because of the division of labour between him and Engels, he wrote little about philosophy in later years. But it is known that he kept up his interest in it to the end, that he left behind extracts from philosophical works copied out in the last year of his life, that he always hoped to write a concise exposition of the dialectic, that there are sporadic philosophical observations in his later works, and finally that he very diligently watched Engels's creative work in philosophy and entirely shared his views. If, as Kolakowski claims, Engels was influenced by Positivist scientism (and it is true that some of the stimuli which affected positivism also influenced the development of Marx and Engels) then so was Marx. If it is true that in 1844 Marx still occupied the idealistic positions in epistemology, close to Jamesian Pragmatism, which Kolakowski wrongly attributes to him, the same Marx in later years voiced different views. For instance, his formulations in the preface to the second German edition of *Capital* are expressly based on the materialist theory of reflection, and so on the classical theory of truth. Should this not be mentioned when we are talking about Marxist epistemology, or the embryo of a Marxist epistemology? If the 'embryo' of 1844 really were incompatible with mature Marxism, then it would not be the real embryo of Marxist epistemology but a potential embryo, later rejected. Is it not nonsense to isolate some early stage in Marx's thought, when he was still an idealist (this is not true in respect of the *Manuscripts* of 1844, but is true for instance of 1841), and to assert that the philosophy of Marxism is idealism; just as it would be nonsense to assert that Marxism in politics is identical with bourgeois radicalism, because in some early period the young Marx did in fact pay homage to that creed? Is this not a typical attempt to oppose the young Marx to the mature Marx, based on the tacit premise that the young Marx, up to about 1844, is the 'true' Marx, whom the later Marx of the *Communist Manifesto* 'betrayed'? . . .

Turning to Kolakowski's observations on the relation of Marxism to the classical theory of truth, let us begin with a general outline of the problem.

The theory of truth is concerned above all with solving the following problem: when is our knowledge true and what do we mean by such a statement? Answers to this question follow one of two main lines.

According to one of them true knowledge exists when we say that something is so and it is in reality as we say. The truth of knowledge depends on its agreement with a reality existing independently of ourselves. Materialists subscribe to this classical theory of truth.

According to the second type of answer, true knowledge occurs when it corresponds to certain norms and principles which we accept. Examples are the theory of coherence, theory of evidence, theory of general agreement, theory of utility (first version of Pragmatism), and the theory of the economy of thought. Such definitions are known as non-classical, and are accepted by the idealistic schools of philosophy.

So then truth in the materialist acceptation consists in the agreement of knowledge with objective reality, which is reflected by human consciousness, while in the subjective idealistic acceptation it consists in the agreement of knowledge with rules dictated by consciousness.

Thus the position of a philosopher on the problem of truth provides a simple test to ascertain his position in the struggle between materialism and idealism—even if like the neo-positivists he proclaims himself neutral.

It is impossible to deny the classical theory of truth without denying materialism. Kolakowski, however, set out to show that the young Marx negated the classical definition of truth and at the same time he promotes the epistemology of which this negation was the result to the status of 'true' Marxism, contrasted with the subsequent falsification by Engels. The only way to achieve this was to show that the author of the *Manuscripts* was not a materialist, but in one way or another an idealist. And Kolakowski makes an obviously strained attempt to represent the young Marx as such an idealist. . . .

Even if the young Marx had evolved an idealistic epistemology there would be no need for us to defend ourselves against it. It would only mean that we had to do with immature views, views in the formative stage, as opposed to the finalized epistemology of Marx in his maturity. But the nub of the matter is that there is no idealistic epistemology where Kolakowski discerns it with the eyes of his imagination.

Delusive phantasy, as usual, hides a methodological error. Kolakowski, as a historian of philosophy, should know that the analysis of a thinker's views, especially those which he held at a period of furious development, cannot abstract from their revolutionary context. It can truly be said with reference to philosophical statements taken out of context that there is nothing new under the sun, in the sense that the same or similar words will have been used by somebody else. But did they have the same meaning? The answer to that must be given by the scholar who studies them in the context of a system, and knows that the meaning of statements formally identical is determined by their context. This is a banal truth for all historians of thought, not just for Marxists. If Marx, James, and Bergson speak of the 'humanization of nature' they are making statements which sound the same but do not mean the same thing.

We know that Marx became a materialist, and with reservations a Feuerbachian, in 1841, and was certainly affected by Feuerbach's anthropological conceptions. We know also that the *Theses on Feuerbach* followed shortly after the *Manuscripts* (in the spring of 1845). They give us the key to the understanding of the often obscure *Manuscripts*, show the direction of Marx's evolution, and decipher various concepts and terms. Soon after came the *German Ideology*, with its materialist interpretation of history. Anyone who reads the *Manuscripts* outside this context is in fact reading only his own thoughts.

Kolakowski bases his crazy construction (not reconstruction) on the fact that Marx introduces *practice* into his theory of knowledge, and asserts not only that man is the creation of nature but that nature is the creation of man. Agreed. The whole question comes down to this: what is understood by the word 'practice', and how do you define the 'humanization of nature'?

Epistemology poses two distinct but interconnected questions concerning the objectivity of knowledge:

(i) whether the object which we know exists objectively, i.e. independently of all consciousness, and

(ii) whether and to what extent knowledge which reflects objective reality is connected with man's practical activity, and how as a result the subjective factor enters into the objective process of cognition.

All materialists acknowledge not only the objective but also the material existence of the object of which we have cognition, but this does not predetermine our attitude to the question of the connection between cognition and man's practical activity.

Marx, unlike mechanistic materialists, and unlike Feuerbach, sees the active aspect of human consciousness, and the practical activity of man engaged in transforming nature as a basic category in his theory of knowledge. In the *Theses on Feuerbach* he stresses that idealism, not materialism, has so far developed the active aspect. As a materialist he postulates the development of the active aspect, not abstractly, after the manner of the idealists, but in the form of practice, of human sensory activity, as he says. If the active aspect is understood in this way it becomes understandable, as Marx says, that not only is man the creation of circumstances, but that circumstances are created by man.

Man, according to this conception, obtains knowledge by acting, by changing the world. Practice understood as human sensory activity is the basis, the source of knowledge. In this sense Marx gives a materialistic interpretation of empiricism.

The *Theses on Feuerbach* are a recapitulation, and a logical conclusion from, the *Manuscripts*. They are devoted to the role of practice in human cognition and social life. But there is not a grain of idealism in them; they are thoroughly materialistic. Whence then did Kolakowski get his construction? Let us see how it is done.

Kolakowski writes: 'The view of the world presented in the *Manuscripts*, in my opinion, originates in attempts to assess man's practical activities as a factor determining his behaviour as a cognitive being.'

Can we agree with this? We can. But here is the next sentence:

'This attempt, from the viewpoint of historical tradition, makes

G

Marx's reflections resemble certain ideas in the doctrine of Spinoza; analogous ideas were to appear later in the analyses of Bergson.'

Here the cat is out of the bag. The author, to put it politely, simply understands his text in a very peculiar way. Anyone who confuses the Marxist with the Pragmatist category of practice, or mixes it up with Bergson's philosophy of creativity, simply does not understand what he has read in the young Marx. . . .

There is a basic confusion here. Kolakowski reasons like this: since man obtains knowledge in the process of practice, he introduces into knowledge a subjective element connected with his perceptual apparatus and his social needs and conditions. So far so good. But here is the unexpected conclusion: because of this we cannot even ask about 'absolutely independent' reality, or being 'in itself'. Here we have a typical *non sequitur*. When we speak of 'absolutely independent' reality or of being 'in itself' we do so in a very definite sense: we are concerned to underline the materialistic thesis that reality is not the creation of consciousness, but exists independently of and outside it. From the assertion that a subjective factor affects our knowledge it does not follow that the object which we know is a subjective creation. The distinction between these two questions is elementary. To blur this distinction is to blur what is basic to materialism—the recognition of the objective existence of material objects. Kolakowski carries this to its logical conclusion, and what is more as Marx's plenipotentiary:

'If it would be correct to say, from Marx's point of view, that consciousness is things thought of, it would be even more accurate to generalize his thought by saying that things are consciousness reified.'

Here Marx has been made into a pure subjective idealist. This in spite of the author's earlier assurances that being 'in itself' cannot, in the light of Marx's doctrine, be deduced from consciousness. Apparently, after all, it can.

But now the way ahead is clear. Kolakowski says expressly that his arguments on the theory of truth are only a conclusion drawn from his general epistemological considerations. Once we understand practice à la Bergson, and objective reality has been reduced to a product of subjective creation, we can boldly assert that Marx negated the classical definition of truth. . . .

In conclusion Schaff says that since the subject of early Marxism has been raised it should now be studied positively, and not just for the purpose of polemics with those who distort it.

xiv. The Debate on Alienation

DANIEL BELL*

There is today, in England and in France, a renewed interest in Marx. One sees this in the pages of the English *Universities and Left Review*, and the French *Arguments*, the magazines of the post-Stalinist left-wing generation in these countries. One hears this in detailed discussion of the writings of the Polish and East German 'revisionists', and particularly of the 'subterranean' ideas of Georg Lukacs, the Hungarian Marxist philosopher, one of the sources of revisionism. One reads this in the literary journals, such as Lucien Goldmann's long essay 'La Réification', in the February-March 1959 issue of *Les Temps Modernes*.

This new interest revolves around the theme of alienation. Marx is read not as an economist or political theorist—not for the labour theory of value or the falling rate of profit, not for the theory of the State or even of social classes, and certainly not as the founder of dialectical materialism—but as a philosopher who first laid bare the estrangement of man from an oppressive society. Alienation is taken to be the critical tool of the Marxist method, and the new canon is

* Presented in a symposium on 'The Nature and Value of Marxism Today', at the meeting of the American Philosophical Association, at Columbia University, December 29, 1959.
The idea of alienation as *derived* from Marx, and employed by intellectuals today, has a double meaning which can best be distinguished as *estrangement* and *reification*. The first is essentially a socio-psychological condition in which the individual experiences a sense of distance, or a divorce from his society or his community; he cannot belong, he is deracinated. The second, a philosophical category with psychological overtones, implies that an individual is treated as an object and turned into a *thing* and loses his identity in the process; in contemporary parlance, he is depersonalized. The two shades of meaning, of estrangement and depersonalization, are sociologically quite distinct.

As Marx used the term, alienation equally had a double, yet obliquely different set of meanings from current usage. The first, of *Entäusserung*, implies the 'externalization' of aspects of one's self, with the overtone that such externalization comes through the sale (in a legal-commercial sense) of one's labour. The product that one sells remains as an object, independent of one's self, but one with which there is the twofold sense of identification and loss. The second term, of *Entfremdung*, implies simple estrangement, or the detaching of one's self from another, of divorce. (Feuerbach's usage, while emphasizing the fact that in religion one externalizes part of one's self, tended to emphasize the sense of estrangement.)

These double usages by Marx are found in the early manuscripts and the unpublished philosophical works. In his later writings, the psychological nuances derived from the early, and in his lifetime unpublished, philosophical manuscripts of Marx. Even non-Marxists accept this new emphasis. Thus in Père Jean-Yves Calvez's comprehensive *La Pensée de Karl Marx*, published in 1956, four hundred and forty of a total of six hundred and forty pages are devoted to the concept of alienation and its use in social and political analysis.

All of this is rather novel. Rarely in the thirties, for example, when the first burst of Marxist scholarship occurred, did one find in the exegetical and expository writings on Marx a discussion of alienation. In Sidney Hook's pioneer account of Marx's intellectual development, *From Hegel to Marx*, published in 1936, the word 'alienation' does not occur *once* in the text. It was not, of course, that Hook was unaware of the idea of alienation and the role it played in Hegelian thought. (His book, based on these early manuscripts, had traced in patient detail Marx's thought to his immediate forebears: to Feuerbach, who, in his discussion of religion, had developed the concept of alienation; to Bruno Bauer, who had emphasized the 'critical method' in philosophy; to Moses Hess, who first sketched the picture of humanistic communism; and to the other young Hegelians for whom the relationship of freedom to necessity was the paramount concern.) But the intellectual problem for Hook, as it was for *all* 'classical' Marxists, was, first, a defence of the idea of materialism as a viable modern philosophy—and this Hook sought to do by reading Marx uniquely as a naturalist—and, second, to resolve the 'contradiction' between Marx's social determinism (i.e. that one's consciousness and knowledge are shaped by one's existence and class position), and Marx's, and Lenin's, class teleology (or the fact that socialist purpose and goal are instilled into the worker from the

---

of the term 'alienation' have disappeared, and in the form in which the idea of alienation appears in *Capital*, as the 'fetishism of commodities', it is clearly in the idea of *reification*. People buy commodities, things, not realizing that each commodity has 'embedded' within it labour power, nor are they aware of the social organization required to produce and distribute products. A serf has a direct obligation to a lord and the relationship is naked and direct. The exchange of products in a market 'hides' the social relationships because the personal ties have become impersonal, and labour, both in the creation of commodities and in the sale of its own labour power, is now an object.

The contemporary use of alienation, as estrangement, is a far cry from the transmuted ideas of alienation as used by Marx in *Capital*. And to a considerable extent, the current usage 'reads back' into Marx overtones of contemporary society that were only dimly heard at the time.

In tracing the idea of alienation, in the present essay, I am concerned largely with the meanings which are present, I think, in the early writings. The larger ambiguous term of alienation is retained because the contemporary political debate begins with that concept.

For a discussion of the terminology, see translator's note to the *Economic-Philosophical Manuscripts* (English-language edition, pp. 10–13), and the citations in Note 6 below.

'outside')[1]—and this Hook sought to do by reading Marx as a pragmatist. The intellectual issue for Marxists in the thirties was the validity of historical materialism.

Different times, different *Zeitgeist*. The reason for this change is clear. In Europe today, a school of neo-Marxists, having rejected Stalinism (and, implicitly, historical materialism, which, in its projection of 'higher' stages of society, had been used to justify the Bolshevik use of terror), has gone back to Marx's early writings to find a new humanist foundation for Socialism. The revisionist philosophers in Eastern Europe do so to find doctrinal support against the official party theologues. The French post-Stalinists, such as Lucien Goldmann or Edgar Morin, see in the idea of alienation a more sophisticated radical critique of contemporary society than the simplified and stilted Marxist analysis of class. And the young English socialists, such as Charles Taylor of All Souls College, see in the concept of alienation a means of reformulating the idea of community.

While all this is a fresh, and even fruitful, way of making a criticism of contemporary society, it is *not* the 'historical Marx'. For, as the following analysis argues, Marx had repudiated the idea of alienation divorced from his specific economic analysis of property relations under capitalism, and, in so doing, had closed off a road which would have given us a broader and more useful analysis of society and personality than the Marxian dogmatics which did prevail. While one may be sympathetic to the idea of alienation, it is only further myth-making to read this concept back as the central theme of Marx. As a political effort by the revisionists, bound within the Marxist camp, it may have some polemical value. As a stage of the pilgrim's progress of those coming out of the Marxist forest, it is understandable. As an intellectual effort, it is false. If the concept of alienation is to have any meaning, it must stand on its own feet, without the crutch of Marx. This, then, is the burden of this paper.

For the 'left-Hegelians', the teachers and colleagues of Marx, the chief task of philosophy was to specify the conditions under which 'Man' could achieve his freedom. They accepted the question which Hegel had opened up; they were dissatisfied with his formulation of the problem.

The goal of Man, Hegel had said, was freedom, a condition, he defined, in which man would be self-willed and where his 'essence'

---

[1] A troublesome issue that still remains unresolved in Marxist theory, for if the intellectuals create the social ideology, while the workers, left to themselves, achieve only trade union consciousness, as Lenin maintained, what, then, is the meaning of Marx's statement that existence determines consciousness, and that class fashions ideology?

would become his own possession—in which he would regain his 'self'. But man was 'separated' from his essence and bound by two conditions which seemed inherent in the world: necessity and alienation. Necessity meant a dependence on nature and the acceptance of the limitations which nature imposed on men, both in the sense of the limitation of natural resources and the limitations of physical strength. Alienation, in its original connotation, was the radical dissociation of the 'self' into both actor and thing, into a *subject* that strives to control its own fate, and an *object* which is manipulated by others.[2] In the development of science, man could, perhaps, overcome necessity and master nature. But how was one to overcome the Orphic separateness of subject and object? Alienation was an ontological fact, in the structure of grammar as well as of life; for the self was not just an 'I' seeking to shape the world according to its intentions, but also a 'me', an object whose identity is built up by the pictures that others have of 'me'. Thus the condition of complete freedom, in which the self seeks only to be an 'I', a shaper of events in accordance with its own will, rather than being shaped by others, is a seeming impossibility. In the face of this irreducible dualism of subject-object, of 'I' and 'me', how does one achieve the goal of being 'self-willed'?

Bruno Bauer, one of the first teachers and friends of Marx, felt that the solution lay in developing a 'critical' philosophy which exposed the 'mystery' of human relationships (i.e. the *real* motives behind social acts). Most human beings born into the world, said Bauer, simply accept it and are oblivious to the sources of their morals and beliefs, of their rationality and irrationality; they are 'determined' by the world. By subjecting all beliefs to criticism, however, men would become self-conscious, reason would be restored to them, and therewith their self-possession. The overcoming of the dualism, therefore, was to be through the achievement of self-consciousness.

Feuerbach, to whom Marx gave credit for making the first real breach in the system of Hegelian abstractions, sought to locate the source of alienation in religious superstition and fetishism. The most radical of all the left-Hegelians, Feuerbach called himself Luther II. Where Luther had sought to demolish an institution that mediated between Man and God, the second Luther sought to destroy God himself. Man would be free, he said, if he could demythologize religion. Man was bound because he took the best of himself, his sensibility, and projected it on to some external object, or spirit,

---

[2] 'For freedom,' says Hegel in his *Logic*, 'it is necessary that we should feel no presence of something, which is not ourselves.' Finitude is bondage, the consciousness of an object is a limitation; freedom is 'that voyage into the open where nothing is below us or above us, and we stand in solitude with ourselves alone' (Wallace edition, pp. 49, 66, cited by Robert Tucker; see footnote 6 below).

which he called divine.[3] But the history of all thought was a history of progressive disenchantment, and if, finally, in Christianity, the image of God had been transformed from a parochial river deity into a universal abstraction, the function of criticism—using the radical tool of alienation or self-estrangement—was to replace theology by anthropology, to dethrone God and enthrone Man. The way to overcome alienation was to bring the divine back into man, to reintegrate himself through a religion of humanity, through a religion of self-love. Men's relation to each other, said Feuerbach, in first employing terms that, ironically, were adopted later by Martin Buber for religious purposes, had to be on an I-Thou basis.[4] Philosophy was to be directed to life, man was to be liberated from the 'spectre of abstractions' and released from the thongs of the supernatural. Religion was only capable of creating 'false consciousness'. Philosophy would reveal 'true consciousness'. And, by placing Man rather than God at the centre of consciousness, Feuerbach sought to bring the 'infinite into the finite'.

This uncompromising attack on religion was equally a sharp attack on all established institutions. But beyond that, the spreading use of the concept of alienation had a more radical consequence in the minds of the left-Hegelians, because it initiated a direct break in the history of philosophy by ushering in the period of modernity. In classical philosophy, the ideal man was the contemplative one. Neither the middle ages nor the transitional period to contemporary times (the seventeenth to the mid-nineteenth century) was ever wholly able to detach itself from the ideal of the Stoa. Even Goethe, who gave us in Faust the first modern man, the man of ambition unchained, reverted, in his ethical image of the human ideal, to the Greek. In discussing freedom, however, Hegel had introduced a new principle, the principle of *action*; for man, in order to realize his self, had to strive actively to overcome the subject-object dualism that bound him. In action a man finds himself; by his choices, he defines his character. For Hegel, however, the principle of action had remained abstract. In Feuerbach, while the principle of alienation is sharply defined and the source of alienation is located in religion, an abstraction remains because Feuerbach was talking of Man in general. In Marx, action was given specificity in a radical new emphasis on *work*. Man becomes man, becomes alive through work, for through work man loses his isolation and becomes a social or co-operative being, and thus learns of himself; and through work he is able to transform nature as well.[5]

[3] See Ludwig Feuerbach, *The Essence of Christianity* (Harper Torchbook edition, 1957), p. 30.

[4] For a discussion of Feuerbach's use of the I-Thou concept, see the introduction by Karl Barth to *The Essence of Christianity, ibid.*, p. xiii.

[5] The key statement of this idea in Marx is to be found, first, in the *Economic-Philosophic Manuscripts of 1844*. An English edition was published in Moscow

In locating man's alienation in work, Marx had taken the revolutionary step of grounding philosophy in concrete human activity. The road by which he 'freed' himself from the Hegelian tyranny of abstraction was a long and difficult one.[6] As a Hegelian, Marx thought first of the alienation of work in terms of idealistic dualities. Man, in working, reifies himself in objective things (i.e. in products which embody his work). This is *labour* (*Arbeit*) and is part of the 'alien and hostile world standing over against him'. In labour, man is 'under the domination, compulsion and yoke of another man'. Against this is the state of freedom where man would transform nature, and himself, by free, conscious, spontaneous, creative work. Two things stood in the way of achieving this freedom: the fact that in the alienation of work man lost control over the *process* of work, and lost control, too, of the *product* of his labour.[7] For Marx, therefore, the answer to Hegel was clear: the alienation of man lay not in some philosophical abstraction of Mind, but in the property system. In the organization of work—in labour becoming a commodity—man became an object used by others, and unable, therefore, to obtain satisfaction in his own activity. By becoming himself a commodity, he lost his sense of identity; he lost the sense of 'him- self'.

The extraordinary thing was that Marx had taken a concept which German philosophy had seen as an ontological fact, and had given it a social content. As ontology, as an ultimate, man could only accept alienation. As a social fact, rooted in a specific system of historical relations, alienation could be overcome by changing the social system. But in narrowing the concept, Marx ran two risks: of falsely identifying the source of alienation only in the private property system; and of introducing a note of utopianism in the idea that once the private property system was abolished man would immediately be free.

The question of why men were propertyless turned Marx to economics. For a man whose name is so inextricably linked with the

in 1959. See pp. 67–84, and especially pages 73–7. A more condensed version of this idea is to be found in Part I of *The German Ideology* (International Publishers, 1939), esp. pp. 7–8.

[6] A comprehensive exposition of the early views of Marx can be found in Robert C. Tucker, *The Self and Revolution: A Moral Critique of Marx*, unpublished Ph.D. dissertation (Harvard, 1957). This study, revised and expanded, will be published by the Cambridge University Press under the title, *The Alienated World of Karl Marx*. I am indebted to Mr Tucker for many insights. A lucid discussion of the nature of Marx's early writings can be found in Jean Hippolyte's *Etudes sur Marx et Hegel* (Librairie Marcel Rivière et Cie, 1955), especially pp. 147–55. An overly simple exposition can be found in H. P. Adams, *Karl Marx in his Early Writings* (London, 1940); a provocative discussion in Hannah Arendt's *The Human Condition* (Chicago, 1958).

[7] For a further discussion, see Herbert Marcuse, *Reason and Revolution: Hegel and the Rise of Social Theory* (New York, 1941), pp. 276–7.

'dismal science', Marx was never really interested in economics. His correspondence with Engels in later years is studded with contemptuous references to the subject and he resented the fact that his detailed explorations prevented him from carrying on other studies. But he continued because, for him, economics was the practical side of philosophy—it would unveil the mystery of alienation—and because he had found in the categories of political economy the material expression of that alienation: the process of economic exploitation.

This development is seen most clearly in the *Economic-Philosophical Manuscripts*, which Marx had written in 1844 at the age of twenty-six. The *Manuscripts*, in the history of Marxist thought, is the bridge from the left-Hegelianism of the early Marx to the Marxism we have come to know. The title itself is both literal and symbolic. Beginning as an anthropology it ends as a political economy. In it one finds the first conceptualization of alienation as rooted in work (rather than in abstract spirit, or religion), and the beginnings of the analysis of property. And in the analysis of property, one finds the direct transmutation, which is so crucial in the development of Marx's thought, of philosophical into economic categories.

In search for an answer to Hegel's question, Marx had sought to pin down concretely the ways in which the human being was 'robbed' of his potential possibilities of realizing his 'self'. For Feuerbach, religion was the means whereby man was alienated from himself; for Marx, now, the idea of the 'self' had become too abstract. The key to the problem was the nature of work—the process whereby man became a social being—but the question remained as to what barred man from realizing his full nature in work. The answer, he thought, lay in the operation of the property system. But how? In the capitalist system, in the bargain made between worker and employer, the individual was formally free. What, then was the means whereby a man, unbeknownst even to himself, was alienated and enslaved? Marx found the answer in money. Money is the most impersonal form of value. It is seemingly neutral. A man who has a direct obligation to another, as a serf does to a master, knows directly the source of power over him. But one who sells his labour power for money may feel himself to be free. The product of the labourer can thus be easily 'abstracted' into money and, through the exchange system, be 'abstracted' from him.[8]

---

[8] 'Money is the alienated *ability of mankind*. That which I am unable to do as a *man*, and of which, therefore all my individual powers are incapable, I am able to do by means of *money*. Money thus turns each of these powers into something which in itself it is not—turns it, that is, into its *contrary*.' *Economic-Philosophical Manuscripts, op. cit.*, p. 139 (italics in the original).

It is this conception of money as the hidden mechanism whereby people became exploited (money 'the common whore . . . (which) confounds all human

Money, thus, is the concrete embodiment of the philosophical abstraction which Hegel had described airily as 'spirit', and the commodity process the means whereby the labourer, by exchanging his labour power for money, is robbed of his freedom unawares. Political economy became for Marx what religion was for Feuerbach, a means whereby human values are 'projected' outside of man and achieve an existence independent of him and over him. And so alienation, conceived initially by Marx as a process whereby an individual lost his capacity to express himself in work, now became seen as exploitation, or the appropriation of a labourer's surplus product by the capitalist. Thus a philosophical expression which embodies, actually, a socio-psychological insight became transformed into an economic category.

The irony, however, was that in moving from 'philosophy' to 'reality', from Hegelian phenomenology to political economy, Marx moved from one kind of abstraction to another. In his system, self-alienation became transformed: man as 'generic man' (i.e. Man writ large) becomes divided into classes of men.[9] For Marx now, the only social reality is not Man, nor the individual, but economic classes. Individuals and their motives count for naught.[10] The only form of

and natural qualities') that lay behind Marx's withering analysis of the Jew, as the dealer in money, in economic society. It is this conception, too, that underlay the extraordinarily naïve act of the Bolshevik regime in the first days after the October Revolution of abolishing all money in an effort to make the relationship of man to man 'direct'. The novel implications of this development in Marx's thought, of the *shift* in the early manuscripts from philosophy to political economy, have been explored in great detail by Professor Tucker (*op. cit.*).

[9] For a neglected discussion of the idea of 'generic man' and 'historical man' in Marx, see Solomon F. Bloom, *The World of Nations: A Study of the National Implications in the Work of Karl Marx* (New York, 1941), Chap. I, pp. 1–10.

[10] In *The German Ideology* Marx poses the question of how individual self-interest becomes transformed into ideology. 'How does it come about,' he asks, 'that personal interests grow, despite the persons, into class-interests, into common interests which win an independent existence over against individual persons, in this independence take on the shape of general interests, enter as such into opposition with the real individuals, and in this opposition, according to which they are defined as general interests, can be conceived by the consciousness as ideal, even as religious, sacred interests?'

Having posed the question so concisely, Marx, exasperatingly, never goes on to answer it. Sidney Hook, in his article on 'Materialism' in the *Encyclopedia of the Social Sciences*, sought to rephrase the problem in these terms: 'What are the specific mechanisms by which the economic conditions influence the habits and motives of classes, granted that individuals are actuated by motives that are not always a function of individual self-interest? Since classes are composed of individuals, how are class interests furthered by the non-economic motives of individuals?' Having rephrased the question even more sharply, Hook, too, left it unanswered. So far no Marxist theoretician has detailed the crucial psychological and institutional nexuses which transform the personifications, or masks of class-role, into the self-identity of the individual.

See *The German Ideology, op. cit.*, p. 203; *E.S.S.*, vol. X, p. 219; and the discussions by Robert Tucker.

consciousness which can be translated into action—and which can explain history, past, present, and future—is class consciousness.

In *The German Ideology*, written in 1846, the idea of the 'self' has disappeared from Marx's writings. Marx now mocks the left-Hegelians for talking of 'human nature, of Man in general who belongs to no class, has no reality and subsists only in the realm of philosophical fantasy'. In attacking the 'true Socialist', Marx writes: 'It is characteristic of all these high-sounding phrases about liberation, etc. that it is always "man" who is liberated . . . it would appear from (their) claims that "wealth" and "money" have ceased to exist. . . .'[11]

In *The Communist Manifesto*, the attack is widened, and made cruelly sardonic. The German *literati*, says Marx, 'wrote their philosophical nonsense beneath the French original. For instance, beneath the French criticism of the economic functions of money, they wrote "alienation of humanity". . . .'. And mocking his erstwhile philosophical comrades, Marx speaks scornfully of 'this transcendental robe in which the German Socialists wrapped their sorry "eternal truths" . . . the robe of speculative cobwebs, embroidered with the flowers of rhetoric, steeped in the dew of sickly sentiment'.[12]

In saying that there is no human nature 'inherent in each separate individual', as Marx does in his sixth thesis on Feuerbach, but only social man, and then only classes, one introduces a new *persona*. Marx makes this explicit in his preface to *Capital*, written in 1867: 'Here individuals are dealt with only insofar as they are the personifications of economic categories, embodiments of particular class-relations and class interests. My standpoint, from which the evolution of the economic formation of society is viewed as a process of natural history, can, less than any other, make the individual responsible for relations whose creature he socially remains, however he may subjectively raise himself above them.'

Thus, individual responsibility is turned into class morality, and the variability of individual action subsumed under impersonal mechanisms. And the ground is laid for the loss of freedom in a new tyranny that finds its justifications in the narrowed view of exploitation which Marx had fashioned.

To sum up the argument thus far: In his early philosophical writings, Marx had seen, against Hegel, that alienation or the failure to realize one's potential as a self, was rooted primarily in work, rather than in the abstract development of consciousness. In the organization of work, men become 'means' for the aggrandisement of others, rather than 'ends' in themselves. As alienated labour, there

[11] *Ibid.*, p. 96.
[12] *The Communist Manifesto*, p. 233, in Karl Marx, *Selected Works* (Moscow, 1935), vol. I.

was a twofold loss: men lost control over the *conditions* of work, and men lost the *product* of their labour. This dual conception is present, in a different form, in the later Marx: the loss of control of work is seen as *dehumanization*, occasioned by the division of labour and intensified by technology; the loss of product, as *exploitation*, because a portion of man's labour (surplus value) was appropriated by the employer.

But except for literary and illustrative references in *Capital* to the dehumanization of labour and the fragmentation of work, this first aspect, as problem, was glossed over by Marx. In common with some later (bourgeois?) sociologists, Marx felt that there was no solution to the loss of 'self' in work inherent in technology. Under communism—in the 'final' society—the division of labour, the cause of dehumanization, would be eliminated so that by variety in work man would be able to develop his varied aptitudes. But these fragmentary discussions take on a utopian hue.[13] In actuality one had to accept not only the division of labour, but hierarchical organization as well. In a polemic against some Italian anarchists who had argued that technology had imposed on man a 'veritable despotism', Engels argued that it was utopian to question the nature of authority in a factory: 'At least with regard to the hours of work one may write upon the portals of these factories: *Lasciate ogni autonomia, vo che entrate!* [leave, ye that enter in, all autonomy behind!]. If man by dint of his knowledge and inventive genius, has subdued the forces of nature, the latter avenge themselves upon him by subjecting him, insofar as he employs them, to a veritable despotism, independent of all social organization. Wanting to abolish authority in large-scale industry is tantamount to wanting to abolish industry itself, to destroy the power loom in order to return to the spinning wheel.'[14]

What became central to *Capital* was the concrete social relationships created by private property, those of employer-and-employee, rather than the processes generated by manufacture. Dehumanization was a creature of technology; exploitation that of capitalism.

---

[13] In *Capital*, Marx writes powerfully of the crippling effects of the detailed division of labour, and then, in a footnote, quotes approvingly the image of work provided by a French workman who had returned from San Francisco: 'I never could have believed that I was capable of working at various occupations I was employed on in California. I was firmly convinced that I was fit for nothing but letterpress printing. . . . Once in the midst of this world of adventurers, who change their occupation as often as they do their shirt, egad, I did as the others. As mining did not turn out remunerative enough, I left it for the town, where in succession I became typographer, slater, plumber, etc. In consequence of thus finding out that I am fit for any sort of work, I feel less of a mollusc and more of a man.' (Marx, *Capital*, Chicago, 1906, Vol. I, Part IV, Section 9, especially pp. 532–5. The footnote is from p. 534.)

[14] F. Engels, 'On Authority', in *Marx & Engels: Basic Writings on Politics & Philosophy*, edited by Lewis S. Feuer (Anchor Books, 1959), p. 483.

The solution was simple, if one-sided: abolish private property, and the system of exploitation would disappear. 'In contemporary capitalist society men are dominated by economic relations created by themselves, by means of production which they have produced, as if by an alien power,' said Engels. 'When society, by taking possession of all means of production and managing them on a planned basis, has freed itself and all of its members from the bondage in which they are at present held by means of production which they themselves have produced but which now confront them as irresistible, alien power; when consequently man no longer proposes, but also disposes—only then will the last alien power which is now reflected in religion vanish. And with it will also vanish the religious reflection itself, for the simple reason that there will be nothing left to reflect.'[15]

When critics argued that technological organization might still 'deform and debilitate' the worker, the Marxist called this utopian. When sceptics asserted that socialism itself might become an exploitative society, the Marxist had a ready answer: the source of exploitation, and of power, was economic, and political office was only an administrative extension of economic power; once economic power was socialized, there could no longer be classes, or a basis whereby man could exploit man. By this extension it became 'clear' that the Soviet Union was a 'workers' state', and no basis for exploitation existed. Thus the concept of alienation came, down one road, to a twisted end.

Having found the answer to the 'mysteries' of Hegel in political economy. Marx promptly forgot all about philosophy. ('The philosophers have only *interpreted* the world differently; the point, however, is to change it,' he had scrawled in his *Theses on Feuerbach*.) In 1846, Marx and Engels had completed a long criticism of post-Hegelian philosophy in two large octavo volumes and (except for some gnomic references in the *Critique of the Gotha Programme* in 1875) neither of them returned to the subject until forty years later when Engels, after the death of Marx, was, to his surprise, asked by the *Neue Zeit*, the German Socialist theoretical magazine, to review a book on Feuerbach by C. N. Starcke, a then well-known anthropologist. Engels reluctantly consented and wrote a long review which, slightly expanded, was published two years later in 1888 as a small brochure entitled *Ludwig Feuerbach and the Outcome of Classical German Philosophy*. In writing the review Engels went back to some mouldering manuscripts of Marx and found among his papers the hastily scribbled eleven theses on Feuerbach, totalling in all a few pages, which he appended to the brochure. In the Foreword, Engels alludes to the large manuscript (without mentioning even its title,

[15] Frederick Engels, *Anti-Dühring* (Chicago, 1935), pp. 332–3.

The German Ideology), and says merely that because of the reluctance of the publishers it was not printed. 'We abandoned the manuscript to the gnawings of the mice all the more willingly,' wrote Engels, 'as we had achieved our main purpose—to clear our own minds.'[16] (The gnawing was literal, since many pages, in fact, had been completely chewed up!)

But it is also clear that while, as young philosophy students, the debates with the other young Hegelians were necessary for the purposes of 'self clarification', the absorption of both into concrete economic study and political activity had made the earlier philosophical problems increasingly unreal to them. In a letter to his American translator, Florence Kelley Wischnewetzky, in February 1886, Engels writes, apropos of his *Anti-Dühring*, 'the semi-Hegelian language of a good many passages of my old book is not only untranslatable but has lost the greater part of its meaning even in German.'[17] And in 1893 a Russian visitor to Engels, Alexis Voden, found Engels incredulous when the question of publishing the early philosophical manuscripts was raised. In a memoir, Voden recalled: 'Our next conversation was on the early works of Marx and Engels. At first Engels was embarrassed when I expressed interest in these works. He mentioned that Marx had also written poetry in his student years, but it could hardly interest anybody. . . . Was not the fragment on Feuerbach which Engels considered the most meaty of the "old works" sufficient?' Which was more important, Engels asked, 'for him to spend the rest of his life publishing old manuscripts from the publicistic works of the 1840's or to set to work, when Book III of *Capital* came out, on the publication of Marx's manuscripts on the history of the theories of surplus value?' And for Engels the answer was obvious. Besides, said Engels, 'in order to penetrate into that "old story" one needed to have an interest in Hegel himself, which was not the case with anybody then, or to be exact, "neither with Kautsky nor with Bernstein".'[18]

In fact, except for *The Holy Family*,[19] a crazy-quilt bag of essays

[16] Frederick Engels, *Ludwig Feuerbach and the Outcome of German Classical Philosophy*, in Karl Marx, *Selected Works, op. cit.*, vol. I, p. 147.

[17] Engels to Florence Kelley Wischnewetzky, February 25, 1886, in Karl Marx and Frederick Engels, *Letters to Americans* (New York, 1953), p. 151.

[18] A. Voden, 'Talks with Engels', in *Reminiscences of Marx and Engels* (Moscow, undated), pp. 330–1.

[19] The first part of *The Holy Family*, subtitled the 'Critique of Critical Critique', is devoted to an alleged misreading by Edgar Bauer of Proudhon's work on property. The book then jumps to a detailed analysis of Eugene Sue's *The Mysteries of Paris* and to the alleged misreading of this volume—which is about the sick and wretched of Paris—by a supporter of Bauer who had used the volume to demonstrate the 'critical method'. The last sections deal with the French Revolution and the Rise of French materialism. In his heavy-handed way, Marx was fond of pinning religious tags on his opponents. Not only are the Bauers called the 'holy family' but in *The German Ideology* Max Stirner is called 'Saint

deriding Bruno Bauer and his two brothers, who with their friends constitute the 'holy family', none of the early philosophical writings of Marx was published either in his lifetime or that of Engels. Nor is it clear whether the major exegetes, Kautsky, Plekhanov, and Lenin, were ever aware of their content. None of the questions of alienation appears in their writing. The chief concern of the post-Marxist writers, when they dealt with philosophy, was simply to defend a materialist viewpoint against idealism.

The contemporary 'rediscovery' of the idea of alienation in Marxist thought is due to Georg Lukacs, the Hungarian philosopher who did have an interest in Hegel. The idea of alienation, because of its natural affinity to romanticism, had already played an important role in German sociology, particularly in the thought of Georg Simmel, who had been a teacher of Lukacs. Simmel, writing about the 'anonymity' of modern man, first located the source of alienation in industrial society, which destroyed man's self-identity by 'dispersing' him into a cluster of separate roles. Later Simmel widened the concept to see alienation as an ineluctable outcome between man's creativity and the pressure of social institutions (not unlike Freud's later image of the inescapable tension between instinct and civilization).

Lukacs, coming to Marx after World War I, was able, without knowing of the early *Manuscripts*, to 'read back' from Marx into Hegel the alienation of labour as the self-alienation of Man from the Absolute Idea. The Kautsky-Lenin generation had construed Marxism as a scientific, non-moral, analysis of society. But in Lukacs's interpretation, Marx's economic analysis of society was turned inside out and became the work, as Morris Watnick put it, 'of a moral philosopher articulating the future of man's existence in the accents of a secular eschatology'. Lukacs's interpretation, which was included in a collection of essays entitled *Geschichte und Klassenbewusstsein* (History and Class Consciousness), published in 1923, smacked of idealism to the orthodox Marxists, and Lukacs quickly came under fire in Moscow. Among the Communists the book was proscribed, although the work continued to enjoy a *sub rosa* reputation among the Communist intelligentsia, less for its discussion of alienation, however, than for another essay which, in covert form, rationalized the elite position of, and the need for outward submission of, the Communist intellectual to the party. When Lukacs fled Germany in the early thirties and took refuge in the Soviet

Max'. Although Marx drew most of his ideas from his peers—self-consciousness from Bauer, alienation from Feuerbach, communism from Moses Hess, the stages of property from Proudhon—he was not content simply to synthesize these ideas, but he had to attack, and usually viciously, all these individuals in the determined effort to appear wholly original.

Union, he was forced, eleven years after the publication of the essays, again to repudiate his book, and this time in an abject act of self-abasement.[20]

When the early philosophical works of Marx were unearthed and published, Lukacs had the satisfaction of seeing how accurately he had been able to reconstruct the thought of the young Marx.[21] But this did not spare him from attack. The dogma, drawn from Lenin, had become fixed.

The early philosophical writings were published in 1932 in Germany. But in the floodtide of Hitlerism, of the destruction of the Social-Democratic and Communist parties, and the dispersal of the German scholarly community, there was little time or incentive to read these inchoate and fragmentary works. In the disillusionments with Stalinism in the late thirties, particularly following the Moscow trials, in some small intellectual radical circles in New York, in the increasing sense of rootlessness felt by a young generation, in the resumption of scholarly activity by a group of German scholars in New York, notably the Frankfurt Institute of Social Research of Max Horkheimer, and the publication of its *Zeitschrift*, first in German and then in English, there arose some small interest in the early writings of Marx, and particularly the idea of alienation. But the application of the idea was psychological and literary and soon found a louder resonance from surprisingly different sources.

The interest in the idea of alienation that unfolded rapidly in the late forties and early fifties came largely from the rediscovery of

[20] This statement is quoted by Morris Watnick in his study, 'Georg Lukacs: An Intellectual Biography', *Soviet Survey*, No. 24, p. 54. Mr Watnick's extended discussion of Lukacs's ideas can be found in *Soviet Survey*, Nos. 23, 24, 25, 27 (1958–59).

Lukacs's book is generally unobtainable here. A chapter from it, under the title 'What is Orthodox Marxism', appeared in *The New International*, Summer, 1957. Sections of the book have been translated into French, in the review *Arguments* published by Les Editions de Minuit. There are some brief, but penetrating remarks on Lukacs—and the problem of the intellectual accepting the soldierly discipline of Communism—in Franz Borkenau's *World Communism* (New York, 1939), pp. 172–5.

[21] The early philosophical writings, principally the incomplete *Economic-Philosophical Manuscripts*, and *The German Ideology* were first published (with small sections missing) in 1932 by S. Landshut and J. P. Mayer under the title of *Der historiche Materialismus*, in two volumes. (Some small fragments of the third part of *The German Ideology*, on Max Stirner, had been published by Eduard Bernstein in *Dokumente des Sozialismus*, in 1902–03.) A detailed description of the early manuscripts, particularly of *The German Ideology*, was published by D. Ryazanov in Volume I of the *Marx-Engels Archiv* in 1927. The complete texts are available in the *Marx-Engels Gesamtausgabe* under the direction of V. Adoratski (Berlin, 1932). A new edition of the early papers was published by S. Landshut in 1953, under the title of *Die Frühschriften von Karl Marx*. A complete guide to the works of Marx can be found in Maximilien Rubel, *Bibliographie des Oeuvres de Karl Marx* (Paris, 1956).

Kierkegaard and Kafka, and from the sense of despair that both epitomized.

Kierkegaard represented the other great, neglected trunk which had emerged from the deep Hegelian roots. Where the 'left-Hegelians' had sought a rational answer to the question of alienation. Kierkegaard argued that none existed. No rational act could overcome the subject-object dualism; any attempt to set rational limits to comprehension ends in the 'absurd'. Only by a 'leap of faith' could man establish a relationship with ultimate powers beyond himself. Thus, from ontology, Kierkegaard took the concept of alienation and gave it a religious content; and where Marx had sought to narrow the description of alienation into the exploitative social relationships created by the economic system, Kierkegaard universalized it as an ineluctable, pervasive condition of man.

There were deep reasons for this attraction to the idea of despair— and faith. The sadism of the Nazis, the ruthlessness of war, the existence of concentration camps, the use of terror, had called into question the deepest beliefs of the generation. One could argue, as did Sidney Hook, for example, that the Stalinist terror grew out of the specific historical circumstances which shaped the Russian dictatorship, and that its existence was no indictment of rationalism. But a more compelling reason—at least, psychologically speaking— seemed to come from the neo-orthodox arguments of Reinhold Niebuhr that such corruption of power was inevitable when men, in their pride, identified their own egos with the demiurge of History, and that rationalism, by encouraging utopian beliefs in man's perfectibility, had left men unarmed against the corruption which lurked in socialism.

From a second source, the 'tragic vein' of German sociology, came new, intellectual support for the idea of alienation. In the influence of Karl Mannheim, and later of Max Weber, the idea of alienation merged with the idea of 'bureaucratization'. The two had absorbed Marx's ideas and gone beyond him. The drift of all society, said Weber, was towards the creation of large-scale organization, hierarchically organized and centrally directed, in which the individual counted for naught. Marx's emphasis on the wage worker as being 'separated' from the means of production became, in Weber's perspective, as Gerth and Mills succinctly put it, 'merely one special case of a universal trend. The modern soldier is equally "separated" from the means of violence, the scientist from the means of enquiry and civil servant from the means of administration.' And the irony, said Weber, is that, from one perspective, capitalism and socialism were simply two different faces of the same, inexorable trend.

Out of all this came the impact of the idea of alienation. The intellectual saw men becoming depersonalized, used as a 'thing' in the operation of society as a machine; the intellectual himself felt increasingly estranged from the society. The idea of alienation, thus, was a judgment *on* society. It also reflected the self-conscious position of the intellectual *in* the society.

The themes of alienation, anomie, bureaucratization, depersonalization, privatization have been common coin in sociological literature for more than a decade and a half. In the light of all this, the recent attempts to proclaim the theme of alienation in the early Marx as a great new theoretical advance in the understanding of contemporary society is indeed strange. The reasons for this—which lie in the sociology of knowledge—are fairly simple. There is today a new political generation in England and France—and in the Communist countries of eastern Europe—whose only political perspective had been Marxism. Following the Khrushchev disclosures at the Twentieth Party Congress and the events in Hungary, this generation became disillusioned about Stalinism. It wants to find its own footing, and, like any generation, has to find it in its own way and in its own language. The post-Stalinist radical generation in England and France still wants to think in political terms (and the dissidents and revisionists in eastern Germany and Poland, by the nature of their situation are forced to argue in philosophical categories)—hence the umbilical cords to Marx.[22]

But the difficulty is that there are no apocalyptic ideas or fresh ideological causes. There may be immediate issues such as nuclear tests or educational policy, but no comprehensive political vision which can fire young imaginations and fill the emotional void that obviously exists. The idea of alienation has gained a new edge because of the disorientation of the radical intellectual in the mass society where tradition, avant-garde, and middle-brow culture all jostle each other uneasily—but that is already a far different topic.

Having started out with the idea that in the young Marx there was a double vision of the nature of alienation, I would like to conclude with some brief remarks about the road that Marxism did not take. Marxist thought developed along one narrow road of economic conceptions of property and exploitation, while the other road, which might have led to new, humanistic concepts of work an labour, was left unexplored.

[22] So eager are the young neo-Marxists to maintain a tie to Marxism or to provide some notion of fresh thinking and discovery that such a bright young Scottish philosopher as Alasdair MacIntyre is led to write such a farrago as appeared in *The Listener* of January 8, 1959, entitled 'Dr Marx and Dr Zhivago': 'Humanity and the one true bearer of the human essence in our time, the industrial proletariat, has to break through and make new forms. So alienated man remakes and regains himself. This is the picture which the young Marx elaborated, the picture out of which the mature Marxist theory grew. In this picture there is a place for those members of bourgeois society who, humane and sensitive as they are, cling to the ideals and culture they know and therefore cannot make the transition to the new society. Such surely is Zhivago.'

In the transmutation of the concept of alienation, a root insight was lost—that alienation is a consequence of the *organization* of work as well, and that in the effort to give a man a sense of meaning in his daily life, one must examine the work process itself. In manufacture, said Marx, the worker is 'deformed into a detail worker', he becomes an appendage to the machine. All this was laid at the door of capitalist society. Yet there is little evidence that the Communist countries have sought to reverse the process, to explore new combinations of work, to re-examine the engineering process, or to question the concept of efficiency that underlies the contemporary organization of work. If anything, in the intense pressure for production, the lack of free trade union movements and independent agencies, which can act as a control or check on the managers and the State, has meant that the workers in the Communist countries are even more exploited than those in western lands. Technology stands as a 'given'.

One need not accept the fatalism of the machine process[23]—or wait for new utopias in automation—to see that changes are possible. These range from such large-scale changes as genuine decentralization, which brings work to the workers rather than transporting large masses of workers to the work place, to the relatively minute but important changes in the pace of work, such as extending job cycles, job enlargement, allowing natural rhythms in work, etc. The 'flow of demand', to use the sociological jargon, must come from the worker rather than from the constraints imposed upon him. If one believes, for example, that the worker is not a commodity, then one should take the step of abolishing wage payment by the piece, or eliminating the distinction whereby one man gets paid a salary and another an hourly wage. If one accepts the heritage of the humanist tradition, then the work place itself, and not the market, must be the centre of determination of the organization of work. The fullness of life can and must be found in the nature of work itself.

[23] For an elaboration of this argument, see my essay 'Work and Its Discontents: The Cult of Efficiency in America' (Beacon Press, 1956).

PART THREE

THE NEW REVISIONISM

xv. The Origins and Significance of East European Revisionism

KARL REYMAN AND HERMAN SINGER

Revisionism in East Europe was a unique historical phenomenon. When the pressures lifted in 1953, after the death of Stalin, the rejection of the Soviet policy of imposing Russian Marxism as the final word of philosophical truth came to the surface. The young intellectuals who had joined the Communist Party after the war did so largely to dissociate themselves from a past which had seen some of the rulers of their countries acquiesce in or accept fascism. Anxious to participate in a socialist rebirth of their countries, they found themselves subjected to regimes employing the phraseology of idealism to impose totalitarian controls. The discrepancy between slogan and reality and the atmosphere which made it impossible for intellectuals to contribute to the social debates of their time combined to create a sense of moral outrage that erupted in 1956, when the Communist rulers were foundering in ideological confusion.

Young Communist intellectuals were, in Paul Kecskemeti's phrase, 'partly privileged and partly frustrated'. Ostensibly part of the ruling elite, they wielded no power. The official youth and student organizations offered no basis for social or intellectual engagement; they had become bodies charged with 'mobilizing' the inert mass to execute Party-ordered tasks.[1]

After Stalin's death, and particularly following the twentieth congress of the CPSU, young Communists took it for granted that reforms would be made within the Party and that free discussion would take place within the framework of socialist principles.

In Poland and Hungary, the intellectuals anxious for reform converted legitimate Party channels into centres of public discussion. *Po Prostu*, previously a little-read weekly published by the Polish student organization, opened its pages to a discussion of reforms, and became overnight a national paper with vastly increased reader-

---

[1] In the Soviet Union, Komsomol members, frustrated by the reduction of the one-time elite corps to a mere 'transmission belt' of Party leadership, suggested that the Komsomol return to a more restrictive membership policy and be entrusted with some major, serious matter—'not just making posters, organizing excursions, and collecting scrap.' These views were specifically condemned in *Komsomolskaya Pravda*, March 20, 1957.

ship. In Hungary, twenty members (seventeen of whom were Communists) of the official youth organization DISZ founded the Petöfi Circle and turned it into a public forum.

Similar developments occurred in Czechoslovakia and East Germany. Young intellectuals, including instructors in Marxism-Leninism at Czechoslovak universities, petitioned the Party for an extraordinary congress to debate the implications of anti-Stalinism. In East Germany, a number of Party intellectuals, led by Wolfgang Harich, pleaded for the creative discussion of Marxist theory. The Stalinist leadership denied public platforms to the advocates of reform but the revisionist current ran strong both in East Germany and Czechoslovakia, encompassing the same theoretical and practical areas as the discussions in Poland and Hungary.

East European Communist intellectuals had accepted the Stalinist myth that 'historical necessity' dictated a choice of fascism or communism. Now 'historical necessity' was destroyed by the admission that Stalinism was not a step towards communism but a megalomaniac's 'cult of personality'. Refusing to accept the thesis of Stalin's 'errors', they wanted to ensure their socialist faith against a similar disillusionment. Against Party discipline they upheld the value of independent moral judgment.

'We are not Communists because we have joined communism as a historical necessity; we are Communists because we have joined the side of the oppressed against their oppressors, the side of the poor against their masters, the side of the persecuted against their persecutors. . . . No one is exempt from the moral duty to fight against a system or rule, a doctrine or social conditions which he considers to be vile and inhuman, by resorting to the argument that he considers them historically necessary' (Leszek Kolakowski, 'Responsibility and History', *Nowa Kultura*, Warsaw, September 1–22, 1957).

This was an echo of Bernstein's argument that the ethical justification of socialism was not derived from economic necessity alone. In his political platform, Harich praised the moral courage of Karl Liebknecht in breaking Party discipline. Czech writers emphasized that 'there is only one morality, human morality, and no other' (for which they were accused of 'Masarykism'). Young Polish Communists quoted Marx in support of the thesis that the use of unjust means would lead to an unjust goal.[2]

The intellectuals extolled civic courage. 'There is no revolutionary movement without revolutionaries, and no one can be a revolutionary who lacks civic courage. Free men must possess civic courage and act according to the principle, "It is better to die standing up than to live kneeling"' (*Po Prostu*, No. 47, 1956). In an almost literal rendition of Bernstein's famous phrase, young Polish revisionists

[2] 'Ein Ziel, das ungerechte Mittel verlangt, ist kein gerechtes Ziel.'

claimed that 'for the Communist the goal is not only communism, but also the movement towards it' (*Po Prostu*, No. 49, 1956).

Bernstein's view that the Socialist programme had to be subordinated to the democratic process reappeared in East European revisionist thinking, which included demands for political freedom, a free press, free elections and a functioning opposition, and an end to police terror. The revisionists took it for granted that political democracy would preserve the socialist character of the state.

In revisionist eyes, Marxism had to be treated as one of many contending concepts. 'We think that Marxism should be subjected to the same methods of scientific verification as any other field of thought. . . . We must never cease to confront it with facts, revising and developing it whenever necessary' (*Po Prostu*, No. 48, 1956). Here again Marx was quoted by Czechoslovakian university instructors: 'In the interest of Marxist philosophy, we should return to Marx's old conception identifying ideology with subjectivism' (*Rude Pravo*, Prague, November 21, 1958). Czechoslovak Party philosophers refused to serve as propagandists and demanded the right of scientific inquiry; some resigned from Party functions on the ground that these forced them to propagandize views which they regarded as un-Marxist (*Zivot Strany*, Prague, November 1957, No. 22). Revisionists were unanimous in denying the existence of an unbridgeable abyss between Marxist and non-Marxist sociology. This resulted in a demand for scientific contacts with the West. A permanent dialogue with Western Democratic Socialists was expressly demanded in Poland, and Harich saw in an ideological rapprochement between the East German Communists and the West German Social Democrats the only workable basis for reunification of Germany under socialist auspices.

The core of East European revisionism, however, was its rejection of Leninism as a doctrine applicable to Eastern Europe. For the first time in a Communist state, Rosa Luxemburg's critique of Leninism was debated publicly. *Po Prostu* (No. 7, 1957) wrote:

'Two ideas of Rosa Luxemburg are of special interest for us today. One is the idea that a degeneration of the Socialist revolution becomes inevitable when in its process law, liberty, and democratic guarantees are destroyed or severely restricted.

'The other is that it is harmful to propose as the model for the revolutionary strategy and tactics of the international working class the experience of the first victorious proletarian revolution, which took place under the specific conditions of a backward and isolated country.

'Both these ideas are valid and tremendously important for our present situation. Today we formulate them both by saying that socialism cannot be built without democracy ... and we talk about specific national roads toward socialism.'

The Polish revisionists, like the Harich group in Germany, placed the blame for the distortion of socialism in the Soviet state on Lenin's Blanquist organizational principles. Harich's political platform, audaciously (if somewhat naïvely) submitted not only to the SED but to the Soviet ambassador in East Germany, asserted that Soviet communism, shaped by backwardness and the absence of democratic traditions, could not be a model for Europe; exported to Eastern Europe after 1945, it had, Harich argued, played a reactionary role.

From this point, the revisionists proceeded to what the Czechoslovak Stalinists called a denial of the class content of the dictatorship of the proletariat. The Czech teachers of Marxism-Leninism, who had asked for a scientific inquiry into what constituted the working class, apparently had in mind the question whether a Party bureaucrat, who received forty times as much as a labourer, and a worker, belonged to the same class.[3] Harich criticized the 'sacred caste of generals', and in Poland the struggle against the Party functionaries was declared to be motivated by class interest. The Workers Councils, under the slogan 'All power to the Councils', would function to keep the bureaucracy in check. Harich's political platform described the resistance to Soviet hegemony 'as an expression of the revolutionary class struggle of the popular masses against the Stalinist Party and government apparatus and its methods'.

Engels's statement that the state is not a power imposed on society from without gained wide currency. The demand for emancipation from Soviet tutelage was thus not completely motivated by nationalist feeling. 'If previously it was said that only socialism guarantees independence and sovereignty, we must now add that only sovereignty and independence can guarantee the building of socialism' (*Nowa Kultura*, Warsaw, No. 44, 1956).

The 'modern' revisionists in Eastern Europe also had to deal with relationships among Communist countries. Their discussion indicated support for neutralism in foreign policy, and an inclination against the use of force. In Poland, the revisionists condemned policies that foment revolutions in a world gripped by fear of a third

---

[3] In Czechoslovakia, the Party organ *Rude Pravo* (June 10, 1958) wrote that a number of revisionists were quite active, but 'thanks to energetic Party action' none of their views was published. 'If all the prevailing incorrect views were compiled and brought out,' the paper conceded, these 'arrogant claims of creatively developing Marxist theory' would amount to a complete revisionist platform such as that which emerged in Poland and Hungary. A notion of these 'arrogant claims' is indicated by a long list of deviations admitted to be current in Czechoslovakia. These included, among others, 'counterposing Marx to Lenin', quoting the young Marx, and admiring the Hungarian Marxist philosopher Georg Lukacs 'as a mind nearly equivalent to the young Marx'.

world war. Kolakowski praised 'reluctant and soft people' who refused to become the tools of fanatics in their efforts 'to impose our concepts on others by means of war, aggression, provocation, blackmail, intimidation, terrorism, murder, and torture' (*Tworczosc*, Warsaw, September 1958).

The emphasis given to the catchphrase that the working class ruled through the instrumentality of the Party was turned against the regime through the promotion of the Workers' Councils, established during the revolts in Poland and Hungary in 1956. In the period between the organization of the Workers' Councils in October 1956 and their liquidation *Po Prostu* (January 6, 1957), reflecting revisionist views, presented a thesis supporting the role of the Councils in a proletarian state:

'The character and tasks of the workers' councils should be analysed against the background of a general conception of the Polish model of socialism. The prevalent theory at the present time is that our model of socialism will be characterized, among other things, by a far-reaching administrative decentralization, in which the decisive part will be played by the Workers' Councils, with the simultaneous maintenance of central leadership in the form of a central plan, central direction for the main lines of development, choice of basic assortments, etc. The realization of this model, however, cannot be accomplished in the form of an artificial fusion of the Workers' Councils with the still existing administrative apparatus set up in the past era. For there is a fundamental difference between bureaucratic centralization and democratic centralization. . . . Therefore, the system of Workers' Councils constitutes a considerable progressive step on the road leading to the restoration of the true significance of the dictatorship of the proletariat. This measure, however, will not endure if obstacles present in other sectors of the ruling system are not overcome, for then the rebirth and entrenchment of the bureaucratic authority apparatus will become inevitable.'

This formulation, stressing the role of the Workers' Councils as an obstacle to any reversion to Stalinism, was part of the essential argument of revisionist thinking: reform could come from within. This view expressed more explicitly than did the Yugoslav Communists—except for the dissident Djilas—the thesis that centralization would have to be neutralized by a variety of other institutions. Before October, the Polish revisionists had little to say concerning the possibility of converting workers' organizations into organs which could operate independently of the state. In Poland, as in Hungary during the Revolt, it was assumed that the first step towards independence was to eliminate Party control of the trade unions. The Workers' Councils, however, became the instruments for giving workers within the factory itself control of decisions affecting their environment. It is significant that the Polish regime dared not condemn the Workers' Councils as subversive of Communist doctrine, although Gomulka, speaking at the Communist Party Central Committee in May 1957, pointed to the possibility that 'If every factory became a kind of co-operative enterprise of the workers, all the laws governing capitalist enterprise would immediately come into effect and produce all the usual results. Central planning and administration . . . would have to disappear' (*Nowe Drogi*, June 1957).

In the midst of the October days in Poland, *Po Prostu* (Warsaw, October 28, 1956) wrote:

'The fact that an important, possibly even a decisive, part was played by the workers and students, gives a special revolutionary character to the October events. They were not a palace initiative; they had the character of a plebeian social movement, led by the most responsible and faithful Party members—the Communists. . . . Workers' self-government was initiated in Yugoslavia essentially as an initiative from above, in the form of a decree, prepared for the most part by comrade Kardelj on a theoretical basis. In our country, as we all know, it was wrested from the ministers by the workers themselves.'

The Hungarian Workers' Councils, which became the backbone of the Hungarian Revolt, went much further in setting up operating procedures in the factories. The Councils not only continued to function for more than a month after the fighting had been suppressed, but were a political force which took the initiative in conducting parleys with the Kadar regime and the Soviet authorities in regard to the reconstruction of Hungary on a non-Communist basis. They differed from their counterparts in Yugoslavia and Poland, too, in seeking to reconstruct worker-management relations on a basis which excluded the Communist Party, or any other political influence, from the factory itself. Hungarian workers had come to feel, because of the pervasiveness of Communist dictatorship during the Rakosi era, that communism and the Communists had so besmirched the slogans of communism, socialism, and democracy that they had to start from scratch in rebuilding the contacts among themselves on a new and honest basis.

Like the Polish workers, the Hungarians had been exposed to discussions of the Yugoslav Workers' Councils through newspaper accounts and talks by trade union leaders who had visited Yugoslavia during the summer and autumn of 1956. The Petöfi Circle had also given some attention to the operation of the Workers' Councils and indicated that their operation might be of significance in reducing or eliminating the pressure of the bureaucracy. There is evidence that these overtures from the Petöfi Circle Clubs were received with restraint by workers because their source was the Communist Party.

Up to the very eve of the Revolt on October 23, Hungarian workers remained suspicious of any promise of improvement of their lot unless it could be seen and felt in the most intimate way—in the factory itself.

The Hungarian Workers' Councils sprang into being with the Revolt itself, and, because of the collapse of the government apparatus and the Communist Party, took on the direction of industry, becoming particularly significant after the second Soviet intervention of November 4. Although the Revolt was crushed, the Workers' Councils, in control of the nation's productive apparatus, continued to deal with the resurrected Communist government as if there was a dual power, setting forth the political conditions under which production would resume—under the direction of the Councils.

On November 21, 1956, the Central Workers' Council of Greater Budapest issued an appeal to 'all factory, district, and county councils', which included the demand that workers be permitted to 'build our social and economic system independently, in the Hungarian way'. The relation of Workers' Councils vis-à-vis the trade unions was not settled during the Hungarian experience; the Councils had no opportunity to set forth a final view as to whether they were to supersede the trade unions or to coexist with them. This indecision was reflected in the statement already cited, which was clear only in holding that the trade unions were to function differently from those under Communist control: 'Our opinion is that there is real need for agencies representing interests, for trade unions and for factory committees, but only such as have been democratically elected from below and in which honest representatives of the working class are the leaders. This is why it is so important that, after the definitive constitution of the workers' councils, factory committees should be elected under completely democratic conditions so that their composition will guarantee the realization of the aims of the revolution.'

The subsequent history of Workers' Councils in Poland and Hungary followed a pattern which had become familiar after 1917. As early as July 1917, Lenin, after his earlier endorsement of the Soviets, found it expedient to withdraw the slogan of 'All Power to the Soviets' on the ground that the Soviets had been infiltrated by elements that might turn out to be enemies of the Revolution. What disturbed Lenin, who had no ideological fondness for an instrument quite as independent as the Soviets, was the fact that they were not firmly under Bolshevik leadership. The reaction of the Communist leaders in Poland and Hungary was similar. The Polish Communist leadership moved quickly to incorporate the Councils into the state, and the Hungarian Communist leaders first endorsed the Councils by pretending that the 'free trade unions' had brought them into being, and then suppressed them.

Aside from the experience of the Workers' Councils—which extended the area of experimentation for creating a new relationship between worker and job—the revisionist doctrines of East Europe on many points came close to the position of European social democracy.

Given the pressures under which East European revisionists found themselves, it would have been surprising if they had made any major theoretical innovations. Discussion ranged from restoration of the original premise of the dictatorship of the proletariat, in which a variety of points of view within communism would be permitted, to the call for a multi-party system as understood in the West. The suggestion that went furthest in the way of 'capitalist restoration' was the possibility, briefly considered within the Hungarian Workers' Councils, of instituting profit-sharing by workers, and even this was to be developed in the context of a socialist society. It is noteworthy that the Kadar regime later introduced a form of profit-sharing.

Underlying the specific demands of the various groups of revisionists was the desire to reassert the value of honest relationships among men. To the official doctrine of Soviet superiority in all spheres of life, the revisionists offered their national traditions within the framework of socialist internationalism. To the pervasive influence of the Party trade union cell, workers responded with the Workers' Councils as a reality rather than a slogan. To offset the daily violations of human dignity, the revisionists sought guarantees of individual freedom and democratic rights. As against the impassiveness of central economic control, the revisionists countered with proposals for decentralization. The Western traditions of free speech and a free press were central to revisionist thinking, although some revisionists did not go so far as to advocate their use by those who opposed socialism. East European revisionism, in effect, repudiated the operational basis of communism. In opting for democracy and in refusing to deify Revolution for its own sake, East European revisionists introduced the corrosive element of democratic socialism into the heart of communism.

What of the revisionists today? They have been silenced, but many remain within the Communist movement, and few have recanted. Early in 1957 the Polish newspaper *Sztandar Mlodych* conducted a poll among its young readers. The second largest group of respondents replied that 'their greatest experience' came during the Polish October. The memory of a period when young persons were vibrant on the social scene will not be easily erased from East European minds. Revisionism reasserted the unity of intellectuals, students, and workers which has sparked democratic revolutions in Europe for over one hundred years. It is hardly likely that this tradition of revolt breathed its last in 1956.

XVI. The Decline and Fall of Revisionism in Eastern Europe

WILLIAM E. GRIFFITH

During the period of ideological ferment in Eastern Europe leading up to the autumn 1956 upheavals in Poland and Hungary, observers in the West became keenly aware of the vital role being played in these developments by the growing numbers of Communist intellectuals who for the first time were daring to speak out against the oppressive and irrational features of Stalinist totalitarianism, and even to challenge certain aspects of hallowed party dogma.[1] The events of the 'Polish October' underlined this role still further, and despite the tragically different outcome of the revolt in Hungary, revisionism—as these tendencies have since come to be known—for several years thereafter continued to be widely regarded as a force which might vitally influence future developments in the Communist world. To many left-wing Western intellectuals, revisionism appeared to hold the promise of an enduring, 'genuinely socialist' and humanitarian 'third force'.[2] On the other hand, those antagonistic to Marxism in any form saw in it primarily a force which might divide and weaken the Communist movement everywhere.

Neither of these hopes has been borne out by the developments of recent years. As the author was able to verify for himself during tours of Eastern Europe in the summers of 1959 and 1960, revisionism has now ceased to be an effective force in the political life of any East European country, not excluding Poland where its influence had been stronger and more persistent than elsewhere. In the Soviet Union itself, revisionist tendencies have been effectively smothered by Khrushchev's double-barrelled policy of continued controls over intellectual life and economic concessions to the population; and in Communist China, such revisionist currents as emerged in the brief 'Hundred Flowers' period have long since been suppressed in the subsequent campaigns against 'rightist deviation'.[3] Nor has revi-

---

[1] This chapter is a revised and expanded version of the author's 'What Happened to Revisionism?', *Problems of Communism*, March-April 1960.

[2] Perhaps the *locus classicus* of these hopes was Jean-Paul Sartre's preface to his magazine's special issue on the Hungarian thaw and rising: 'Le fantôme de Staline', *Les Temps Modernes*, November-December 1956–January 1957.

[3] Roderick MacFarquhar, *The Hundred Flowers Campaign and the Chinese Intellectuals* (New York: Praeger, 1960); Shau Wing Chan, 'Literature in Com-

sionism fared much better even in the West, where its advocates have for the most part quit, or been purged from, the Communist Party organizations without being able to exert any significant degree of influence on the democratic socialist parties of the Left, with the single exception of Nenni's Socialist Party in Italy.

The causes of this universal decline of revisionist influence are a great deal more complex than might at first appear. Certainly, the measures which have been taken by all the Communist bloc regimes since 1957 to retighten ideological controls, curb the public expression of revisionist views, and purge the revisionists have been one major cause—and no doubt the one most directly responsible for forcing revisionism beneath the surface. Another and perhaps more significant cause lies in the fact that, in Eastern Europe certainly and probably elsewhere as well, many if not most revisionists have come to the conclusion that revisionism, insofar as it postulates reform within the Marxist-Leninist framework, offers little hope of genuine liberalization.

REVISIONISM DEFINED

As it emerged in Eastern Europe after Stalin's death in 1953 (and in Yugoslavia as exemplified by Milovan Djilas), revisionism was a conscious effort on the part of Communist intellectuals to revitalize Marxism-Leninism in ideology and practice, so as to restore to it some of Marxism's earlier qualities of idealism, notably its emphasis on humanist values, genuine internationalism, and advancement of the general welfare of mankind. There was nothing basically new in the content of Eastern European revisionism: it combined ideas from Bernstein, Bakunin, Bukharin, and Trotsky. Nor was it static; as with its predecessors, Eastern European revisionism was a dynamic process. Because of both outside pressures and internal development, most revisionists abandoned Marxism-Leninism itself and embraced many of the tenets of democratic socialism.

Eastern European revisionism derived its initial impetus from growing intellectual disillusionment—especially among the younger intellectuals, many of whom had supported Stalinism—with the practical consequences of Stalinist rule: the complete suppression of individual liberties and cultural freedom of expression, widespread economic suffering, and the reign of police terror. Its first manifestations in 1955 were largely confined to protests against rigid party controls over cultural activity, but following Khrushchev's revelation of Stalin's crimes at the 20th CPSU Congress, the revolt rapidly spread into the areas of politics, economics, and party

munist China', *Problems of Communism*, January-February 1959; Merle R. Goldman, 'Re-educating the Literati', and P. J. Honey, 'Ho Chi Minh and the Intellectuals', *Soviet Survey*, April-June 1959.

ideology.[4] Refusing to accept the Soviet explanation of Stalin's crimes as merely the result of the 'cult of personality', the revisionists saw the deeper causes of Stalinist misrule in defects inherent in the Communist system itself, and this in turn led them to challenge the validity of certain basic principles, first of Stalinist, then of Leninist, and finally —in some cases—even Marxist dogma. While it embraced varying shades and degrees of opinion, revisionist thinking on the main points at issue may be briefly summarized as follows:

1. In regard to the position of the Soviet Union and the CPSU vis-à-vis other Communist states and parties, the revisionists generally rejected the Stalinist interpretation of 'proletarian internationalism' which required the complete subordination of the lesser regimes to 'the leading role of the Soviet Union'. Instead, they insisted that intra-bloc relations be based on genuine national and party equality. It was this revisionist principle which the Soviet Union opposed most inflexibly, and which—in the extreme form it took in Hungary—led to Soviet armed intervention. Revisionism also stressed the principle of 'separate roads to socialism', which had received official Soviet recognition in the June 1955 Khrushchev-Tito joint declaration at Belgrade and again in Khrushchev's official 20th Congress report.

2. In the crucial area of political doctrine, the revisionists strongly opposed the narrow concept of 'the dictatorship of the proletariat' on the ground that it meant, in effect, absolute party dictatorship and inevitably led to 'bureaucratism' and 'state capitalism'. To forestall a recurrence of these dangers, they urged the establishment of a dual system of institutional safeguards against over-concentration of power; on the one hand, genuine democratization of the inner-party structure, procedures, and rules of discipline; and, on the other, external checks upon the party's power in the form of a more authoritative role for parliament and—in the more radical forms of revisionism—the institution of a limited multi-party system which would allow the independent existence of other parties subscribing to socialist principles. Some extreme revisionists made the decidedly un-Leninist suggestion that the party should act primarily as political educator of the masses; contrary to the Yugoslav Titoists, they wished to deprive the party of decisive political control.

3. In the economic sphere, revisionism placed major emphasis on ending the rigid application of certain policies which, under Stalin, had acquired the force of economic doctrine; principally, forced collectivization of agriculture, priority for heavy industry at the expense of consumer needs, extreme centralization of economic authority, and severely exploitative labour practices. The revisionists stood for a gradualist approach to collectivization, greater emphasis on the

---

[4] The best available overall account of the intellectual thaw in post-Stalin Eastern Europe is Heinz Kersten, *Aufstand der Intellektuellen* (Stuttgart: Seewald, 1957).

H

production of consumer goods, economic decentralization, reduced capital investment programmes, more rational and balanced planning, restoration of a free market in some sectors of the economy, lower production quotas for workers, profit-sharing, and—above all —greater 'economic democracy' through workers' councils functioning as organs of factory self-government.[5] Some of the more radical revisionists, however, went so far as to challenge fundamental Marxist theories regarding the evolution of capitalism (pauperization of the working class, etc.) and the ultimate necessity of its overthrow by proletarian revolution. Arguing that modern technology and industrial organization have tended to transform capitalist relations of production, and espousing Bernstein's thesis that socialism deals not with goals but process, they foresaw a progressive emancipation of the working class under capitalism and a gradual rapprochement between the capitalist and socialist systems of production and social organization, eliminating the necessity for violent revolution.

4. Finally, in the intellectual and cultural sphere, revisionism stood for the complete sweeping away of Stalinist restrictions upon freedom of thought and expression, including restrictions upon the freedom to criticize and re-evaluate party ideology. It also called for a return to Marxist 'humanism' as an indispensable basis for preventing a recurrence of the flagrant abuses of power and mass crimes of the Stalinist era. It was revulsion against the crimes and inhumanities of Stalinist rule that imparted to revisionism its 'dynamic of

[5] For workers' councils, see Kazimierz Grzybowski, 'Workmen's Councils in Poland', *Problems of Communism*, July-August 1957; Hannah Arendt, *The Origins of Totalitarianism*, 2nd ed. (New York, 1958), pp. 497–501; Oskar Anweiler, 'Die Arbeiterselbstverwaltung in Polen', *Osteuropa*, April 1958, and 'Die Räte in der Ungarischen Revolution, 1956', *Osteuropa*, June 1958; Wolfgang Eggers, 'Das System der Arbeiterräte im kommunistischen Bereich', *Osteuropa Wirtschaft*, December 1957. For the post-1953 developments in Soviet economic theory (they can hardly, at least as yet, be called revisionist) see A. Nove, 'Recent Developments in Economic Ideas', *Soviet Survey*, November-December 1957; Robert W. Campbell, 'Some Recent Changes in Soviet Economic Policy', *World Politics*, October 1956; Alfred Zauberman, 'Economic Orthodoxy and Revisionism', *Soviet Survey*, October-December 1958; Gregory Grossman, 'Economic Nationalism and Political "Thaw" ', *Problems of Communism*, March-April 1957; Ernst Halperin, 'The Metamorphosis of the New Class', *Problems of Communism*, July-August 1959, and 'Totale Planwirtschaft oder Marktwirtschaft', *Osteuropa*, December 1957; for liberalization of Soviet economic theory and influence of Leontief's input-output theory on it, Oskar Lange, *Balans zatrat i vypuska produktsii* (balance of outlays and output of production) preface by Academician V. S. Nemchinov (Moscow, 1958), and the best recent overall survey, the symposium edited by Gregory Grossman, *Value and Plan* (Berkeley and Los Angeles: California, 1960); for post-1956 Polish developments, see 'Poland's Economy', *East Europe*, June 1959; Alexander Erlich, 'The Polish Economy after October, 1956: Background and Outlook', *American Economic Review*, May 1959; J. M. Montias, 'The Polish "Economic Model" ', *Problems of Communism*, March-April 1960; for 1956, P. J. D. Wiles, 'Changing Economic Thought in Poland', *Oxford Economic Papers* (new series), vol. IX, June 2, 1957.

disillusionment', best reflected in revisionist literary writing.[6]

So much for the Eastern European revisionists' programme; what of the social forces and psychological attitudes they represented? Sociologically, revisionism was largely a revolt of Party intellectuals against the *apparatchiki*, a demand for the priority of ethical standards over those organizational considerations to which Lenin, notably in his *What Is To Be Done*, had always given first place. It reached its heights where, as in Poland and Hungary, the pre-war Communist Parties had been initially so small and thereafter so decimated by the Stalinist purges that after 1945 newly-recruited young intellectual cadres had to be rapidly pushed into positions of influence; it was easily controlled in those other countries (Czechoslovakia, East Germany) where adequate numbers of *apparatchiki* were available, where (as in Yugoslavia and to some extent in Albania) war-time Partisan *esprit de corps* and the tie of nationalism had produced a strong, mass-based Party, or where, as in Yugoslavia, Bulgaria, Rumania and Albania, the tradition of intellectual dissent was recent and weak. The revolt of the Party intellectuals represented their (largely unconscious) return to the fold of the traditional intelligentsia, its Western traditions and (the factor which consciously attracted them) its self-imposed privilege and duty to incarnate and represent the national ideals and purpose.[7]

Roughly speaking, there were two major and (unconsciously) revived currents in revisionist thought: the Luxemburgist and/or Trotskyist one of genuine internationalism and emphasis on mass spontaneity, and the older Bakuninist and Soviet Workers' Opposition one of anarcho-syndicalism. Particularly in Poland and Hungary, many of the revisionists were Jewish; Stalin's pathological and Khrushchev's pragmatic anti-Semitism were influential in their revolt. Theirs was above all a moral revolt, against the gap between Leninist theory and Eastern European Communist reality; more specifically, against the abyss between the Western and humanist aspects of Marxist-Leninist ethics and the Stalinist reality of lies, purge trials, slave labour camps, and murder. Like many of the Jacobins or the early Bolsheviks, they were suffused with and energized by a moral passion in rebellion against the increasingly irrational Stalinist perversion of the original Communist moral fanaticism.

[6] For translated collections, see *Les Temps Modernes, loc. cit.* (for Hungary), February-March 1957, 'Le socialisme polonais'; Edmund Stillman, ed., *Bitter Harvest* (New York: Praeger, 1959), for a general collection; for Poland, Pawel Mayewski, ed., *The Broken Mirror* (New York: Random House, 1958); for Hungary, William Juhasz and Abraham Rothberg, ed., *Flashes in the Night* (New York: Random House, 1958), and George Palozi-Horvath, ed., *One Sentence on Tyranny: Hungarian Literary Gazette Anthology* (London: Waverley, 1957); for poetry, Robert Conquest, ed., *Back to Life* (London: Hutchinson, 1958).

[7] Cf. K. A. Jelenski, 'The Genealogy of the Polish Intelligentsia', *Survey*, July-September 1959.

By their commitment to the internationalist and humanistic aspects of Marxist socialism, the East European revisionists were also philosophically committed to Western rationalist and humanist thinking, itself alien to Lenin's moral relativism. It was this commitment which explained the hostility of many of them to the economic and social injustices of pre-1939 Eastern Europe and to the irrational horrors of Nazism; and it made it impossible for them to go on accepting and justifying such Stalinist excesses as the Slansky trial and the 'Doctors' Plot'.

These, then, were the main currents of revisionist thought which were steadily gaining strength in East European Communist ranks in the months leading up to the historic upheavals of October 1956. In Poland and Hungary, where the ferment of ideas was more pronounced and public than in the other East European satellites, revisionism became the intellectual spearhead of the forces of anti-Stalinist revolt; as such, it played a decisive part in bringing about the October explosions in both countries. In the end, however, the two took drastically different turns. In Poland, revisionist support of Gomulka contributed greatly to his success in containing the 'Polish October' within limits that would not provoke prompt Soviet reprisal or jeopardize continued Communist Party control. In Hungary, on the other hand, revisionism was overwhelmed by the much more powerful forces of nationalism and the yearning for political liberty. Its inability to contain these forces resulted in the brutal tragedy of Soviet armed intervention.

THE ANTI-REVISIONIST CAMPAIGN

As a consequence of the Polish and Hungarian upheavals, and more particularly of the part played by revisionism, Soviet intra-bloc policy in 1957 was marked by a renewed insistence upon rigid ideological conformity. The new policy was given formal expression by the Moscow twelve-party declaration of November 1957,[8] which designated revisionism as the 'main danger' to world communism and thus sounded the signal for a bloc-wide anti-revisionist campaign.

The twelve-party declaration, to which the Yugoslav Communists refused to subscribe, also marked a further step towards the new rupture in bloc relations with Tito, which finally took place following publication of the Yugoslav party's 'Draft Programme' of April 1958.[9] Although the contents of the programme were in no way novel, its publication was in effect a renewed Yugoslav ideological

---

[8] *Pravda*, November 22, 1957.

[9] The Draft Programme is in the Belgrade Journal of *International Affairs*, June 1, 1958; the final version is in *Yugoslavia's Way*, tr. Stoyan Pribichevitch (New York, 1959); and the first Soviet attack on it in P. Fedoseev, I. Pomelov, and V. Cherpakov, 'On the Draft Programme of the League of Communists of Yugoslavia', *Kommunist*, No. 6, 1958.

challenge to the Sino-Soviet bloc. Sino-Soviet propaganda promptly seized upon it as a pretext for casting Tito and the Yugoslav Communists in the role of arch-villains of the 'revisionist' conspiracy.

In its anti-Yugoslav phase, the bloc campaign against revisionism displayed striking variations in intensity. China, foreshadowing the Sino-Soviet differences which became apparent in 1960, played a leading and extremely aggressive role from the outset,[10] although on balance it still seems unlikely that Peking, rather than Moscow, was the decisive factor in the anti-Tito assault. In Eastern Europe, Albania and Bulgaria, both with territorial grievances against Yugoslavia, were quick to join in the assault, and Czechoslovakia (which had never repudiated the Slansky trial) likewise took an active part. Poland was the last member of the bloc to join the attack, and then only with obvious reluctance.

Concurrently with the propaganda war against revisionism, the Communist regimes in Eastern Europe—again with variations in speed and intensity—moved to curb or eradicate revisionist influences by means of internal 'administrative measures'.[11] These naturally were applied most speedily and severely by the Kadar regime in Hungary, reaching their climax in June 1958 with the 'trial' and execution of ex-Premier Nagy and other leaders of the October 1956 revolt. (A notable feature of the trial was the virtual attempt to equate revisionism with 'counter-revolutionary treason'.) Of the other East European satellites, Poland again was the last and most reluctant to follow suit, but there, too, the revisionists have gradually been silenced through stricter censorship and publication controls, the purging of editorial staffs, and other constraints on intellectual freedom, all of which represent an attenuation of the gains of the 'Polish October'.

[10] E.g., Hu Chi-pang, 'Yugoslav Revisionism Viewed Through the Case of the Counter-revolutionary Nagy', *Jen-min jih-pao*, Peking, June 18, 1958; 'Modern Revisionism Must be Criticized', *ibid.*, May 5, 1958; Ch'en Po-ta, 'Yugoslav Revisionism—Product of Imperialist Policy', *Hung Ch'i*, June 1, 1958.

[11] Lack of space prevents their detailed description and documentation here: vd. *East Europe, Osteuropa* and *Osteuropa-Wirtschaft, passim* and (for documents concerning the renewed Soviet-Yugoslav break), *The Soviet-Yugoslav Controversy, 1948–1958: A Documentary Record*, Robert Bass and Elizabeth Marbury, eds. (New York: Prospect Books, 1959), pp. 61–225, and *The Second Soviet-Yugoslav Dispute*, Vaclav L. Benes *et al.*, eds. (Bloomington, Ind.: Indiana University Publications, Slavic and Eastern European Series, vol. 14, 1959). Vd. also the articles in the two recent symposia concerning Eastern Europe: *Annals of the American Academy of Political and Social Science*, CCCXVII (May 1958), 'The Satellites in Eastern Europe', John H. Hallowell, ed., *The Soviet Satellite Nations: A Study of the New Imperialism*, reprinted from the February 1958 issue of the *Journal of Politics* (Gainesville, Fla.: Kallman, 1958). For general documentation, vd. Paul E. Zinner, ed., *National Communism and Popular Revolt in Eastern Europe* (New York: Columbia, 1956), and for the best and most recent summary, Zbigniew Brzezinski, *The Soviet Bloc: Unity and Conflict* (Cambridge, Mass.: Harvard, 1960), pp. 308–32.

In Poland and Yugoslavia, as Gomulka and Tito clearly realized, revisionists like Kolakowski and Djilas who initially wished to reform a system which they felt obsolete, were now dangerous obstacles to the peaceful continuation of such reforms as the Party leadership considered desirable; on the contrary, their influence was disruptive and unsettling. Being genuine internationalists, Eastern European revisionists, like that Soviet-proclaimed 'revisionist' Tito, had international ambitions, though different in character. Like Rosa Luxemburg, they felt that they and their Communist Parties had an international mission to reform and revitalize the world Communist movement. But, unlike Tito, Gomulka was a 'native' Polish Communist whose ambitions did not go beyond the Polish boundaries, while Nagy and his closest supporters wanted to adopt for Hungary Austrian-style neutrality. Gomulka immediately came to terms with the Polish Church and its leader Cardinal Wyszynski on the basis of their common interest in preventing Soviet intervention; neither Gomulka nor the Cardinal (for different reasons) had any desire to preserve the influence which the Polish Party revisionists had in 1956. Together they controlled the power and authority existing in Poland; once the revolutionary fervour of late 1956 ebbed, the Polish revisionists were soon isolated. Furthermore, some of them, primarily Party activists rather than literary intellectuals, appalled by the prospect the Hungarian Revolution had revealed of communism's total collapse and desirous (like the non-Communist majority of the Polish nation) of avoiding Soviet military intervention à la Budapest, felt that the Polish Party mechanism, so near disintegration, had to be reconstructed even at the cost of curbing the literary revisionists' freedom.

The Hungarian Revolution was the great caesura for the Eastern European and Soviet and Yugoslav Communist regimes and for the revisionists themselves. For in fact, during those hectic days in Budapest, not only did the Hungarian Communist regime collapse, but the Communist revisionists themselves saw that their own dreams were clearly going awry. The Nagy government's withdrawal from the Warsaw Pact, its acceptance of a multi-party system, the dissolution of the Hungarian Communist Party, were all forced by non-Communist popular pressure. Had the Hungarian Revolution succeeded, the result would have probably been similar to that of post-1945 Austria; a minuscule Communist Party, nationalization of large-scale industry coupled with small peasant and artisan proprietorship, a Western-style parliamentary regime, and neutralism in foreign policy. When the Hungarian Revolution tore away the Communist film from Hungarian reality, all Communists, followers of the regime and revisionists, realized that the popular disgust and fury with them was so great that there was no serious possibility of reviving any variety of Leninism. This realization was crucial for

Khrushchev, Gomulka, Kadar, and the other Eastern European rulers, and for Tito as well: revisionism of communism in Eastern Europe, they now clearly saw, meant its inevitable collapse there, and its replacement by a Western-orientated parliamentary democracy.[12]

These pressures, plus their own ideological evolution, led the revisionists to the belief that the attempt to reform communism while remaining *within* the basic Marxist-Leninist framework was bound to fail. This was strikingly corroborated by discussions which the author had in the summers of 1959 and 1960 with a number of Polish ex-revisionists, who almost unanimously expressed the conviction that there is at present no possible 'third way' between Khrushchev's (and Gomulka's) new orthodoxy and non-Communist, democratic forms of socialism. They acknowledged that they themselves had abandoned the revisionist viewpoint and consciously become—in fact, if not in name—democratic socialists.

This change in their thinking is a complex but by no means unprecedented phenomenon. In fact, it parallels almost exactly the political and ideological development of the Yugoslav ex-Communist intellectual, Milovan Djilas, who also realized the impracticability of a Titoist (or Gomulkaist) mid-way position between Leninism and democratic socialism, and found himself inevitably drawn towards the latter.[13] There was one notable difference, however, between Djilas's earlier experience and that of the present-day East European revisionists. Djilas broke with 'national communism' prior to the Hungarian Revolution, when it was still possible to believe —as many revisionists undoubtedly did—in the feasibility of the national-Communist formula of an intermediate position between Soviet domination on the one hand, and true national independence and democratic freedom, on the other. The East European revisionists, however, had before them the lesson of Hungary, where the national-Communist (i.e. revisionist) phase of the October revolution lasted but a few days, quickly yielding place to a kind of democratic

[12] See the author's 'The Revolt Reconsidered', *East Europe*, July 1960, and his 'Background of Revolution: Rethinking Modern Hungarian History', *ibid.*, November 1960.

[13] Contrast Djilas's 1953–54 *Borba* and *Nova Misao* articles, now available in Abraham Rothberg, ed., *Anatomy of a Moral* (New York: Praeger, 1959) with his *The New Class* (New York: Praeger, 1957) and his November 19, 1956 *New Leader* article on the Hungarian Revolution ('The Storm in Eastern Europe') which led to his imprisonment. For Western leftist reflection of these two viewpoints, vd. François Fejtö's pro-revisionist 'Changes in the Communist World' and Henry Pachter's ex-revisionist 'A Critical Comment', *Dissent*, Spring 1959. Cf. Alvin Z. Rubinstein and J. Roffe Wike III, 'The Djilas Heresy: Its Beginning and Development', *Western Political Quarterly*, December 1958; Thomas Taylor Hammond, 'The Djilas Affair and Jugoslav Communism', *Foreign Affairs*, January 1955; Ernst Halperin, *The Triumphant Heretic* (London: Heinemann, 1958), pp. 216–44.

socialism—all this, of course, *before* the second Soviet intervention. The only conclusion the post-Djilas revisionists can draw from this is that national communism would, at best, be only a brief and transitory phase for any East European country attempting to free itself from the shackles of Soviet orthodoxy and control.

LIMITATIONS OF REVISIONISM

Looking more closely at the Hungarian and Polish Revolutions, one can discern some of the reasons underlying the failure of revisionism to become a stronger and more lasting political force. Both the Hungarian uprising and the Polish October were characterized by a resurgence of profound romantic patriotism, accompanied by a reassertion of many traditional nationalistic and religious patterns. But both nationalism and religion were quite alien to many of the strongly internationalist and anti-clerical intellectuals, who consequently underestimated the popular strength of these forces, intensified as they were by Soviet attempts to crush them.

As another consequence of their intellectual orientation, the revisionists—with a few important exceptions—had little support among the peasants who, outside Czechoslovakia and East Germany, still remain the most numerous element in East European society. Thus in Hungary, for example, the 'third force' Populist ideology, best represented in the writings of Istvan Bibo, was more in line with the political propensities of the Hungarian rural population, and as a leftist (but non-Marxist and hence non-revisionist), nationalist and neutralist alternative to Rakosi's Stalinism and pre-war Hungarian authoritarianism. It made a strong appeal to large sections of the intelligentsia and the workers as well. The fact, moreover, that it is the peasants, rather than the workers and the intelligentsia, who in Poland and to a far lesser extent in Hungary have preserved most of the gains of the October 1956 reforms, has further diminished any chances the revisionists may have had of securing mass support.

Poland and Hungary are largely agrarian countries. But it is safe to assume that even in such highly industrialized countries as Czechoslovakia and East Germany, revisionism would sooner or later have to give way before the greater popular strength of more indigenous political movements and ideologies. For, no matter how great the moral prestige of men, say, like Wolfgang Harich (the leading East German revisionist, now in jail), there is little doubt that his concept of a 'liberal communism' has far weaker roots in Germany than the old socialist and trade union traditions. Furthermore, the pull of West Germany on its Eastern counterpart, and of the SPD on the SED, both engendered by the deep longing of East Germans, including most SED members, for reunification, had a very special effect on Harich and other East German revisionists: aware that any other position would forfeit them popular support, they became in fact democratic socialists although (for reasons of tactics vis-à-vis the SED leadership) they continued publicly to profess their Leninist fundamentalism.[14]

During the glorious but brief heyday of the 'thaw' in Poland and Hungary, the revisionists there felt that they had genuine contact with, and even leadership of, the masses. Polish and Hungarian revisionist writers and student and youth leaders were certainly in the forefront of the movement, but this was largely because, as Communists, they were the only critics of the *status quo* who had access to the means of communication and thus were able to provide leadership in the drive for liberalization. Paradoxically, the revisionists were unwittingly paving the way for their own loss of political leadership. For the more they succeeded in arousing latent popular forces of opposition, the more they tended to be displaced in popular favour by 'legitimate' spokesmen of the older political and social trends— i.e. peasant, worker, and religious leaders deriving their popular support from past positions of influence and their adherence to traditional patterns of national patriotism and social and parliamentary democracy.

Viewed in this light, the prominence of revisionism during 1955–56 appears to have been an exceptional phenomenon, and its subsequent rapid decline becomes more readily understandable. In Poland particularly, and to a lesser extent in Hungary, revisionism has now given way to a 'neo-realist' philosophy—referred to in Poland by the term 'organic work'—of economic co-operation with the regime combined with continued non-acceptance of its official ideology. The people at large, and particularly the young people, have ceased for the present to take any interest in communism or any other political ideology. Their hopes are now centred on gradual economic improvement rather than apocalyptic Communist political salvation.[15]

A LOOK BACK

To point out that revisionism has ceased to be an effective force in Communist life, and will probably remain quiescent for some time to come, is not at all to minimize the importance of its past achievements, or of its potential for the long-range future. For all the brevity of its hour in the limelight, revisionism played a major role in the historic drama that unfolded in the Soviet East European empire in the years of crisis between the death of Stalin and the end of 1956. It may be well, therefore, to look back briefly at the record of its past

[14] The writer discussed this point with some of Harich's associates, now in West Germany, in late summer 1960.

[15] See, e.g. Stanislaw Stomma, 'The Shade of Winkelried', *Tygodnik Powszechny*, June 21, 1959; Jerzy Turowicz, '*Tygodnik Powszechny* After Fifteen Years', *Tygodnik Powszechny*, March 27, 1960. Cf. Czeslaw Milosz, 'Das Ende der Apokalypse', *Forum*, July-August 1959.

contributions before offering some final speculations with regard to the prospects of a future revival.

There can be no question that the East European revisionists played a vital and even indispensable part in exploiting the political thaw which followed Stalin's death. As pointed out earlier, only they could have performed this task, because, as Communists, they had access to the means of mass communication. Moreover, because they had in most cases been identified as Stalinists themselves, their ultimate revulsion against the excesses and crimes of Stalinism when these were bared by Khrushchev was that much more intense. It infused their writings with a 'dynamic of disillusionment' which made them particularly moving and effective.

The flowering of revisionism brought out the fact that a good many Communist intellectuals had never been genuine, ideologically convinced Stalinists, even though they had outwardly worn the Stalinist label. Their advocacy of Stalinist ideas had stemmed more from fear than from conviction, and once the reign of police terror was attenuated and a few chinks opened in the armour of thought controls, their courage and scepticism rapidly asserted themselves. Revisionism also exposed the weaknesses of an ideology which, under Stalin, had taken on qualities of irrationality and an almost theological dogmatism that were glaringly inconsistent with the original rationalist inspiration and spirit of Marxism.

The revisionists played one other significant political role. Their initial leadership of the liberalization movements in Poland and Hungary served to some extent as a restraining influence upon the tendency of the masses to rush impetuously into revolt. This, of course, was more true in Poland than in Hungary, particularly after the Poznan rising of June 1956 demonstrated the dangers of a runaway development. It was less true in Hungary, primarily because the relative weakness and extreme Stalinism of the party apparatus tended to make the forces of popular revolt more volatile and less amenable to restraining influence, especially an influence from an element within the party.

A LOOK AHEAD

What, then, are the prospects for a future resurgence of revisionism? It is probable that a large proportion of yesterday's leading East European revisionists—whether or not they remain nominally Communist Party members—have become today's convinced, albeit to a large extent politically ineffective, democratic socialists. However, revisionism—still in the strict sense of a movement to reform communism within the Marxist-Leninist framework—is undoubtedly an ever-present potential force which tends to generate new vigour under conditions of Stalinism, or even perhaps (though more slowly) of Khrushchev's neo-orthodoxy. Like molten lava in a volcano, revisionism is always there and may spring to life when a confluence of certain essential factors occurs to release it.

What these factors are may be clarified by reference to the conditions which made possible the thaw of 1955–57. The two most essential were: (1) factionalism in the Soviet and satellite parties arising out of the post-1953 struggle for power among Stalin's successors; and (2) mass popular unrest caused mainly by economic discontent and further heightened in East Europe by nationalist dissatisfactions.

Thus, it is evident first of all that developments in the Soviet Union will be a vital key to the future course of developments in Eastern Europe. With regard to the CPSU, Khrushchev's elimination of all serious challengers would appear to have assured him full Party control for the near future. However, the Soviet leader's relatively advanced age is one of the most important political facts in the Communist world today. When the problem of his succession eventually arises, the new struggle for power and its reverberations in the satellites could again create conditions favourable to the start of a new liberalization trend, and hence to a resurgence of revisionism. Moreover, just as the thaw of the post-Stalin period had its start in the Soviet Union before spreading to the satellites, so any new thaw in Eastern Europe will probably take its cue from prior developments in the USSR.

It seems likely that in the next cycle, whenever it occurs, revisionism will have more 'cover' and fewer content aspects, it will become increasingly a mechanism of concealment, a 'ketman' to hide the genuinely democratic socialist thinking of its proponents, and its economic aspects, because easier to propagate and achieve, will become more important.

But it is not only in this respect that Soviet developments will affect those in the East European orbit. Soviet policies in relation to the Bloc countries have an important bearing on the second factor mentioned above, i.e. popular unrest. For the present, Khrushchev's concessions to economic and nationalist dissatisfactions have somewhat lessened the acuteness of popular unrest, but discontent has probably only subsided. History suggests that economic concessions do not, in the long run, satiate the popular hunger but rather whet the appetite for more.

A reversal of Khrushchev's economic liberation policies both at home and vis-à-vis the Bloc countries seems unlikely during his lifetime, and the increasingly deep effect they are having on Soviet and satellite life make it improbable that his successors will be willing or able to hazard reversing them (most certainly not while they are competing for his throne). Even more than Khrushchev, they will stand before at least two historic alternatives: either to move farther in the direction of what Professor W. W. Rostow calls a 'mass consumption society' (and therefore a less totalitarian one), or to divert the vastly augmented industrial capacity of the Bloc into foreign adventures. Should the first alternative be chosen, resulting in an increased diffusion of economic and political power, and should the party's continual drive to justify its increasingly anomalous role gradually give way to a more 'efficiency-oriented' bureaucratic ethos, then the chances for further liberalization, perhaps more economically than politically oriented, *may* eventually improve.[16] This does not necessarily mean that the Soviet expansionist threat to the non-Communist world will diminish; indeed, a more rational totalitarian system may in this respect be more dangerous. But perhaps Khrushchev's successors, like himself, will decide to steer a course between two alternatives: to adopt a more rational, 'enlightened' totalitarianism[17] and to confine foreign expansionism to what Khrushchev has called 'wars of national liberation' and thus to maintain control of the USSR and the Bloc. And, what is more, they may well succeed.

One final and very tentative point: the course during 1960 of the Sino-Soviet dispute, and in particular the apparent line-up of Albania with Peking rather than with Moscow, suggest that ideological and organizational unity within the Bloc and among the Eastern European Communist Party leaderships is diminishing.[18]

It is important to realize both the similarities and differences between the Sino-Soviet differences of 1960 and thereafter and the Eastern European crisis of 1956. Then, Gomulka wanted a certain degree of domestic autonomy and internal deviation (notably in agriculture), which Khrushchev was eventually willing to allow. The Hungarian Revolution brought withdrawal from the Bloc and the collapse of the Hungarian Communist Party; this all Communist leaders (Khrushchev, Mao, Gomulka, and even Tito) rejected, and the Red Army crushed. In 1960 and 1961, Hoxha's deviation was

[16] The best overall recent analysis of probable future Soviet developments is to my mind Raymond Aron's 'Soviet Society in Transition', *Problems of Communism*, vol. 6, November-December 1957; see also his 'Une Revolution totalitaire', Suppl. a *Preuves*, December 1957; Adam B. Ulam, 'Soviet Ideology and Soviet Foreign Policy', *World Politics*, January 1959, and 'Expansion and Coexistence: Counterpoint in Soviet Foreign Policy', *Problems of Communism*, September-October 1959; Isaac Deutscher, *Russia; What Next?* (New York: Oxford, 1953), and his 'The Future of Russian Society', *Dissent*, Summer 1954; various replies to him in the same and the subsequent two issues, and Deutscher's rejoinder, 'Russia in Transition', *Dissent*, Winter 1955.

[17] Vd. Adam B. Ulam, 'The New Face of Soviet Totalitarianism', *World Politics*, April 1960, pp. 391–412, and Herbert Ritvo, 'Totalitarianism without Coercion?', *Problems of Communism*, May-June 1960, pp. 19-29.

[18] D. F. Zagoria, 'Strains in the Sino-Soviet Alliance', *Problems of Communism*, May-June 1960; Z. K. Brzezinski, 'Patterns and Limits of the Sino-Soviet Dispute', *ibid.*, September-October 1960; ok., 'Chruschtschews Kampf mit der Chinesischen Konkurrenz', *Neue Zurcher Zeitung*, November 11, 1960; Boris Meissner, 'Zur Auseinandersetzung Moskau-Peking', *Ost-Probleme*, February 3, 1961, pp. 87–9; R. Lowenthal, 'Diplomacy and Revolution: The Dialectics of a Dispute', *China Quarterly*, No. 5, January-March 1961.

not on domestic policy, but on foreign policy (the proper posture towards Yugoslavia and the United States) and ideology (the relative priority for the struggle against revisionism and dogmatism). In 1956, after initial gestures of support to Ochab and Gomulka, occasioned probably by their own desire for a greater degree of autonomy from Moscow, the Chinese, appalled by the course of the Hungarian Revolution, supported Moscow against Gomulka and Tito. In 1960 and thereafter, the Chinese, now differing strongly with Moscow on a whole range of issues of foreign and domestic policy and ideology, had no intention of breaking with the Russians, who in turn did not wish to break with them. However, just as the Sino-Soviet differences of 1960 involved *inter alia* the struggle for the control of world-wide Communist front organizations and for influence in various non-Bloc parties, so in the case of Albania they involved a struggle for influence over a ruling party within the Bloc, but one whose geographical isolation prevented the Soviets from bringing it immediately to heel, as did (perhaps more importantly) their desire to avoid a rupture with Albania's protector China.

Although Albania's deviation was 'dogmatist' (i.e. 'extremist') this might eventually favour a renewed rise of its opposite—revisionism. In the first place, the primary cause of the Albanian deviation was the same as that of Poland's and Hungary's in 1956 (and Yugoslavia's in 1948): nationalism. The Albanians hate and fear the Yugoslavs, one of their many historic enemies and in 1944–48 their masters. They prefer as their protectors the Chinese (also violently anti-Yugoslav) to the Russians, who in 1955–56 favoured the Yugoslavs and may (the Albanians fear) again, and who are in any case geographically closer, and therefore more of a threat to their independence, than are the Chinese. Furthermore, the course of the Sino-Soviet dispute in 1960 and 1961, and particularly the eighty-one-party Moscow meeting in November 1960, indicated that the Soviets, competing with the Chinese for support in the international Communist movement, both within and without the Bloc, in large measure won, obtaining support particularly from the Poles. But support, in such a situation, had its price. At the beginning of 1961 there were already signs that the Poles were utilizing Moscow's need for their support against Peking to favour their own continuing 'national peculiarities'.[19] All this was still far from a renewed rise of revisionism, but, organizationally, if the Sino-Soviet dispute were to continue and intensify, it would probably bring with it that increased room for manoeuvre, both for Eastern European regimes and for right-wing dissident elements within them, which was such an indis-

[19] Gomulka at Katowice, *Trybuna Ludu*, December 4, 1960; Artur Starewicz, 'On Reading the Declaration of the World Communist Movement', *Polityka*, December 17, 1960; 'The Debate of Communists from 81 Countries', *Nowe Drogi*, January 1961.

pensable pre-condition for the 1956 revisionist wave.

In any event, the experience of the last five years has shown that neither the East European Communist intellectuals' drive for humanist, internationalist, democratic socialism, nor the aspirations of the masses under Communist rule for economic improvement and true national independence, can be indefinitely suppressed, much less transformed into willing acquiescence. Like the thirst for freedom and justice, in which it has its roots, revisionism is self-generating.

XVII. East German Revisionism: The Spectre and the Reality

MELVIN CROAN*

Before the Harich affair and the SED's slanderous campaign against revisionism, East German intellectuals were widely regarded as essentially subservient to the Ulbricht regime. Intellectual quiescence during the workers' uprising of June 1953 seemed to illustrate all too poignantly a conclusion which had already been argued in terms which variously stressed the effectiveness of political controls, the success of the regime in corrupting intellectuals through an excess of material rewards, and the predominance of commitment on the part of East German writers, artists, and scholars to the doctrines of Marxism-Leninism. But the 1956 intellectual ferment upset all such calculations. Almost overnight the intelligentsia appeared to be the Achilles heel of the entire system. And even today, although public expression of intellectual dissidence has again been suppressed, the expectation persists that in East Germany, as elsewhere in the Soviet bloc, the future may yet belong to the critical spirit.

In a sense, interpretation of the political fate of the East German intelligentsia has been somewhat obscured by the still unresolved controversy about the role of the intellectual under Communist totalitarianism in general. Students of the mechanics (or, as some would insist, the dynamics) of totalitarian rule *per se* have long denied the intellectual any fate other than that of self-compromising subordination. Other observers, however, have recently struck a somewhat different note. Those who look forward to an eventual transformation of the Soviet and satellite dictatorships envisage a special role for the intellectual committed to Marxism. In essence, proponents of this view ascribe to the Marxist intellectual the functions of guardian of the democratic and humanistic elements in the doctrine, critic of the political practices of Stalinist totalitarianism, and guide to the reformation of Soviet-style dictatorship. The first assessment thus postulates the obliteration of the critical spirit by political power, while the other point of view anticipates that the

* The author wishes to acknowledge his appreciation of the support and assistance of the Russian Research Center, Harvard University. This paper forms part of a chapter of a forthcoming book on *The East German Political System*.

committed intellect may restrain and eventually transform power itself.

Unfortunately, the unique dilemmas of East German revisionism are obscured by both these divergent interpretations, neither of which adequately reflects the multiple predicament of the East German intelligentsia. In the first place, despite extensive intellectual antipathy towards party policies no less than towards Ulbricht personally, it is surely rather deceptive shorthand to introduce such set categories as 'the intelligentsia' versus 'the regime' (or vice versa). It may well be that the SED has appeared to represent a monolithic entity with fixed objectives. Thus, although lively disagreements raged within the highest party councils on the proper methods of countering the unrest of students and intellectuals during 1956, such disputes were carried on entirely *in camera*, with the result that the intellectual rebels never did have access to real political power and were readily subdued. More important, however, is the fact that the dissident intellectuals of 1956 never accounted for more than a fraction of the entire 'intelligentsia'. Indeed, to impute a cohesion of composition or a singleness of purpose to the East German intelligentsia—in 1956 or at any other time before or since—is grossly misleading.

Unlike the intelligentsia in Poland, German intellectuals have never formed a distinct and homogeneous social class. Officially, the SED regime often talks as if there were but a single intellectual stratum, comprising both 'progressive' recruits from the pre-1945 generation and all of the post-war graduates. Transparently, the terms of the party's discourse have been borrowed from the vocabulary of Soviet sociology. Accordingly, the regime has also had occasion, if only for purposes of classification, to draw the distinction between the technical intelligentsia (*technische Intelligenz*) and the intellectuals of the humanistic disciplines (*geisteswissenschaftliche Intelligenz*). The division of the intelligentsia suggested by the regime's formal classification is both a socially realistic and politically vital one. In fact, there exist neither bonds of sentiment nor a sense of mutual affiliation between the two categories of the *Intelligenz*.

The technical intelligentsia comprises a variety of technical and professional callings; engineers, economic planners, industrial managers, doctors, and the like, while the humanistic intelligentsia includes artists, musicians, poets, writers, scholars, and university teachers. University students, always a special case, have shown a special sensitivity to the eddies and swells of opinion among the humanistic intelligentsia.

To a very large extent the ranks of the technical intelligentsia are still staffed by non-working class elements. In the main, these representatives of what is officially designated the 'old intelligentsia' have little interest in and probably less sympathy for Marxism-Leninism as political doctrine. Ultimately, of course, the regime would like to replace all such people with new 'socialist cadres'. Its efforts in this direction are underscored by a *numerus clausus* providing that at least 60 per cent of annual university admissions shall be drawn from applicants of working class or peasant background, and by the establishment of special Workers-and-Peasants Faculties to provide immediate managerial and professional training for the talented and reliable from shop bench and collective farm. But the notorious persistence of class attitudes has impeded the speedy realization of the regime's goal.[1] So far, at least, the social transformation of the technical intelligentsia has not even kept pace with the increasing demands for such talent generated by the 'socialist transformation' of the East German economy and society.

Nonetheless, the continued importance of the 'old intelligentsia' has proved embarrassing more in ideological than in political terms. The disdain of most members of the technical intelligentsia for Marxism-Leninism is but one manifestation of a more general political apathy on their part. The high degree of specialization of function, together with the traditional German expert's attitude of political neutrality, have contributed to the isolation of the technical intelligentsia from their humanistic counterparts. The very same factors have facilitated dutiful service on the part of most technicians and professionals.[2] Although the SED basically distrusts these people, in the way and for the reasons the ideology dictates that it should, the regime recognizes full well the need for their services and therefore early decided to purchase the required talents at a generous rate of exchange.

The extent of the material benefits offered to the technical intelligentsia, regardless of social origin, seems to lend substance to the charge levelled by West German critics that the loyalty of the managers and professionals has been bought by the regime. In accepting the accusation, however, one must bear in mind the essentially apolitical background and attitude of almost all of the people involved. The allegiance of the technical intelligentsia has proved quite fragile whenever the regime, contrary to its repeated promises, has exerted political and ideological pressures. Members of the technical intelligentsia figured significantly, for example, among the large num-

---

[1] See Hans Köhler, *Zur geistigen und seelischen Situation der Menschen in der Sowjetzone*, Bonn, 1954, who quotes as typical the response of one young worker: 'I am not going to sell myself. If I don't do what they want in school, they'll throw me out and I won't have learned anything anyhow. I would rather remain a worker' (p. 29).

[2] It is typical that the complaints of the technical intelligentsia against the regime are for the most part directed to such technical questions as the efficiency of centralized planning, distribution, and the like. For a list of such criticisms, see the anonymous survey, 'Die Opposition gegen den Stalinismus in Mitteldeutschland', Beilage, *Das Parliament*, June 11, 1958, p. 296.

bers who fled the DDR in the course of the 'construction of socialism' drive during 1952–53. To a real extent these departures should be read as a sign of political protest. Not that the technical intelligentsia sought to remonstrate against Marxism as such; much less against the 'construction of socialism'. It was rather the case that the regime's declaration of class warfare in July 1952 inspired local SED militants to treat the technical intelligentsia as 'second class citizens', as the party euphemistically confessed at a subsequent date.[3] Specifically, bourgeois technicians and professionals were beset by incessant political agitation and bureaucratically deprived of a number of privileges which the regime had prescribed for them.

The unintended flight of technical and professional cadres during 1952–53 and the SED's reaction to it proved indicative of what has since become a recurring sequence. Long before the introduction of the New Course, special concessions were made to win back the technical intelligentsia. Thus, in March 1953, the regime decreed still further privileges involving increased rations, an inflated salary scale, and a number of new social perquisites. Moreover, party function-aries were directed in quite explicit terms to cease political persecution and ideological pressure.[4]

Almost the very same sequence was repeated more recently when the frenzy against 'revisionism' and the militancy of the current drive for 'an accelerated tempo in the construction of socialism' generated vexatious pressures against bourgeois technicians. In this instance members of the medical profession were particularly affected, with the result that during 1958 the DDR experienced a 'flight from the Republic' of large numbers of doctors. This distressing situation, however, prompted a specific Politburo decree countermanding the pressures.[5]

Clearly no occupational category, no matter how useful to the regime, can be guaranteed permanent political immunity under totalitarianism. The point is rather that the technical intelligentsia in the DDR has fared as well as the behavioural characteristics of this particular regime can allow. Both the special treatment and the underlying factors which have made it possible have, in turn, further contributed to the isolation of the technical and professional people from the humanistic intelligentsia.

Separated from the technical intelligentsia—and, it should be added, from most other social and occupational groupings in East Germany—intellectuals of the humanistic disciplines have never dis-

[3] 'Mehr Achtung den Angehörigen der Intelligenz!', *Neues Deutschland*, May 23, 1953.

[4] See 'Die Bedeutung der Intelligenz beim Aufbau des Sozialismus', *Neues Deutschland*, May 24, 1953.

[5] Cf. 'Fragen, die unsere Ärzte stellen', *Neues Deutschland*, September 13, 1958, and 'Kommunique des Politburos zur Ärztefrage', *ibid.*, September 18, 1958.

played the unity that the regime imputes to them. Disciplinary specialization, so traditional to German intellectual life, continues to be significant. On to this divisive factor there has been superimposed a divergence of temper between the pre-war left intelligentsia and the younger ranks so pronounced as to merit seriously the designation of a 'conflict of generations'.[6]

Whatever cultural resplendence the DDR can claim, it owes to intellectual notables of another era. Consider the reputations and biographies of writers like Anna Seghers, Arnold Zweig, Heinrich Mann, Stefan Heym, and Ludwig Renn, literary critics like Hans Mayer and Alfred Kantorowicz, the playwright Bertolt Brecht, and the philosopher Ernst Bloch. Without exception, members of this older generation of Weimar intellectuals had been in exile in the West. Having made the conscious and voluntary decision to return to the homeland, each chose East Germany. Ostentatiously received by the Communist authorities, intellectuals of the older school have been publicly celebrated and munificently remunerated. Altogether the arts and letters have been magnanimously supported by the regime, although it is scarcely necessary to add that ever since 1951 and the fifth plenum of the SED Central Committee, standards of socialist realism have been rigidly enforced.

Of the psychology of the older generation as a whole, it should be said that a common animus against bourgeois society and the capitalist West have sustained its support of the East German regime. The fascinations of nihilism and anarchism that once enthralled the alienated café society of inter-war Berlin and intellectual members of the German Communist Party have faded into the social history of the Weimar period. But why this demise? And, even more to the point, how could a regime so unmistakably stamped with the Ulbricht personality have ever attracted such brilliant and sensitive psyches?

The attitude of the older intellectuals toward the German Communist functionary of the Ulbricht stamp has from the outset indeed been an amalgam of contradictory responses. Consider the outraged comment of Heinrich Mann to the effect that he had 'found it impossible to sit at the same table with a man like Ulbricht who might suddenly assert that the table was no table at all but rather a duck pond and then employ every means to compel acceptance of his definition'.[7] All the same, such open contempt has been combined with a ready if not always enthusiastic acceptance. The apparent paradox is psychologically quite understandable. Contemplation of the despised self-satisfaction of the bourgeois West and, more especially, the memory of the horrors of the Nazi period, set within

[6] See the very pointed and perceptive observations of Gerhard Zwerenz,'Junge Intelligenz unter Ulbricht', *Die Neue Gesellschaft*, July-August 1958, pp. 311–14.

[7] Quoted by Alfred Kantorowicz, 'Kantorowicz berichtet', *Die Welt*, September 12, 1957.

a framework which regards the entire national history as the story of 'German misery', have all played a part. Given the resentments and antipathies of the older intellectuals, there has simply been no alternative to which the Ulbricht regime has not seemed 'the lesser evil'.[8]

The contrast between the intellectual exhilaration of the Weimar Republic and the austere atmosphere of the 'construction of socialism' in the DDR needs no comment. Not surprisingly, the oppressive conditions of party regimentation have resulted in a pronounced sterility of the older generation of writers and artists. Anna Seghers, for example, renowned for her *Seventh Cross*, has since the war published but two novels, separated by a decade, and neither has been exactly a brilliant literary success. A similar lack of distinction has characterized the few published efforts of Arnold Zweig and the late Bert Brecht. Stefan Heym, who marked his return from America with the solemn profession to the effect that the creative muses of the 'new Germany' would allow him little diversion, has been able to write little if anything. The situation was described by Wolfgang Harich in 1953 as nothing less than 'a crisis of intellectual creativity of psychotic character among those who support our republic without the slightest political hesitation'.[9]

The absence of creativity, the 'failure to produce', has been interpreted by the regime as a sign of political protest. This may well be the case. The SED at least views the passivity of the older generation as a real challenge to party authority. The point was made quite explicitly at the thirty-third plenum of the Central Committee (October 1957) when, during a general discussion of intellectual attitudes, Hans Rodenberg, a party functionary with special responsibilities in the cinematic and literary realms, denounced 'silence' as the 'most dangerous of all behaviour'.[10]

Yet, if the older generation of writers and artists is practising an inner emigration through silence, its external attitude towards the regime has been quite correct. Thus *Der Sonntag*, a cultural journal controlled by the youthful intellectual dissidents during 1956, felt it necessary to complain about the insensitivity of their elders to the new currents of fermentation and protest. In essence, the complaint was exactly that of the regime, albeit directed towards a different end: 'Where is the voice of our German writers in the newspapers, journals,

---

[8] Zwerenz, *loc. cit.*, p. 312. Kantorowicz remarks, '. . . I believed for too long that these crude, stupid and violent [party] men were still . . . honest allies in the struggle against Nazism. . . .', 'Evidence', *The Review* (Imre Nagy Institute), October 2, 1959, pp. 77.

[9] Wolfgang Harich, 'Es geht um den Realismus', *Berliner Zeitung*, July 14, 1953.

[10] Quoted from an internal party document, *Aus dem Wortprotokoll der 33. Tagung des Zentralkomitees der SED Vom 16.–19. Oktober 1957*, p. 124.

at public meetings—in short, in public?'[11] The externally correct
attitude of the older intellectuals was manifested all too clearly in
the declarations against the Hungarian uprising which the regime
sought and obtained from them even before the crackdown within
the DDR. A blank verse poem written by Gerhard Zwerenz conveys
something of the sense of bitterness and betrayal which such behaviour produced among the younger East German intellectual rebels:

> When they were young
> They drew the sword impetuously,
> Too impetuously
> So they now suppose.
> Having grown old,
> They are prudent and wise——
> And run the young ones through
> With the thrust of
> Their wisdom.[12]

II

What, then, is one to make of the manifestations of revisionism
uncovered by the SED in all spheres of East German intellectual
life? It is entirely characteristic of Communist functionaries of the
Ulbricht cut that critical ideas of whatever direction and magnitude
should appear as powerful weapons of the enemy. In the eyes of the
Ulbricht leadership of the SED, there is little difference between
criticism of the standards of socialist realism in literature and a programme of outright opposition such as that drawn up by Wolfgang
Harich. All such currents, in this view, 'turn into open counter-
revolution'.[13] In the longer scheme of things the assessment may
contain elements of self-fulfilling prophecy; for the shorter run it
only obscures the divergent strands of a multi-hued revisionism.

Merely to list all the entries in the SED's current catalogue of
revisionist heresies would entail a protracted effort. But it would be
pointless, for the category itself is little more than a pejorative one
without fixed meaning or content. It covers thought as philosophically
potent as that of Ernst Bloch, and also misdemeanours as devoid of
formal intellectual content as the support offered by party functionaries to the Schirdewan-Wollweber 'faction'.[14] Some of the most

[11] *Der Sonntag*, October 28, 1956.

[12] 'Die alten Dichter', in Gerhard Zwerenz, *Galgenlieder vom Heute*, Berlin,
n.d.

[13] W. Ulbricht, 'Some Aspects of the Ideological Work of the Socialist Unity
Party of Germany', *World Marxist Review*, October 1958, p. 19.

[14] It should be emphasized that the anti-Ulbricht faction within the highest
echelons of the SED at no time sought to rally the intellectual dissidents.

prominent manifestations of revisionism in several different fields of intellectual endeavour do, however, deserve comment. The account of the regime's reaction to all such phenomena will illustrate the larger point: Much of what came to be labelled 'revisionism' represented not so much a total challenge to the SED dictatorship as a response to an official invitation to strike out on new lines of 'creativity' during the period of doctrinal flexibility in 1956. That such efforts brought to the surface ideas which infuriated and possibly genuinely terrified the Ulbricht leadership of the party tells more about its own psychology than about that of the critical thinkers.

The events of 1956 in East Germany did bequeath at least one radical programme of opposition to the SED dictatorship, that drafted by Wolfgang Harich. Harich himself, widely regarded as a typical and brilliant representative of the younger intellectual generation in the DDR, is in many ways much more of an individualist than is usually supposed. The extraordinarily successful career which he made for himself in the realm of Marxist philosophy has tended to obscure Harich's bourgeois background, truly atypical of his breed, as well as his own earlier fascination with Buddhism and Catholicism. But biography aside, it is true that the ideas associated with his programme, and more generally with this kind of intellectual protest, were far from uniquely German. On the contrary, the inspiration was provided by the Polish protagonists of 'humanitarian socialism' as well as by friends and teachers of the Hungarian Petöfi circle.

Nonetheless, Harich's 'testament', as it has been called in the West, does have independent significance. It is not so much that the thoughts which it expressed may have been widely shared. Certainly they were. Rather more important is the conclusion towards which the several contradictions of the programme itself seem to point. The very attempt to apply Hungarian and Polish notions of 'the special national road' to the East German situation only underlined the political infeasibility of 'national communism' in the DDR.

In essence, the Harich programme demanded a doctrinal and organizational transformation of the SED in order to attenuate the party dictatorship over East Germany. The image of a liberalized DDR which Harich suggested was that of a democratic collectivist rival to the present German Federal Republic which would display such economic characteristics as an abundance of consumer goods, profit-sharing, and industrial management by Workers' Councils. Furthermore, collective farms were to be dissolved, full intellectual and religious freedom restored, and a parliamentary coalition government established—albeit with the proviso that 'a reformed SED should remain in control'. Neither the order of significance of these several goals, nor even the issue of their compatibility is touched upon. But that deficiency, forgivable enough in an 'action programme', is far from the major point. What is more significant about Harich's proposals is the fact that the attainment of the entire programme of reform is viewed as providing only a *transitory* stage, to lead logically and speedily to German national reunification. That a political relaxation according to the prospects of the 'special German road to socialism' would require the liquidation of the DDR is reasonable enough, but for that reason alone it is improbable that such a programme could ever have been accorded Soviet support, much less the support of those who actually wielded power within the SED.

How, then, is one to interpret the opposition of Wolfgang Harich and his associates? In the West, Harich has earned a share of the admiration which has developed for the intellectual rebels under Communist rule who, in one fashion or another, have undergone martyrdom. The further claim of one of Harich's rebellious colleagues that Harich should be celebrated because he in fact attained that elusive national quality, a synthesis of thought and action,[15] can only be regarded with scepticism.

Too little is known about Harich's political thought to make a definitive judgment on its quality. Certainly it would be a mistake to attach any particular intellectual significance to his programme of opposition, the 'testament', as such. Not only does it abound in potential programmatic contradictions of the sort already indicated, but its search for theoretical foundations is entirely abortive. Consider the following mixed bag of those called into service to 'enhance Marxism-Leninism':

[Marxist-Leninist theory] must be enhanced and enlarged through the perceptions of Trotsky and above all those of Bukharin; it must be enhanced and enlarged through the thought of Rosa Luxemberg and, partially, Karl Kautsky. We must take into Marxism-Leninism worthwhile elements from the theories of Fritz Sternberg and other Social-Democratic theorists. We must adopt aspects of the Yugoslav experience and those new elements which mark theoretical discussion in Poland and China. . . . '[16]

To develop Marxism-Leninism simultaneously along these many lines would indeed be a challenging, if not wholly baffling exercise. It makes greater sense to suppose that Harich only intended to draw from each of the sources mentioned a justification for his own opposition to some specific aspect of SED rule in East Germany. As far as more constructive, and perhaps more profound analysis is concerned, it is known that Harich, in the German manner, did prepare a set of

[15] G. Zwerenz, 'Aus dem Tagebuch eines Geflohenen', *Der Monat*, December 1959, p. 48.
[16] 'Die politische Plattform Harichs', *SBZ-Archiv*, Sondernummer (1957), p. 8.

sixteen theses, on 'the further development of Marxism-Leninism'. These he submitted to the editorial board of the *Deutsche Zeitschrift für Philosophie*, apparently in late summer 1956. The philosophy journal refused to publish them because the theses contended ex- plicitly that Marxism was relevant only to nineteenth-century con- ditions. A further important source for the intellectual biography of Wolfgang Harich, a more substantial manuscript on 'humanistic Marxism' which was being written at the time of his arrest, reportedly fell into the hands of the secret police.

Leaving aside the substance of the youthful philosopher's thought, his lack of aptitude in synthesizing thought with action can be demon- strated all too readily. Convinced of the merits of his own position, Harich first sought to present his programme to the SED leaders. In particular, he wanted to interest the recently rehabilitated Paul Merker and Fritz Dahlem. That failing, Harich closeted himself for a conference lasting four hours with Soviet Ambassador Pushkin. When Ulbricht, having been informed of these goings-on, summoned Harich to provide a list of all who shared his point of view, Harich grew angry and took his schemes elsewhere, this time to the West. Rudolph Augstein, editor of *Der Spiegel*, has given a truly staggering picture of the incoherence of Harich's optimism and the arrogance of his self-righteousness. Harich had become so convinced of the historical inevitability of his proposals as to believe that Ulbricht himself might adopt them to save his own position (*sic!*).[17] In the case of Wolfgang Harich, the conclusion seems inescapable that how- ever much he may have precipitated the expression of East German intellectual discontent, he himself was far too much the typical romantic and erratic intellectual to translate 'thought into action'. The real hiatus between political power and the critical spirit in a sense foredoomed Harich, as it had so many other critical intellectuals throughout German history, to an erratic romanticism.

If Harich's self-acknowledged revisionism perished stillborn, what is one to make of the many other manifestations of 'revisionism' uncovered by the SED after the thirtieth Central Committee plenum of January 1957? Given the party's proclivity to regard unorthodox thought in the light of the Hungarian uprising, the creative strivings in East Germany which had been tolerated and, indeed, encouraged during the previous six months had to be denounced as ideological heresy. In fact, by the standards of orthodoxy which had been dropped in 1956 only to be restored in 1957, a good deal of such speculation did amount to precisely that.

Consider the realm of Marxist philosophy. Those who had taken seriously the SED's resolution calling for a struggle against dogma- tism and for the 'further development' of Marxism demonstrated lively interest in the younger Marx and devoted painstaking effort to

[17] *Der Spiegel*, March 20, 1957, p. 10.

such other tasks as reconciling Marxism with the findings of modern physics. The work of many young philosophers, including Richard Lorenz, Günther Zehm (both pupils of Ernst Bloch), Martin Strauss, and Friedrich Herneck (two young Marxist philosophers of science) was not undistinguished. The direction taken in these inquiries was not likely to appeal to those interested in the preservation of ideological infallibility. Herneck, for example, openly challenged the applicability of dialectical materialism to research in the natural sciences, and even made a case, in the light of the theory of relativity and the quantum theory, against the scientific pretensions of philosophical generalizations derived from the principles of dialectical materialism. To be sure, all such heretical thought was countered at every turn by the remaining guardians of philosophical orthodoxy. On the other hand, the party leadership, with transparently little understanding of the substantive issues at dispute, stood aside, applauding the vigorous 'conflict of opinion'.

The consequences of the sudden change in the SED's attitude which was precipitated by the Hungarian events may be illustrated by reference to the case of the dean of DDR philosophers, Ernst Bloch. Bloch's unorthodox Marxism had long been tolerated, if only grudgingly. After the thirtieth plenum he was forcibly retired from his chair at the Karl Marx University, hounded as a revisionist, and challenged to renounce his deviant philosophical tenets. Unfortunately for him, the events of 1956 put Bloch's notion of teleogical indeterminacy, the uncertainty of history, in a dangerous light. Pupils of his school turned out to be in the forefront of those critics of the regime who insisted upon investigating the social causation of Stalinism. Further, Bloch had lent the weight of his philosophical authority to demands for the abolition of the compulsory university course in Marxist-Leninist social science, a course which he had described as 'narrow-gauge Marxism'. As a result of all this, according to the regime, 'his philosophy had become—politics'.[18]

Politics indeed! The SED's post-1956 review of the 'conflict of opinion' uncovered politics, and dissident politics at that, in every intellectual domain. Thus the example of the Harich case was employed to beat down Professor Hans Mayer, the Leipzig literary critic, who had followed up a criticism of literature as the science of engineering the human soul with an unfavourable survey of Soviet and East German literature. That kind of assessment, official spokesmen said in warning, represented 'capitulation to the forces of imperialist restoration and bourgeois decadence' and was to be combated by 'ideological and organizational measures'.[19]

[18] 'Der Kampf gegen die bürgerliche Ideologie und den Revisionismus', *Einheit*, February 1957, p. 137.
[19] K. Schwalbe, 'Wichtige Aufgaben unserer Literaturwissenschaft', *Neues Deutschland*, February 9, 1957.

How much more appalling for the Ulbricht regime to discover that revisionism had also infected economic theory and tainted almost all of its leading economists. In particular, the entire faculty of the German Academy of Economic Science, which had previously been regarded as a bastion of party loyalty, had pursued the 'conflict of opinion' with spirited discussions of the problems of the withering away of the state. The Director of the Central Statistical Administration, Professor Fritz Behrens, and his assistant, Arne Benary, had even drawn up specific blueprints.[20] Extending the tentative analysis of Professor Gunther Kohlmey, Director of the Economics Institute of the German Academy of Sciences, Behrens and Benary had concluded that the time was ripe for a far-ranging decentralization of the East German economy. Decentralization had become possible, they postulated, because the DDR had already passed into a more 'mature' phase of the 'construction of socialism'. While 'administrative' and 'bureaucratic' direction of the economy had earlier been necessary in order to 'suppress the class enemy', the retention of such methods was running counter to economic rationality and, specifically, was crippling the productivity of labour. Accordingly, Benary called for autonomy for individual industrial enterprises in such matters as the organization of work, distribution of profits, and the like. Behrens argued that adequate centralized direction and proper economic equilibrium could be maintained by the Central Reserve Bank, which would take into account actual economic demands and real economic values. All of this would be entirely feasible, according to Benary, because of the 'dialectical unity between consciousness and spontaneity', a position which he sought to defend by elaborating some new thoughts on 'the spontaneity of the masses'. These theses bore for the party an uncanny resemblance to certain Yugoslav theories. And worse still, they one and all 'diminished the leading role of the party'.[21]

A similarly 'disruptive' proposal emanated from Professor Kurt Vieweg, Director of the Institute for Agricultural Economics. Like Behrens and Benary, Vieweg also challenged principles of planning and control heretofore sacrosanct. Pointing to recurring difficulties in the area of agricultural production, Vieweg offered a truly radical solution: unprofitable collective farms were simply to be dissolved. Once the fetish of collectivization had been given up, the countryside could develop more in keeping with realistic economic considerations. State supported, but otherwise independent, 'family farms' of 30–40 hectares (75–100 acres) were especially to be encouraged. Such co-

[20] See Fritz Behrens, 'Zum Problem der Ausnutzung ökonomischer Gesetze in der Ubergangsperiode', and Arne Benary, 'Zu Grundprobleme der politischen Ökonomie des Sozialismus in der Ubergangsperiode', *Wirtschaftswissenschaft*, 3. Sonderheft, 1957.

[21] 'Der Kampf gegen die bürgerliche Ideologie und den Revisionismus', *loc. cit.*, p. 135.

operative farming ventures would compete (Vieweg thought successfully) with both private farms hiring agricultural labourers and the
few remaining collectives. Disregarding the political functions of the
machine tractor stations, Vieweg further recommended that the
MTS be transformed into repair shops to service the agricultural
machinery which he suggested might properly be transferred outright, in time, to the family farms as well as to collective farms which
had proved their viability.

The theories of Behrens, Benary, and Vieweg are singularly instruc-
tive. To all intents and purposes all three men were loyal supporters
of the regime and certainly had nothing in common with the Harich
opposition. Given the more relaxed atmosphere of 1956, they had
registered the expert's response to specific economic pressures and
popular discontents. For Behrens and Benary the problems of labour
productivity and the overplanned and entirely inefficient distribution
and supply systems were central. For Vieweg it was the perpetual
crisis of agricultural production and the dissatisfaction of the peasantry. All of these formulations were prepared at a time when it seemed
that they might at least be welcomed as contributions to the 'conflict
of scientific opinion'.

The several manifestations of 'revisionism', in philosophy, literary
criticism, and economics may serve to point up the relationship
between revisionism and the location of the party line. The doctrinal
orthodoxy of Stalinism at least established well-defined categories.
Until late 1957 and Khrushchev's own clarification of the menace
of revisionism, the SED, no less than other satellite parties, had to
proceed cautiously. The lack of clarity in the specifics of doctrine, as
well as the elements of change and fluidity in Soviet interpretation
and practice, confounded both SED functionaries and East German
intellectuals loyal to the regime.

The case of Professor Jürgen Kuczynski, who occupies the chair of
Economic History in the Humboldt University, illustrates the situation. In the spirit of the 1956 campaign against dogmatism, Professor
Kuczynski ventured to protest against the dogmatic conception of
'party-mindedness' governing historical research, and had even composed a very moderate appeal for limited criticism. However,
Kuczynski was careful to point out that he did not mean to invoke
'the useless criticism of bourgeois liberalism'.[22] The following revealing exchange between Ulbricht and Kuczynski transpired some
months later at a conference of the editors of *Einheit* and party
intellectuals and functionaries:

Ulbricht: . . . the theoretical journal is to play a leading role both
in the formation of new questions and in the struggle against

[22] Jürgen Kuczynski, 'Meinungsstreit, Dogmatismus, und "liberale Kritik" ',
Einheit, May 1957, pp. 603–11.

bourgeois ideology For that reason *Einheit* carries articles which provoke discussion. But often nobody replies to such articles. This was the crux of the matter in the case of the theses of Comrade Kohlmey. Just what will happen to the article of Comrade Kuczynski, I cannot foretell.

Kuczynski: I know already!

Ulbricht: Well, I really don't know yet. Perhaps you have already spoken with other comrades who want to take a stand on it. But perhaps a half dozen comrades who have quite different viewpoints will express themselves. That will be quite interesting.[23]

Kuczynski had obviously gone too far in his pronouncements against dogmatism. Did this mean that he too was to be adjudged a revisionist? Even Ulbricht was uncertain! It required a protracted and highly scholastic examination of virtually every potentially divergent phrase of Kuczynski's piece before the party concluded that he had indeed been guilty of revisionism.[24]

The striking incidence of revisionism uncovered in East Germany, especially in 1957–58, must therefore at least partially be understood in terms of the shortsightedness of loyal party intellectuals in not anticipating the retroactive shift of the SED line. When Kuczynski undertook self-criticism at the Third SED Conference on Higher Education in March 1958, his remarks revealed a sense of frustration of the sort only a loyal Communist could experience over the shift of the party line in the course of his own scholarly work.[25] The point was made even more explicitly at the same conference by Professor Behrens, who announced that he had 'thrown overboard' his proposals for economic decentralization:

'I confess that objectively the conception which I developed was directed against the party and that therefore it was revisionist. There is no need for me to deny that the Twentieth Party Congress prompted me to work out my theory. . . . I also acknowledge that it was quite wrong to have directed the main attack against dogmatism. Rather it must [now] be directed against revisionism.'[26]

In a real sense, the emphasis on party-mindedness which once

---

[23] 'Theoretische und praktische Probleme der Übergangsperiode und die Aufgaben der "Einheit" ', *Einheit*, June 1957, p. 669.

[24] In Professor Kuczynski's case the conclusion was facilitated by the publication of his study of German Social Democracy on the eve of World War I (*Der Ausbruch des ersten Weltkrieges und die deutsche Sozialdemokratie*, Berlin: Akademie Verlag, 1957) in which it was argued that the leaders of the pre-war SPD 'were not primarily responsible for the attitude of the masses during August 1914' (p. 145).

[25] 'Forschung mit Kampf verbinden', *Neues Deutschland*, March 12, 1958.

[26] 'Meine Konzeption war revisionistisch', *Neues Deutschland*, March 4, 1958.

again dominates every intellectual pursuit in the DDR has simplified the problems of both intellectuals and functionaries. The indeterminacy of the party line which led unsuspecting intellectuals into the camp of revisionism along with the rebellious ones, also impeded attempts of loyal functionaries to block the route. Consider the plea of Paul Wandel, under attack for having shown a 'hesitant and wavering' attitude towards intellectual currents in his realm:

'It is necessary that many things be changed. In the very first place the ideological struggle must be waged differently from 1956. It must be waged more according to principle. Unclarified questions therefore need to be clarified and quickly.'[27]

The triumph of Ulbricht in the intra-party struggle has brought the desired clarification of doctrine. In the longer scheme of things there remains, of course, the potential menace that today's ideological 'revisionism' might become tomorrow's orthodoxy on certification from Moscow itself. More immediately, there is still the problem of intellectuals who, having once been exposed to the more liberal atmosphere, can no longer accept Ulbricht's clarifications as doctrine binding them to the SED.

The most prominent exponents of intellectual criticism during 1956, Harich and his associates, have been removed bodily from public life. They were joined in gaol by a number of other young intellectuals who, in the course of the SED's review of 1956 events, were found to have spoken provocatively to students or, as was the case with Ernst Bloch's pupils, Richard Lorenz, Gunther Zehm, and Erich Loest, to have written seditiously. Revisionists of the older generation found it somewhat easier to make their peace with the regime. Behrens, Benary, and Kuczynski have all submitted to the required self-criticism, even if without the total self-immolation so pleasing to Ulbricht. Professor Bloch, too hoary and, in his own view, too venerable to write off an entire lifetime of philosophic work, has nonetheless expressed at least passing regard for the drive against revisionism.[28] Professor Vieweg acted more impetuously, fleeing to West Germany in April 1957, only to return to the DDR in November. Such indecisive behaviour led to his arrest on charges of having betrayed economic secrets to the Bonn Government. *Caveant alii.*

Once again a pall of party-mindedness hangs heavily over every intellectual pursuit in East Germany. Party doctrine has become fixed and party controls manifest renewed efficacy. The lessons of the Harich case have been hammered home in connection with a thorough exposition of the many potential forms and appearances

[27] *Aus dem Wortprotokoll der 33. Tagung des Zentralkomitees der SED*, p. 116.
[28] Ernst Bloch, 'Ich stehe auf dem Boden der DDR', *Neues Deutschland* April 20, 1958.

of revisionism. Under such banners as 'Storm the Heights of Culture' and 'Seize the Pen, Mate', the regime has undertaken a new cultural offensive. Changes in organization and transfers of personnel have been effected to assure that these campaigns will receive attentive hearing and obedient response. And no company of scholars and intellectuals is deprived of the presence of some representative of the omnipresent secret police.

The gulf between generations opened up by the quiescence of the older generation during 1956 has certainly not been closed. If anything, the behaviour of the older group has tended to confirm the charges of the militant young critics of the regime, that their elders have been corrupted by an excess of material benefits. One is reminded of Heinz Kahlau's remark to the 1956 Congress of Young Writers and Artists:

'One can as little expect militant controversy from [intellectuals] who are concerned with their household comforts as one can from functionaries who constantly travel about in their official cars.'[29]

The disillusionment of the younger generation with its mentors has been given poetic expression in precisely these terms by Gerhard Zwerenz:

> The times are morose
> Writers are silent
> From fear
> And critics lecture
> At command
> And there is a literature
> Which no one believes
> But fees are paid.[30]

Yet, for all the elements of real truth in such recriminations, they do not do entire justice to the greater predicament which encompasses intellectuals, elderly as well as youthful. Consider the fate of Alfred Kantorowicz who fled to the West in August 1957. A literary critic and Professor of Modern Literature at the East Berlin Humboldt University, Kantorowicz had been the recipient of all the material benefits the regime could afford, including a handsome salary, a villa, servants, and a private limousine. During 1956 Kantorowicz had remained splendidly aloof from the intellectual rebels, his only protest a privately devised strategem which enabled him to avoid having to add his signature to those of other writers on the declaration in favour of the Kadar regime.[21]

[29] 'Revoluzzer?', Forum, 12, 1956.
[30] Zwerenz, Galgenlieder vom Heute, p. 28.
[31] See Kantorowicz's own account in 'Evidence', loc. cit., p. 82.

The reasons why Kantorowicz fled when he did, therefore, make for particularly interesting speculation. Kantorowicz's case is all the more revealing precisely because he refuses to answer the question in that form, but prefers to address himself to the reasons for his prolonged sojourn in the DDR. In essence, he shows how a concatenation of basically divergent factors—material rewards, repression, and inner migration together—had made him a part of the system.

Kantorowicz is fond of citing the sentiments of Carl Ossietzky, the much abused German pacifist who refused to flee from Hitler's power, to the effect that intellectuals who aspire to purify an infected national spirit must share its fate. Whether the quotation applies to Kantorowicz himself is not particularly important, for surely it does illuminate the predicament of East German intellectuals, especially the more youthful critics of the Ulbricht regime. How misleading is the contention that the dissident intellectuals, no less than others persecuted by the regime, have the easy option of flight to the West, an option supposedly made more attractive by the fact that in quitting the DDR for West Germany, they need not leave their country, its language or culture. To be sure, many an intellectual, menaced by the threat of arrest, has taken this path. For the others, however, the decision is not at all an easy and obvious one. Psychological factors reinforce personal considerations. For the young Marxist intellectual, flight from the DDR in fact means exile in a strange land. The very commitments and concerns which have driven him into opposition to Ulbricht are nowhere understood, much less shared, in the Federal Republic.

Not surprisingly, then, the logic of the totalitarian situation in East Germany involves the twofold phenomenon of the intellectual in subservience and the intellect in opposition. While it remains true that the intellectual by himself can do little to resist, oppose, or mitigate total power, changes in the structure or in the manner of exercise of such power may well induce a change of intellectual behaviour from external acquiescence to criticism and open opposition. That 'revisionism' may be set in the interstices of dictatorship is certainly one lesson of the events of 1956. However, another relationship seems no less compelling. It is but one manifestation of the general truth that the psychology of the intellectual in any society is determined in real measure by his effectiveness that, under totalitarianism, the individual behaviour and specific attitudes of the intellectual are conditioned by the effective exercise of political power. The repressive power of totalitarian dictatorship may not only preclude the expression of intellectual opposition but may even alter the attitude and psychology of intellectuals subjected to it.

The crucial inter-relation between intellectual attitudes and the efficacy of political power is one that the Ulbricht leadership of the

SED seems to appreciate especially keenly. The intolerance and even obscurantism which have characterized the reimposition of party controls over intellectual pursuits since 1956 seem ill-designed to assuage intellectual disaffection. But in the short run such measures at least preclude articulate opposition. In the longer term, they may well operate once again to repress entirely the critical spirit.

XVIII. Tito—A Reluctant Revisionist

ALFRED SHERMAN

The terms *Revisionism* and *Titoism*[1] are liable to introduce misleading connotations. *Revisionism* has come to mean the re-examination of certain tenets of one Marxist orthodoxy or another in the light of experience and changed conditions, and the subsequent formulation of a revised doctrine. The very word *Titoism* suggests that the Yugoslav Communist hierarchy has worked out a specific doctrine which can be more or less definitely stated and compared with rival bodies of Marxist doctrine.

In fact its origins and significance are fundamentally different from those of earlier revisionist schools—either Bernstein and his contemporaries inside the social-democratic movement, or 'deviationists' like Bukharin or Lovestone inside the Communist movement. *Titoism* is essentially the *post-factum* doctrinal legitimation of expedients forced on the Yugoslav Communist leaders by the exigencies of their relations with the Soviet Communist leaders, in which their twin aims are to remain independent of the Soviet leadership and to retain absolute power in Yugoslavia. Titoism's significance lies in the light it throws on the problems arising from the existence of more than one Communist State. These problems include the impact of Communist co-existence on doctrinal orthodoxy and on internal policy.

Because *Titoist* doctrines have fluctuated so violently with the vicissitudes of Yugoslav-Soviet relations (which in turn are shaped by many factors which are quite uninfluenced by Yugoslav policies), it is fruitless to collate Titoist theoretical statements made during the past decade and try to deduce from them a coherent body of doctrine. What was a central tenet of Titoism in 1953 may have been abandoned and reversed in 1955, and hesitantly re-adopted again in 1960. These contradictions and tergiversations, however incompatible they

---

[1] The Leaders of the Yugoslav League of Communists (formerly Communist Party of Yugoslavia) deny that they are Revisionists or that there is such a thing as Titoism or National Communism. Yugoslav Communists—said Kardelj in introducing the Programme of the League in 1948—are true Marxist-Leninists, applying the general principles of Marxism-Leninism to Yugoslavia's specific conditions. The Yugoslav leaders claim to be the only Communist Party which has succeeded in retaining its foothold on the narrow path between revisionism and dogmatism, and between their related twin evils of anarchism and bureaucratism.

I

may be with a neat theoretical formula, are an integral part of Titoism. They add further dimensions to our picture of the range of possible contingencies in inter-Communist relations, and their impact on Communist society.

It may therefore be useful to begin with a historical sketch of *Titoism*, as it emerged from within a broader political context, before examining its principal doctrines.

Though both Soviet and Yugoslav propaganda have from time to time claimed that differences of doctrine or approach between the two parties ante-dated and played a part in bringing about the conflict in 1948, all the available evidence suggests that the CPY leaders considered themselves to be impeccably orthodox Stalinists when the conflict broke out, and subsequently were extremely reluctant to revise their doctrines. The proceedings of the Fifth Congress of the CPY, held in July 1948, a month after the Cominform resolution, were characterized not only by the absence of recognisable 'deviations' but also by repeated assertions of Stalinist orthodoxy.[2] For the best part of the year that followed, the CPY leaders explicitly avoided any revisionist statements or aspersions on the Soviet Union and its leaders. For this there were good reasons. First, they still hoped that the dispute could be settled and Yugoslavia 're-admitted to the Socialist camp,' and were therefore unwilling to say anything which would make subsequent reconciliation more difficult. Secondly, they were well aware of the difficulties involved in demolishing the doctrines and beliefs they had so sedulously inculcated into their supporters. Thirdly, they realized that any denigration of Stalin and the USSR would be liable to have repercussions on their own position.

However, Titoism was thrust upon them by Soviet policies.[3] The Communist bloc imposed a damaging economic blockade on Yugoslavia, incited Yugoslav Communists and national minorities in the border regions to revolt and sabotage, showed far more bitter hostility to Yugoslavia than to the Western powers, and gave the Yugoslav leaders cause for suspecting—rightly or wrongly—that an armed attack might be contemplated. The CPY leaders, therefore, had to prepare their cadres, the rank and file, and the population as a whole for a long and bitter struggle against their erstwhile allies; they had to ferret out and imprison thousands of Cominform sympathizers who had recently been among their most devout supporters; and

[2] *Proceedings of the Fifth Congress of the Communist Party of Yugoslavia*, Belgrade, 1948.

[3] There are several works which discuss these developments in detail. Two which show considerable insight are Adam Ulam's *Titoism and the Cominform*, Harvard University Press, 1952, and Ernst Halperin's *The Triumphant Heretic*, London, 1958. The first, unfortunately, stops with 'High Titoism' in 1952; the second is less heavily documented.

they had to turn to the West for economic and later for military aid and political support.

Stalinism proved to be an unsatisfactory doctrine for rationalizing these policies and generating *esprit de corps*; the CPY leaders therefore began reluctantly to revise it. This revision was to continue stage by stage for the next four years or so. Some steps were taken under the pressure of external events; others followed logically from steps already taken, and the course began to develop a momentum of its own, with unforeseen consequences.

The first tenet of Communist doctrine to undergo revision concerned, logically enough, 'proletarian internationalism' and the relations between Communist parties. The CPY continued to recognize in theory the 'leading role' of the Soviet Communist Party and the obligation to maintain monolithic Communist unity long after they had been compelled to violate it in practice. (It transpired from the exchange of letters between the two parties that the Yugoslav leaders had at one time envisaged Yugoslavia's ultimate absorption into the USSR.) An article by Djilas, published in September 1949 in the party daily *Borba* and the theoretical journal *Kommunist*, rejected this thesis, and recognized that the national question remained after Communist parties assumed power. So long as the Soviet Union was the only socialist state—the thesis ran—Communists had a special duty towards the Soviet Union and Communist Party. But the emergence of other Communist-ruled states created a new situation for which the old rules no longer held good. In the new conditions absolute equality between Communist parties and reciprocal non-interference became essential, since the leading role or hegemony of one party over another would entail effective rule by one state over another, thereby infringing national independence.

The advent of Communist power, Djilas pointed out, did not automatically ensure that Governments would act correctly in their relation with other states, eschewing arrogance, 'hegemonism', or even economic exploitation. The significance of this argument—which remained the irreducible core of Titoism—for future relations between Communist states was overshadowed at the time by Yugoslav criticism of Soviet rule and doctrine as such. Having demonstrated that Communist theory did not preclude the Soviet Government's acting immorally toward Yugoslavia, the CPY leaders had to explain why it had actually done so. Since they regarded it as axiomatic that a country's foreign policy directly reflected its social system, and that a socialist foreign policy was by definition a moral one, they naturally set out to prove that the Soviet Union was not really socialist at all.

According to the new thesis, the Soviet Union was a state-capitalist despotism, ruled by a bureaucratic caste, and broadly comparable to fascism. Having established complete economic monopoly at home, its ruling caste naturally proceeded, like all monopolists, to an imperialist policy bent on world hegemony.[4] The theoretical argument underlying this thesis ran broadly as follows: any proletarian revolution inevitably begins by establishing a strong state apparatus, to defend the revolution against counter-revolutionaries and to reorganize the economy on a socialist basis. The more backward the country the stronger this apparatus must be. At first, the bureaucracy's role is a progressive one, but unless it is kept under firm control by the masses it becomes the seedbed for a bureaucratic caste. This caste will merge with the ruling party, become independent of the working masses, and rule over them. It will then turn into an independent social force following laws of social development inherent in its own make-up. This bureaucratic degeneration represents a far greater danger to socialism than opposition by remnants of the old classes, since the latter can only slow down development, whereas 'bureaucratism' can do socialism immense harm, and indeed, the Soviet bureaucratic caste had ruined the socialist heritage of the October revolution and become an enemy of the progress of world socialism in general. Furthermore, this system had long since ceased to play a progressive role in the economy, and had become a drag on the further development of the Soviet economic potential.

From late 1950 onwards, CPY spokesmen drew a parallel between 'bureaucratic dictatorship of the Soviet type' and fascism; according to their contention, fascism occurs when the bourgeoisie as a class is no longer capable of retaining power, while the proletariat is still too weak to capture it; the Soviet type of regime occurs when the proletariat assumes power but is too weak and culturally or politically too backward to retain it, with the result that the 'new men' who control the state, the economic bureaucracy and the party apparatus suppress and eliminate working class influence over the administration and turn into absolute rulers. This phenomenon is reflected, in turn, in the cult of the individual, growing inequality between social strata, and bureaucratic caste dictatorship over all forms of social activity, including the arts.

In the Western democracies, on the other hand, the thesis ran, the objective laws of social development were leading to a growth of socialist forms, albeit rather haphazardly and unevenly. In spite of resistance by the capitalist class, reforms were being introduced, working-class conditions improved, and some measure of planning imposed. These changes, though they had reached a far lower level of development than they had in Yugoslavia, were nevertheless on the right road.

---

[4] The new thesis was developed step by step in a number of speeches and articles published by party leaders between mid-1950 and Stalin's death. Cf. Tito's speech in the National Assembly introducing the Bill for the Establishment of Workers' Management, and Kardelj's address to the Federal Assembly on April 1, 1952, introducing the General Law on Local Authorities.

Taken as a whole, the argument met an obvious need in rationalizing Yugoslavia's changing relations with the Soviet Union and the West, and had the advantage of being considerably closer to ascertainable reality than the pre-1948 theory had been. But it created a new dichotomy between theory and practice at home.

Yugoslav society had been closely modelled on the Soviet Union until well into 1950, and even after the break all speeches and articles on internal economic and political policies had been buttressed more by quotations from Stalin and appeals to Soviet practice than by statistics. The Titoist critique of Soviet society naturally called domestic arrangements and their underlying theoretical justification into question. Since the need for support against Soviet pressure had made the leaders far more dependent on the active goodwill of their party-members and the public at large than previously these implicit or explicit questions had to be answered.

The CPY leaders set out to satisfy the questioners in a variety of ways. In the first place, they baldly asserted that Yugoslavia had always been different from the USSR. Our attitude was sometimes too uncritical; sometimes we transplanted institutions without due regard to Yugoslav conditions, but things never went far enough to do serious harm, and by now we have set things right—this was the case now advanced. But in itself it was quite insufficient to allay the serious misgivings experienced by many party members, confronted day in day out by the evidence of their own eyes. In order to make Yugoslav 'Democratic Socialism' demonstrably different from Soviet 'bureaucratism', two methods were used: first, real reforms were introduced on peripheral matters; secondly, a theory of socialist development was evolved to guide and explain Yugoslavia's unique way to socialist democracy.

The new theory followed logically from the critique of Soviet society. Whereas Soviet rule had degenerated into bureaucracy by allowing the state apparatus to grow too strong, Yugoslav socialism was said to have been accompanied, from the very beginning, by a gradual withering away of the state, as its functions, primarily in economic life, were handed over to the working people by decentralization of administration and economic life, and by turning over factories and economic enterprises to the working people themselves to manage. 'In the Soviet Union after thirty-one years the factories belong to the State, not to the people . . . they are run by civil servants . . . workers have the right to work but this is not very different from the position in capitalist countries,' Tito said.

According to this thesis it was quite wrong for the State to hold on to all its powers until a high degree of industrialization and all other material conditions for full socialism had been reached; the state must begin withering away step by step, even while productive forces are still relatively backward and cultural levels low. (This was remarkably similar to the 'sprouting of communism' thesis elaborated by the Chinese Communist leaders in 1958. It is not difficult to trace certain similarities in the conditions which gave rise to it: the need to revivify the morale of their cadres after rather depressing occurrences, and the need to demonstrate moral superiority—in a Communist sense—to the Soviet Union to compensate for the latter's obvious technological and economic superiority and Communist 'seniority'.)

This new doctrine in its turn set in train, or was accompanied by, a number of practical steps. In the first place the social and economic inequalities between the various grades and strata were diminished, and some privileges abolished. Efforts were made to cut down administrative staff and to send party officials back to work in outlying districts. Many measures which anticipated the post-Stalin 'thaw' in the Soviet Union were introduced, or decreed. Emphasis was placed on 'socialist legality', compulsory participation in political activities was substantially reduced, and a measure of real freedom was permitted in the arts and literature.

These fruits of the conflict between the Yugoslav and Soviet Communist Parties created fresh political problems for the CPY leadership. In the first place, extensions of political democracy, far from reconciling the public to socialism, provided weapons by which it effectively resisted official social and economic policy. Peasants took advantage of their right to leave the collectives, many of which collapsed overnight; once the fear of arbitrary arrest and imprisonment was lessened, people became increasingly intractable. Some of the younger and more idealistic sections of the party pressed for even further democratization. Other sections of the party came to resent the new dispensation with growing bitterness, as their privileges were curtailed, or at least threatened, and as they were increasingly deprived of the means of coercion in order to implement policies which could not be implemented in any other way. Their opposition to further progress on Titoist lines took the form of passive resistance— privileges were maintained in defiance of regulations, socialist legality was violated, etc., and was also expressed politically, partly in new outbreaks of pro-Stalinism and partly in overt opposition at the highest level. In November 1962 Blagoe Neskovic, a member of the politburo, who tried to cry 'halt', was obliged to resign all his party posts and vanished from public life.

In spite of all their misgivings at the rumbling from their own party and the intransigence of the population, the leaders of the CPY saw no alternative but to press on with their Titoism; the logic of their relations with the USSR seemed to leave them no alternative. Stalin's death changed the situation radically, for a time at least. Negotiations between the two governments began almost immediately and in June 1953 a few months after Stalin died, 'normalization' of relations between the two states was announced. Press attacks ceased. Before the month was out the Central Committee of the League of Yugoslav Communists (as it came to be called after the Sixth Congress in 1952) had met at Brioni and issued a statement calling for a general tightening up of party discipline and 'democratic centralism', and for an assault on reaction and 'anarchism'.

The next two years saw the retreat from the 'high Titoism' of 1951–53 and increasingly cordial relations with the Soviet Union. One of the first casualties of this change was Milovan Djilas, who not only resisted the retreat from high Titoism, but attempted to take the new doctrine to its logical conclusion by advocating the abolition of the political monopoly of the Communist Party.

Djilas wanted freedom of discussion for critics of the CPY, recognition that the party itself can become an obstacle to the further development of democracy, abolition of the party's official status and power and its conversion into an association concerned with the dissemination of ideas and influence only, and liquidation of the professional party machine. He also showed how the party's monopoly of power had turned the cadres into a morally corrupt caste in Yugoslavia no less than in the USSR. Above all, he broke through the accepted convention in Titoist theorizing of dealing with the 'withering away of the state' in isolation from the party's role as an integral part of state power.

The Party's answer to Djilas was fundamentally a re-statement of Stalin's thesis on the State, with the term 'party' substituted for the term 'state'. The withering away of the Party must be a lengthy process, Tito insisted, and cannot be expected to take place before the last class enemy has been rendered incapable of action, before Socialist consciousness has permeated all layers of the population. Till then neither liquidation nor withering away of the Party could be considered; on the contrary, it would need strengthening. The class struggle which the Party would have to conduct would continue for a long time, until the construction of Socialism was complete and Communism was finally reached.

Djilas's own statement before the Plenum of the Central Committee expressed Titoism's predicament most clearly. In the course of the campaign against the Soviet Union, Djilas confessed he had gone on to criticize things in Yugoslavia which appeared similar, and, apprehensive of the dangers of 'bureaucratism', had step by step carried his criticism further. This had led him into abstract democratic theory, favourable to the petty bourgeoisie and 'Social-democratism' of the Western stamp.

In other words, criticism of the Soviet system led ineluctably to criticism of Yugoslav Communism. But the decision whether or not to criticize the Soviet system never depended on the CPY leaders alone; in 1954, when discussions for the complete liquidation of the

1948 'misunderstanding' were proceeding, and the groundwork for Khrushchev's visit to Belgrade was being laid, it was relatively simple for the CPY to suspend criticism of the Soviet Union and to assert that Soviet society had proved healthy enough to overcome distortions introduced by the 'personality cult', and that all major defects had been repaired since Stalin's death.

But whenever Moscow or Peking begins again to exert pressure on the Yugoslavs to fall into line, and again begins to 'use weapons from the arsenal of the Cominform'—as Belgrade puts it—then the CPY, however reluctantly, is again forced to renew its criticism of Soviet, Chinese and satellite 'bureaucratism' and 'dogmatism'.

This predicament runs through subsequent attempts to codify Yugoslav Communist theory, of which the 1958 'Programme of the League of Yugoslav Communists'[5] is the most representative and thoroughgoing. (The Programme was already out of date by the time it was printed. Increasing Soviet and Chinese pressure on Yugoslavia provoked hostile reactions from Belgrade,[6] which inevitably involved less favourable appraisals of the Soviet and Chinese regimes.)

The Programme represents an attempt to provide a coherent ideology for independent Communism, reconciling absolute power of the Communist Party within the boundaries of the national—or multinational—state with undiminished state sovereignty vis-à-vis other states, Communist and non-Communist alike.

This requires a fine balance between incompatibles. On the one hand the programme insists on the sole truth of 'scientific socialism', the reactionary nature of capitalism, its increasing tendency to apply fascist and other anti-democratic methods in suppressing revolutionary and democratic movements, its intensified exploitation of the labouring classes, the evils of imperialism, and the danger of further wars. On the other hand it insists that Marxist thought has, for some decades, been lagging behind events, and that Communist countries can reproduce the negative features associated with capitalism.

On the one hand the programme insists on the principle of 'proletarian internationalism', which includes solidarity with the working-class struggle for socialism everywhere; on the other hand it denounces all interference by one country in the internal affairs of another. On the one hand it insists that capitalism has exhausted all its possibilities and can no longer endanger or obstruct the advance of the socialist forces, and on the other hand it insists that 'imperialist hegemony' constantly threatens a new world war. On the one hand it asserts that

[5] Seventh Congress of the League of Communists of Yugoslavia, *Kultura*, Belgrade, 1958.

[6] *Kommunist*, Belgrade, May 1958; Tito, June 15, 1958; Kardelj in *Socialism and War—a review of Chinese criticism of the Policy of Co-Existence*. Yugoslav statements on Chinese policies manage to combine the suggestion that the Chinese variant of Marxism produces something strange, barbaric, and hardly recognizable, with the assertion that Moscow's influence is really to blame.

a country's economic and cultural level determines its social relationships and the rate at which it can liberate itself from bureaucratic
tendencies; on the other hand it claims that Yugoslavia has the most
advanced social system of any country, though it is economically
and culturally backward not only vis-à-vis the West but also in comparison with other Communist-ruled countries. The programme
denounces dogma but insists that the 'scientific truths' and prophecies
of Marx and Engels are above question.

The entire programme is made up of contradictions of this kind;
there is scarcely a single thesis in it that is not followed by its antithesis. The reader might be tempted to dismiss it as a farrago of
nonsense; yet it was put out, after careful and detailed discussion, by
representatives of a party which had proved capable of seizing and
retaining power under quite difficult conditions, and of extracting
large-scale economic aid from wealthier states. It is also a party
which understands contradictions; the answer to this apparent inconsistency is that the contradictions which fill the programme are real
contradictions faced by Yugoslav 'National Communism'.

Any criticism of Marxism-Leninism, or the admission that 'bourgeois democracy' has progressive features, threatens to undermine
the ideological justification for the party's monopoly of power. Yet
the CPY leadership must retain complete freedom to denounce the
Soviet system and ideology whenever relations between the two
countries deteriorate, in order to defend itself from Soviet allegations
of disloyalty to the Socialist camp. It must also have justifications of
the West ready to hand in case it is again forced to rely on the West
for economic, military, and political aid. So its theory has to be
ambiguous.

Current CPY theory has nothing to say on the impact of inter-
Communist feuding on developments inside the Communist countries, Yugoslavia in particular. While Titoism was still defined mainly
by opposition to Soviet pressure, there was general empirical recognition that the split had served to initiate a reconsideration of doctrine
and an amelioration of the regime. Now this is no longer admitted,
though many benefits of de-Stalinization remain.

The programme avoids analysing the implications of the problem
of relations between Communist states, where power must be legiti-
mized by theory, and where disagreement is tantamount to challenging
legitimacy. It argues that so long as nations themselves do not wither
away, Communism will have to remain within the framework of
national states. It does not admit the possibility of a conflict between
Communist and state interests, or recognize the tendency for nationalism to reassert itself inside the Communist world as Communist parties
become rooted.

The glimmerings of self-criticism sparked by the struggle with the
Soviet Union did not survive the Djilas affair. In particular, where

the role of the Communist Party is concerned, the CPY is again portrayed as a *deus ex machina*, a vanguard exempt from tendencies which may affect other mortals. 'The mechanism of our political and economic system is an insurmountable barrier to a bureaucratization of the League of Communists of Yugoslavia . . . the League, in addition to creating conditions for a more complete development of Socialism, protects itself against the possibility of bureaucratization . . . against methods of dragooning the people . . . of becoming a brake on further progress.'[7]

It is now thirteen years since the break between the CPY and CPSU came into the open, and a decade since Titoism developed its most characteristic features. Since then Yugoslav revisionism has inevitably been overshadowed by much greater changes in other parts of the Communist world following Stalin's death. In fact, whereas this event brought about the 'thaw' in the USSR, the satellites, and, belatedly, in China, it marked the beginning of the re-freeze in Yugoslavia, though, of course, many beneficial effects of the Titoist thaw have remained in operation in Yugoslavia.

In addition to revisionist ideas or practices inherent in the Yugoslav-Soviet conflict, and denounced by Soviet spokesmen, the CPY leaders have introduced departures from Stalinist practice which have invited less severe Soviet criticism. The most important is in economic planning, which gives the market a role to play. 'The present social plan of Yugoslavia establishes the basic proportions in social production and distribution, assuming within these ratios free initiative of economic enterprises under market conditions and state regulation.' These measures are supervised, according to the Programme, by Workers' Councils and the Party. Ironically enough, the theoretical justification for this development—namely that 'at present . . . the laws of commodity production also operate in the economic system of Yugoslavia. . . . Denying the laws of value and other laws of the market does not strengthen the socialist elements in the economy but weakens them, chains initiative, and does harm. . . .'—does not basically differ from the views expressed by Stalin in his 1952 treatise on the laws of value under Socialism.

In any evaluation of Yugoslav revisionism it has to be borne in mind that at any given time the CPY, like any other Communist Party, is likely to be deliberately underplaying or overplaying differences of doctrine out of political considerations. During the 1948–53 period, first the Russians, then the Yugoslavs, did their best to magnify the difference between them; during the reconciliation period they did their best to minimize them; during the subsequent deteri-

---

[7] The 'withering away of the state', in the sense of exercising party control through a range of media other than the Central Government, has become a commonplace in the USSR, and China, as well as in Yugoslavia. See 'Totalitarianism without Coercion?' by H. Ritvo in *Problems of Communism*, 6/1960.

oration of relations Soviet publicists did their best to exaggerate differences, the Yugoslavs to minimize them.[8]

More emphasis has been given in this essay to political developments and less to analysis of the ideas themselves than might seem necessary in dealing with political theory. But if any sense at all is to be made out of Tito's amazing tergiversations, it is that the ideology with which tactical manoeuvres are ritualized has an innate tendency to acquire an independent life of its own, and to lead to results its creators had never intended. If Djilas, pygmalion-like, was overjoyed when his creation came to life, the majority of his comrades were embarrassed, and the subsequent history of Titoism can only be understood as the quest for an equilibrium between independence and orthodoxy. This quest is still continuing. Though Tito has solved the problem of 'co-existence with states of a different regime and philosophy', his efforts to find a basis for co-existence with his fellow-Communists have met with considerably less success.

[8] Cf. *Kommunist*, 6/1958.

XIX. The Revisionism in Soviet Economics

ALFRED ZAUBERMAN

Before setting out to write this short sketch I had tried to make sure of my terms of reference. My bearings have been provided by the standard definition of revisionism. I shall attempt then to trace the 're-examination, distortion and negation' of Marxist doctrine in Soviet economic thinking, but admit that I am rather at a loss as to the qualifying criterion which is, that this should tend to 'debase, emasculate, destroy' Marxism, and should do so specifically 'for the benefit of the bourgeoisie'. Routine Soviet comment on revisionism in economics is mainly concerned with developments in non-Soviet writing; hence most of the issues it conventionally treats lie outside the compass of this note. Nor shall I try to consider the reference to my subject of a significant statement in a recent Soviet symposium, to the effect that 'in no [previous] historical epoch was there such a *spiritual closeness* of revisionism, reformism and bourgeois political economy as there is at present'.[1] My general contention will be that developments in Soviet economic life are gradually pushing the operative doctrine away from Marxism, and that such a long-term trend—revisionist in the sense just defined—is distinctly discernible.

It will become clear that the developments in Soviet thought with which we shall deal centre on Marx's theory of value. It may therefore be useful at this stage to say something on the history of its critique and to relate it to these developments. In this the role of the theory of value as the heart of Marxian doctrine and ideology will be brought into relief. We shall not dwell on individual critics such as Mrs Joan Robinson (her famous aside on 'Hegelian stuff and nonsense'),[2] or the Oskar Lange[3] of a quarter of a century ago, who deny

---

[1] *Kritika sovremennykh burzhuaznykh, reformistkikh i revizionnistskikh uchenii,* Moscow, 1960, p. 33. My italics.

[2] *On Re-Reading Marx,* London, 1950.

[3] He said a quarter of a century ago that the labour theory of value . . . 'has no qualities which would make it, from the Marxist point of view, superior to modern elaborate theory of economic equilibrium. It is only a more primitive form of the latter restricted to the narrow field of pure competition, and not without its limitations even in this field.' *Review of Economic Studies,* June 1935, p. 195.

the necessity of a value theory as such; or Rudolf Schlesinger,[4] to whom the labour theory of value seems useful as a methodological approach but with no influence on price relations—something like a deity presiding over a system without ruling it. We have to concern ourselves more with criticism from the standpoint of alternative value theories, since this has relevance for what is happening in Soviet economics today.

The first frontal attack on Marx's theory of value was launched by Böhm-Bawerk. Within two years of the publication of the third volume of *Capital*, *Zum Abschluss des Marxschen Systems*[5] appeared (1896) from the pen of this brilliant representative of the Austrian school; and the years have detracted little from its importance as the classic refutation of Marx's value conception. Böhm-Bawerk was the first to point out the inconsistencies which still worry its students; having tried to bring the conflicting elements of the first and third volume of *Capital* to some common denominator, he contended that 'Marx has not deduced from facts the fundamental principles of his system, either by means of a sound empiricism or a solid economico-psychological analysis'. In his reasoning he lays the main stress on the latter, but the bulk of the essay is devoted to demonstrating that 'the system (i.e. Marx's value-theory system) runs in one direction, facts go in another', that this is indeed its radical fault 'at its birth', which begets other contradictions. Böhm-Bawerk concludes that Marx's system, founded 'on no firmer ground than a formal dialectic' has 'a past and a present but no abiding future', it is surely doomed as are all scientific systems 'based on a hollow dialectic'.[6]

Before long Böhm-Bawerk's critique obtained further powerful support from one of the founding fathers of modern mathematical economics. Pareto's reasoning on the subject in *Les Systemes Socialistes*[7] runs parallel to that of Böhm-Bawerk. He questions in particular the validity of a system in which crystallized labour is taken as the substance of value of commodities, but exchange ratios agree with this proposition only in a specific demand/supply situation, thus depriving it of generality. As in Böhm-Bawerk, the original Paretian challenge has been made from positions of marginal-utility but it linked the critique with the mathematical school's basic equilibrium approach in general, and thus with its subsequent ramifications and refinements.

Rigorous argument apart, Pareto was able to point to the religious

[4] *Marx, His Times and Ours*, London, 1950.
[5] The latest English translation is contained in *Karl Marx and the Close of his System*, edited with a very interesting introduction by Paul M. Sweezy. The book contains also a translation of Hilferding's critique of Böhm-Bawerk's essay.
[6] All quotations from *op. cit.*, Sweezy's edition, p. 101.
[7] See in particular the chapters 'L'économie marxiste' and 'La théorie matérialiste de l'histoire et la lutte des classes', in Vilfredo Pareto, *Les Systèmes Socialistes*, 1st ed., Paris, 1902; there is no English translation.

character which Marx's theory of value and the 'law' based on it had acquired.[8] At the time he wrote *Les Systemes* it was already the basis of the ideological platform of the Marxist movement. Since, according to the 'law of value', surplus value was proportionate only to that part of capital which is paid out in wages, the theory became the basis of the doctrine of the capitalist exploitation of wage-earners. Hence it became to the Marxist movement the theoretical justification of the call for a revolutionary overthrow of the capitalist economic, social and political formation.

Thus the battle royal between Marxist and non-Marxist thought was joined twenty years before the October Revolution, and the principal battlefield was marginalism versus labour theory of value. In the realm of theory, marginalism became for dogmatic Marxians arch-enemy No. 1, and their implacable hostility embraced the Lausanne variant, the mathematical school and approach (whether there was an explicit utility concept underlying it or not). Its method, its analysis of intra-economy relationships, and its apparatus became Trojan horses that could not be allowed to pass the labour-theory-of-value trenches of Marxism. Moreover, because of its ideological significance, the value theory obtained a very strict stamp of *non-varietur*: true, certain attempts have been made to reconcile the two antagonist approaches—they still continue today—but the very attempt at reconciliation came to be considered by Marxist doctrinaires as revisionist. Dr Meek[9] has tried to justify this attitude in a way which is in itself eloquent: Marxists have been encouraged in their opposition to suggestions to reconcile the labour theory of value with the marginal utility theory, as well as to suggestions to

[8] Note his general remarks on Marx's theoretical thinking: 'Mais il y a chez Marx une partie sociologique, qui est supérieure aux autres, et qui se trouve souvent d'accord avec la réalité. Marx a une idée très nette: celle de la lutte des classes; c'est cette idée qui inspire toute son action pratique, et il lui subordonne toutes ses recherches théoriques. Celles-ci ne sont qu'un moyen pour atteindre un but qui existe indépendamment de ces recherches. C'est ce qui distingue la foi de la science; la foi admet que ses vérités soient confirmées par la science, mais elle ne tolère pas que la science les contredise.' Cf. *Les Systèmes Socialistes*, 2nd ed., vol. II, p. 338.

On Marxists' mode of interpretation of Marx's doctrine, he wrote: 'Si vous élevez des objections contre un passage du *Capital*, dont le sens vous parait incontestable, on peut vous en citer un autre, dont le sens est entierèment différent. C'est toujours la fable de la chauve-souris. Si vous adoptez un sens, on vous repond:

> Je suis oiseau; voyez mes ailes;
> Vive gent qui fend les airs!

Et si vous adoptez l'autre, on vous dit:

> Je suis souris; vivent les rats;
> Jupiter confonde les chats!'

Ibid., p. 342.

[9] *Studies in the Labour Theory of Value*, London, 1956. This is a scholarly account of the critique of the labour theory of value, written from a strictly Marxist point of view.

eliminate it from Marxist doctrine, by the observable fact 'that many of those within their own rank who have criticized the labour theory of value have eventually shown themselves to be interested not so much in purging labour theory from Marxism as in *purging Marxism itself from the ideology of the labour movement*' (our italics).

Such mental and indeed emotional attitudes, set long before the Bolsheviks seized power in Russia, formed part of their intellectual and ideological heritage. Apparently it never occurred to any of their thinkers that, nearly half a century after they took over control of the Russian economy, the question might arise of empirically testing the validity of the two irreconcilable rival approaches to the value theory in the light of facts; that is, testing it on the ground suggested by Böhm-Bawerk.

This raises another point of considerable relevance. It is that Marxists, when in control of a society heading towards communism, could not really envisage a test of value theories within it, if only because they would not expect the phenomenon of value to survive capitalism. Marx's vision of the post-capitalist society remained nebulous in his writing. But in one of the very few references to it, in an *obiter dictum* of the *Critique of the Gotha Programme*, he gave it as his opinion that 'within the co-operative society based on common ownership of the means of production, the producers do not exchange their products; *just as little does the labour employed on the products appear here as the value of products*, as the material quality possessed by them, since now, in contrast to capitalist society, individual labour no longer exists in an indirect fashion, but directly as a component part of the labour' (our italics). Obscure and contradictory as Marx's other indications of the distribution principles may be, this one clearly sounded the death-knell of the 'law' of value. And indeed what else could be compatible in logic with a theory which deals with exchange value as distinct from use value? Could the 'law' survive once exchange had been eliminated? It is exchange which in Marx's system turns goods into commodities. Such, at any rate, was the traditional interpretation of Marx's view of post-capitalist society, which again fitted in well ideologically with the socialists' emotional attitudes, their anti-money idiosyncrasies— Kautsky traced them as far back as Thomas More's *Utopia*.[10]

Against this background, it is not surprising that the focal issue on which the revisionist movement centres in Soviet economics is that of value both as a concept and a historical phenomenon. To begin with the latter; the first important stage in the revision of the doctrine was its attempted reconciliation with the survival of commodity relations in a post-capitalist society which, in the 1930s, was proclaimed to have reached the stage of socialism.[11] Apart from the

[10] *Thomas More and His Utopia*, English translation, New York, 1927.
[11] See on this my remarks in *Review of Economic Studies*, vol. XVI, p. 1.

crude interlude of War Communism, born of disasters and itself disastrous, the first phase of the planning era—in which the economy was controlled by central administrative fiat, framed basically in physical terms with little reference to price—seemed to support and feed the nostalgic Marxist hankering after a money-free, price-free society; the hankering that formed such a strong emotional under-current in pre-revolutionary Russian Marxism. As the economy grew and became increasingly complex, the Marxian conception was showing itself patently more and more unrealistic. More recently, the Khrushchev era has seen the elimination of certain obstinate 'natural', non-money, elements in the Soviet economy inherited from the past —the abolition of compulsory deliveries of farm produce, and of payment in kind for the services of machine and tractor stations, and the gradual substitution of wage-type remuneration for dividends in kind as part-reward for the labour of collective farmers.

Stalin perceived the clash between the needs of the maturing eco-nomy and the accepted teaching, encouraged revisionist thinking on this subject in the '40s, and eventually himself revised the doctrine in his last contribution to the theory of socialism.[12] He did so, however, for no more than a circumscribed sphere of economic life, accepting as a fact the existence of commodity and exchange relations outside but not within the socialist sector par excellence (that is, the State sector). *Ce n'est que le premier pas qui coûte.* Once Marx had been put in the wrong on this point, other changes were bound to follow. The role of money and price as instruments of planning and control grew in the second part of the fifties as a result of changes in the economic environment and the institutional and organizational re-forms carried out by the Khrushchev administration. The general climate has been in any case somewhat more favourable to pragmatic thinking. In the latter fifties a great debate was initiated, with obvious official blessing and the clear purpose of completing the revision of the Marxist tenet. (For those interested in the way it performed its task there is already a voluminous and tedious Soviet literature on the subject.[13]) Apart from a few dissidents, the general conclusion estab-lished in the process is that, far from dying-off as Marx expected, the 'law of value' strengthens its sway in a society as it approaches com-munism. Appearances have been saved by the acceptance of the tenet that, by some dialectical leap vaguely hinted at, the 'law' will lose its hold at the point of its final consummation.

Once the rule of the 'law' under socialism was doctrinally estab-lished, the next issue to be tackled was that of its quantification, that is, of devising a rational price formula. Apart from being very arbi-trarily applied, the formula traditionally adopted by Soviet practice

[12] In his *Economic Problems of Socialism in the USSR*, Moscow, 1952.
[13] For an account see my: 'The Soviet Debate on the Law of Value and Price Formation' in *Value and Plan*, ed. G. Grossman, Berkeley, 1960.

(based on circumscribed average prime cost, plus a negligible profit margin related to it) has proved a highly insensitive tool for the central planners in their economic choice-making, and irrational as a guide for lower echelons of the economy. During the debate of the fifties one or two more important seeds of deviation from Marx on this subject were planted, but on the whole the discussion remained rather inconclusive and has had little effect on Soviet practice.[14] It gained in depth and intensity around the turn of the decade, when it was rechannelled into exploration of mathematical avenues in the planning and running of an economy. How the 'invasion of Soviet economics by mathematics and machines' came about calls for a special study: Kulev, a participant in a Soviet conference on the subject held in April 1960, remarked that the post-1957, organizationally restructured Soviet economy, lent itself to a more adequate description in simple equations. Another and eminent Soviet economist, Prof. Notkin, suggested in his address to the same conference that as the Soviet economy grows—I would say as its growth becomes stabilized—'its optimality becomes more and more synthesized in a few categories of political economy':[15] which may seem to make easier a mathematical formulation and solution of its problems. The indefatigable promotion of mathematical concepts in the economic thinking practice of the Soviet Union—and the countries in its orbit —is especially closely connected with two distinguished names, Academician Nemchinov in the Soviet Union, and Professor Oskar Lange in Poland.

Lange's role certainly merits an exceptional emphasis. Attention should be drawn in particular to his essays, published three years ago, on Marxism and bourgeois economics.[16] He proceeds there from the Marxian proposition that economic thinking is inevitably class conditioned, and his further argument is broadly this: The neo-classics, from Marshall onwards, made a breach in 'vulgarized' political economy; marginalism has become the basis of petty-bourgeois criticism at the monopolist stage of capitalism, and paved the way for a fruitful analysis of monopoly, oligopoly and imperfect competition. Welfare economics thus appears as a critique of monopoly capitalism from the angle of socio-economic rationality. Moreover, for a variety of reasons, the monopolist, in contrast to the earlier capitalist entrepreneur, has an interest in an effective and correct analysis of the

[14] The present state of the debate is clearly reflected in *Zakon Stoimosti i evo ispolzovanie v narodnom Khoziaistve SSSR*, ed. Ya. Ya. Kronrod, Moscow, 1959, a collection of essays by authors covering the whole range of views. A useful exposition of the price controversy may be found in T. Khachaturov, *Voprosy Ekonomiki*, No. 1, 1961. A valuable discussion of the wider issues of planning and control involved in the methodology of pricing is contained in A. Nove's textbook on Soviet economics, to be published shortly.

[15] *Voprosy Ekonomiki*, No. 8, 1960.

[16] *Polityka*, Nos. 9 and 10, 1958.

market as a basis for his profit, output, and price policies. For similar reasons the capitalist State, as it becomes more and more interventionist, looks for guidance to scientific economics. Lastly, the professionalization of bourgeois economics has been another factor favouring the return of bourgeois economics to its earlier intellectual integrity. The renaissance in bourgeois economics happened at the time when the construction of socialism in the first socialist country was already nearing completion: at any rate, its builders were affected by prejudices inherited from the apologetist phase of bourgeois economics. Their self-imposed isolation, however, condemned them to 'primitive empiricist methods'. Worse still, Soviet economics had turned into a defence of 'the interests of some social groups, interests in conflict with the requirements of further social progress'. The shoe was now on the other foot: in its turn, Marxist economics fell into an 'apologetico-dogmatic' degeneration.

These ideas of Lange have been partly expanded and supplemented in his subsequent attempt[17] to formulate—in a systematized treatise —a philosophical frame for the assimilation of post-Marx Western concepts and techniques. Central to his argument there is his inquiry into the principle of rationality in economic activities (a subject hitherto studiously shunned in Soviet and Soviet-influenced literature, clearly because of the danger that some taboos and dogmas would be undermined). This has led Lange to a general theory of purposeful human activity, or the efficiency dilemma. The approach would bring into relief the general place taken by the modern armoury of theoretical and applied economics in the quest for the most efficient ways of using means in the pursuit of ends; this is a problem to which the Soviet Union of the Khrushchev era has become increasingly sensitive as its economy moves from a highly extensive to a more intensive phase of development.

The signal lack of any violent reaction in Soviet writing to Lange's bitter words (there have been only sporadic outbursts of criticism), may support the hypothesis that it was not unwelcome to those in control of such matters to have the ticklish issues of a rejuvenation of Marxist economics—and especially the question of the doctrinally safe limits for borrowing from Western thought—thrashed out in the orbit rather than at home. The decisive consideration must have been the possible gains for the Soviet mechanism of planning and control, whose inadequacy was by that time widely recognized.

It should be pointed out that Soviet economics has hitherto had a deep distrust of econometrics, looked upon as *per se* revisionist; its deeply ingrained conservatism in any case militated against any innovation, and economists confined themselves largely to the ideologically safe restatement of dogmas. Questions relating to the quantification of economic phenomena were carefully dodged; 'quantitative

[17] See his *Ekonomia Polityczna—Zagadnienia Ogolne*, Warsaw, 1959.

analysis—Academician Nemchinov incisively remarked—has now become one of the "bottlenecks" of Soviet economic science'.[18] This may appear a true paradox in a country where the very nature of a planned economy would appear to call for a sophisticated theory of the quantitative examination of economic life, as the foundation for consciously influencing it. But then, as the famous Soviet mathematician Kantorovich noted, not without a touch of sarcasm, Soviet planning too is 'qualitative' rather than quantitative: hence, he says, the constituent parts of the plan are ill-fitting, the choices accidental, the planning decisions outdated, 'the best solutions are only rarely adopted'.[19] However, fortunately for themselves, the champions of the econometric approach have been able to unearth some useful *obiter dicta* in the classics to show that they were not really hostile to mathematics: indeed, its use by Marx in his equations of 'expanded reproduction', and by Lenin in his description of the marketing of social product—elementary as it is in both cases—has become a useful argument in support of Marxist-Leninist respectability for these novelties.

However, the remarkable fact is that once the plea for the assimilation of mathematical methodologies in Soviet economics became acceptable, it was discovered that the Soviet Union possessed the nucleus of a brilliant mathematical school; one which hitherto had had no influence on either theory or practice. We may in this context ignore the Soviet claim that the mind of Professor Leontief, the famous American author of input-output analysis, i.e. of analysis of inter-industrial inter-dependencies, was initially fertilized by the experience gained and the ideas imbibed in the Soviet milieu of the twenties. In any case, the conceptual scaffolding and the computational procedures for linear programming (a powerful mathematical technique for selecting the most efficient among feasible solutions, which enables technological and economic problems to be put into the simplified form of a 'straight-line' equation constrained by 'straight-line' inequalities) were devised in the late 1930s, independently of and indeed chronologically even before the similar Western achievement, by the famous Soviet mathematician Kantorovich.[20] There has now been discovered a galaxy of first-class scholars—pure and applied mathematicians—who can be drawn upon to develop Soviet econometrics and mathematical techniques rapidly. There can be no doubt that they have already succeeded in inspiring a good deal of confidence in—and indeed enthusiasm for—mathematical economics among a large part of the economic profession.

[18] In *Voprosy Ekonomiki*, No. 6, 1960, p. 13.
[19] *Ekonomicheski raschet nailuchshevo ispolzovaniya resursov*, Moscow, 1959, p. 9.
[20] In his *Matematicheskiye Metody organizatsii i planirovanya proizvodstva*, Leningrad, 1939, reprinted in *Primenenye matematiki v ekonomicheskikh issledovanyakh*, ed. V. S. Nemchinov, Moscow, 1959, pp. 251–309.

I shall say nothing here on the technical side of the methodologies, which are of course decisive. Nor shall I try to predict their ultimate effect in improving the planners' box of tools, though I would mention in passing that a good deal of experimenting is going on with this box in the USSR, Poland, and Hungary, and that these experiments have shown gains in terms of time and precision as well as certain weaknesses. In particular, the Polish experiments, perhaps the most conclusive so far, seem to have led to rather cautious and gradualist attitudes. They would suggest that, with the vast number of decision variables and constraints involved, at the present stage of 'modelling' and of computational routines and equipment, mathematical techniques of choice-making still have a limited scope at the level of the economy as a whole. But even at this stage they have been found helpful in providing an important all-economy analytical insight, in securing a fair degree of growth-equilibrium in the system, and in devising a system of rational prices. (This is the crucial point, since faulty prices are one of the most vulnerable features of the Soviet economic mechanism.)

The point is, however, that the price arrived at in the calculus—like the one implied in the optimal-solution—turns out to be in unmistakable conflict with that derived from Marx. Marx's price is a cost price, while the conservative Soviet critics of the two representative protagonists of the mathematical scheme, Kantorovich and Novozhilov,[21] correctly identified their value-weights as scarcity prices, typically marginalist in their nature. Many of these critics—especially Boyarski, Kats, Kronrod, Gatovski[22]—have rightly pointed to the deep roots of the mathematicians' price in the subjective value concept, and to its incompatibility with Marx's objective value, reducible to 'congealed' socially-necessary labour. 'L. V. Kantorovich,' the two last-named critics remarked in an article published in the central organ of the party, 'has connected his elaboration of mathematical methods designed for the economic calculus in the all-economy scale with a re-examination [in the original 's peresmotrom'—a milder term for revisionism] of the Marxist labour theory of value. In its essence his conception rests on an attempt to reconcile the irreconcilable, Marx's value theory with a variant of the "theory

[21] For Kantorovich's system see his *Ekonomicheskiy raschet* . . . , *op. cit.*; *Matematicheskie metody* . . . , *op. cit.*, and 'Dalneysheye razvitye matematicheskikh metodov i perspektivy ikh primenenya v planirovanii i ekonomike' in *Matematicheskie metody* . . . , ed. Nemchinov, *op. cit.*, and *Voprosy Ekonomiki*, No. 1, 1960. For Novozhilov's system see his 'Izmerenie zatrat i ikh rezultatov v sotsialisticheskom khoziaistve' in *Matematicheskie metody* . . . , ed. Nemchinov, and *Voprosy Ekonomiki*, No. 2, 1961.

[22] For this criticism see Boyarski in *Planovoe Khoziaistvo*, No. 1, 1960, p. 93, and *ibid.*, No. 7, 1960, p. 70; and *Voprosy Ekonomiki*, No. 2, 1961; Kats, *Voprosy Ekonomiki*, No. 5, 1960, p. 107, *ibid.*, No. 11, 1960; see also contributions by them and Kronrod and Gatovski at the conference mentioned, *Voprosy Ekonomiki*, No. 8, 1960, pp. 100ff.

of marginal utility", with marginal systems of valuation (these valuations are constructed, not on the basis of social-labour expenditure, but by the yardstick of "marginal utility" that is of the utility of the last unit of a given product which meets the buyer's least indispensable need).'[23]

It is highly characteristic of the present climate that Soviet economists—especially Nemchinov and Novozhilov—have rediscovered and found inspiration in a Russian mathematical economist, of exceptional brilliance, who wrote at the beginning of this century and in many respects anticipated the trend in contemporary thought. His remarkable work, long forgotten and now unearthed, had a significant sub-title: 'Attempt of an organic synthesis of the labour theory of value [in its Ricardian version—A.Z.] with the marginal utility theory.'[24]

One ideological implication is particularly worrying to the conservative Marxist. In Marx, the productive contributions of prime factors other than labour are passed on to the new product without adding to its value. This tenet stems logically from a scheme in which value is identified with 'objective' labour productivity, without the latter being broken down into its contributive elements. But the tenet was detached from its qualifying assumptions and acquired the rank of an absolute unqualified dogma. In its dogmatic formulation, the way value is transferred to products has an almost transcendental character, and indeed forms one of the metaphysical elements in Marxist materialism. In contrast, in the mathematician's scheme, the portmanteau concept of labour productivity is broken down. Each prime factor is revealed as an independent contributor to the product-value, and the relative scarcity of each of them (under given supply-demand and technological conditions) emerges as the measure of its own value. It is in this way that the basis of rational pricing of factors —of land, equipment, of this or that kind of skill, of unskilled labour and so on—is established. The clash with Marx's teaching, as traditionally expounded, is here so acute that it is not really surprising that it became the rallying point for the anti-revisionists. (Other points in their critique of the price structure arrived at by the mathematicians—in particular that it may at best correspond to a static situation, that it does not allow for technological progress; that it is consequently unsuitable for constructing a dynamic plan, that indeed it would inhibit the growth of the economy—all these points, though deserving serious consideration, lie outside the scope of our present theme and are therefore disregarded here.)

Here we may pause in our discussion of the purely economic aspects

[23] *Kommunist*, No. 15, 1960, p. 86.
[24] V. K. Dmitrev, *Ekonomicheskie Ocherki*, St Petersburg, 1904. For an interesting discussion of his approach see Ladislaus von Bortkiewicz, *Archiv fuer Sozialwissenschaft und Sozialpolitik*, 1907, vol. 25, especially pp. 28ff.

of the revision of Marx's reasoning, and turn to its projection into the domain of social and political relations. The doctrine of labour as the exclusive value-building factor is the basis of Marx's teaching on surplus value. It therefore forms the basis of Marx's social diagnosis and his system of social and political morality. It underlies the critique of capitalist society from the ethical angle as well as his critique of the efficiency of an atomistic, free-enterprise market mechanism. In this sense it forms the very cornerstone of the Marxian *Weltanschaung*. *Per contra*, in a scheme where valuations measure the availability of productive facilities, technologically necessary to produce the flow of goods of desired kind and quantity, value becomes ethically neutral. This is why it robs Marxian economics of much of its emotional load, why revision on this point is branded as apologetist (apologetist, that is, for a capitalist society). Whatever the merits of the mathematician's price as an efficiency instrument, it was bound to cause serious concern because of its repercussions on the ideological heart of Marx's doctrine.

One or two further points deserve attention here. The very mode of thinking, characteristic of the mathematical school, is unfamiliar to the Soviet Marxist traditionalist. The elementary efficiency concept which underlies Kantorovich's scheme of valuations is that—at an optimum—marginal products with alternative uses which *compete* for scarce resources should be made equal: it is precisely this *competition*, which equalizes opportunities so that the overall yield cannot be improved by any allocational shift in any direction, which is the logic of its being *the* optimum. Hence the best the planner can do in his office is to imitate an equilibrium model of a perfectly *competitive* model, to stage in his calculations a *competitive* struggle. I shall not discuss whether and in what sense this clashes with Marx's efficiency concept, but to the Soviet economist it is psychologically repugnant.

The Soviet mathematical school has no doubt put a good deal of genuine effort into fitting themselves into the Marxian framework, at least semantically. But their thought is essentially alien to Marx; its parentage by-passes him and leads to Jevons, Menger, Walras, Cassel, Pareto, Barone, Schumpeter, and contemporary Western econometrics. One can appreciate the Soviet economists' intellectual predicament. It was aired at the conference (referred to previously in this note) by Academician Kronrod as restatement of the Schumpeter thesis that it is to non-Marxian Western thought that socialism owes the fundamentals of a rational theory of its economy.[25]

Over the last two or three years, the links between Soviet and Western non-Marxist economic thought have grown in a remarkable way owing to the mathematicians. There are in this process certain rules of play to which the Soviet economists adhere. For example: a

[25] *Voprosy Ekonomiki*, No. 8, 1960, p. 106.

Soviet academic writer will take up the theme of the 'apologetic nature of the econometric theory of strategic games' (this is the actual title of a paper published in a theoretical journal).[26] Then he or someone else will acquaint the Soviet reader with the equivalence between the model of one class of these games and the model of linear programming, hence with its relevance for efficient planning; hence with its practical interest for Soviet economics.

Of course there is, and understandably enough, a good deal of resistance to this osmosis. Even where the ideological implications are not as clear and as profound as they are on the points discussed here, resistance comes from the economist's inertia (a point rightly made by Academician Nesmeyanov[27]) and his vested intellectual interests. There is in it a good deal of sincere confusion and embarrassment. On the one hand economists exhort each other to be selective in borrowing from non-Marxist economics, to be vigilant in an area strewn with revisionist traps. Did not Lenin himself say à propos bourgeois economics: '*Not one* professor of political economy, though capable of producing most valuable works in the field of factual, special research, can be trusted *with a single word* where the general theory of political economy is concerned'?[28] On the other hand, there is a good deal of conscience-soothing justification; recently Academician Kolmogorov, a mathematician of world repute, credited with the calculus for the Sputnik, lent his authority in its support: 'Do not be concerned about the purity of your Marxism,'[29] he tells the Soviet economists, 'because of a certain similarity between the mathematical instruments adopted for a theory of socialist economy and some elements of bourgeois economics. After all, they must have a common mathematical apparatus.'

The impetus in the growing rapprochement between Soviet and post-Marx non-Marxist economics—grudging as it may be—and in generous Soviet borrowing from the latter, robs of sense the tenet that these economics will move inexorably towards decay and 'vulgarization'. It was permissible to find common roots for Marxist and non-Marxist economics up to Ricardo, but not later. The dividing line now is not so clear.

One final remark is relevant. The rigorous reasoning which the mathematicians have brought into Soviet economics has also had some influence on the vision of the goal towards which a socialist economy is heading. Novozhilov has had the courage to explode the myth of a scarcity-free millenium under ultimate communism, and Nemchinov has argued that consequently the need for subtle and precise instruments of value-measuring is bound to increase rather

[26] S. Nikitin, *Vestnik Statistiki*, No. 7, 1960.

[27] *Voprosy Ekonomiki*, No. 8, 1960.

[28] *Sochineniya* (Collected works, 4th ed., vol. 14, p. 328). Italics in the original.

[29] *Voprosy Ekonomiki*, No. 8, 1960, p. 114.

than to decline. Utopia is thus being reduced to a somewhat retarded institutional variant of an affluent society.

This briefly indicates the movement in Soviet thinking produced by pressures from the economy, as it matures and stabilizes its growth. In the picture so drawn, Stalin appears as the first major revisionist, and the trend he initiated is seen to gain momentum in recent developments in Soviet thought, to undermine some ideologically important cornerstones of Marx's economic teaching, and to make its impact on Marxian economic and social eschatology.

Being a creed as well as a school of thought, Marxism has been understandably inclined towards an integrationalist attitude. To tinker with any of its building bricks—let alone such an important segment as its value theory—has always been regarded as a threat to the entire structure. It is from this angle—and from that of the precedence economics traditionally takes in the Marxian hierarchy of disciplines, not unlike theology in the Middle Ages—that the trend sketched out in these lines reveals its full significance.

xx. Prospects for the Soviet Dictatorship: Otto Bauer

MELVIN CROAN*

This paper first appeared in the Journal of Politics (*Gainesville, Florida*), vol. 21, November 1959, under the title 'The Politics of Marxist Sovietology: Otto Bauer's Vision', and is reproduced here through the kind permission ot the editors of that journal.

The reader may well inquire what light, if any, can be shed upon recent manifestations of revisionism in East-Central Europe by examining a political issue that divided European Social Democracy thirty years ago. The answer is neither obvious nor simple.

That basic Marxist assumptions may as easily lead to apologetic acceptance of the Soviet dictatorship as to criticism of any of its features is clearly demonstrated by Otto Bauer's thought. It may well be argued that Marxism can never provide an adequate philosophical basis upon which to ground a moral protest against Soviet totalitarianism. After all, ethical standards are not usually deducible from historical analysis. Not surprisingly, then, the revisionism of, say, a Kolakowski leads beyond Marxism to Kantianism. But what of such revisionist critics as Wolfgang Harich, whose revisionism was expounded primarily in historical terms? To be sure, Harich himself was a sufficiently skilled dialectician to construct a critical case against 'Stalinism' founded on a distinction between 'progressive' and 'reactionary' phases of Soviet internal development and of Soviet relations with the People's Democracies. (See Wolfgang Harich, 'The Testament of a Party Rebel', in E. Stillman (Ed.), Bitter Harvest, New York, 1959.) But immanent criticism is subject to the same kind of rebuttal. 'Objective circumstances', both internal and international, can always be called upon in order to justify disagreeable aspects of the Soviet dictatorship. Is this not precisely the logic of the line advanced by such anti-revisionist ideologues as Adam Schaff? And, psychologically speaking, to read history as hope for the future may well be to blunt conscience in the present. If the polemical language is discounted, there may yet be some

* The author wishes to acknowledge his gratitude to the International Institute for Social History, Amsterdam, for allowing him access to certain private materials for the preparation of this paper. Thanks are also due the Russian Research Center, Harvard University, for its support and assistance as well as to Mr Morris Watnick for his stimulating comments and criticisms.

truth in Trotsky's evaluation of Bauer and his ilk as 'scared opportunists'. 'The essence of their nature,' continued Trotsky, 'is adaptation, yielding to force. . . .' (Diary in Exile, Cambridge, Mass., 1958, p. 27). Marxist revisionism that does not transcend Marxism is all too vulnerable to the logic of 'yielding to force'.

Discussion of the meaning of the Soviet experience and attempts to predict its future are all the fashion today. And this is as it should be. No other development of our age constitutes a greater challenge to scholarly comprehension or a greater burden to responsible statesmanship. All the more reason, therefore, to be history-minded, not only about the problem itself but also with regard to the various approaches to it which are current today.

Consider, for example, what has been called the contemporary 'Marxist' analysis of the Soviet dictatorship. In its best known form this analysis insists that totalitarian dictatorship, having brought about the industrialization of the Soviet Union, has *eo ipso* prepared the way for its own evolution into a socialist democracy. Marxist Sovietology therefore anticipates a gradual dismantling of total political control, beginning with the curbing of mass terror (which in fact has happened since the death of Stalin), to be followed by an increasingly scrupulous observance of the rule of law (something which may now be occurring), and later by the removal of restrictions on freedom of thought and expression. But such an evolution is invariably predicated upon the relaxation of international tensions, from which it follows that the West, particularly the United States, should do everything to encourage the anticipated outcome, even if this entails the utmost accommodation toward the Soviet Union.[1]

That the optimism of this theory and the policy prescription suggested by it are based on a set of questionable premises hardly needs to be laboured. What does need to be added is that the theory itself derives directly from earlier Marxist origins still largely overlooked but important nonetheless for their bearing on its optimistic outlook. It is now almost entirely forgotten that much of the discussion of 'developmental trends and possibilities' of Soviet society since the death of Stalin was originally propounded over a quarter of a century ago by Otto Bauer, one of the foremost theorists of Austrian and international Social Democracy. The neglect of Bauer's thought is all the more regrettable since he employed almost the very categories of analysis and vocabulary of discourse which today clamour for our attention. Yet, if Bauer finds a permanent place in the annals of the history of political thought, it may be only on account of his con-

---

[1] The 'classic' exposition of these views occurs in Isaac Deutscher, *Russia: What Next?* (New York, 1953). For a cursory survey of the Marxist approach and an introduction to the other schools of analysis, see Daniel Bell, 'Ten Theories in Search of Reality', *World Politics*, vol. X (April 1958).

tribution to the theory of nationalism. This would be indeed unfortunate, for Bauer's treatment of social and economic change in the inter-war period is significant not only for the history of the times but even for the policy of the present.[2] For this reason the reader will be introduced to the content and evolution of Bauer's thought about Soviet Russia, and thus to the earliest version of Marxist Sovietology. The parallel between current optimism and Bauer's vision will emerge clearly in the course of the presentation. What remains to be added is no less important for it is now possible to reach a definitive conclusion about the psychological and political *function* of Bauer's analysis and therefore to open a new approach to the latter day Marxist Sovietologists.

II

For European Marxism as a political movement, the profoundest consequence of the Bolshevik Revolution was the division of the continental working class into Communist and Social Democratic parties. It was the problem that specially occupied Otto Bauer and, in a sense, all of his theoretical writing was devoted to the vision of a reconciliation within Marxism. As a leading protagonist of the international 'Marxian Centre' and later of the doctrine of 'integral socialism', Bauer sought — without success, as it turned out — to fashion a theoretical position which would overcome the split between the Comintern and the Second, later the Labour and Socialist International. Within the democratic Socialist camp Bauer was regarded as the leading Russian expert. His opinions exercised great influence in shaping Socialist attitudes and policy toward the Soviet regime. And always, even when he was most critical of the regime, Bauer exercised his authority in the international socialist movement to keep open every possibility for a rapprochement with the Communists.

Otto Bauer's expertise on Russian affairs, to some extent at least, was an accident. Called into active military service at the start of World War I, Bauer was taken prisoner by the Russians in the fall of 1914 and consigned to the Troitskolavsk prisoner of war camp in

<hr/>

[2] Bauer's *Nationalitätenfrage und die Sozialdemokratie* (1907) represented a brilliant application of Marxist theory to a problem which Marxists up to that time had conveniently glossed over. But Bauer's treatment of the nationality question ought not to exhaust his claim to recognition as an independent thinker within democratic Marxism. As the outstanding theoretician of post World War I Austro-Marxism, Bauer achieved, perhaps involuntarily, a rather unique accommodation of reformist practice to consciously radical theory. In addition, he did publish the beginnings of a major theoretical analysis of structural changes within capitalism. (*Kapitalismus und Sozialismus nach dem Weltkrieg*, 1931, and *Zwischen Zwei Weltkriegen?*, 1936.) But history seems to have its own judgment. When democratic socialism was overwhelmed by problems which its theory could not comprehend, Otto Bauer's writings entered oblivion.

the Zabaikal'skii district. It was here that Bauer was able to perfect his knowledge of the Russian language, though, as he complained in a Red Cross prisoner of war card to his revered mentor, Karl Kautsky, this was at the expense of the 'pursuit of theory'.[3]

Bauer was not repatriated to Austria until August 1917, and thus had a chance to observe Petersburg during a period of revolutionary ferment. Having fallen out with the right wing party leadership at home, Bauer found that his sympathies were with the Martov-Internationalist wing of the Menshevik party. All the other Mensheviki, in his opinion, were too timid for the requirements of the revolutionary situation and thus 'objectively' abettors of reaction. The Bolsheviks, on the other hand, were a cocky lot who had mistaken notions about 'the supreme power of the machine gun' in making history.[4] A dictatorship of the proletariat was out of the question, much less a socialist society in a country like Russia where the proletariat was still a minority.[5]

Nevertheless, when Lenin and his associates did succeed in making history through 'the power of the machine gun', Bauer acquiesced. Indeed he was inclined to blame the Mensheviki in the first instance for having forced the Bolsheviks to seize power in order to save the revolution. Bauer contested the propriety of right wing Social Democratic attacks on the Bolsheviks, even going so far as to insist that the October revolution had to be accounted 'a victory for the proletariat'.[6]

During the years immediately following Lenin's seizure of power, Bauer became more critical of the theory and practice of Bolshevism. But his major concern was not Russia. Rather he sought to deny the pertinence of Bolshevik methods to the problems of Central European and particularly Austrian Social Democracy. 'I am not a Bolshevik,' Bauer wrote in 1919, 'because although Bolshevism might mean a temporary victory for the proletariat, it would be followed by a fateful defeat.'[7] That defeat, he believed, was a foregone conclusion because of the conservatism of the peasantry and the certainty that the victorious allies would impose sanctions to strangle Austria economically.[8] Bolshevism might triumph in Russia and perhaps

[3] The Kautsky Archives of the International Institute for Social History, Item 489, postcard from Bauer to Kautsky 27/3/16 (?). (Although not indicated, 1916 is the probable year of this communication.)

[4] Kautsky Archives, Item 500, letter from Bauer to Kautsky, 28/9/17.

[5] Heinrich Weber (Otto Bauer), *Die russische Revolution und das europäische Proletariat* (Vienna, 1917), p. 26.

[6] Heinrich Weber (Otto Bauer), 'Die Bolshewiki und Wir', *Der Kampf*, vol. XI (March 1918), p. 147. Cf. also Bauer's protest against the publication of the *Leipziger Volkzeitung* of various attacks on the Bolsheviks. Kautsky Archives, Item 503, letter from Bauer to Kautsky, 4/1/18.

[7] Otto Bauer, *Acht Monate Auswärtiger Politik* (Vienna, 1919), p. 9.

[8] Otto Bauer, 'Die historiche Funktion des Bolshewismus', *Wiener Arbeiter-Zeitung* (June 28, 1919), p. 1, subsequently reprinted as part of the essay *Welt-*

even survive temporarily in Hungary because these countries were far more immune to such pressures. In both countries, the peasantry was politically backward but economically revolutionary. Moreover, the sheer size of Russia, its underdeveloped economy and its distance from the centres of world politics gave it a chance to defeat allied intervention.[9] Thus Bauer refused to draw a general indictment of Bolshevism, arguing that:

'The question is not whether the Bolsheviks are right or wrong as far as Russia is concerned. Rather the question is whether we *here* in *our* country can and should imitate the Russian example.'[10]

Bauer's approach to the Bolshevik question was based, as he candidly admitted in private correspondence, on a desire to preserve the unity of the Austrian working class. He recognized the evident fascination of certain segments of the workers with immediate Bolshevik victories and feared that this would offer an opening wedge for the Austrian Communists. To condemn Bolshevism in Russia as the right wing leaders of the majority SPD were doing might result in a division of proletarian forces as serious as that in Germany.[11]

Not that Bauer's notion of the circumstantial impossibility of Bolshevism in Europe carried with it approval of the specific policies of the Bolshevik regime in Russia. In 1920 Bauer published an analysis of 'war communism', criticizing it as 'despotic socialism', prompted by a misdirected utopianism—despotic socialism, based on brute force and rampant terror, in contrast to 'democratic socialism' for which social, cultural, and economic development were preparing the rest of Europe.[12]

Bauer's terminology here is in a sense misleading. To a Marxist of his school, Bolshevism could not build socialism, despotic or otherwise, because socialism was the end result of a democratic capitalism and, as such, an order marked by the greatest degree of individual freedom and industrial democracy. Indeed, Bauer at this time was an ardent exponent of the precepts of Guild Socialism.[13] In using the term 'despotic socialism' to describe war communism, then, Bauer was merely groping for a way of damning Bolshevism but with faint

revolution (Vienna, 1919). Cf. also Bauer's post-mortem on Soviet Hungary, *Die Österreichische Revolution* (Vienna, 1923), pp. 136–8.

[9] *Ibid.*
[10] Otto Bauer, 'Das russische Vorbild', *Wiener Arbeiter-Zeitung* (March 25, 1919), p. 1, subsequently reprinted as part of the essay, *Rätediktatur oder Demokratie?* (Vienna, 1919).
[11] Kautsky Archives, Item 513, letter from Bauer to Kautsky, 29/3/20.
[12] Otto Bauer, *Bolshewismus oder Sozialdemokratie* (Vienna, 1920), pp. 88–92.
[13] Otto Bauer, *Der Weg zum Sozialismus* (Vienna), 12th ed., 1921, pp. 1–5, *Bolshewismus oder Sozialdemokratie*, pp. 88–99, and *Die Österreichische Revolution*, pp. 171–2, where Bauer specifically acknowledges the influence of G. D. H. Cole upon his thinking.

praise—groping, in other words, for a critical position which would still stop short of the kind of bitter polemic which, in his view, was so dangerous to the unity of the working class. That 'despotic socialism' was anything but socialist to a mind like Bauer's is indicated by his expectation that the despotic Soviet regime, for all of its socialist experiments, would have to give way to controlled capitalism. He observed that capitalism was in its infancy in Russia and would require a long period of growth before socialism were even thinkable. The revolution had been made for the most part by the peasantry and this overwhelming majority of the Russian population simply would not abide socialist experimentation.[14] Not surprisingly, then, Bauer took the introduction of the New Course (NEP) as a vindication of his prophecy that brute political force could never prevail over stubborn economic realities. The Bolsheviks could not build socialism because:

'Neither dictatorship, nor terror, nor power can force upon a country a social order to which its productive forces and productive relations have not matured.'[15]

Accordingly, Bauer urged the Soviet regime to return to legality and to develop democratic procedures, in keeping with the needs of the New Economic Policy. Failure to do so, he warned, would doom NEP and pave the way for reaction.[16]

Throughout the twenties, Bauer reiterated the basic attitude toward Soviet power in Russia which he had formulated between 1917 and 1921. Commenting on Trotsky's removal and the promulgation of the doctrine of 'socialism in one country', Bauer wrote once again that:

'No government, whatever its dictatorial powers, can lead a capitalist economic organization to socialism unless there are first strong and mature social organizations which are organic to it and which have been developed in the free and democratic activity of the masses. . . .'[17]

---

[14] Otto Bauer, *Bolshewismus oder Sozialdemokratie*, pp. 35–42, and Part I, 'Die sozialen Voraussetzungen der russischen Revolution', pp. 7–26. Also *Der 'neue Kurs' in Sowjetrussland* (Vienna, 1921), pp. 30–5. In this connection there is a brief indication of Bauer's attitudes at this time in that monumental and (as far as Austrian socialism is concerned) sympathetic study of Charles A. Gulick, *Austria From Hapsburg to Hitler* (Berkeley and Los Angeles, 1948), vol. II, p. 1398.
[15] *Der 'neue Kurs' in Sowjetrussland*, p. 20.
[16] *Ibid.*, pp. 33–6.
[17] Otto Bauer, 'Voraussetzungen des Sozialismus. Die ökonomischen Grundlagen des Falles Trotzki', *Wiener Arbeiter-Zeitung* (December 25, 1924), as reprinted in Grigorii Dimitroff, (ed.) *Die Tragödie Trotzki* (Berlin, 1925), p. 68.

His approach, together with the accompanying criticism of the Bolshevik dictatorship, was shared by almost all European Socialists, most notably by Karl Kautsky.[18]

Nevertheless, this agreement on the fundamentals of theory went hand in hand with a bitter dispute about the practical policy of international socialism toward Soviet Russia. Kautsky, for one, argued that the Socialist International should welcome and even assume the leadership of any general uprising which might occur against the regime. For him, the Soviet dictatorship had already gone the full length of reaction; its successor could never be worse. Kautsky's position was hotly contested both by the Russian Mensheviki in exile and by Austro-Marxists. Bauer did not directly participate in the discussion which was precipitated by the publication of Kautsky's *Die Internationale und Sowjetrussland*, but his fundamental rejection of Kautsky's proposals is indicated by his activities in other areas. A leading participant in the Vienna, or Second and a Half International, which had sought, in its own way, to re-establish the broken international ties between Bolshevism and Social Democracy, Bauer was willing to concede, as we have seen, that given the circumstances in Russia in 1917, the Bolshevik seizure of power was not only possible but even objectively 'necessary'. He was all the more disappointed that the Bolsheviks were unwilling to admit the possibility of roads to socialism other than their own.[19] Since the Comintern stood dogmatically by the Twenty-One Conditions of 1920, the Vienna International had no choice but to declare at the Hamburg Congress of 1923 its return to the fold of the Labour and Socialist International.

But Bauer's belief in the desirability of a reunification of all Marxist parties persisted. To be sure this was out of the question as long as the Bolsheviks maintained their aggressive parochialism, but Bauer felt that the very problems of government in Russia which had led to the introduction of NEP would eventually mellow Leninist dogmatism and lead Communist parties back to the mainstream of European Social Democracy. On the other hand, this was not likely to happen if Socialists assumed an attitude of implacable hostility toward Soviet Russia and looked forward to its overthrow. Thus at successive Congresses of the Labour and Socialist International Bauer championed resolutions favouring the acceptance of Bolshevik power in Russia

[18] See especially Kautsky's *Terrorismus und Kommunismus* (Berlin, 1919) and the second edition (Berlin, 1925), *Von der Demokratie zur Staatssklaverei* (Berlin, 1921), *Die proletarische Revolution und ihr Programm* (Berlin, 1922). Bauer indicated approval of Kautsky's harsh indictment in *Von der Demokratie* in a letter to Kautsky 16/9/21, Kautsky Archives, Item 517.

[19] Otto Bauer, 'Sozialdemokratie und Kommunismus', *Wiener Arbeiter-Zeitung* (June 29, 1919), p. 2, subsequently reprinted in the pamphlet, *Die Weltrevolution* (Vienna, 1919).

and admonishing the European powers to keep 'hands off Soviet Russia'.[20]

III

Despite disagreement within the Socialist International on practical matters of policy toward Soviet Russia, a disagreement which was never fully resolved, the unanimous view during the twenties was that the Soviet regime was not and indeed could not be building socialism. It was Otto Bauer who first challenged this consensus and, incidentally, his own earlier appraisal of the regime.

Bauer's reappraisal of Soviet Russian society was first outlined in 1931 at the conclusion of the first volume of what was to have been a general analysis of contemporary capitalism. In this work, subtitled *Rationalisierung-Fehlrationalisierung*,[21] the chapter devoted to 'Rationalization and Socialism' conceded the possibility that the introduction of the First Five-Year Plan might enable the Soviet regime to build socialism after all, without first having passed through a period of capitalism. Bauer clung to this conclusion until his death in 1938, giving it an ever more positive expression in *Zwischen Zwei Weltkriegen?* (1936) and in his other writings of the period. An examination of the major lines of Bauer's analysis leaves no doubt that the Sovietology which in the post-Stalin era has been advancing the vision of an inexorable democratic evolution of the totalitarian regime is far from startlingly new.

For Bauer, the industrialization of Russia amounted to the distinctive Soviet version of economic rationalization which, despite the severe dislocation of the 1929 crisis, he regarded as the dominant secular trend of the times. The term *Rationalisierung* was standard usage in Europe. It referred to those techniques and procedures within individual plants and in the economy as a whole which result in the maximization of productivity and the minimization of cost—introduction of efficiency methods, greater mechanization and the like. The concept of rationalization was thus employed by Bauer in the first instance as a tool of economic analysis. What makes Bauer's use of this concept uniquely important, however, is the fact that he added an explicit causal relationship between rationalization in the strictly

---

[20] Cf. Bauer's report, 'Der internationale Kampf gegen die internationale Reaktion', *Protokoll des Internationalen Sozialistischen Arbeiterkongresses in Hamburg 21. bis 25. Mai 1923* (Berlin, 1923), pp. 23ff., his report on 'The Dangers of War in the East', *Second Congress of the Labour and Socialist International at Marseilles, 22nd to 27th August 1925*, English Edition (London, 1925), pp. 265–71, and Bauer's comments, 'Der Kongress in Marseilles', *Der Kampf*, vol. XVIII (August-September 1925), pp. 281–5. Also Bauer's report on 'The World Political Situation and the International Labour Movement', *The Third Congress of the Labour and Socialist International, Brussels, 5th to 11th August 1928* (London, 1928), pp. 153ff.

[21] Otto Bauer, *Kapitalismus und Sozialismus nach dem Weltkrieg, Erster Band: Rationalisierung-Fehlrationalisierung* (Vienna, 1931).

economic sense and rationality in society as a whole. The political expression of such social rationality, he argued, was democracy:

'Rationalization advances a style of thought appropriate to engineers, a matter-of-fact, positivistic, relativistic style of thought which reckons in terms of measurable results, seeking to reach desired goals at the least possible cost. This style of thought avoids everything that cannot be calculated; it shuns every risk, every uncertain adventure. Therefore it will always attempt to bring about social change only if and only to the extent that the majority of the people, "public opinion", can be won over and only as long as such support is maintained. Modern democracy is rooted in this style of thought.'[22]

Industrialization, Bauer argued, be it a spontaneous development as in nineteenth-century England or a consciously directed policy as in twentieth-century Russia, in all cases means a transitional process fraught with frightful social consequences. The forced industrialization of Russia, moreover, had to proceed against the handicap of the immense cultural and economic backwardness of Russian society. However reprehensible terror might be in abstract moral terms, it was the 'historical' prerequisite to successful industrialization in such circumstances. But in the very course of the process of industrialization, terror would begin to loose its economic rationale. Indeed, he felt in 1931, that political terror against Soviet technicians had already become irrational, i.e. economically self-defeating. The requirements of the successful industrialization of society included the guarantee of the inviolability of the persons of the industrial bureaucracy. As the new managers, engineers and technicians became part of the regime itself, terror against the industrial sector would abate since, at least in Otto Bauer's mind, rationalization in industry and rationality in politics were indissolubly linked.[23]

The collectivization of agriculture presented a somewhat special problem. For the short run, Bauer argued, collectivization would have to be labelled as a case of 'misapplied rationalization'. This was true because agricultural production had declined precipitously as the result of the uprooting of the peasantry. But he expected that the agricultural crisis would be overcome and mechanized efficiency introduced to the countryside, thus at once extending economic rationalization from industry to agriculture and political rationality from urban to rural areas.[24] Industrialization, and with it collectivization, would be a success. And that very success, engineered by the brute political power of a wilful dictatorship, offered the hope of the eventual democratization of the dictatorship itself. In 1931 Bauer's

[22] *Ibid.*, p. 225.
[23] *Ibid.*, pp. 207–13.
[24] *Ibid.*, pp. 216–18.

K

vision was one of cautious optimism. Nonetheless he expressed confidence that:

'The terroristic dictatorship will be overcome and will be dismantled to the degree that the standard of living of the masses is improved. The Soviet regime can be democratized. If the dictatorship which controls the state owned machinery of production is replaced by a system of democratic control by the workers, there will emerge from dictatorial state capitalism, a socialist order of society.'[25]

Those who have criticized the more recent versions of Bauer's analysis usually point to a single defect of reasoning: while it may be true that an industrial order is dependent for its successful operation upon a degree of political rationality, it scarcely follows that the industrial process by itself necessarily permeates the entire social structure within which it functions with rationality. Interestingly enough, Bauer himself was aware of the limits of rationality in a rationalized industrial order. Consider the following appraisal:

'[Rationalization] chains the worker to an uninterrupted rhythm . . . it chains the employee to the adding machine . . . it condemns the masses to jobs which can offer neither excitement nor satisfaction and which provide no outlet for personal initiative, imagination and responsibility. What is denied them in their work people seek on an evening off in the movies, at the sports arena and in public life. This craving to have some more meaningful experience, to take a chance, to experience a sense of adventure leads some to Fascism, others to Bolshevism.'[26]

Why did Bauer's concession that a rationalized industrial order might harbour personal dissatisfactions of so serious a sort as to produce, or at least contribute to irrational political movements fail to disturb his vision of a democratization of the Soviet Union? However unsatisfactory an answer it may be for us, Bauer's answer was a simple, and in his own terms, an obvious one: there was a qualitative difference between rationalization in a capitalist society and in a socialist society. Here the Marxist's faith in the basic Marxist postulates about the ownership of the means of production was sufficient to be decisive.[27]

Given this line of analysis, it is all the more interesting to recall that it was Bauer himself among the Marxists who, long before the Communists seized power in Russia, had challenged the very assumption that socialism would invariably mean the liquidation of all

[25] *Ibid.*, p. 223.
[26] *Ibid.*, p. 225.
[27] Cf. *ibid.*, p. 226.

elements of cultural irrationality. In his treatise on the nationality problem Bauer had, indeed, argued just the opposite case: that the 'socialization of the nation' would strengthen rather than weaken the stubborn psychological residuum of extrarational attachment to nationalism.[28] But, writing in the thirties with reference to Russia's future, Bauer evinced no awareness of this inconsistency with his earlier thought. Assuming the basic incompatibility of an industrial order with a political dictatorship, he concluded that the dictatorship would have to give way, gradually to be sure, but nonetheless certainly:

'A sudden transition from the Soviet dictatorship to a democracy is certainly not possible . . . (but) the gradual democratization of the Soviet constitution will become necessary to the degree to which the Soviet people develop in the course of a rapid cultural climb to self-conscious citizens (*Kulturmenschen*) who are not prepared to obey bureaucratic absolutism, who demand personal freedom, intellectual freedom, and the freedom of personal decision and self-government.'[29]

Bauer admitted the probability of resistence against a democratic evolution of the regime on the part of the established political bureaucracy. But in the long run the selfish desires of men could not prevail over the logic of the underlying social changes which they themselves had instituted. He was confident that history would do its work well. Moral inquiries about the human cost of such historical enterprises were dismissed as beside the point.[30]

IV

Otto Bauer's optimistic predictions about the future of Soviet Russia were not accepted uncritically by other Socialists. Indeed something of a major polemic developed against him. Although Bauer's views were discussed in terms of the question of whether or not the Soviet regime could build socialism, the substance of the debate was in fact

---

[28] The development of this interesting point is obviously beyond the scope of this article. The reader is referred to *Die Nationalitätenfrage und die Sozialdemokratie* (first published in 1907), 2nd ed. (Vienna, 1924), pp. 94–108 and 507–21. Bauer's preface to the Second edition in which he acknowledges his earlier adherence to Kantian epistemology and subsequent recovery from the 'Kantian diseases of childhood' (pp. XI–XII) is especially noteworthy.

[29] Otto Bauer, *Zwischen Zwei Weltkriegen?* (Bratislava, 1936), p. 166.

[30] Cf. *ibid.*, pp. 145–168. For an indication of Bauer's appreciation of the 'historical function' of the Stalinist dictatorship, see his review of Boris Souvarine's *Staline*, 'Der Diktator in der Diktatur', *Der Kampf*, vol. II (October 1935), pp. 457–61. As an exercise in the genealogy of ideas, it is fascinating to observe the extent to which this article's anticipated the major thesis of Isaac Deutscher's *Stalin: A Political Biography*.

concerned with the possibility of a democratic evolution of the dictatorship.

Karl Kautsky was most vehement in denying such an outcome. Indeed, he even doubted the success of the Five-Year Plan and went so far as to predict a miscarriage so serious as to end in the collapse of Bolshevik rule. Kautsky argued that democratic socialism could not emerge from Bolshevism because the political dictatorship had so degraded the Russian population and its working class that it could never attain the degree of maturity and sense of responsibility which democracy requires without first overthrowing the Bolshevik regime. But the dictatorship, for Kautsky a form of 'Asiatic absolutism', was now attempting to force prodigious social and economic change; however Marxism teaches that economic reality makes politics and not vice versa, and therefore Kautsky believed that the Bolshevik programme of industrialization was doomed to failure.[31] In these and similar terms Bauer's prognosis was contested by a number of Russian Mensheviki, notably Theodor Dan and Raphael Abramovich.[32]

The substantive and logical merits of Bauer's position and that of his opponents aside, the entire controversy needs to be placed within the context of the times. A deepening economic crisis and the spread of Fascism were darkening the horizons of democratic socialism everywhere in Europe. By 1934, Social Democracy had been outlawed in Italy, Germany and Austria, as well as in a host of smaller Central and Eastern European countries. Only in this context can the psychological and political function of Bauer's optimism concerning the possibility of a democratic evolution of the Soviet Union be understood. Such an evolution represented really the final hope for Central European socialism and, as Bauer saw it, the only chance for peace in Europe. A closer examination of Bauer's thought in terms of the politics of the period will clarify the relationship.

Marxism, armed with an assurance of the inexorability of its own ultimate triumph, is essentially an optimistic creed. Otto Bauer, however, was not only a theoretician but also a practical politician for whom the political fortunes or misfortunes of his own party were of immediate concern. If Bauer's analysis of the 1929 crash as only a passing 'crisis of rationalization' had been correct, as patently it was

---

[31] See Kautsky's review of Bauer's *Rationalisierung-Fehlrationalisierung*, 'Die Aussichten des Sozialismus in Sowjetrussland', *Die Gesellschaft*, vol. VIII (November 1931), pp. 420–44. Cf. also Kautsky's *Der Bolshewismus in der Sackgasse* (Berlin, 1930) and his article, 'Die Aussichten des Fünfjahrplanes', *Die Gesellschaft*, vol. VIII (March 1931), pp. 255–64.

[32] Cf. Theodor Dan, 'Der Kampf um die Demokratie', *Der Kampf*, vol. XXIV (July-August 1931), pp. 285–91. R. Abramowitsch, 'Fünfjahrplan und Sozialismus', *Die Gesellschaft*, vol. VIII (July 1931). See also T. Dan, *Wohin steuert die Generallinie?* (Berlin, 1931), especially pp. 123ff., and D. Dalin, 'Vokrug Pjatiletki', *Sotsialisticheskii Vestnik* (June 13, 1931).

not, then capitalist society did indeed possess great resilience. Politically, the economic recovery which Bauer expected at best would have preserved intact the 'balance of class forces' which, according to his analysis elsewhere, had held Austrian and European Socialism in a debilitating stalemate.[33] In fact the political consequences of the economic crisis were far more ominous. In the Marxist view, the bourgeoisie, in order to preserve its own power, forsook democracy for fascist dictatorship. This pitifully inadequate deduction scarcely served to explain the baffling fact that the masses were deserting Socialist and democratic parties. In the face of such an incomprehensible and overpowering situation, Soviet Russia seemed to offer a last ray of hope. To be sure, the version of Marxism which held sway in Russia was a perverted one. But if that perversion could be shown to have been historically necessary and if history itself were working to correct it, a bastion of democratic socialist strength might emerge in the East to salvage the international movement as a whole. *Ex oriente lux.*

That Bauer's post-1931 view of the Soviet Union must be treated in this light may be demonstrated by closer scrutiny of the controversy which his analysis raised among spokesmen for Social Democracy. The rejection of Bauer's ideas by Kautsky and the Russian Mensheviks led to a series of anti-Bauer polemics. The very intensity of the attacks against him should have required that he respond in kind for such is the tradition of Marxist disputation. Yet this is precisely what Bauer refused to do. In a letter to Kautsky in 1931 Bauer expressed regret that his old friend rejected his views but sought to defend himself only in terms of his study of and expertise on Soviet affairs.[34] When the Kautsky-Bauer dialogue burst the bounds of a semi-private exchange, it was Friedrich Adler, the Secretary of the Socialist and Labour International, who engaged Karl Kautsky.

The Adler-Kautsky exchange, published in the Austro-Marxist journal, *Der Kampf*, in February 1933, is itself also revealing. Adler did not at all share Bauer's views, since he doubted that a socialist democracy was a likely outcome of Soviet industrialization. Rather he feared that successful industrialization would mean the further development and strengthening of the state capitalist dictatorship. Unlike Kautsky, however, Friedrich Adler expected that the industrialization of Russia by the Communists would succeed.[35] Adler was quite candid about his reasons for defending Bauer even though

[33] Otto Bauer, *Die Österreichische Revolution* (Vienna, 1923), especially Part IV, 'Die Zeit des Gleichgewichts der Klassenkräfte', pp. 196–247.

[34] Kautsky Archives, Item 523, letter from Bauer to Kautsky 6/10/31.

[35] Friedrich Adler's own 'theory' of state capitalistic dictatorship was developed in an essay entitled, 'Das Stalinsche Experiment und der Sozialismus', *Der Kampf*, XXV (January 1932), pp. 4–16.

he could not agree with the latter's optimism. 'Not the hope for (democratic) socialism in Soviet Russia,' he wrote, 'but *the real dangers resulting from a collapse* of Bolshevik rule are decisive for our position.'[36] Kautsky's point that socialism could only grow out of capitalist democracy was dangerously irrelevant. Moreover the grand master's contention that the Bolshevik regime was bound to collapse and in fact it might be overthrown by exploiting the difficulties of industrialization was politically inadmissable. Adler made the point of Kautsky's disservice to the Socialist International so plainly that Kautsky took it as a personal affront.[37]

The question of why Bauer so conspicuously refused to debate with Kautsky and his other critics requires an answer. Theodor Dan reported in 1932 that Bauer rejected the challenge on account of his desire, for political reasons internal to the Austrian party, to avoid also having to contest Adler's less sanguine approach to Soviet Russia.[38] Dan was not convinced. The real reason for Bauer's reticence, he felt, was Bauer's inability to defend his own position. This, in turn, was so because Bauer's position was not a scientific analysis at all but rather an article of faith in a situation immanent with despair:

'What is really serious about Bauer is not that the working class is following him but that he is following the working class which in its confusion and hopelessness is groping for miracles. And Bauer transforms this belief in miracles into a 'theory'. I don't believe he himself feels especially strongly. If he did, he would not have avoided discussion as in fact he is doing. . . .'[39]

For Dan, Bauer's 'Marxist analysis' of the developmental potentialities of the Soviet regime was sheer illusion 'born out of the distress and unmentionable difficulties of the international labour movement'.[40] This is indeed a sad commentary on the general decline of the supposed objectivity of Marxist thought. In biographic terms, it is a no more flattering observation of the uses to which the analytic powers of the author of *Die Nationalitätenfrage* were being employed. Yet within the advantage of hindsight we must conclude that Dan's evaluation of Bauer's position was in all likelihood quite valid.

[36] *Ibid.*, p. 14. Italics in original.

[37] The whole discussion, originally in the form of an exchange of letters, took place as a result of the reluctance of the editors of *Der Kampf* to publish an article by Karl Kautsky which attacked Bauer's vision. The article, 'Demokratie und Diktatur', together with an expurgated version of the Adler-Kautsky correspondence appeared in the February 1933 number of *Der Kampf*, XXVI, 2, pp. 45–69.

[38] Kautsky Archives, unnumbered item, letter from Dan to Kautsky, 11/2/32.

[39] *Ibid.*

[40] Theodor Dan, 'Der Kampf um die Demokratie', *op. cit.*, p. 290.

The theoretician's tools had been put to the service of the immediate needs of the faltering political movement.

Such a conclusion is further prompted by the one article which Bauer did undertake in his own defence. In this piece, directed to the question of the future of Russian Social Democracy, Bauer dealt with the practical problems of the Mensheviki. Dan and Abramovich had criticized Bauer in practical as well as theoretical terms.[41] If it were true that the dictatorship in Russia should labour to bring forth socialist democracy, did it not follow that the Russian Social Democracy in exile had lost its *raison d'être*? Ought not the Mensheviki, completely cut off from Soviet society, dissolve their organization? This practical conclusion specifically raised by the Mensheviki, presented Bauer with another problem of the international movement—a problem which, although of lesser significance than that of the future of Soviet Russia, nonetheless was troublesome because of its obvious relation to the larger issue. Therefore Bauer was impelled to record a protest against those who had taken him to mean that the Mensheviki should disband:

'I believe that the Mensheviki can still fulfil a great historical task. Indeed the fulfilment of that task will only become feasible as a result of the economic consequences of the dictatorship. That task is to be the leader, or at least one of the leaders of the Russian proletariat in the struggle for the gradual democratization of the Soviet regime. . . .'[42]

Bauer's treatment of the Russian problem in these terms and at this level of practical internal Socialist politics is indeed suggestive. Max Adler, the outstanding philosophical mind in Austrian Marxism, who subscribed to Bauer's optimistic vision of Soviet democracy, but was less directly involved in politics, easily pointed to the analytical inconsistency. For Bauer had granted a wholly unwarranted dispensation to the Mensheviki. If the dictatorship were really creating the preconditions for its own liquidation internally, one could only advise the Russian Social Democrats, as Max Adler in fact did, to accept and support 'the regime as it is'.[43]

During the thirties Bauer affirmed his belief in the democratic evolution of the Soviet regime with increasing confidence. If, in the first instance, his 1931 analysis had been prompted by the precipitous decline of democratic socialism, the subsequent affirmation was certainly prompted by the threat of a general European war. Again,

---

[41] *Ibid.*, and Abramovich, *loc. cit.*
[42] Otto Bauer, 'Die Zukunft der russischen Sozialdemokratie', *Der Kampf*, XXIV (December 1931), pp. 513–19, p. 517.
[43] Max Adler, 'Zur Diskussion über Sowjetrussland', *Der Kampf*, XXV (July 1932), p. 311.

like certain contemporaries, Bauer was fearful lest international tensions perpetuate, or even tighten, the existing dictatorial controls over Russian society.[44] The logic of international politics in the thirties did not allow a plea to the major powers 'to seek peace and follow it' —the exhortation to the United States of those current commentators who claim to be concerned with the impact of international events upon the internal evolution of the USSR. Nor had the Marxists of a quarter of a century ago yet been reduced to such conscious voluntarism. Bauer, for one, showed considerable aptitude in interpreting every major international disaster between 1934 and 1939 as additional proof of the immanent triumph of socialism. The inadequacies of his interpretations of international politics during this period make painful recitation. Fortunately, there is little need to discuss them here.[45] It will suffice to summarize his conclusions: history had doomed both the Communist dictatorship in the USSR and Social Democracy in Europe. The creative destruction of the historical process required a new unified movement, an 'integral socialism'. Integral socialism was to be higher synthesis rather than a mere fusion of its twin antecedents and would impart Bolshevik militance to European socialism as well as socialist appreciation of democracy to the Soviet Union.[46]

Otto Bauer would be the first to agree that history makes definitive judgments. History found him overwhelmingly wrong in his predictions about international politics, in his hopes for an organic union of Communism and Social Democracy, in his expectation of a speedy evolution of the Soviet dictatorship into a constitutional democracy. In each of these cases, the wish was father to the thought. The vision of a democratic and socialist colossus dispelled immanent despair and Bauer, at least, died before the final collapse of the world which he had known. But now Bauer's image of the Soviet future has emerged once again. The foregoing investigation of the psychological and political motivation behind Bauer's misplaced optimism suggests a single question: is it not possible that present-day optimism is only a mask for an essential pessimism—a pessimism all the more profound because this time it is not the working class, rent by division that is at stake but rather the whole of mankind, threatened with nuclear holocaust?

[44] Bauer, *Zwischen Zwei Weltkriegen?*, pp. 167, 223–32.

[45] For a severe criticism of Bauer's views on international politics during this period, see Joseph Buttinger, *In the Twilight of Socialism* (New York, 1953).

[46] Bauer, *Zwischen Zwei Weltkriegen?*, pp. 312–35, and also *Die illegale Partei* (Paris, 1939), *passim*.

PART FOUR

THE NEW LEFT

XXI. Britain: The New Reasoners

G. L. ARNOLD

'Hungary and Suez' are commonly regarded as the crucial events in the formation of what is currently styled the 'New Left' in Britain. Certainly most of its adherents would subscribe to this view—notably those who until that date maintained an uneasy relationship of activity in, or co-operation with, the Communist Party. Yet some of the insurgent tendencies which came to a head in October-November 1956 had already been at work for some time. The crisis of that autumn—preceded some months earlier by the shock of Khrushchev's disclosures about Stalin—gave form to a movement which until that date possessed for its only identifiable political signature a generalized dislike of nuclear weapons and a demand for disarmament; and while 'Hungary' came to matter most to those who under the impulsion of this event left the CP, 'Suez' achieved similar status for left-wing elements in and around the Labour Party who had simultaneously become concerned over the racial struggle in South Africa and East Africa, and over the emerging colour problem in Britain consequent upon the post-war arrival of West Indian immigrants.

One may say that all these topics have coalesced to generate something like a unified attitude on the part of a left-wing intelligentsia for whom emancipation from Stalinism had somehow acquired an importance similar to—but not markedly greater than—concern over colonialism in Africa, or dislike of 'the Establishment'. The fact that these issues all tend to inhabit the same emotional plane, and to be debated with an approximately equal degree of seriousness, testifies to the truth—otherwise perceptible from the literary manifestations of the school—that the entire 'movement' is still in the main confined to intellectuals. This, however, is the normal condition of a new political grouping in its early phase, and does not necessarily signify that one is witnessing a mere coffee-house revolt. In fact, the public response to the Campaign for Nuclear Disarmament suggests that at least one sector of the political 'front' has been affected by the new stirrings: not surprisingly perhaps when one considers that the campaign has received the blessings of Lord Russell, who for the rest can hardly be considered a suitable patron-saint of either neo-Marxism or neo-existentialism. The New Left in fact has its traditionalist aspects: a circumstance which invests it with a certain charm for the beholder who recalls the similar enterprises of the 1930s.

So general a characterization, however, misses at least one important element in this politico-intellectual ferment: the 'new thinking' within the Labour Party provoked by the electoral defeat of 1955, and rendered more agonizing by that of 1959. It was in response to the earlier of these setbacks that Mr Gaitskell obtained the leadership of the Party with a programme of modernization; and it was to satisfy the demand for a more streamlined version of Socialist thinking that Mr Crosland in 1956 published the massive volume which has come to be regarded as the basic document of the Labour leadership's Keynesian faith.[1] It may seem strange to couple this bulky manifesto of Labour's New Right with the very different professions of the New Left; but the intellectual tension between neo-Fabianism and neo-Marxism is very much part of the background against which Socialist thinking in Britain currently seeks to define itself. If Mr Gaitskell and his friends—notably Mr Crosland and Mr Douglas Jay —are Fabians who have moved so far towards Keynes as to be at times almost indistinguishable from the more advanced Liberals, the Left can be described as neo-Marxian in view of its continued insistence on the central importance of public ownership. And though adherence to public ownership as the criterion of a distinctively Socialist policy can on occasions be combined with a sophisticated acceptance of modern industrial society,[2] it nonetheless implies a conception of socio-economic planning sharply divergent from the Keynesian faith in the efficacy of monetary management. It is the Left's insistence on ownership and/or control of the great monopolistic concentrations of power, together with its hostility to the entrenched managerial stratum, which sets its attitude off sharply from the Right's belief that modern capitalism is quite compatible with both democracy and the welfare state.[3] At present this quarrel appears to lack political relevance, in view of the Labour Party's recent inability to make even a moderate programme of reform palatable to a majority of the voters; but it is precisely this failure which has sharpened the conflict between the two schools and thus created something like a permanent tie-up between the political 'Left' of the pacifist Campaign for Nuclear Disarmament, the anti-colonial movement, and the intellectuals of the 'New Left'. But for the struggle over socialization, the not very original railing against 'the Establishment'—the cant term for the ruling stratum in its non-

---

[1] C. A. R. Crosland, *The Future of Socialism* (London, 1956).

[2] Cf. Robin Marris, in *Socialist Commentary*, January 1960; Harold Wilson, 'A Four-Year Plan for Britain', *New Statesman*, March 24, 1961.

[3] Not that Mr Crosland and his friends would claim a state of perfection under Conservative rule. On the contrary, they are quite aware that it implies a high degree of social stratification; but it is their belief that this problem can be solved without wholesale socialization of the economy and the effective displacement of the present managerial stratum.

political, cultural and social aspect—would long ago have died of its own triviality.

It is against the background of this debate that one must judge the relevance of Mr John Strachey's ambitious attempt to reconcile Marxism and Keynesianism along the lines suggested in his two noteworthy studies, *Contemporary Capitalism* (1956) and *The End of Empire* (1959). Mr Strachey can scarcely be called a neo-Marxist; it would perhaps be more accurate to describe him as an ex-Marxist who by a roundabout way has arrived at the traditional Fabian position of gradualism in practice and empiricism in theory: yet with the difference, that, having at one time absorbed a good deal of Marxian thinking (though mostly relating to economics), he has emerged as a neo-Fabian who uses Marx rather than Keynes as the starting point for his theorizing. *Contemporary Capitalism* was an attempt to show in what respects economic reality and economic doctrine have moved away from the pattern traced by Marx; yet the mere fact that the book's critique centred on Marx rather than Keynes made it unpalatable to the majority of reviewers, while orthodox Marxists for their part deplored the author's failure to penetrate the inmost significance of Marx's theorizing.[4] The political significance of this apparently doctrinal dispute lay in the fact that Mr Strachey had attempted to outline what might be called a Social-Democratic position, midway between the Keynesian neo-Liberalism of the 'New Right' and the vestigial Leninism of the 'New Left'; a tendency even more marked in his second work, where the standard critique of Western colonialism was balanced by an appreciation of its historic achievement and a considered rebuttal of the familiar Leninist doctrine that Western living standards depend on the exploitation of backward countries.[5] This balanced approach—natural enough to a writer with Mr Strachey's personal experience of public affairs—does not come easily to the more strident ideologists of the New Left. But neither does his quiet acceptance of the end of British—if not Western —supremacy in world affairs appeal to the deeply ingrained outlook of his countrymen, whatever their party affiliation. It is a circumstance well known to candid observers of the British scene that the 'imperial' nostalgia is shared by all classes and is by no means the special preserve of either the ruling stratum or the Tory defenders of tradition. Yet the painful discovery of this fact at the time of the Suez crisis in 1956 produced something like a traumatic shock on the Left: nowhere more so than among the London literary intelligentsia, which had naïvely attributed its own pacifist outlook to the majority of its countrymen, and was appalled to find that such senti-

---

[4] Cf. Ronald L. Meek, 'Economics for the Age of Oligopoly', in *The New Reasoner*, Spring 1959, pp. 41ff.; cf. also Mr Strachey's brief reply in the Autumn issue of the same periodical, pp. 107–8.

[5] *The End of Empire*, London, 1960, pp. 98ff.

ments evoked only the barest echo from the average Labour supporter.

With these observations we have insensibly crossed the frontier dividing politics from literature, and must now turn to that widely misunderstood phenomenon: the 'revolt against the Establishment'. For all its overtones of bohemianism, erotomania, and downright silliness, this has been very much part of the spiritual and emotional ambience of the New Left, ever since the now historic moment in May 1956 when Mr John Osborne presented his play *Look Back In Anger* at the Royal Court Theatre. Among other literary manifestos reflecting the new radical mood, mention may briefly be made of the symposium entitled *Declaration*, published in October 1957 with contributions from a number of well-known writers and critics; its rather more serious and reputable companion-volume *Conviction* (1958); Mr Wayland Young's writings on nuclear radiation and allied subjects;[6] the noteworthy sociological studies of popular culture published by Mr Richard Hoggart[7] and Mr Raymond Williams;[8] and, in a lighter vein, the novels of Mr Kingsley Amis and Miss Iris Murdoch, who as a philosopher also contributed a severely formal essay to the symposium entitled *Conviction*. Except that it has little direct topical relevance, Mr Ernest Gellner's assault on linguistic philosophy in general, and the Oxford school in particular,[9] may be included in this list, notwithstanding the impeccably liberal and non-Marxist convictions of its author.

From this brief enumeration it will be seen that the New Left is far from being a uniform phenomenon; indeed where it broadens out into an attack on the *status quo* in the universities or in popular entertainment, its existentialist tendencies are more in evidence than the neo-Marxian philosophy of its Socialist adherents. Nonetheless it is Socialism that gives coherence to the movement, while cultural 'modernism' may be said to be among the features it has in common with the more orthodox Liberalism of the 'old' Left.[10] Socially this division between the 'old' and the 'new' Left—apart from the inevitable hiatus produced by the war, and the obvious difference between the political line-up of the 1930s and the 1960s—appears to reflect the cleavage between dissident 'Establishment' intellectuals and the new post-war intelligentsia which has come up by way of scholarships and lacks some of the social graces (as well as the

---

[6] Cf. *Encounter*, February 1957, November 1958, and the Penguin volume *Strategy for Survival* (1959), stressing the dangers of nuclear war.

[7] *The Uses of Literacy* (1957).

[8] *Culture and Society* (1958); *The Long Revolution* (1961).

[9] *Words and Things* (1959).

[10] It is not quite clear where the *New Statesman* stands in this matter. Its cultural attitudes represent a curious amalgam of Bloomsbury and St Germain-des-Prés; of late a certain infusion of 'New Left' ideology has been observable, but it is too early to tell.

characteristic snobberies) of its predecessors. A sociology of this intelligentsia (of largely working-class and lower middle-class background) would probably disclose that it prefers films to the theatre, American to French literature, modern to classical music, etc.; but it does not follow that these tastes are shared by all its more articulate spokesmen.

So far we have mostly dealt in generalities. It is time now to consider how far the tendencies under discussion are reflected in the two periodicals which since 1957 have served as the principal vehicles of the new trend, prior to their amalgamation late in 1959, when the *New Reasoner* and the *Universities and Left Review* combined to form the bi-monthly *New Left Review*, with an estimated circulation of eight to ten thousand, and a board of editors suggesting a careful balance of former Communists and traditional left-wing Socialists, with a slight numerical preponderance of the latter.[11]

The first point to note is that the fusion concerned two groups whose antecedents differed not only with respect to politics and general outlook, but also age-wise, the *Universities and Left Review* (ULR) founders belonging to the post-war generation and being mostly in their late twenties, while the *New Reasoner* (NR) group were on an average several years older, and included people with political experience going back to the 1930s. Having been closely linked to the Communist Party until the 1956 upheaval, NR tended to view political matters through Leninist spectacles even after the formal break with the CP, whereas the original ULR caucus at Oxford, which crystallized in the student excitement over Suez and Budapest, had no such ideological ballast to get rid of. There was the further important difference that the NR group was centred on Yorkshire, included some trade unionists, and in general showed a different social composition, some of its intellectual spokesmen having a working-class background. It was thus doubly outside the 'Establishment', a circumstance which lent a specific ring to its radicalism and likewise made it more dangerous to the CP than the rather more traditional (in British terms) London-Oxford, middle-class and student, rebelliousness of the ULR. The latter group, while larger, more ebullient, and with better facilities for spreading its views among students in London and at the two ancient seats of learning,[12] was

[11] This distinction takes no account of the original public appeal on behalf of the *New Left Review* signed by a number of fairly eminent sponsors, including some well-known transatlantic names. These might be thought to constitute a rather more representative cross-section of both Liberal and Socialist opinion, inside and outside the academic world, than the regular staff of the *Review* which exudes a somewhat sectarian flavour.

[12] ULR began in Oxford and thereafter spread to Cambridge, thus reversing a movement which in the 1930s turned Cambridge into the Communist Party's most important recruiting centre among intellectuals. At present the London-Oxford axis would still seem to be predominant.

politically inchoate, and to former Communists with some experience must have looked like a collection of youthful amateurs rather than a serious competitor. That in fact it turned out to be more successful in terms of public resonance (ULR's circulation steadily topped 8,000 almost from the first, while NR never got much above 2,500, including—it is claimed—some 250 in Eastern Europe), and able to hold its own ideologically as well, must be attributed to the fact that some of its contributors had from the start struck a distinctive note, of which more later. Practically, the growing convergence of NR and ULR thinking, as reflected in the editorial policy of both journals, gradually established the pre-conditions of a fusion which was consummated at the end of 1959. If the offspring of this union, now styled the *New Left Review* (NLR), soon displayed a very marked falling off in intellectual standards compared with its parent journals, the amateurishness inherited from ULR days probably had more to do with this than any sectarian narrowness which the new journal might be thought to have carried over from the past.

A glance at the composition of the editorial boards of these journals, before and after their fusion, discloses a family resemblance strong enough to outweigh the differences in origin already referred to. These must have seemed important at a time when the *New Reasoner* had not emerged from the caterpillar stage of an irregular stencilled discussion sheet (then still known as *The Reasoner*) circulated within the CP by dissident members of that organization who had been shocked into heresy by the disclosures made at the Twentieth Congress of the CPSU. By the time ULR's first issue appeared on the news-stalls in the spring of 1957 (with contributions from Mr Isaac Deutscher, M. Claude Bourdet, Professor G. D. H. Cole, and Mrs Joan Robinson), the gap had already so far narrowed that not only Mr E. P. Thompson (one of NR's two original editors) but even Mr E. J. Hobsbawm—presumably a revisionist, but certainly not an open rebel against the CP leadership—felt able to contribute articles to the new venture. The distinction—one cannot speak of a division —between former Communists and left-wing Socialists was further narrowed when ULR began to carry Marxist analyses of the British economy, while NR gradually moved away from its overriding concern with the USSR and Eastern Europe to give more space to domestic developments; and it vanished altogether when both journals adopted virtually identical attitudes towards the Labour Party's conduct of the 1959 election campaign. By then it was evident that the former Communists no longer regarded a 'reform' of the CP as possible, while the left-wing Socialists thought of the 'New Left' as a *movement* with a distinctive orientation, rather than a 'ginger group' within the Labour Party. Symbolically, the editorship of the combined journal was entrusted, by mutual consent, to a former ULR editor whose West Indian background, social origins, and quasi-

Trotskyist pre-1956 affiliations, seemed to mark him out as the embodiment of all those tendencies—anti-colonial, intellectual, neo-Marxist—which the New Left might be supposed to incarnate.

The *New Left Review*, whose first issue hit the news-stalls early in January 1960, thus presented itself as the distillation of a trend which had already found expression in its parent journals and in the two symposia, *Declaration* and *Conviction*, referred to earlier. Taking them together one may distinguish three distinct areas of interest common to the groups and individuals revolving around these various editorial platforms over the past four or five years: (1) World affairs, with special reference to nuclear disarmament and, latterly, racialism and anti-colonialism in Africa; (2) Socialism and Labour politics in post-war Britain, with special emphasis on the socio-cultural problems of industrial society in the age of full employment and the mass media; (3) Re-thinking of Marxism in the light of post-Stalinist disillusionment with the USSR and its particular brand of 'socialism'. The last-named subject was perhaps of greater initial concern to the NR group, but the more original contributions have tended to come from writers associated with the ULR whose approach to Marxism may be described as existentialist, in one case at least Christian-existentialist.[13] This is an aspect of the New Left which links it with similar currents across the Channel, but it is only one tendency among several. If the entire group, as now constituted, were run through an intellectual spectroscope, the picture would refract into a number of distinctive shades, running from more or less orthodox Marxism-Leninism (mainly in economics), by way of 'third force' Socialist neutralism and pacifism, to something like Christian existentialism in philosophy, as represented, with different degrees of emphasis, by Alasdair MacIntyre, Iris Murdoch, and Charles Taylor.[14] The same kind of 'spectrum analysis', when applied to the corresponding group around the Paris monthly *Arguments*, would disclose a similar result;

[13] Cf. Charles Taylor, 'Alienation and Community' (ULR, No. 5, Autumn 1958) and the same author's pamphlet *Is Marxism a Humanism?* The attitude reflected in these writings appears to have more in common with that of recent French and Polish discussions of Marxian philosophy than with the somewhat more traditional formulations of the NR group. For the latter cf. above all Mr E. P. Thompson's essay 'Socialist Humanism' (NR, Summer 1957, pp. 105ff.) and the same author's 'Socialism and the Intellectuals' (ULR, No. 1, Spring 1957).

[14] For the orthodox Marxist strain cf. in particular Mr E. J. Hobsbawm's paper 'Dr Marx and the Victorian Critics', in NR, 1, and Mr Ronald Meek's series of essays under the joint title 'Economics for the Age of Oligopoly', in NR, 8, 9, and 10.

Since NR began as a dissident Communist journal, it is not surprising that some of the early contributions—e.g. Professor Hyman Levy's 'Soviet Socialism' in No. 1—should have sounded the old ideological battlecries. The growing sophistication reflected in subsequent issues of NR doubtless helped to promote the eventual fusion with the ULR group.

and here too the political tie-up with the non-Communist Left (in this case the left-wing Socialist group associated with the weekly *France-Observateur*: the counterpart of the London weekly *Tribune*) has manifested itself in the somewhat excessive weight given to issues which happen to be of importance to Britain and France as ex-colonial powers: imperialism, racialism, pacifism. This is an aspect of the New Left of which its adherents tend to be unaware. It does not seem to occur to them, for example, that their relative indifference to the fate of people in Eastern Europe, as against their almost obsessive concern with even quite minor happenings in Britain's and France's former African dependencies, reflects a kind of West European parochialism. The same might be said of the anti-American strain which affects their thinking, seemingly unconsciously and without any awareness that the underlying sentiments are of a fairly traditional kind.

International affairs are the Achilles heel of the New Left. This was already evident from the *Conviction* symposium, where the two weakest and most pretentious essays were devoted to the subject. By contrast, economics and sociology are more effectively represented. *Conviction* indeed was barren of economics, but included some noteworthy analyses of the Welfare State, and detailed excursions into popular culture by Hoggart and Williams. Like the contributors to this volume, the ULR group from the start showed a desire to link the sociology of capitalism with the critique of modern culture, and some of its more original efforts were directed to that end. Others, e.g. Mr Michael Barrat-Brown's lengthy three-part study of the managerial organization of British industry and banking,[15] or Mr Ralph Samuel's essays on class society in Britain,[16] reflected the impact of transatlantic sociological thinking in general, and the example of Mr C. Wright Mills in particular. A contributing motivation may have been supplied by the desire to underpin the conviction of the Labour left-wing that effective control over the British economy has remained oligarchical and needs to be radically democratized. This theme was not always clearly distinguished from the related subject of 'class' in the peculiar British sense of 'caste'. A degree of confusion on this subject is traditionally endemic among all left-wing movements in Britain, though less so among writers whose Marxist training enables them to perceive the relevant distinction between 'class' as the embodiment of social control by a minority and 'class' as the (more or less illusory) possession of conventional

---

[15] 'The Controllers', ULR, Nos. 5, 6, and 7, sub-titled 'A Research Document on the British Power Elite'.

[16] 'Class and Classlessness', ULR, No. 6; 'The Boss as Hero', ULR, No. 7, and 'The Deference Voter', NLR, No. 1. Cf. also Stuart Hall, 'A Sense of Classlessness', ULR, No. 5, and Norman Birnbaum, 'Social Constraints and Academic Freedom', *ibid*.

marks of social distinction. It is the latter, not the former, sense of the term which is commonly intended when it is said that the aim of Socialism is to establish a classless society. Nonetheless the two subjects are linked in the minds of most writers adhering to the New Left, and it is this fact which sets them off from the 'new thinkers' on Labour's right wing, for whom 'class' in the traditional, or Marxian, sense has little or no significance.[17]

Taking all these themes together, and ignoring the differences arising from variations in personal and political background, the common ground occupied by the adherents of the New Left can perhaps be described somewhat as follows:

(1) World affairs since 1945—the *terminus a quo* for nearly all the writers adhering to the movement—are envisaged mainly in 'neutralist' or pacifist terms, as a competition between two rival blocs whose latent enmity threatens to bring about a global conflict fought with nuclear weapons. This is in conformity with Mr Nehru's well-known views, and it is not surprising to find that his position is regarded with sympathy. But it also accords with at least some of the sentiments voiced in Lord Russell's (Bertrand Russell's) writings since 1957, and it is this strand of thinking which connects the New Left most closely with the Campaign for Nuclear Disarmament and with the factional warfare inside the Labour Party. The borderline between pacifist and neutralist thinking—e.g. the CND's demand that Britain leave NATO, which would appear to be a political rather than a moral issue—tends to be somewhat blurred. For the rest, racial problems (now that colonialism is as good as dead) are mainly envisaged in terms common to Socialist and Liberal democrats all over the Western world. There is a marked reluctance to admit that working-class attitudes in this respect are not particularly 'progressive', and that middle-class Liberals—or even big business organizations—have been noticeably ahead of the 'common man' in working for racial equality.[18]

[17] The subject is too complicated to be dealt with here, and one can only say that the authors in question are evidently struggling with a post-Marxian formulation of what post-bourgeois society appears to be like. To date, the most substantial contribution to this discussion appears to have been made by Mr Raymond Williams, whose writings—notably *The Long Revolution*—are expressly concerned with the sociology of class and caste stratification and the chances of a genuinely democratic culture. This concern goes back to the 'Philosophic Radicalism' of the early nineteenth century, but Mr Williams is clearly influenced by William Morris rather than Bentham.

[18] Mr Ralph Samuel's article, 'The Deference Voter' (NLR, No. 1), provides a partial exception, in that it alludes—though rather casually—to the strength of traditional racial prejudices among working-class voters, who on these grounds supported the Conservative Party in the 1959 elections. But such candid admissions are rare. If the 'New Left' has yet grasped that 'Suez' lost the Labour Party hundreds of thousands of working-class votes, it has at any rate not said so in public.

(2) The analysis of capitalism in general, and of British society in particular, has broken away both from Fabianism and from rigid Leninist theorizing, but has not yet attained a theoretical level commensurate with the declared aim of providing the Labour movement with an up-to-date Socialist doctrine. The general tendency is to make a rigid distinction between Soviet society—as being in some sense 'socialist', though not democratic—and Western capitalism. This makes it excessively difficult to perceive that Western society has become 'post-bourgeois'. On the other hand, the factual analysis of Britain's 'mixed economy' is fairly close to the realities.[19]

(3) There is considerable uncertainty over doctrinal foundations. Here, as noted before, the spectrum runs all the way from orthodox Marxism, via a kind of traditional Socialist militancy as reflected in Mr E. P. Thompson's writings, to a species of Christian humanism. It is noteworthy that the writings devoted to these topics are much superior, as regards their intellectual level, to the amateurish and somewhat jejune pronouncements often made on 'ordinary' political or international matters. The same might be said of the more strictly 'literary' contributions, which are occasionally as good as anything published by the most exacting 'Establishment' organs.[20] This curious hiatus seems to reflect the somewhat accidental make-up of the inner circle, its overriding concern with matters of importance to intellectuals, and its comparative indifference to the boring trivia of public affairs. It would not be surprising to find the New Left giving birth to some quite genuinely novel and important ideas in the field of philosophy, whereas there are few signs so far that it is thinking hard about international politics.

In terms of intellectual history, perhaps the most striking feature of the New Left is its (largely unconscious) dependence on French existentialism, a dependence which goes hand in hand with a certain naïve insularity.[21] The latter is clearly perceived as a danger in philosophy (cf. Iris Murdoch's essay in *Conviction*), but otherwise does not get much attention. The liberation from Stalinism—which was the fundamental experience of the ex-Communists in the group,

---

[19] Cf. Brian Abel-Smith, 'Whose Welfare State?' in *Conviction*; and Peter Townsend, 'A Society for People', *ibid*. The bewilderment which seized hold of the Labour Party after 1955 is adequately portrayed in Norman Mackenzie's introductory essay to the volume, 'After the Stalemate'. Cf. also Ralph Milliband, 'The Sickness of Labourism', NLR, No. 1.

[20] If not better; cf. in particular the discussion on *Dr Zhivago* (ULR, Nos. 5 and 6), and on the Polish film *Ashes and Diamonds* (ULR, No. 7).

[21] De Gaulle's coming in 1958 even provoked something like a chauvinist outburst on the part of New Leftists. This began to look rather embarrassing when Gaullism turned out to be distinctly more progressive in regard to Algeria and Africa than the previous democratic regime. The latter, of course, was more responsive to popular pressures and *for this reason* more obscurantist. This is the kind of thought which, if it ever penetrates the minds of the New Left's ideologues, may be expected to give considerable pain to some very estimable people.

and to some extent affected the entire New Left—has brought in its wake, along with more desirable and better advertised features, a certain tendency to relapse into 'Little Englandism'. This is, however, held in check by the obvious circumstances that Paris (though not New York) continues to exercise a good deal of intellectual fascination. East of the Rhine, Marxism now tends to be identified with the heresies of Georg Lukacs and Bertolt Brecht (neither of them quite as heretical as the New Left is inclined to suppose). 'Socialist realism', for obvious reasons, makes no appeal to writers whose overriding concern with personal sincerity causes them to be on their guard against every species of officially sponsored make-believe.

Generally speaking, the future of the New Left must obviously depend on the development of the Socialist movement in Britain. Its current tie-up with the rebellious left wing of the Labour Party gives it a certain political resonance, but also increases the danger that political attitudes will become stereotyped. In contrast, the intellectual level of its more strictly theoretical pronouncements suggests the possibility of something like a genuine break-through in the fields of philosophy, literary and art criticism, and possibly the sociology of modern industrial culture. Both the characteristic weaknesses and some of the more promising traits of the movement were put on display with the publication, in the summer of 1960, of yet another volume of collected essays, entitled *Out of Apathy* and apparently intended to offer a synthesis of long-range philosophical reflections and short-term political recommendations.

In his prefatory remarks, the editor, Mr E. P. Thompson, made a valiant attempt to pull together the conflicting strands of Socialist internationalism and more specifically national concern with the state of society in modern Britain: the connection being provided by hostility to the Atlantic Alliance as the supposed primary source of conservative-traditionalist attitudes at home and abroad. With the outbreak of intensified strife inside the Labour Party over the Party leadership's refusal to adhere to 'unilateral' disarmament slogans, this theme has served to link the New Left more firmly to its political allies and turn it into the focus of a pacifist revolt in which the ingrained attitudes of the old non-conformist Bevanite movement have found fresh expression. At a deeper—or at any rate more literary—level, 'Natopolis'—Mr Thompson's term for the part of the world organized under US leadership—was discovered to be the breeding-ground of a 'Natopolitan' ideology of despairing quietism about politics. The problem for Socialists anxious to emerge from the 'Age of Apathy' was to get 'Outside the Whale', the 'Whale' being acceptance of the Cold War as unalterable; and the escape-hatch offered to the Socialist Jonah was the assertion that the British have it in their power to save themselves by their exertion, if not the rest of the world by their example. To quote from a contributor to the volume, Mr Peter Worsley:

'Britain is in a unique position in all this. What India has achieved would be as nothing compared to the immense pressure Britain could generate, in alliance with India, Ghana, Yugoslavia [sic] and backed by the uncommitted countries, for world peace and active neutrality. And most of these uncommitted nations are countries which could, under such stimulus, move towards socialism . . . India, Austria, Israel, Indonesia, Ghana, to name a few . . . not forming another frozen bloc, but trading and communicating freely, gradually breaking down the existing barriers on both sides.'

So bald a summary of the political programme outlined in this essay necessarily fails to do justice to the thinking that underlines the New Left's concrete specifications for pulling the Socialist rabbit out of the neutralist hat. Still, one could not help noticing that New Zealand and Sweden—both ruled by Labour governments—did not figure in a list which included the democracies governed by Marshal Tito and President Soekarno: New Zealand doubtless because it had committed the unforgivable sin of linking its defences with the USA; Sweden perhaps because, although neutral, it had been toying with the idea of acquiring a nuclear carapace. This leads to the reflection that a Socialist government which armed itself with atomic weapons for the purpose of guarding its neutrality would pose an exceedingly tough ideological problem for New Leftists who are also nuclear disarmers. What comes first: breaking free of 'Natopolis' or being disarmed? And what if these aims should conflict?

The real importance of this collection of essays fortunately was not exhausted by these exercises in wishful thinking. *Out of Apathy* contained no earth-shaking revelations, but it was a respectable contribution to the debate now going on within the Labour movement, and some of the essays did break new ground. Mr Thompson, when not busy denouncing the Natopolitan corruption of other intellectuals, had something important to say about the political morality of a generation which has at any rate managed to get outside the Stalinist whale; Mr Alasdair MacIntyre outlined the kind of sophisticated Hegelian neo-Marxism which has for years been debated in France, Italy, and Poland (and in the USA and West Germany too, though he fails to realize it); Mr Ralph Samuel, Mr Stuart Hall, and Mr Kenneth Alexander have all written trenchantly about corporate capitalism and the limits of the welfare state; and Mr Worsley, when not haunted by ghosts from the political past, was able to document the growing irrelevance of Conservative imperialism (though his rhetorical antithesis 'Renaissance or off-shore island?' begged all the real questions concerning Britain's status in Europe). Compared with the rather amateurish writings brought together in *Declaration* and *Conviction*, this symposium of New Left theorizing represented a step forward. At least the contributors displayed a standard of professional competence not always evident in the earlier essay collections.

Why was it finally not possible to feel that the authors had managed to pull Socialist theory and practice together into a new whole? The trouble would seem to lie at the political level. There were elements of a genuinely novel, fruitful, and undogmatic kind of thinking in Mr MacIntyre's critique of utilitarianism or in Mr Thompson's challenge to the apathetic 'realism' which grew out of the political stalemate of the '50s; but these ideas were not pursued to the end because the authors were too impatient to translate their insights into the language of practical politics. 'Natopolis' (a grotesque conceit no less surrealist than Orwell's fantasies, whose effect on the young was deplored by Mr Thompson) was invoked to render plausible the assertion that at bottom East and West are pretty much alike; a futile attempt was made to rekindle the emotions of the Spanish Civil War and the Second World War (which was not just an anti-Fascist crusade); the illusions of 1945—which were not shared by everyone—were treated as sacrosanct, and their loss blamed in unequal parts on Stalin and on the Americans (who appeared to be the real culprits). There was no recognition that the Western world might be held together by something besides capitalism and the Bomb. Characteristically, the intensification of the Cold War in 1948 was noted without any mention that Berlin served as a catalyst, and that it was the democratic Labour movement which bore the brunt of the Soviet offensive.

The reader of these essays is thus made to feel that their authors are primarily men of letters with an urge to bring about that fusion of theory and practice which Marxism demands, but which intellectuals are rarely able to achieve. Even in the more reflective pieces, the edge of the argument is often blunted by polemical irrelevancies arising from impatience to have done with theorizing and get into the arena of Aldermaston marches and other forms of political shadow-boxing. In this respect, Mr Thompson is perhaps the chief sinner, but Mr Alasdair MacIntyre, too, has his King Charles's Head; it is—Trotsky! The reader of his essay is urged to decide between 'Keynes with his peerage, Trotsky with an icepick in his skull. They are the twin lives between which intellectual choice in our society lies.' Between patrician liberalism on the one hand, and the utopian expectations of 1917 on the other, there is a no-man's-land uninhabited by any political formation to which this writer can honestly lend his allegiance. Fortunately, some of his colleagues seem less wedded to romanticism.

It would be unfair to conclude this appraisal without referring once more to a point already mentioned: the connection between the New

Left as a political grouping and certain purely intellectual trends pointing to a departure from liberalism and empiricism in philosophy. Though tenuous, the connection certainly exists. It has been exemplified in the work of Mr Alasdair MacIntyre—when he is not carried away by political romanticism, but sticks to philosophical analysis— and in a slightly different context by Miss Iris Murdoch's concern with existentialism as a possible alternative to, or complement of, empiricism. What it comes down to—at any rate in the opinion of the present writer—is a kind of auto-critique on the part of intellectuals for whom the traditional liberal emphasis on personal freedom of choice has come to seem bloodless and academic, because unrelated to *political* choice. Hence the interest in Marx and the early Hegel, with their conception of man as a being who freely creates his own world; and hence too the existentialist flavour of this somewhat idiosyncratic Marxism, which is certainly not that of Moscow. The subject is too complex to be pursued here. Suffice it to say that insofar as they have entered this particular arena of debate, the left-wing intellectuals in Britain may be said to form part of the growing current of European Marxist 'revisionism'.

Even the now fashionable concern with human 'alienation' in society is conducted in terms which at least raise the discussion to the level it has attained in New York and Paris since the last war. And here it is only fair to note that those former Communists who were at an early stage inoculated with Marxism have taken their share in working out an approach which is still in the Hegelian-Marxian tradition without being committed to the peculiar *Weltanschauung* of Soviet Marxism, or Marxism-Leninism. The achievement is no less significant for being somewhat belated. It is really two-fold, for in addition to emancipating themselves from Soviet Marxism, the writers in question have also transcended the increasingly rigid and inadequate framework of traditional British Empiricism and its political counterpart in the Socialist movement: the Fabian orthodoxy of 'social engineering' which in the last analysis derives from Bentham and the utilitarians. However highly one values the historic achievement of this school, it must be admitted that its international significance has diminished in a world in which the frontiers of the mind have widened, while those of the British empire have shrunk. It was comparatively easy, as late as 1914, to work on the assumption that the intellectual framework of British empiricism —and consequently of British liberalism and Fabianism—was broadly applicable to the world as a whole. Today it is evident that this is not the case. In facing this unpalatable fact, and in trying to overcome the traditional separation of British from European thought, the New Left—perhaps unconsciously—is making a minor but not insignificant contribution to the gradual emergence of a common international outlook.

XXII. France: The Neo-Marxists

JEAN DUVIGNAUD

It is not easy to pronounce upon the present course of revisionism in France without reference to the unfavourable conditions that France has presented for penetration by Marxism. This invites us to begin with a brief review of the past.

Although the working-class movement proclaimed itself, towards the end of the last century, as one of 'scientific Socialism', we cannot say that Marxism had been discussed and illustrated in France as it had been in central Europe during the same period. We might even speak of a *resistance* to it by the 'intellectual class' that had been nourished for more than a century on liberal ideas, and then upon the utopianisms of the '48.

The hard core of this resistance was, no doubt, in University circles: although we could not, as in the case of Italy, speak of a 'dictatorship of idealism' (for no French philosopher, not even Bergson, imposed himself with such force as Croce), it must be allowed that the French University had elevated a subtle synthesis of Kant and Comte to dogmatic status. During the second third of the nineteenth century this synthesis became the ideology of the higher ranks of the administration and of philosophic teaching. The centralized and strongly bureaucratic University system as Napoleon had founded it, and as it had been consolidated by the attacks of its adversaries themselves, therefore had its own dogmatic—a dogmatic that excluded dialectics as well as materialism.

Moreover, one could say of Marx and Hegel what has so often been said lately with regard to Husserl or Freud or Max Weber— that the invasions of the great ideas, while they were spreading widely in central Europe, were repulsed in France by the chauvinism and traditionalism of official bodies, right up to the last war.

The infiltration of Hegel and Marx was clandestine: before the war of 1914, it took place in the privacy of the Ecole Normale Supérieure, around the personality of Lucien Herr.[1] Later, in the days of Surrealism, some young University philosophers in conflict with the Sorbonne tried to introduce the use of the 'revolutionary

---

[1] Lucien Herr belongs to that race of men who write little, but whose influence is greater than their works. One of his rare publications was the article that he wrote for the *Encyclopédie* upon Hegel, which long remained almost the only reference to that philosopher in France!

dialectic'. But neither Georges Politzer,[2] nor Paul Nizan,[3] nor, above all, Henri Lefèbvre (whom we shall find again among the contemporary 'revisionists') succeeded in this aggressive enterprise. We had to wait until the last war before Hegel and Marx received the 'freedom of the city' at the Sorbonne and in the University curricula. And it was doubtless by becoming 'authors among the rest' that they became contestable authorities—being now deprived of their mystery.

Another reason for the feeble impact of Marxism upon France lies in the relations that the 'intellectual class' maintains with the political class. Indeed, the French intelligentsia, although ever since the eighteenth century it has demanded a control over politics, has claimed to exercise supervision over the recruitment of the elites, and has sought to possess means of direct intervention in social and political life, has never seemed to be very particular about the choice of its representatives! One remembers how Diderot and Voltaire acclaimed Frederick II and Catherine II as 'enlightened sovereigns', as mediators between Reason and the Peoples at the moment when those two rulers were behaving with vulgar rapacity. Such delegation of power to a man or a group regarded as the incarnation of Reason pretty clearly exemplifies the 'enlightened-ruler complex' that afflicts the intelligentsia of this country.

Thus, many of those who rallied to communism during the two great phases of the expansion of the party (the Popular Front and the Resistance) delegated to that organization not only their rights of control over its power, but worse still, their own right to criticize. The creation of a political 'higher self', as it were, had the effect of weakening all independent reflection. Their philosophy thus became ideology, and their reflection mere justification of slogans or catchwords given out by the hierarchy. One might say that the French intelligentsia that rallied round the Communist Party was returning both to the popery of the Catholics, implying obedience to a dogmatic

[2] Politzer, an *agrégé* in philosophy, was at first concerned to make certain German psychological researches known in France. Later, he was converted to militant Marxism, joined the CP and disowned his earlier 'illusions'. Denounced and arrested during the occupation, he was shot by the Nazis.

[3] Nizan was undoubtedly, with Sartre and Malraux, the most brilliant writer of his generation. A 'Normalien *agrégé* in philosophy, he wrote a pamphlet against Brunschvicg, his master at the Sorbonne—*Les Chiens de Garde*. His novel, *La Conspiration*, is one of the best descriptions of the situation before 1940. Having become a communist, he wrote the diplomatic page in *l'Humanité*; then revolted against the Soviet-German Pact, left the party, enlisted in the army, and disappeared during the siege of Dunkirk. In 1960, an avant-garde publisher, Maspero, had the idea of republishing *Les Chiens de Garde* with a preface by Sartre. This became one of last year's best sellers. Sartre, however, in his introduction, is less concerned to discuss fundamental criticism than to evoke the visage of his old friend, which he does with much fire and vigour.

imposed from abroad, and to the Cartesian intellectualism which despises all dialectics!

Twice over, this same mechanical reaction took place. First, at the advent of Surrealism, younger philosophers such as Nizan, Politzer, and Lefèbvre had no sooner entered into the party organization than they almost immediately ceased to illustrate and expound Marxism as 'a universal and complete conception of the world'. And again, after the Liberation, their successors of a younger generation encountered the same resistances and yielded to them in the same way.

As for the other two categories of French 'Marxists' or 'Marxians', they are of no direct interest to us here. The first is of those who wanted to remain true to the principles of their youth, and did not join the Communist Party. Adherents of various Trotskyist groups, they have produced work of quality and often of importance (such as that of Daniel Guérin on the French Revolution, and Pierre Naville's on Human Labour), but one could not expect them to 'revise' their system of thought. Secondly, there are those Catholics who have sought to expound the thought of Marx in the pastoral-social departments of their seminaries. Their works, such as those of Calvez or Bigot, are always fair and correct; and we cannot expect *them*, allergic as they are to the spirit of heresy, to understand how the Marxist system may be broken!

In view of these impediments to the development of Marxism in France, and of the belated acceptance of dialectical thinking, it is easy to see why Marxist revisionism should have been almost contemporary with the spread of Marxism itself! And it is a remarkable fact that the criticism of Marxism has, for the last ten years, provoked more passion and more philosophic activity than the defence of it.

Here we shall pay attention only to the revisionism proposed by sociologists and philosophers trained in Marxism who have at some time in their lives been members of the Communist Party.

It will be necessary, then, to leave aside all that has been written by the adversaries of Marxism, or by the existentialist philosophers who, at the end of the war, were trying to combine dialectical materialism with phenomenology. Thus, the well-known works of Raymond Aron obviously anticipate contemporary revisionism, but they did not really attain their full meaning until the moment when younger men than he arrived by experience at ideas nearly approaching his own (a moment, too, when Aron moved towards the 'Left' in his opposition to the war in Algeria). Nor do the essays of Merleau-Ponty concern us here, since they take no account of the experimental reality of Marxism but put themselves upon a plane of pure ideas, applicable only to pure speculation about an 'ideal communism'.

Similarly, we shall not here make use of evidence supplied by novelists who broke with communism (such as Jean Cassou, Edith Thomas, Clara Malraux, J. F. Rolland), nor by poets (like Pierre

Emmanuel or Francis Ponge) because they bear only upon the moral and aesthetic aspects of Stalinism, and our concern here is to see what it is that has raised the whole question of Marxism itself—and even of socialism—as a political vision.

We shall therefore examine the ideas of those who, at the present day, are asking themselves, and trying to answer, these two questions:

(1) Is Marxism, in whatever form it is embodied, the best means of realizing the socialist ideal?

(2) Is equalitarian socialism—a dream of the last century, contemporary with the beginnings of capitalism—still a reasonable ideal, or does it now belong to the museum of imaginary politics?

There is one sphere in which revisionism might have developed in freedom—almost without political consequences—namely, that of the 'social sciences'. But for this to have happened, scientific works of Marxist inspiration and indisputable quality would have had to be already in existence: which was hardly the case.

For the reasons we have examined above, Marxism never struck root in the body of French scientific research. Some specialists like H. Wallon, P. Georges, or L. Dresch may have produced works of authority in psychology, demography, or geography, but it would be very hard to find in these works any reflection upon questions of importance to Marxism—even orthodox Marxism.

These scientists call themselves Marxists or communists. But Marxism is of no service to them in their work, where they simply make use of the traditional methods and modes of thought appropriate to the domain of science that each is developing. And elsewhere, how much Marxism do they remember beyond a vague scientism or a 'Comtiste' positivism, which is scarcely compromising?

In a recent study devoted to French historical works and to the school of Marc Bloch-Lucien Febvre, Fernand Brandel notes 'how little' Marxism has 'besieged' the profession of history. Here and there, it is true, some influences penetrate, but these are but partial, fragmentary solicitations: 'The one thing lacking, in this early twentieth century, is a master-work of Marxist history which could have provided a model and a rallying-point: we are still waiting for it.'[4]

The absence of Marxism from the 'social sciences' upon which it should have made an impression, is remarkable. In history, one can find hardly anything worthy of the name, beyond the work of Albert Soboul.[5] Soboul, a Marxist, revised the Stalinian conception of the French Revolution which, by comparing Robespierre to Stalin, had conjured away the reality of the popular movements.

Revisionism among the Marxist 'scientists' being non-existent, as non-existent as works of Marxist inspiration, the task of not only

[4] *Traité de sociologie* (1959).
[5] *Les Sansculottes parisiens en l'An II* (1959).

restoring the real vision of Marx has devolved upon non-Marxists. Here I am thinking of the books by J. Y. Calvez and of P. Bigot about Marx, and above all of the courses delivered at the Sorbonne by G. Gurvitch, on the notion of class and on the Marxian sociology.[6] By referring back to the confusion and hesitations of the 'founder', by re-establishing the standpoint of research and the historical context of his work, Gurvitch has undoubtedly done much to dispel ready-made ideas. The large number of students who have followed these courses know, from now onward, that certain stupidities about Marx are not allowable.

The importance of French revisionism is undoubtedly due to this—that the communists found themselves in a situation analogous, in its way, to that of the intellectuals in a 'popular democracy'. The rude remarks that they made about the communist apparatus are analogous to those passed upon it by the men of the Petöfi circle in Hungary or of the review *Po Prostu* in Poland.

This, it is true, was their situation only in a moral sense: there were no police in France who compelled the communist intellectuals to live in the 'ideological ghetto' of the party. But everyone knows that the psychological and social solicitations that follow from the creation of the political 'super-ego' we mentioned just now can exert a mental tyranny symbolically comparable to police pressure. French Marxists knew that they were living in a democratic country, but they themselves were getting lost in a political prison, the bars and walls of which they were helping to construct. Thus we can say, without much risk of error, that most of the French revisionists' ideas correspond to the revisionist ideas in the popular democracies, since the intellectuals in this country too had, for some time, put themselves into a situation formally comparable to that which obtains over there.

But before examining these revisionist ideas, we ought surely to make the distinction that was drawn by Edgar Morin,[7] in a recent number of the review *Arguments*,[8] between *restricted* and *general* revisionism.

Restricted revisionism is concerned only with the external aspects of Marxism. It does not call into question the system of socialist

---

[6] C.D.U., 1954, 1956.

[7] Morin belongs to the generation now entering into its forties. Having become communist during the war, he took up the study of the forms of magic in contemporary civilization. He was expelled from the CP, and applied his own methods to himself; it was then that he wrote *L'Autocritique*, in which he related his political experiences in order to analyse the magical forms they exemplified.

[8] *Arguments*, a review published by the Editions de Minuit, was founded by Edgar Morin and the writer of this article in 1957. It has published the majority of the revisionist texts, and has made known the thought of foreign philosophers in quest of a new political position. Today, this latter preoccupation tends to overshadow all the rest, in a review liberated from the Marxist 'taboos'.

ideas or the actual tissue of the 'revolutionary dialogue'. It admits, in general, that socialism will be 'regenerated' when it has swept away the ashes of Stalinism and of the military dictatorship.

General revisionism, on the other hand, demands quite a different effort and a more sustained application. It concedes nothing at all to utopianism, and endeavours to apply the Marxist criticism to Marxism itself, regardless of the immediate consequences that might ensue from such a total restatement of the question.

The themes that we outline here certainly do not all imply their authors' acceptance of *general* revisionism (neither Mascolo[9] nor Lefèbvre would agree to so complete a revision of their values), but they enable us to follow the often complex proceedings of this critical movement, in which a great many writers and philosophers are engaged.

When he went to Poland a little while after the events of October 1956, Dionys Mascolo found himself embarrassed among his foreign friends: the French intellectuals had been unable to hinder either the colonial war or the establishment of Stalinism. Petty cowardices, disavowals, capitulations, grotesque trivialities had reduced the French intellectuals, both of the right and the left, to the status of 'sympathizers' who ratify without protest the dismal fate allotted to them. Stalinism plays a special part in this degradation, for these 'officials appointed to the tasks of propaganda falsely called cultural' are betraying both the revolution and the authentic communism to which Mascolo refers.

To this 'corruption of the intellectuals' Edgar Morin returns in his *Autocritique*, and suggests a political explanation for it. In his sociological works, Morin has studied the survival, or the persistence, of magic in the consciousness of civilized, industrial man. Applying the same methods to his own adventures, he now discovers the *magical* nature of Stalinism, and indeed of Marxism too. Man in history, as he is pictured by Marx, is no longer the real man, but a phantom, and into this phantom the living man projects all his own resources of energy—to the point of losing himself in a logical but hysterical frenzy. Thinking then loses its meaning: Marxism has supplanted it!

In a recently published essay, *Le Marxisme en question*, Pierre Fougeyrollas[10] shows that the Marxist analysis is one of the great

[9] Mascolo is of the same generation as Morin. He joined the CP during the war, and was expelled about 1950. His *Polish Letter on the intellectual poverty in France* was published in 1957 by the Editions de Minuit.

[10] Fougeyrollas, who also belongs to the generation of Morin and Mascolo, was condemned to death by the Nazis during the war, but became one of the liberators of Limoges. Professor of philosophy in Paris, he resigned from the CP at the time of the Hungarian affair; his *Marxisme en question* was published in 1959.

philosophies directed to the emancipation of man—but *only one* of those philosophies. To the classical Marxist theory of 'super-structures' ineluctably fastened to 'infra-structures' that determine them, Fougeyrollas opposes a more elastic conception of social dynamics, and tries to show that the 'models' or 'patterns' proposed by Marx do not correspond to permanent situations. Society is capable of infinite accommodations and variations, and the forms specified by Marx are only aspects of these. If, therefore, we want to understand something of the real history of our times, we had better repudiate the *fixed* patterns laid down by Marx, and measure the extent to which a still fluid society renders possible all kinds of relationships between classes and the means of production. Thus the privilege that is claimed for Marxism, as the regulator of all socialist or historical reflection, breaks down.

That privilege is contested also by Henri Lefèbvre[11] in *La Somme et le Reste*, but on the strictly philosophic plane. Comparing Marxism with other forms of thought that he had previously found seductive —such as Schelling's and that of Nietzsche—he comes to the conclusion that the materialist dialectic is *one of the possible reflections* upon Being and Becoming. One could even say, pursuing Lefèbvre's line of thought, that Marxism is like a symbol into which one reads everything that one desires. Immersed in the communist experience and subjected to the pressures of ideology and dogma, the philosopher thus transmutes the thought of Marx into a total system, able to replace all the others. In the end, Marxism becomes an 'all-purpose philosophy' and consequently good for nothing.[12]

In the course of several journeys through the popular democracies, I have personally had opportunity to see that the imposition of Marxism upon certain countries (such as Eastern Germany, for instance) causes a setback of several years in their development. By this I mean that the directorate of a few, which is constituted by the professional revolutionaries, having planted itself upon a country whose social forms are already well developed in conjunction with its industrial growth, is obliged to bring that country back again to the stage at which it was when Marx made his analysis of an earlier

[11] Lefèbvre, who belongs to the generation born at the turn of the century, is the only French Marxist philosopher. In the early days of Surrealism, he tried to illustrate the conception of the Marxist world, and his works on *La Conscience mystifiée* (in collaboration with N. Gutermann) and *Le Matérialisme dialectique* have had an enormous influence. After becoming a communist, he exchanged philosophy for ideology, which he sought to apply to literary analysis, publishing books on Rabelais, Pascal and Musset. After expulsion from the CP he wrote a book dealing with the history of his thought, *La Somme et le Reste* and won the 'Prix des Critiques'.

[12] Here I may be allowed to mention my own critical essay on the foundations of Marxism and of political ideologies: *Pour entrer dans le XXème siècle* (Grasset, 1960).

capitalism. If Marx is to be justified, everything seems to show that the social reality must be *magically* reduced to what it was at the time of the first railways—although at the same time certain technological sectors are being developed with the most modern means.

That there is such a divergence is the conclusion reached by François Fejto, in his analyses of the Popular Democracies.

Surveying the imposition of Stalinism upon Hungary and the other countries of Central Europe, Fejto shows that the forms of association imposed by dogma correspond in no way to the expansion of the human personality in a socialist environment. And if the institutions representing the transition to communism have not proved favourable to man it is not likely that the system they are leading to will be any more so. To think so is to forget that institutions, once set up, no longer obey their founders' intentions but have their own way of life; and that one is no longer allowed to mention reform, as soon as men have stopped talking of revolution.

To a lesser degree we find the same theme in the *Autocritique* of Morin, where the notion of the Party as the sole means of leading the masses to socialism is subjected to a severe criticism. Examining the processes of bureaucratization and 'cretinization' in the Party apparatus, and trying to view this apparatus in the more general perspectives of one class, of an ideal collective, of one country, and of the divergent outlooks that constitute the warp and weft of social reality, Morin concludes that this organization 'alienates' the working class and, in the end, cheats it of its own objectives.

There are two kinds of Marxist concepts—those that belong to the 'canon' of the doctrine (such as class, ideology, revolution, surplus-value, etc.), and those that come out of the 'vulgate', having been brought to light or invented by the Marxists of the end of the last century or the beginning of the present one (such as alienation, mystification, reification, etc.). If the former belong to a concrete analysis of the economic and sociological reality of the time of Marx, and are founded upon realities of the nineteenth century, the latter are only so many attempts to enrich the poverty of Marxism by adding to it. The work of Bernstein, Kautsky, Lukacs, Walther Benjamin, Korsch, Ernst Bloch, or even of Adorno or of Horkheimer, has always consisted in the creation of a phantasy of Marxism around Marx. The official hierarchy may occasionally complain about this phantasy; nevertheless, such a cloud of smoke is quite useful to it, serving as it does to drug the brains of certain philosophers.

Such 'Marxist' concepts as alienation and reification still have a certain success in France; for, following upon the works of Lefèbvre, such as *La Conscience mystifiée*, certain talented epigoni did, to a certain extent, embellish and illustrate them by means of a set of new terms borrowed from the dictionaries of the Austro-German universities. But these are not essential concepts: one can dispute them without thereby questioning the Marxist teaching itself.

Only a much more searching analysis can take the key concepts—those of class, ideology, revolution, surplus-value, or of the circulation of industrial capital—and subject them to examination. That is what Fougeyrollas attempts in *Le Marxisme en question*: the confusion of different meanings of the word 'class' brings him to recognize that we must either abandon this concept or, at least, reconsider its constituent elements. Has not modern industrial progress profoundly modified the social stratification in contemporary societies, bringing about the appearance of what is now called the 'tertiary sector'? Ought not the use of ideas of so little precision, which in their classical form are indeed out-of-date, be given up?

As for ideologies, Fougeyrollas argues that these are not simply reflections of the economic sub-structures. A closer analysis constrains the analyst to abandon concepts that have become meaningless. Even the concept of revolution itself is subjected to a stringent criticism, both by Fougeyrollas and by Lefèbvre. Not that either of them denies the effervescence and mobility of society, or the power of a group of men to break down the existing structures of a society by violence, in order to bring the great masses of humanity into a rational order. But both of them—and Lefèbvre especially—regard 'the Revolution' as an epiphytic myth, all too liable to dry up the thought of the individual investigator or philosopher. *La Somme et le Reste* is like an Odyssey, a tale of the distressing voyage of a consciousness unluckily caught between the Hegelian Charybdis of the 'absolute' Revolution and the Scylla of an opportunist ideology. If the Revolution still has a meaning, ought it not to be defined anew?[13]

If the fundamental Marxist concepts have thus to be revised in the light of contemporary economic realities and of modern industrial civilization; if the whole of the ideology, all the forms of thought, both revolutionary and simply political, have to be broken up and replaced by new perspectives, does this not amount to saying that we had better have done with the formulas of Marxism? The social levelling is a fact; it is going on without the socializing ideologies which are invented to justify it. Economic progress is another fact: it makes nonsense of the philosophies of history, for it is being realized in America without the famous 'crises' which Marx thought inseparable from and essential to capitalism; and is being realized in

---

[13] It is in connection with the revaluation of this word 'revolution' that one should read the vivid and polemical analyses of Pierre Hervé in his books *La Révolution des Fétiches*, and *Dieu et César, sont-ils communistes?* Hervé was expelled from the CP for having been a 'Khrushchevian' before Khrushchev had made his most celebrated speech. Here he examines the various illusions shared by most of the French communist leaders, and sheds a harsh critical light upon the prejudices and ready-made ideas entertained by the responsible ideologists of the Party.

L

the USSR in the teeth of those who did not *want* to build up a capitalist accumulation, but have done so all the same—by calling it 'socialist accumulation'! Clearly, then, every 'limited revisionism'— however little it may be true to its own logic or however deficient it may be in courage—can only lead to 'general revisionism'.

Two successive numbers of the review *Arguments* (14 and 16) were devoted to such a radical revisionism. 'Everyone ought to confess to himself where he now stands,' was the opening declaration of this collective examination of political and social values.

It was Kostas Axelos,[14] undoubtedly, who carried this logical enquiry the farthest, by drawing the ultimate conclusions which could not fail to follow from the criticisms that were formulated and presented, among other aspects of general revisionism, by the review *Arguments*.

After the great controversy aroused by the Hungarian affair, which went on for nearly two years, the revisionist movement was weakened. Setting aside the polemical work of J. Baby, published in the autumn of 1960, which criticizes the political methods practised in the French party (but does not start a fundamental debate), we find no further attempt to call the foundations of Marxism in question.

It may be that the establishment of the Gaullist regime is bringing about contradictory consequences. Opposition to the centre of power is re-grouping a few small movements of intellectuals into virulent and ineffectual sects, in which the 'big words' of the Marxist vocabulary regain currency—the class struggle, the armed rising of the workers, the dictatorship of the proletariat, etc. There are also groups publishing, at great expense, confidential reviews like *l'Internationale situationniste*, where the most elementary thinking mingles with the most unpleasant vulgarity.

Other groups try to restore to life some policy which drew inspiration from Marxist concepts. These groups are more effective, because they find themselves back again in organizations like the Parti Socialiste Unitaire. The Workers' University, founded in the autumn of 1960, is a response to the demand for some magical restoration of the nineteenth-century past. The Franco-Swiss review *Médiations*, too, is another attempt to regroup young, rather immature, provincial intellectuals, with a few nostalgic elders of the 'great old days'.

A majority of the intellectuals who have been involved in Marxism have withdrawn from it without attempting any authentic criticism of its fundamentals.

As for the attempt by Sartre, in his *La Critique de la Raison dialectique*, published in 1960, this is not an attempt to reopen the

[14] Axelos, after the revolution and civil war in Greece, in which he took an active part as a communist, took refuge in France, and left the Party. He is one of the Editors of *Arguments*.

question. Sartre, abandoning certain existentialist positions, but criticizing certain aspects of Marxism, is attempting not so much a radical analysis of fundamentals, as a synthesis. Moreover, the philosopher seems concerned, above all, to resolve the very old problem of 'free will or determinism'; he is not asking himself whether the mental attitudes of the nineteenth century are still suitable in our days.

The dreams of the nineteenth century doubtless corresponded to the most elementary necessities of men, to the great hunger that had depressed human societies for thousands of years, separating them into classes in accordance with economic requirements. And capitalism, in its creative phase, did not destroy these ancient forms, but even accentuated them. In its infancy, it was indeed that frightful monster of which Engels speaks for Great Britain, and that Marx analysed with genius in *Das Kapital*. That was all true enough, and if the proletarian revolution had broken out at that time, as Marx expected, it might have justified his hopes. But that time passed; and, more than the time, it was the growth of the economy and the pace of events that modified the ways of life and overturned the old structures of nineteenth-century social and economic capitalism. How could the dreams of men still be the same today as they were a hundred years ago, when the Parisian workers came out for the Commune? With the satisfaction of men's primary demands, which the West has appeased wherever it has imposed a liberal democracy, are not new needs arising—and new dreams? Or are we to go on vegetating in the utopias of the last century, and setting up idols in front of men who altogether repudiate them? The best service and the sincerest homage that we can render to the memory of Marx, is to deal with Marxism as he dealt with the systems of his age. That is, to challenge the social organization set up in his name, realizing that new dreams must be invented for a new world.

XXIII. Italy: The Choice for the Left

GIORGIO GALLI

The Twentieth Congress of the CPSU and the events connected with it reawakened in Italy the ideological debate between the various trends of opinion basing themselves on Marxism. Following a period of lively discussion and polemics, their respective standpoints may now be considered to be fairly well established, if less rigidly than was the case up to 1956. In order to understand the nature and details of this ideological process it is necessary first to consider in broad outline the general situation in that year. Since the various ideological standpoints were each of them related more or less directly to political movements, any attempt to identify the trends of opinion must inevitably include reference to those movements.

The various ideological standpoints defining themselves as Marxist can be classified as follows:

(i) The two great 'mass' parties, the Communist Party (PCI) and the Socialist Party (PSI), both of which still described themselves as Marxist-Leninist. They claimed to accept Marxism according to the interpretation given to it by Lenin. But the need to adapt Lenin's views to the conduct of political action over a long period under a democratic parliamentary regime (a situation in which Lenin had never been placed) inevitably gave rise to a whole series of adjustments and modifications of the Russian revolutionary's ideas; and consequently the theoretical basis of these parties acquired a confused and contradictory character. In addition to this there was the need to justify at all times the internal and foreign policy of the USSR, a constant preoccupation shared at that time both by the PCI and the PSI, which introduced further elements of ambiguity on the theoretical no less than on the political plane. According to this interpretation, the USSR was a socialist State at the head of the 'socialist camp' which was threatened by aggression on the part of Western, and particularly American, imperialism; and in order to carry out this aggressive policy in the international sphere, and to avoid internal difficulties, Western capitalism tended to move on to a more openly Fascist plane. Hence the need for the working-class movement to struggle, in the first place, to maintain peace, and secondly to defend democratic liberties whose banner—to quote Stalin's well-known phrase—the bourgeoisie had let fall.

(ii) The Social-Democratic Party (PSDI), which also affirmed the primary need to defend democratic liberties—but which saw the main threat to those liberties in the PCI, a totalitarian party under the orders of a totalitarian State (the USSR), where not socialism but a dictatorial regime of State capitalism reigned. In the PSDI's view, within the framework of parliamentary democracy, which acted as the bulwark against totalitarian threats, economic and social reforms should be carried out, with the aim of attracting to the democratic State the masses who were under the influence of the PCI and, even more, the PSI.

(iii) The small intermediary groups consisting of ex-Communists and ex-members of the two socialist parties, who were critical alike of Stalinism and of traditional Social-Democracy (such as, for example the Unione Socialisti Indipendenti (USI)), or who drew their inspiration from a so-called 'liberal socialism' deriving from the pre-war clandestine anti-Fascist movement *Giustizia e Libertá* (for example, the Unitá Popolare (UP) group.[1]

(iv) The trends deriving from the left wing of the Third International, i.e. the Partito Comunista Internazionalista (Internationalist Communist Party)[2] centred round Bordiga, a former first secretary of the PCI at its foundation, and the Revolutionary Communist Groups (Trotskyists) adhering to the Fourth International. These small groups, with no influence on the masses, criticized the Stalinist distortion and the abandonment by the Russian leaders of Leninist principles both on the internal and the international plane; the distinction between them lay in the fact that the former regarded the USSR as a regime of State capitalism, while the latter, following Trotsky's well-known analysis, considered it a 'degenerate working-class State' governed by a bureaucracy.

(v) The politically uninvolved or only marginally involved intellectuals, among whom an interesting group was that centring round the review *Ragionamenti*, linked to the French group of *Arguments*, which as early as 1955 foreshadowed the type of thinking which was later to be described as 'revisionist'.

In addition, within the framework of the larger parties there existed trends more or less openly critical of the official line. Thus, within the PCI, from the summer of 1954 onwards, there was the *Azione comunista* group, which from a left-wing standpoint criticized the leadership especially for its failure to exploit the revolutionary situation which, in the group's view, existed in Italy immediately after the war, and also for its parliamentary policy; their organ was the *Lettere ai compagni*, which circulated inside the party. Within the PSI, it was well known that certain influential personalities and intellectuals adopted an attitude of reserve, and that their ideas,

---

[1] The USI organ was the weekly *Risorgimento Socialista*, the UP published the weekly *Nuova Republica*.

[2] Its organ is the fortnightly *Il programma comunista*.

whether from Leninist, Luxemburgist, or Marxist-gradualist influence, did not coincide with the party line. In the PSDI, criticism of the majority line (which favoured passive collaboration in the 'bourgeois' government) was particularly lively among the trend deriving its inspiration from *Critica Sociale*, the first Italian Socialist review, founded by Filippo Turati in 1891. This review had remained independent and still adhered to its line of democratic Marxism.

What was the reaction, from the ideological angle, of these various trends to the Soviet Communist Party's Twentieth Congress, the Poznan rebellion, and the events of October 1956 in Poland and Hungary, and what new trends emerged as a result of these events?

Within the PCI, in the first instance, the official line was to stress Khrushchev's dictum that, in the new situation resulting from the 'victory of socialism' in a third of the world, it was possible for Communist parties in capitalist countries to gain power by democratic parliamentary means. This thesis, the opposite of Lenin's hypotheses in the period after the first World War, had been maintained by the PCI, and in particular by its secretary Togliatti, ever since 1944, and it was now reiterated afresh after a partial eclipse during the 'cold-war' years. On the one hand it was averred that the launching of the sixth Five-Year Plan provided further proof of the validity and efficiency of the Soviet system; on the other hand, the modification of one of Lenin's central ideas was seen as a consequence of the change in power relationships between socialism and capitalism at world level. Criticisms of the Stalinist period were represented as a process of internal correction within the system involving no ideological problems.

At the first meeting of the PCI Central Committee after the Twentieth Congress, Togliatti launched the slogan of the 'Italian way to socialism'—thus resuming once more his own original standpoint—in these words: 'New conditions have been created by the existence of the socialist camp and by the consequent modifications in the world structure and in relation to the struggle for socialism . . . what we are doing today would have been neither possible nor right thirty years ago—it would have been pure opportunism, as indeed at that time we said it was.' In support of this position, now presented as no longer opportunist because of the changed situation, Togliatti discovered its remote origins in the philosophy of Antonio Gramsci, a leading Italian Marxist who had directed the PCI from 1924 to 1926 and died in prison in 1937 during the Fascist dictatorship. Togliatti declared: 'The search for an Italian road towards socialism has been our constant preoccupation. I believe I can say that it was also a preoccupation with Antonio Gramsci, who in all his political action, and particularly in the last period of his life, was concerned to provide an Italian version of the lessons of the Russian revolution.'[3]

After Khrushchev's celebrated 'secret report' was made public at the beginning of June, Togliatti, after speaking of 'certain forms of degeneration' occurring in the USSR, arrived at the ideologically most advanced point to be reached within the framework of the communist movement with his famous assertion that communism was now becoming polycentric. This is what he said: 'The Soviet model cannot and must not any longer be obligatory. . . . The whole complex of the system is becoming polycentric, and within the communist movement itself it is no longer possible to speak of a single guide. . . . Out of the criticism of Stalin a general problem arises, common to the whole movement.'[4]

But while the Poznan rebellion was being suppressed, the Soviet leaders took up a position against revisionism with their resolution of June 30, in which they directly criticized Togliatti for his attitude about the 'forms of degeneration', maintaining that 'There is no basis for raising such a question.' The PCI leader then published an editorial about the events in Poland under the title 'The presence of the enemy',[5] in which he swiftly returned to the customary thesis that the main cause for the disturbances in eastern Europe lay in the manoeuvres of imperialism. This was the line which the PCI ultimately adopted during the crisis of 1956: on the one hand stress was laid on the possibility of attaining power in the West by democratic and parliamentary means; on the other hand it was made clear that criticisms of Stalinism were not to bring into discussion the criteria for wielding power within the Soviet system. On the first point, precise affirmation is given in the theses for the Eighth Congress of the PCI (December 1956), although an element of reserve remains in the statement that 'the "peaceful", painless development will depend on a complex network of conditions of which some depend on us, while others depend on the enemy's actions. . . . We can never say that there is absolute certainty of a peaceful development.'[6]

---

[3] These quotations are taken from the PCI daily *Unità*, March 15, 1956. Gramsci's writings were published after the war and exerted a considerable influence in the intellectual as well as the political world. It should be borne in mind that his philosophy underwent various phases. Originally (1919–20) he attached great importance to the role of the factory councils, especially in Turin, seeing in them the possible Italian Soviets. Later, in 1920–21, he accepted the pre-eminent function of the party; and lastly (1924–26) he became concerned with the importance of an alliance between the industrial workers of the North and the impoverished peasants of Italy's backward South as a decisive element in an eventual Italian revolution. By emphasizing one or other aspect of his philosophy it can be utilized to support theses which are sometimes divergent, as was in fact the case in the years under consideration.

[4] *L'Unità*, June 17, 1956.

[5] *L'Unità*, July 3, 1956.

[6] Togliatti in *Rinascita* (PCI monthly), July 1956.

While outside events were moving rapidly, the 'centrist' position adopted by the party leadership favoured the development within the PCI of two different trends. The *Azione comunista* group began in June 1956 the publication of a fortnightly in which it criticized the parliamentary line adopted by the PCI from 1944 onwards. This group considered that the existence of the 'socialist camp' did not justify abandoning the Leninist thesis that the conquest of power can only come about by revolutionary means. At the same time, starting out from an examination of the origins of Stalinism, they modified their opinion concerning the socialist character of the Soviet system and, without defining it precisely, accepted the criticisms about its distortion advanced by the left wing. The events in Poland and Hungary accentuated this development, and the group, whose members were expelled from the PCI, showed an increasing tendency to resemble, from the ideological standpoint, the old left-wing opposition groups which quitted the Third International, rejecting alike the opportunism of communism in the West and the forms it had assumed in the East. [7]

At the same time a 'revisionist' opposition group developed within the PCI, which aimed at carrying to extreme lengths the new ideas about the utilization of parliamentary democracy. This faction, which, given the structure of the PCI, did not succeed in becoming an organized trend, claimed that the leadership's passive acceptance of the theoretical bases and political implications of Stalinism had restricted the PCI's possibilities of action during the preceding decade, and that approval by the leadership of the dictatorial governments thrown up by the Soviet system, and even more of the repression exercised in Hungary, made it impossible for the party to present itself as a champion of those libertarian and democratic values which it claimed to accept.

This trend, which through its various groups fought first within and later outside the PCI, thus tended to adopt a position similar to the traditional outlook of gradualist Marxism, which regarded democratic freedoms as being limited by the economic structure of bourgeois society but nevertheless as a permanent acquisition of mankind, to be developed with the advent of socialism. Grafted on to this traditional standpoint was the influence of modern sociology, of neo-positivism, of Gramsci in his factory-council period, and of the idea of the 'leadership of the proletariat', in antithesis to the more rigid conception of dictatorship. Collaboration between this trend and the intellectuals gave rise to two reviews which afforded a clear

[7] In 1957 the *Azione comunista* group merged with the small libertarian communist movement GAAP (*Gruppi anarchici di azione proletaria*—Anarchist Groups of Proletarian Action) which some years previously had detached itself from the anarchist movement FAI (*Federazione anarchica italiana*) and which published the monthly *L'Impulso*.

expression of their attitudes: *Tempi Moderni*, edited by Fabrizio Onofri, a former member of the PCI Central Committee, and *Passato e Presente*, under the influence of Antonio Giolitti, a communist Deputy and former Under-Secretary for Foreign Affairs at the time when the PCI participated in the Government, who is now a PSI Deputy.[8] Another group, led by Eugenio Reale, a former Senator and member of the PCI Directorate, produced the weekly *Corrispondenza socialista*, an organ of political struggle rather than ideological enquiry; the group, which took the name of 'Alleanza socialista', accepted the theoretical standpoint of the PSDI (described above) and in fact eventually joined that party.

Reactions to the events of 1956 outside the PCI were of even greater importance. In the PSDI, they were interpreted as the confirmation of the rightness of the party's views, for the PSDI had all along denounced the totalitarian and oppressive character of the Soviet regime. But in the party as a whole no effort was made either to analyse from a social and economic point of view the changes that were going on in the USSR, or to examine the problems raised by the new situation for European and in particular for Italian socialism. The left-wing trend alone, and especially *Critica Sociale*, while seizing the opportunity to stress the characteristics of its own brand of Marxism, sought to face questions which went beyond the immediate situation. Among what they regarded as the theoretical tasks of socialism were:

'An analysis of the nature of the regimes in the Russo-Chinese bloc, which may be represented either as the most advanced and "concentrated" form of capitalism (transformed into State capitalism) or as a new economico-social form differing from both capitalism and socialism; the problem of the conquest of power, after historical experience has shown how the evolutionary method encounters limitations which appear insuperable, because the State incorporates certain social duties (e.g. the Welfare State) without modifying its class structure—while at the same time the revolutionary method has shown itself to be adapted only to promoting the industrialization of backward countries, arousing them from the torpor of primitive social regimes and systems, but without then knowing how to embark on the road towards an authentic democratic and socialist development; the problem of wielding power in such ways that the abolition of capitalist society will not involve the destruction of political and civil

---

[8] Onofri's theories, inspired by Gramsci, were outlined in the essay 'La via sovietica (leninista) alla conquista del potere e la via italiana, aperta da Gramsci' (The [Leninist] Soviet way to the conquest of power and the Italian way, opened up by Gramsci), in *Nuovi Argomenti*, No. 23–4, 1957. The main exposition of Giolitti's views is to be found in his book *Riforme o rivoluzione* (Turin, 1957).

liberties won by the liberal revolution and which have become the common heritage of the socialist movement.'[9]

In the PSI, the events of 1956 brought about a re-examination of the party's whole ideological position. Nenni, the party secretary, stated clearly that 'as far as we are concerned . . . it must be recognized that a certain tendency towards historical justification which we used to apply to whatever we regarded as unjust or worthy of condemnation in the communist dictatorships has limited the critical appraisal of events. . . . Even in the attack on the "shameful facts" denounced in K's secret report, there is an indication to the working class movement to place itself without reserve on the plane of the democratic and socialist struggle . . . engaging itself to the hilt in order that the changes which are necessary may come about within the framework of democracy and by consent.'[10] On the purely theoretical plane, Nenni, maintaining that criticism of Stalinism should go back to Leninism as well, tended to interpret the position of the 'PSI as a synthesis of various Marxist trends: 'Intuitively, the party had already solved some of the present-day problems thirty-six years ago. . . . Then and later the party always harked back to the validity of the Marxist analysis of historical revolution in general and of the development of capitalism in particular, an analysis enriched by Lenin with the theory of imperialism. . . . Though accepting the Marxist idea of the dictatorship of the proletariat, the party had freed it from the elements of terrorism inherent in the Bolshevik experiment. . . . In this field Austro-Marxism, in substantial agreement with us, conducted between the wars studies which are still valid and which found expression in the Linz programme, one of the most concrete documents of socialist policy.'[11]

In effect, the PSI revised and brought up to date its formal Leninism (which, as we have said, was in practice contradicted by the party's post-war policy), and in relation to problems of the conquest and conduct of power it aligned itself with the views of the left wing of the Socialist International after the first World War. As to the definition of Soviet society, the party continued for the most part to define it as 'socialist' without going into details about the meaning accorded to that term. It was admitted that power was not exercised there in democratic forms even after the 'transition phase' of the dictatorship of the proletariat had come to an end—a fact which made it impossible for the system to be regarded as 'socialist' in the Marxist sense of the word. The adjective therefore only meant (as

[9] 'Tesi di *Critica Sociale* per l'unità e il rinnovamento socialista' (Theses of *Critica Sociale* for unity and Socialist revival), in *Critica Sociale*, November 20, 1958.

[10] *Avanti!*, June 24, 1956.

[11] *Avanti!*, July 29, 1956.

indeed was understood even by non-Marxist and non-socialist scholars and intellectuals) that private ownership of the principal means of production had been abolished and the economy was planned.

The new position of the PSI was confirmed by its estimate of the events in Poland and Hungary, which the party saw as authentic working-class and popular insurrections against police regimes where the policies adopted had created the situation which had led to rebellion.

On the ideological plane it is also interesting to note that while in the matter of the conquest and conduct of power the whole party adopted the traditional standpoint of gradualist Marxism, a left-wing group in the party's monthly review *Mondo Operaio* took up once more the theme of the factory councils, of workers' control of factory management, and of socialism developing within the very heart of the capitalist centres of production. These themes were identical with the 'socialism of the Workers Councils' advocated in the period after the first World War (in Russia, Hungary, and Bavaria), and in English Guild Socialism, themes which in Italy had found their expression in the factory councils, especially in Turin, and in the first phase of Gramsci's philosophy, and which now once again became actual, since it was precisely the Workers' Councils, both in Warsaw and in Budapest, which were the centres of working-class action against the Stalinist regimes in Poland and Hungary.

Lastly, as far as the lesser groups are concerned, the new position of the PSI coincided pretty closely with those of the USI and the UP, in that while on the one hand it criticized Stalinism, on the other it did not accept as completely valid the position of the European Social-Democratic parties. These groups therefore merged in the PSI, except for a minority of the USI which became absorbed in the PSDI.

By contrast, the Trotskyist and Internationalist Communist groups found in the events of 1956 the confirmation of the rightness of their own standpoint, and indeed they saw in them that alone. Thus, the Trotskyists laid stress on Khrushchev's criticisms of bureaucracy, and on the 'anti-bureaucratic' character of the Polish and Hungarian workers' claims, in order to reaffirm Trotsky's traditional view of the social structure of the USSR; while the International Communists placed the emphasis on Khrushchev's reforms in order to illustrate the increasingly capitalist characteristics (market economy, diminution of state ownership of the means of production) which these reforms were introducing into the social and economic structure of the USSR.

Thus during 1956–57 the ideological dispute centred on two main questions: the type of power existing in the USSR, and hence the whole significance of the Soviet experiment; and the possibility of evolution towards socialism in the West as it presented itself in consequence of a development of capitalism which appeared to involve the exclusion of revolutionary solutions.[12]

The launching of the first Sputnik, a year after the events in Hungary, and the simultaneous period of economic recession in the USA and its subsequent repercussions in Europe, modified the terms of the debate. The PCI and the intellectuals who shared its theoretical standpoints found arguments—in Soviet space technology, in the new objectives of the Seven-Year Plan, and in Khrushchev's reforms in general—to substantiate their affirmation of the superiority of the USSR. After the demotion of the Malenkov group and of Zhukov, the struggle for power in Moscow seemed to be concluded, with a victory for Khrushchev; and this fact made it possible to present the first post-Stalin phase as a period of readjustment in which the foundations had been laid for fresh advances. At the same time, the recession in the West was presented as a proof of the permanent validity of the Marxist critique of capitalism; revisionist positions were identified with those of so-called 'neo-capitalism' (mass capitalism, popular capitalism, etc.) and were consequently discredited, on the one hand, as being foreign to the class movement, and on the other as being refuted by the facts (e.g. the recession). The strengthening of right-wing forces in Europe (de Gaulle's advent to power) was regarded as further proof that capitalism was running along its old anti-democratic lines of violence and authoritarian regimes.

The following quotations are typical of the interpretation of Marxism given by leaders and intellectuals of the PCI during the period in question:

'Once again the laws elaborated by Marx concerning capitalist economy have been proved valid. There is an excess of production in relation to capacity of consumption. . . . The result is unbalance, violent ruptures, crises. Emergency measures can only mask and retard these phenomena; they cannot overcome or permanently conquer them.

'History is no longer made by military cliques and joint-stock companies. . . . It is the working class which is the protagonist of history. . . . There is the Communist movement, which governs a third of the world, to set turning the wheel of history. . . . There is a tendency on the part of large-scale capital to embark upon the road to Fascism, clerical totalitarianism, and war.

[12] John Strachey's book *Contemporary Capitalism* (London, 1956) had a considerable influence in this direction; it was widely discussed especially in France. Cf. *Conquiste democratiche e capitalismo contemporaneo* (Milan, 1957), which includes essays by Strachey, Lange, Sauvy, J. Robinson, Bettelheim, Basso, etc.

'Against the convulsions of the capitalist world, generating wars, poverty, reaction, and violence, the action of the socialist world for peace and progress shows up in luminous contrast . . . the third Sputnik shows how far man can go when imperialism and the regime of exploitation are overthrown. . . . The socialist world has history and reason on its side.'[13]

In a situation thus dramatically presented, the PCI nevertheless maintained that it was still possible to achieve power in the West by democratic methods: 'for a democratic government of the working classes' was the slogan launched by the PCI in its Eighth Congress and adopted in its electoral campaign of 1958, in which the call was for 'a vote for peace and unity'.[14]

It was this contrast between the apocalyptic and manichean character of its Leninist enunciations and the moderate and 'possibilist' nature of its estimates of the situation in Italy which prevented the PCI from exerting an ideological influence comparable to that of the pre-destalinization period and from recovering the positions it had lost in 1956. The intellectuals refused to identify socialism with the USSR's advances in the space-race, and instead turned their attention towards problems of the structure of contemporary societies in the East, in the West, in the 'Third World'—such problems as bureaucracy, economic planning in a backward or an advanced society, the relationship of planning to the democratic conduct of power, the validity of the 'class' concept and its significance in the light of socio-economic and technological changes. In this way they strove to find for twentieth-century socialism a meaning independent of Soviet successes and prestige.

On the more strictly political plane, the PSI at its Naples Congress in January 1959 consolidated its autonomy in relation to the PCI, already affirmed at the Venice Congress of February 1957, when all formal alliance had been broken off. It thus offered a centre of attraction to the intellectuals and groups which had been thrown into ferment by the 1956 crisis and which did not wish to confine themselves to purely theoretical debate. It is significant that this power of attraction extended over a fairly wide range, running from the left wing of the PSDI, by tradition social-democratic, to that section of *Azione comunista* which was most sensitive to the claims of libertarian socialism. This was made possible by the fact that so-called 'democratic centralism', signifying ideological conformity, had been discarded in 1956, and consequently there was now more opportunity for the circulation of different ideas within the PSI.

From the purely ideological point of view, the various attitudes

[13] *L'Unità*, April 10, 1958; May 16, 1958; May 17, 1958.
[14] Communiqué of the PCI Directorate, *L'Unità*, May 17, 1958.

within the PSI differed chiefly according to the degree of emphasis
attached to the questions considered above—namely, the guarantee
of a democratic character in the conquest and conduct of power,
and the view taken about forms of power existing in the Soviet bloc.
Since no trend postulated as indispensable the violent conquest of
power (Lenin), and none regarded the USSR as the 'leading State'
(Stalin), distinctions were rather to be found among the more recon-
dite ideological nuances. Thus, while the majority of the party
reduced to a minimum any reference to the USSR and its role and
emphasized the democratic guarantees provided by socialism, the
trend favouring a close alliance with the Communists (their journal
is *Mondo Nuovo*) expressed solidarity with the present leadership in
the East, which it identified with power in the hands of the working
class. An intermediary position, though nearer to the latter group,
was to be found in the trend led by Lelio Basso, an intellectual who
was formerly deputy party secretary and who has been particularly
influenced by Lenin, Trotsky, and Rosa Luxemburg. (They publish
the monthly *Problemi del Socialismo*.)

The statements made in the motions presented by these three
trends at the Naples Congress reflect these differences. On the subject
of socialism's guarantees of democracy, the document of the majority
trend laid down among its requirements 'a form of socialist state as
an organization of mass democracy which eliminates class differences
through the assumption by the workers of control of production and
distribution; which realizes in concrete fashion the democracy of the
working masses, freed from exploitation and from all economic and
spiritual subjection; and which assures at every rank and level direct
popular control over public powers and productive activity. . . . The
choice of the democratic method as the way to socialism, not from
motives of political opportunism, but as an organic necessity of
socialist action, whether in carrying on the struggle for the conquest
of power or in its exercise towards the end of building up the socialist
society and state. . . . The absolute guarantee of fundamental civil
liberties which, inasmuch as they ensure the dignity and full development of human personality, are part of the very substance of socialism.'[15]

The statements of the Basso trend and of the wing favouring close
alliance with the PCI are much more synthetic. The former says:

'The PSI . . . renews the pledge . . . to operate on the basis of autonomy and class unity for the democratic way to socialism;'

and the latter:

'Socialist autonomy is consistent . . . with the practice of social

[15] Stenographic report of the 33rd National Congress of the PSI (Milan, 1959),
p. 405. The five quotations which follow are from pp. 417, 415, 409, 421, 415.

democracy in the course of the struggle itself and not only as a final goal.'

On the other hand, on the subject of the USSR and its role, it is the majority trend which is synthetic: 'The PSI does not identify itself with any position of States or blocs, but with the will of the workers of all countries to reconstitute in peace the unity of the world. ... The PSI stands side by side with all the peoples who are struggling against colonialism and imperialism.' The other two trends are more explicit. The Basso trend affirms: 'In the present historical period the advance of socialism is not bound up with the expansion of the Soviet bloc: it is the socialist forces in each country who must autonomously ensure, in a form suited to the particular situation, the advance towards socialism, within the framework of international solidarity, while the existence of the Soviet Union plays an immense part in the struggle against imperialism, especially in the sphere of the emancipation of colonial peoples.' And the wing favouring close collaboration with the PCI says: 'The socialists reaffirm, in contradistinction to the theory and practice of the leading-State, the revolutionary autonomy of the Italian working-class movement and the national ways to socialism. With this autonomy as its point of departure, solidarity is reaffirmed with the October Revolution, with the social organization that has emerged from it, and with the countries in which the working class is in power: a solidarity within whose framework disagreements can be expressed and within which can be realized the continuing task of socialists to work towards prospects of renewal: a solidarity which naturally does not exclude the widest relations with the other working-class parties of the world.'

The new phase of détente and the further Soviet successes in the space-race have not modified the PSI's ideological position. The party secretary recently emphasized, in speaking of the PSI's relations with the PCI, 'a fundamental divergence, which not long ago touched anguished depths, on the problems of the conquest and exercise of power, on the regimes within which individual liberty and the democratic life of the masses are organized and find their guarantee'. In this it may be possible to detect the influence of those trends of opinion mentioned earlier which are attempting to analyse on a sociological basis, going beyond ideological theories and categories, the socio-economic structures of the USA and the USSR and of the countries which to a greater or lesser extent are following their respective models.

Thus, after several years of far-flung debate, the positions of the different trends of Marxist opinion may today be considered to have become stabilized. By that I mean that the PCI and the intellectuals who move within its orbit are to all intents firmly fixed, if naturally with more elasticity and less dogmatism, in the views they held in 1955; but at the same time the PSI and the intellectuals linked with it, and the autonomous scholars of Marxist inspiration, have withdrawn themselves perceptibly, from the ideological point of view, from the influence of the 'Made in Russia' brand of Marxism, linked formerly with the myth and prestige of Stalin and today with the dynamism and prestige of Khrushchev.

XXIV. Germany: Marxismus-Studien

IRING FETSCHER

In the last thirty years the influence of politics has been deeper and more decisive in Germany than in almost any other European country. In view of the well-known remoteness from politics of German intellectuals this may seem paradoxical, but in fact it was just this apparently a-political attitude of wide circles of the cultured middle class which made it possible for Germany to fall for twelve years under the heel of the most unintellectual and brutal exponents of its society and to be exposed to the dictatorship of a barbaric ideology. It is important to remember this political background when considering the post-war discussion of Marxism in Germany. However grotesque the utterances of Nazi writers may seem to us, it is necessary to recall their theses to see where political discussion had to start from after 1945, to appreciate the prejudices it had to overcome, and the errors it had to correct.

In the Nazi view Marxism was above all 'Western' and 'Jewish' and therefore 'un-German' in a double sense. In a Nazi manual on political-ideological training we read:

'The founder of this doctrine (Marxism) was Karl Marx. Marx was a Jew and this fact in itself explains the whole nature and influence of his views. He was no proletarian but came from a bourgeois-Jewish background. He was also not a labour leader but a typical littérateur. He was deeply influenced by the liberal-capitalist writings of the English economists. There is no greater antithesis than between Karl Marx and Adolf Hitler.'[1]

This account of Marx contains all the fictitious figures whom the Nazis declared to be their 'enemies': the Jew, the intellectual, the bourgeois, the capitalist, the English. The description was intended to combine a number of firmly established prejudices. The romantic attack on the Enlightenment, on reason and modern economic methods, was fused into an extremely telling symbol and set against the incarnation of the Good in Adolf Hitler. The intellectual discussion of Marxism was rejected as superfluous and even dangerous. Anti-semitism was also called in to help destroy the bridge between

[1] Dr H. Männel, *Politische Fibel*, Richtlinien für die politische-weltanschauliche Schulung, Berlin, 1940, p. 115.

the alleged 'socialism' of the Nazis and that of the Marxists. In accordance with the myth of the Jewish conspiracy it was stated that 'the aim of Marxism is the same as that of capitalism: the dominion of World Jewry' (ibid., p. 119).

Adolf Hitler tried to exploit the widespread prejudice against Hegal and Marx for his own ends and to play off the rights of the individual against Marx's collectivism. The Jew was unmasked once again as the mysterious power behind the scenes of world history:

'Marxism represents the purest form of the Jewish attempt to elimi-nate the outstanding personality from all spheres of human life and to replace it by the masses.' (Mein Kampf, II, p. 438.)

Consciously or unconsciously, Hitler was speculating on the resent-ment of the little men who are lost in the masses but like to think of themselves as 'outstanding personalities' and are happy to be supplied with a plausible reason for their own failures, which also allows them to transfer their resentment to an 'enemy'.

The Nazis did not tone down this hostility to Marx and Marxism even during the brief period of friendship with Stalin, whom they regarded as the liquidator of Marxist internationalism and—though they did not admit this openly—the creator of a totalitarian system which appeared to be akin to their own. During the war against the Soviet Union far more stress was laid on the alleged 'inferiority of the East' than on Soviet Marxism, and this was made the pretext for their own behaviour in Russia.

When the war ended in 1945 with the total defeat of the Nazis, many Germans knew scarcely anything of Marx except the name and that he was a Jew. Apart from Sigmund Freud, hardly any of the great thinkers had fallen so much into oblivion or been inter-preted so one-sidedly as Marx. From the outset, however, intellectual life developed in opposite directions in the Eastern and Western zones of Germany. Whereas in the Eastern zone the German Com-munists who had returned home developed large-scale Communist propaganda and an educational programme under the protection of the Red Army's bayonets, cultural and political life in the Western zones was able to develop with a large measure of freedom. The few Communists who banded together in the Western zones were, con-sidering the smallness of their numbers, astonishingly active, but they achieved few successes outside the circle of their old supporters. Under the leadership of Kurt Schumacher, social-democracy had turned its back on Marxism completely, though it continued to honour the memory of Marx himself.

Marxism would, however, certainly have stood a chance in Western Germany if it had not appeared in the shape of the Soviet Marxism, as an instrument of the Stalinist imperialism of which millions of

Germans had had direct bitter personal experience. They might other-wise have been attracted by the fact that it could provide a relatively plausible explanation of the phenomenon of National Socialism, and one less superficial than ascribing it to the pathological qualities of Adolf Hitler and his subordinates or making out that all Germans were devils. For the Marxists, Nazi totalitarianism was a political form which a completely obsolete capitalism was bound to assume in its latest phase in order to maintain itself vis-à-vis the discontented masses; Nazi ideology was a smoke-screen hiding the interests of the monopolistic capitalists.

This thesis would certainly have fallen on more receptive ears if it had not been counter-balanced by the experiences undergone by German prisoners of war and the victims of the transfers of popula-tion, and also by the hostility towards 'Eastern ideology' which was still felt by many former Nazis. In a free competition of ideas Marxism had no political prospects whatsoever.

That is the reason why the serious study of Marx and Marxism was taken in hand exclusively by those circles which—though not personally interested in Marxism—thought it necessary to come to grips with it in view of developments in the Eastern part of Germany. In the first place, the two main Christian denominations have for ten years devoted themselves to this task and produced an ever in-creasing output of publications on the subject. At the same time, there have been the beginnings of a critical discussion of the econo-mic theories of Marx and Soviet Marxism in trade union circles.[2] Finally, scholars with no party axe to grind have repeatedly referred to the philosophical anthropology of the young Marx or based cultural analyses on his theory.[3] As far as the discussion of Marxism in the Soviet zone of Germany is concerned, it is so dependent on Soviet Marxism that so far it has not merited separate treatment.[4]

THE CATHOLIC CRITICISM OF MARXISM

Even though the Catholic church had occupied itself with the study

[2] Cf. for example Ernst Bose, 'Das Elend der Verelendungstheorie', in *Gewerk-schaftliche Monatshefte*, January 1958, and also Karl Kühne, 'Karl Marx und die moderne Nationaloekonomie', in *Die neue Gesellschaft*, II, pp. 1-4, 1955.

[3] Cf. above all the following works by Theodor Adorno and Max Horkheimer: Horkheimer-Adorno, *Dialektik der Aufklärung*, Amsterdam 1947; Adorno, *Minima Moralia*, Reflexionen aus dem beschädigten Leben, Frankfurt, 1951; *Prismen, Kulturkritik und Gesellschaft*, Frankfurt, 1955.

[4] This applies anyway to the work of writers living in the Soviet zone of Ger-many with the exception of the special case of Ernst Bloch, whose work belongs, however, to the period before 1933. Georg Lukacs had, until 1956, a considerable influence, above all on the younger intellectuals in the Soviet zone, through his writings which were published by the Aufbau Verlag, a firm which does not belong to the Party. He was, however, always regarded with a certain amount of suspicion by the SED, and has been described as an 'enemy of Marxism'.

of Socialist ideas long before 1945, it was the developments of the post-war period that made it necessary for the Church to come to closer grips with Marxism. In the countries of the Eastern bloc a predominantly Catholic population was for the first time exposed to the unremitting influence of Marxism as an official State doctrine (Poland, Hungary, Czechoslovakia), and two of the oldest Catholic countries (Italy and France) came to have the largest Communist parties in the Western world. Quite soon after the war there appeared the Italian edition of a book on Soviet Dialectical Materialism by Father Gustav Wetter, S.J., Professor at the Pontificum Institutum Russicum in Rome.[5] This book, which has since become a standard work, provides a historical survey which becomes more detailed from Plekhanov onwards, and it then expounds systematically the main principles of the dialectical materialism of the Stalin era which it criticizes objectively and in purely philosophical terms. In the first edition the author's catholic and indulgent approach was more evident than in the later editions: he endeavoured to discover the positive qualities in dialectical materialism and points of contact for a future Catholic mission. Among the positive elements which he discovered were first of all the epistemological realism of Leninism which, though blended with an ontological materialism, can be logically separated and made a 'valuable precondition' for the development of a genuine (Thomist) philosophy. Secondly, Wetter emphasizes the difference between a dialectical materialism which acknowledges the qualitative differences between the various spheres of existence and the mechanical, vulgar materialism which is the only kind of which most people are aware. Finally, however, he tries, like so many Catholic authors who have followed him, to play off the dialectic of Soviet Marxism against materialism itself and to establish their mutual incompatibility. Incidentally, he takes dialectical materialism perfectly seriously as a philosophy—in spite of its low level formally—and he examines and criticizes it in all its aspects and peculiarities with great care and patience.

Catholic scholars may have been helped in their appreciation of Soviet philosophy by a certain similarity between the argumentative method which it employs and the method of the scholastics.

At the same time as the Austrian Wetter's great work appeared, the works of the Polish emigrant J. M. Bochenski were beginning to be known in Germany.[6] Bochenski is a Professor of Philosophy and head of the Eastern European department in the Swiss university of Fribourg. He starts out from a more pronounced philosophical position than the historian Wetter. Above all, he has provided valuable analyses of the Soviet discussion of logic (from 1951 onwards).

[5] Gustav A. Wetter, S.J., *Dialectical Materialism*, London, 1958.
[6] I. M. Bochenski O.P., *Der sowjetrussische dialektische Materialismus (Diamat)*, Berne and Munich, 1950 (2nd ed.; 1956).

Like most other Catholic authors, however (de Vries, Ogiermann, Meurer, for example),[7] Wetter and Bochenski display a comparative remoteness from history and a lack of familiarity with the historical dialectic of Hegel. Apart from the Thomist point of departure, the reason for their remoteness from history is that they have studied Marxism primarily as it appears, in a decayed form, in present-day Russia, rather than in its original shape. It would appear, however, that some of the above-mentioned authors are now endeavouring to overcome this one-sided approach. Their interpretations are also to some extent one-sided inasmuch as they approach in purely philosophical terms phenomena the objective meaning of which can often be explained only by examining the function they are intended to fulfil in the execution of certain political or economic decisions. In other words, they imply that Soviet philosophy enjoys an autonomy which is not in accordance with the facts.

One of these Catholic writers has, however, devoted himself to a critical study of the young Marx and the revolutionary élan which he kindled: Jakob Hommes, Professor of Catholic Philosophy in the Philosophical-Theological College of Regensburg.[8]

For Hommes Marxism is a product of the decay of the theory of natural law of the Christian Middle Ages, the restoration of which is probably his fundamental concern. His criticism of Marxism is therefore combined with a criticism of modern ideas in general (cf. Jacques Maritain in France and Gerhard Krüger in Germany). For him the distinguishing mark of Marxism is its radical humanism and historicism, its dissolution of all established traditional structures and their abandonment to the sovereignty of man. Hommes no doubt appreciates the original intentions of Marxism better than the other Catholic writers, but by passing sentence on the whole intellectual development of modern times he places himself in a hopeless position and deprives himself of all means of mastering the modern reality. The weakness of his interpretation of Marxism lies, however, not so much in his hopelessly conservative approach as in the reversal of the error committed by Wetter and Bochenski. Whereas they identify Soviet Marxism with Marxism itself, Hommes overlooks the fundamental change that has taken place in Marxist thinking since the time of the young Marx.

The future development of Catholic criticism of Marxism will probably consist in the mutual correction of these one-sided positions and in the reception of dialectical elements into Catholic

[7] Josef de Vries. *Die Erkenntnistheorie des dialektischen Materialismus*, 1958; Helmut Ogiermann, *Materialistische Dialektik*, 1958; Joseph Meurers, *Wissenschaft im Kollektiv, ein neuer Versuch zum Verständnis des dialektischen Materialismus*, 1959.

[8] Jakob Hommes, *Der technische Eros*, das Wesen der materialistischen Geschichtsauffassung, 1955; by the same author, *Krise der Freiheit*, Hegel-Marx-Heidegger, 1958.

thought itself. It is almost inevitable that Thomas will be supplemented and enriched by Hegel if a historical philosophy equal to authentic Marxism is to be developed. A number of French Catholics have already taken a lead in this direction.

THE EVANGELICAL STUDY GROUP'S COMMISSION ON MARXISM[9]

The only institutional centre of Marxist research in the German Federal Republic is the Commission on Marxism of the Evangelical Study Group which was set up in the Spring of 1951. It is made up of scholars of the most diverse disciplines, theologians, philosophers, lawyers, historians, economists, slavists, political scientists, who usually meet twice a year for working sessions. The original centre and organizer of the circle was Erwin Metzke, the Tübingen Professor of Philosophy who died in 1956. It was thanks mainly to his skill and far-sightedness that it was possible for such a heterogeneous circle to develop so quickly into a vital working fellowship. It is typical of the way in which Marxism was regarded by the Commission that it conceived it from the outset not as something alien and remote, which confronts modern man entirely from the outside, but as a doctrine which is still capable of facing us with important questions and which can cause us to re-think our historical position. This readiness to question one's own position is characteristic of Evangelical Christianity, which regards the Christian faith and ideological fixations as complete opposites. Just because a man is committed to a faith he is freed from the necessity of protecting himself ideologically and is able to discard the encasement in which his contemporaries secure and exclude themselves from reality.

In the search for what is relevant to modern man in Marxism, the Commission soon came upon the anthropology of the young Marx and his criticism of the modern world as 'alienated'.[10] Just because it was intent not on mere contradiction but on discovering the real strength of Marxism, it had to return to this part of Marxist thought even though it has been neglected or even thrown overboard, as 'pre-Marxist', by Soviet Marxism. It was impossible, however, to stop at the young Marx, since it is scarcely possible to understand his thought without referring still further back to that of Hegel. Most of the philosophical contributions to the Marxist Studies published by the Commission culminated in a detailed study of Marx's universal

[9] Some of the papers read at the meetings of the Commission have been published in the three volumes of *Marxismusstudien* which appeared in 1954, 1957, and 1960 (Tübingen, Verlag, J. C. B. Mohr, Paul Siebeck).

[10] Apart from the contributions published in the *Studien* the following have been published by members of the Commission: Helmut Gollwitzer, 'Zum Verständnis des Menschen beim jungen Marx', in *Festschrift Günther Dehn*, 1957, pp. 183–203; Erich Thier, *Das Menschenbild des jungen Marx*, Göttingen, 1957.

dependence on and antithesis to Hegel.[11] Erwin Metzke pointed out that Hegel, who has been so often decried as unrealistic, is in fact far more realistic than Marx for whom in the end historical existence is something to be used and manipulated.

No doubt certain of the ideas suggested in this context owe their origin to Martin Heidegger, the greatest contemporary German thinker, and especially to his 'Letter on Humanism'.[12] Heidegger now interprets the whole development of the West as the result of a 'forgetfulness of Being' which has been the mark of all metaphysical thinking since Aristotle. A forgetfulness of Being has been man's fate since that time. The decline has culminated in the absolute rule of technical thinking and led to the terrible homelessness of modern man, and it must be superseded by a new era of which there are already certain signs, which Being will itself bring about and to which we have to attune our thinking. From this angle Heidegger finds a kindred concern in Marx:

'Homelessness is becoming the fate of the whole world. It is therefore necessary to think of it in terms of the history of Being. What Marx discerned as the alienation of man, deriving this insight in an essential and significant sense from Hegel, reaches back in its roots to the homelessness of modern man, which has been brought about by metaphysics, consolidated by it and concealed as homelessness. Because Marx, through his experience of the alienation of modern man, is aware of a fundamental dimension of history, the Marxist view of history is superior to all other views (p. 27).'

The kinship of Heidegger's thought to that of Marx arises from the fact that for both of them the modern alienation of man and its expression (which Heidegger finds in metaphysics, Marx in ideology) are the result of a basic process by which man is overwhelmed. Heidegger leaves it unexplained, describing it as 'a fate of Being', whilst Marx interprets it as an inevitable social and economic development. Disregarding this important difference, it might be possible to identify the theories of the two thinkers, as Jakob Hommes has done though in a negative rather than a positive way.

At this point, however, the disciples of Heidegger will rightly point out that for him the distinguishing mark of 'Being' is that it is essentially outside human control: it is not 'available' to man, whereas Marx believes that it is possible for the proletariat to take in hand its own destiny and that of humanity in general. It is therefore hardly

[11] This applies to the papers by Ludwig Landgrebe in the first and third series of the *Studien*, by Erich Metzke in the second, and by me in the second and third series.

[12] Martin Heidegger, 'Über den Humanismus' in *Platons Lehre von der Wahrheit*, Bern, 1947 (written in the autumn of 1946 as a letter to Jean Beaufret), reprinted Frankfurt a.M., no date.

right to condemn both Marx and Heidegger as representing a 'technical eros', as Hommes has done, since Heidegger's rejection of the whole of metaphysics arises from the charge that it has exalted a type of purely technical thinking which is entirely 'forgetful of Being'. The difference between Heidegger and Marx vanishes only if one disregards Marx's reference to revolutionary action and only takes into account the no-longer-controllable past. But this no-longer-controllable past has itself given rise to the proletariat, which has the power to put an end to its own passively endured fate and turn it into 'real history', moulded and controlled by itself as the 'subject-object' of history. There are echoes of Heidegger's position above all in the works of Erwin Metzke and Ludwig Landgrebe, though they both give a markedly Protestant turn to his thought.

As the interest of the Commission on Marxism was centred on the young Marx, it became necessary to define more closely the relationship of the early to the later Marx and also to Friedrich Engels and the later Russian and Central European Marxists.

Quite a number of publications included in the *Studies of Marxism* have been devoted to this topic. In a detailed analysis of Engels's preliminary work on the *Communist Manifesto*, Hermann Bollnow[13] has shown that the 'Principles of Communism' of 1847 already contain features typical of Engels, as distinct from Marx himself, which were to emerge more clearly after the death of Marx: a type of thinking based more on natural law and straight-line progressivism as opposed to the historical-dialectical thinking of Marx; a greater appreciation of scientific technical progress as such, and a relative blindness to the phenomenon of 'alienation' analysed by Marx. These characteristics explain, incidentally, the confusion, observed by Georg Lukacs, of 'revolutionary action' with industrial production of Engels's *Anti-Dühring*, a lapse which shows how little Engels had assimilated the idea that in capitalist society men are not at all the free subjects of their own actions but dependent on an overruling objective context, that they are, as Lukacs puts it, 'not actors but acted upon'.

Other works, including those of Richard Nürnberger, H. H. Schrey, and myself,[14] deal with the characteristic qualities of Leninist

[13] H. Bollnow, 'Engels Auffassung von Revolution und Entwicklung in seinen "Grundsätzen des Kommunismus" (1847)', *Marxismusstudien* (first series), pp. 77–144.

[14] Richard Nürnberger, 'Lenins Revolutionstheorie, eine Studie über Staat und Revolution', *Marxismusstudien* (first series), pp. 161–72; the same, 'Die Französische Revolution im revolutionären Selbstverständnis des Marxismus', *loc. cit.* (second series), pp. 61–76. H. H. Schrey, 'Geschichte oder Mythos bei Marx und Lenin', *loc. cit.* (first series), pp. 145–60. This work has been strongly criticized by members of the Commission because it obliterates the essential difference between the thought of Sorel and Lenin. I. Fetscher, 'Von der Philosophie des Proletariats zur proletarischen Weltanschauung', *loc. cit.* (second series), pp. 26–60; the same, 'Das Verhältnis des Marxismus zu Hegel', *loc. cit.* (third series), pp. 66–169.

Marxism, with copious illustrations. Erich Mathias and Christian Gneuss have described the ideology of German Social-Democracy as it appeared before the first World War in its two most characteristic personalities: Kautsky and Eduard Bernstein. It is clear from these studies that even before 1914 German Social-Democracy was already far removed from revolutionary Marxism.

The idea that Engels served to some extent as a bridge between revolutionary and revisionist Marxism cannot be entirely rejected even after a study of the unabridged text of his preface to Marx's *Civil War in France*. Certain statements in his correspondence with Bebel are very revealing: for example, the praise which he bestows on Lord Randolph Churchill for his nonchalant criticism of the government of his own Tory party (May 12, 1891), and his whole emphasis on the constitutional freedom enjoyed in England, which is expressed in numerous letters written during the later years of his life. It is also typical of Engels that he admits a preference for Eduard Bernstein 'as the exact opposite of Kautsky' on account of his greater degree of realism (cf. his letter of August 25, 1881).

My own essays in the second and third volumes of the *Studies* are an attempt to analyse sociologically and critically the whole development of thought from the young Marx right up to Stalinism and its disintegration: an analysis from which emerges the picture of a tragic dialectical change from a humanistic point of departure to an anti-human end. At the same time my study is intended to reveal the inner tension which lies in the Soviet system, with its Marxist pretensions, which differs fundamentally, in this respect, from Nazi totalitarianism, the ideology of which was entirely homogeneous with the reigning system of terror.

The tension between Marxist ideology and Stalinist practice formed one of the driving forces behind the October crises in Poland and Hungary. Young intellectuals were able to express their displeasure with Stalinist tyranny with the aid of categories which they had acquired from the study of Marx's early writings.

The demand, made by the young Marx, for the abolition of all ideology with its deceptive appearance of independence, by means of a new definition of the relationship between historical consciousness and historical action, had been abandoned. That is already clear from the fact that the word 'ideology' has ceased to be used critically but has been adapted to the American usage which makes it possible to say, for example, 'my ideology is christian'. Soviet Communists boast likewise of having a 'marxist ideology'. Both obviously run counter to the original conceptions of Christianity and Marxism alike.

The result of the investigations into the changed relationships between Marxism and Hegel was similar. The question illustrates the whole change in function and meaning which Marxism had undergone. Here too, though he regarded Hegel's philosophy as limited only by the limits imposed on philosophy as such, Marx tried to surpass those limits by transforming theory into revolutionary activity, whereas Engels and his Soviet followers turned Marxism into a materialist philosophy in competition with other ideologies: a philosophy which has to emphasize its opposition to Hegel the more blatantly, the more the difference in fact tends to disappear. The development may be summarized in the form of a paradox: Soviet ideologists turned increasingly away from Hegel the more their political practice became Hegelian and the more their dialectical materialist ontology acquired characteristics of the Hegelian system. It is not surprising that such criticism, based as it was on Marxism itself, was especially unwelcome to the apologists of the Soviet system who claim to be Marx's sole heirs. For this reason they have repeatedly attacked the *Studies of Marxism*, though they have been unable to produce any cogent philosophical arguments worth mentioning. The weakness of these anti-critics is evident from the fact that in defending themselves against arguments based on Lukacs, Bloch, Korsch, etc., they have the presumption to maintain that these writers were never Marxists.[15]

In contrast to the sterility of these polemical attacks, the criticism which Jürgen Habermas has made of certain of the *Marxist Studies* —and indirectly of the whole contemporary discussion of Marxism —really does pinpoint a weakness due to the neglect of a fundamental aspect of Marxist thought.

A CRITICISM OF THE DISCUSSION OF MARXISM IN POST-WAR GERMANY

It is remarkable how intensely the present-day discussion of Marxism

[15] Cf. D. Bergner, W. Jahn, *Der Krezuzzug der evangelischen Akademien gegen den Marxismus*, Berlin, 1960. The following statements, which are contrary to the facts, are there made concerning Lukacs and Bloch: 'Both represent the left wing of the Frankfurt Circle for Social Research and are certainly sympathetic to the workers' movement. But there is a difference between sympathizing with the working class and standing by them on their own ground.' [Lukacs entered the Party a month after the foundation of the Hungarian Communist Party and from March 1919 onwards he was a member of the Central Committee, deputy People's Commissar for Education in the government of Bela Kun, etc. I.F.] 'Politically decisive situations show where the individual belongs. When the counter-revolution raged in Hungary in 1956 Lukacs stood objectively on the side of the counter-revolutionaries, and Bloch on the side of the revisionists in Poland and Germany. Ideologically neither of them has *ever taken the position of Marxism-Leninism*' (p. 16).

Another work attacking the criticism of Marxism, described as the 'joint work of the Chair of Philosophy in the Institute for Social Sciences in the Central Committee of the SED' and which is entitled *Die Philosophie des Verbrechens* (The Philosophy of Crime), Berlin, VEB Deutscher Verlag der Wissenschaften, 1959, is even sharper in its tone and even weaker in its arguments.

in Germany is concentrated on philosophical topics and how little attention is paid to the scientific claims and the empirical scientific components of Marxist theory.[16] In the Catholic thinkers this one-sidedness is due partly to the fact that they concentrate entirely on the contemporary form of Marxism in the Soviet Union, which exhibits a tendency to isolate the ideological philosophical element which has only latterly begun to be corrected. In the Evangelical authors and the scholars associated with them, the reason for this one-sidedness is to be found, however, more in an idealistic conviction, which is not clearly expressed, according to which the ultimately decisive driving force behind the movements of history is to be sought in philosophy. They therefore presuppose something that should first be proved—against Marx. Jürgen Habermas has made this the starting-point for his attack. He criticizes Landgrebe, Metzke, Popitz and others[17] for mistakenly making Marx's biographically important descent from Hegel the systematic basis of his theory. He continues:

'In strict accordance with the remaining of a materialistic dialectic, philosophy starts by reflecting on the position in which it finds itself; it proceeds therefore from the alienation which it at once experiences and from an awareness of the practical necessity for the alienation to be overcome. This consciousness rises to the level of self-consciousness where philosophy sees itself as an expression of the very situation which has to be annulled and henceforward makes the aim of its critical practice criticism by practice. It knows that it is working towards the abolition of itself qua philosophy to the extent that it is endeavouring to realize its own immanent existence. Such criticism leaves . . . the stage of contemplation. It has seen through the façade

---

[16] I have dealt with the 'scientific claims of dialectical materialism' in a radio talk which is printed in the collective volume *Christen oder Bolschewisten*, Stuttgart, 1957, pp. 81–96. But I did not deal with the question of the scientific nature of a differentiated economic analysis in the spirit of Marx, but only with the claim of the Soviet dogmatists.

[17] Heinrich Popitz, *Der entfremdete Mensch*, Basel, 1953, in a dissertation prepared under the supervision of Karl Jaspers which is far above the usual level of German dissertations and the first recent work to renew interest in the humanist approach of the young Marx. Karl Jaspers's own critical position in relation to Marxism was already apparent in his small book *Die geistige Situation der Zeit*, 1931. In the first place he criticizes Marxism, from the point of view of Max Weber's conception of science, on account of its claim to make binding and scientific statements about situations which are based ultimately on the free value judgments of men. Secondly, Jaspers attacks in the Marxist system a form of thinking below the level of the great philosophies which has always tried to limit the open horizon of human endeavour. His stand against Marxism coincides with his fight against other creators of philosophical systems such as Hegel, Schelling, Heidegger. Simplifying the matter a little, one might call this criticism existential Kantianism.

of its own autonomy by which it has been led to believe that it is able both to prove and to realize itself.'[18]

At this point, however, where philosophy recognizes its own limitations and the abolition of the reality by which it is conditioned as its true goal, it proves that it is dependent on an empirical scientific understanding of the facts from which the conditions making this abolition (i.e. the Revolution) feasible can alone be derived: 'The dependence of criticism on science, on empirical historical, sociological and economic analyses is so fin l and unalterable that, within the theory, it can only be refuted scientifically. That does not mean, however, that it could be proved sufficiently by scientific means. Once given the scientifically ascertainable conditions for a potential revolution, the revolution itself would still need the grasping of the possibility . . . the practice stimulated but not determined by an understanding of the practical necessity.'[19]

Habermas here points to a distinction which is overlooked by present-day Marxists—or left in the dark for propaganda reasons: the distinction between a theoretical necessity which imposes itself with the inevitability of a natural law, and a practical necessity which is dependent for its realization on deliberate human action. According to the Marxian analysis the development of the capitalist method, which imposes itself against the will of individual persons, is a theoretical necessity. On the other hand, the socialist revolution which is by no means already determined by the mere recognition that it is possible, is a practical necessity. Where the distinction is ignored, the essential difference between the deductive Hegelian dialectic, as opposed to the dialectical empiricism of Marx, is lost.

According to Habermas's interpretation of Marx, the necessity of progress is a practical, not a theoretical one, since '. . . otherwise historical dialectic would not be historical and also not contingent, and the assertion that Marx had based himself, without discussion, on Hegel's *Preface*, would be correct. In the face of such a presupposition all empirical analyses would be a mere epilogue, deprived of their power of falsification without which it is impossible for science to achieve any scientific stringency.'[20]

Habermas is doubtless right. But it has to be said that his Marxism is merely one possible form and not the one propagated in the Soviet Union today and presumably also not the one for which Marx himself stood. Certainly, in later life Marx wanted to investigate the conditions making for the possibility of revolution and referred again and again to the empirical situation but, since at that time the facts

[18] Jürgen Habermas, 'Zur philosophischen Diskussion um Marx und den Marxismus', in *Philos. Rundschau*, V (1957), pp. 165–235, p. 192.
[19] *Ibid.*, pp. 192ff.
[20] *Ibid.*, pp. 193ff.

seemed more or less in accordance with the trend for which he hoped, he did not, like present-day Marxists, undergo the embarrassment of having to falsify his hopes.

The point that Habermas makes with the greatest ease in the last part of his essay, that the contemporary proletariat in industrial countries is neither able nor inclined to abolish by revolution the conditions under which it lives, in order to make an unalienated existence possible for all men, would have meant for Marx the surrender of his lifelong hopes. It is hardly to be assumed that he would have reconciled himself to a position from which Marxists living in the West today still shrink. Even with this qualification, however, there remains a good deal of positive value in Habermas's critical enquiry.[21] He is, for example, perfectly right to point out that for thinkers who do not acknowledge the dependence of Marxist theory on empirical research, the 'surplus' over and above the rational elements in Marxism seems like a secularized theology[22] or gnostic cosmology (Ernst Bloch). Even in Habermas himself, however, there is a surplus: the impulse which has to be added to the mere recognition of the possibility of revolution in order to transform it into reality.

It can hardly be called anything but an ethical impulse. And thus we reach the ethical motivation of Marxian socialism which has been constantly rejected by Marxists of all schools. The alternative is only too clear: either deterministic materialism or an ethical motivation for the socialist revolution.

Germany was once the intellectual home of Marxism. Only since 1945, however, has it been possible to discuss Marxism freely once again. In Eastern Germany it takes the form of a Soviet Russian import and, at any rate partly, denies its origin. In Western Germany there is something abstract and unreal about the discussion of Marxism, which is hardly carried on at all by its followers and believers. The discussion has been concentrated on purely philosophical problems and has only rarely dealt—for example in the analysis of the Soviet world with the aid of Marxian categories—with the society of the present day. Conversation with scholars of other

[21] Incidentally, in a footnote, Habermas himself points out that the distinction between the two kinds of necessity was later 'obliterated in particular in the preface to the first volume of *Das Kapital* and in the final paragraphs of that work', and he attributes responsibility for this development to the influence of Engels and his, 'in the metaphysical sense, "materialistic" thinking'. Note 48, p. 193, *loc. cit.*

[22] In his book *Weltgeschichte und Heilsgeschehen* (Stuttgart, 1953) Karl Löwith has described Marxism as the 'story of salvation in the language of economics'. In his other works (*Von Hegel zu Nietzsche*) and above all in the *Gesammelten Abhandlungen*, Stuttgart, 1960 (which contain the long essay on Max Weber and Karl Marx of 1932), Löwith goes beyond this one-sided view of Marxism.

countries, for example, England, America, Poland or France, might help to liberate the German discussion of Marxism from this one-sidedness. What seems most desirable, however, is the inclusion of economic and sociological problems. Only when the whole range of questions which Marx confronted and combined in himself has come into view again will the criticism of Marxism reach the point of enriching and fertilizing learning in the free world generally.

xxv. USA: Marxists at Bay

LEWIS A. COSER

The historian of American Marxist groups in the post-war period cannot but feel a certain kinship with those anthropologists who rush into the field because they fear that their tribe may soon become extinct. The American Marxist has become a rare species.

While the Marxist Left, outside of the Communist Party, never numbered more than a few thousand adherents, it yet showed in the 'thirties and early 'forties great intellectual fertility, a liveliness and zest for ideas, and vigour in theoretical analysis. Most of this disappeared in the late 'forties and the 'fifties. There have not been any intellectually exciting debates such as those in which men like Sidney Hook, James Burnham, Lewis Corey, Meyer Schapiro, Max Shachtman, Bertram D. Wolfe, and a host of other talented writers attempted to delineate a non-Stalinist Marxist theory; there have been no discussions which could measure up to the debates on the character of Russian society which took place inside and on the periphery of the Trotskyist movement.

By and large, whatever remains of Marxist thought is imitative and permeated by a strongly nostalgic view of the 'thirties. The bland 'fifties, with their temporary disappearance of major dramatic political issues and the prosperity which large strata of American society enjoy, have dried up the major sources of recruitment of the Marxist left, have severed it almost completely from the Labour movement, and have drained off most of its intellectual vitality. The various Marxist groups which I shall discuss have all attempted in some way to come to terms with the realities of the 'fifties—but so far have met with indifferent success.

This survey might perhaps best begin with a discussion of the group of pro-Eastern Marxist intellectuals assembled around the magazine *Monthly Review*. Founded in the late 'forties by Paul M. Sweezy, the well-known economist, and Leo Huberman, a left-wing popularizer, the magazine seems fairly representative of that trend of thought which has consistently stood for 'defence of the Soviet Union as a socialist country'. The programmatic statement in its first issue, which is reprinted from time to time, defines socialism as 'first, public ownership of the decisive sectors of the economy, and second, comprehensive planning of production for the benefit of the producers themselves'. Given this definition it is hardly surprising that the editors of the *Monthly Review* consider that 'Socialism became a reality with the introduction of the first five-year plan in Soviet Russia in 1928'.

The magazine has consistently adhered to this stand, even though it has also maintained that it does 'not accept the view that the USSR is above criticism simply because it is socialist'. On balance, materials devoted to the defence of the Soviet Union have been preponderant and criticism has appeared only here and there, usually in rather muted tones. Admiration for the Soviet Union was grounded chiefly on the pragmatic or pseudo-pragmatic argument that it 'worked'. Thus Paul Sweezy has written: 'It is the Soviet Union's military success in the war against Germany which more than anything else has convinced the world that socialism really works. This is a fact which historians of the future may well rank in importance with the October Revolution itself.'[1] Sweezy and his co-thinkers recognized that there were, as they delicately put it, 'restrictions on liberty' in the Soviet Union, but they argued that 'the restrictions on liberty which are characteristic of Soviet Russia are far less symptomatic of the times than the crisis of liberty in the United States.'[2]

After the death of Stalin, 'one of the greatest men of all times,'[3] and especially after Khrushchev's revelations to the Twentieth Congress of the CPSU, the tone of the *Monthly Review* became more critical. An editorial (October 1957) commenting upon Khrushchev's victory over his rivals makes the point that 'terror is an integral part of the system; it kept the other parts in balance; without it, the system is visibly beginning to fall apart,' and it predicts that the drift of events in Russia points to the emergence of a military dictatorship which could be stopped only if the Communist Party took steps 'to democratize its own rule'. There has also appeared a number of rather sharply worded articles and comments on the Soviet Union in the last few years, although the November 1959 issue of the magazine reaffirms editorially that Khrushchev is 'a Marxist' and 'the leader of a socialist country.'

While the *Monthly Review* has in the last few years wavered in its attitude towards the Soviet Union, it has been almost unqualified in its enthusiasm for Mao's China. In its March 1959 issue, for example, it published an article by the Indian scientist D. D. Kosombi in which the communes were hailed as the beginning of the withering away of the state:

'Certain small but nevertheless important parts of the state machinery have vanished altogether. To that extent the *state machinery has begun to wither away*. Control over people has been replaced by

[1] *Socialism*, 1949, p. 29.
[2] *Ibid.*, p. 261.
[3] *Monthly Review*, IV, p. 449.

the people's control over things. Though predicted by Marx and Engels, this is the first known example of the kind in actual practice. . . . The Chinese people have been the first to take the great step toward the real beginning in human history' (p. 462).

The main reason why the contributors to the *Monthly Review* are so fascinated by 'socialist' developments abroad is their deep pessimism about the possibilities of socialism at home. This leads Paul Sweezy[4] to write about what he calls 'the great paradox of the modern world,' namely that 'capitalism has so poisoned its immediate victims as to paralyse them, and at the same time it has awakened and set in motion the vast masses of the backward countries who are now the ones to bear undisguisedly the burdens of the irrationalities of capitalism.'[5] 'The advanced countries,' Sweezy continues, 'and especially the United States, have lost their chance to lead the way. They will be overtaken and surpassed economically by the centrally planned economies. . . . World leadership, for better or for worse, is on the point of passing out of the hands of Western white civilization and into those of a new Eastern and predominantly coloured civilization. One can regret it, but I don't think I do. . . . As for us Americans, if the world survives at all, we will of course rejoin the procession sooner or later.'[6]

The somewhat weary tone of this passage is characteristic of much of Paul Sweezy's more recent writings. One senses in them a pervasive alienation from American society, disgust with its values, premises, and assumptions, together with a fundamental disbelief in any hopeful socialist development on the American scene in the foreseeable future. Sweezy wrote in 1949 that to 'say that the Western European and American working classes have so far failed to fulfil the role of "grave diggers" of capitalism is not equivalent to asserting that they never will do so. Marx and Engels were certainly wrong in their timing, but we believe that their basic theory of capitalism and of the manner of its transformation into socialism remains valid and is no less applicable to Western Europe and America than to other parts of the world.'[7] But more recently Sweezy wrote that Marx had believed that the working class in the most advanced countries would bring about a socialist society but that 'Alas, he was wrong.'[8]

Hopelessness with respect to the possibility of working class socialist action is thus combined with a desperate clinging to the belief that the 'socialist countries' despite 'mistakes', 'corruptions', etc., still carry the socialist flag forward. *Monthly Review* represents

[4] *Monthly Review*, October 1958.
[5] *Ibid.*, p. 221.
[6] *Ibid.*, pp. 222–3.
[7] *The Present as History*, 1953, pp. 26–7.
[8] *Monthly Review*, October 1958, p. 221.

M

a curious variant of Marxism in which belief in the working class has been replaced by what, for want of a better term, one might call a consistently Eastern orientation.

The *Monthly Review*'s assessment of the American scene has been wavering over the years. During the McCarthy period and even after the McCarthy wave had receded, the dangers of impending fascism in America were painted, as might have been expected, in the most vivid colours. 'American political life is slowly but surely degenerating into a strange state, part anarchy and part fascism,' ran an editorial as late as October 1954. In 1952 Sweezy wrote that 'there is a very strong probability that the election of Eisenhower and Nixon would be the point of no-return on the road to fascism and World War III.'[9] A month earlier an anonymous collaborator had stated that 'whatever the forms of its specific actions, the Big Business-military coalition in the United States assumes all the *functions* of a fascist regime. It undertakes all the basic assignments of fascist rule.'[10] A few months earlier still an editorial stated that 'anti-communism in practice is nothing more nor less than the American form of fascism.'[11]

In more recent years the fascist perspective slowly disappeared from the pages of the review which, however, continued to characterize American society as dominated by monopoly capitalism. But, as distinct from a number of other Marxist publications, the *Monthly Review* did not indulge in periodic speculations about an impending crisis of the capitalist economy. Sweezy, who is a highly competent economist and whose *Theory of Capitalist Development* (1942) is one of the most lucid expositions of Marxist economics in any language, has been influenced by Keynesian thinking in a number of respects. He has therefore tended to reject theories of catastrophic breakdown, admitting that a certain degree of direction and planning of the economy is compatible with the maintenance of capitalist domination. His general prognosis for the economy has thus been based on the expectation of 'creeping stagnation', a lack of expansion, a general dependence on military expenditure, and a gradual lagging behind the expansive forces of the 'socialist countries'. Such a perspective clearly fits in well with the general orientation sketched earlier. Not only the failure of the American working class but also the dominant trends in the American economy, as he perceives them, lead Sweezy to see no immediate possibilities for socialist action in America.

Peaceful coexistence, a peaceful competition between rival systems, but a competition which must inevitably reveal the superiority of the 'socialist' countries and the stagnation and decay of the West—this

[9] *Monthly Review*, vol. **IV**, p. 231.
[10] *Ibid.*, vol. **IV**, p. 189.
[11] *Ibid.*, vol. **IV**, p. 70.

is the perspective that Sweezy and many, though not all, of his collaborators envisage. In the meantime all they can do is to hold the fort, and serve as a meeting ground for that saving remnant of pro-Eastern Marxists and semi-Marxists who read *Monthly Review* and the books it publishes.

While Sweezy represents the tired wing of the *Monthly Review*, Paul Baran, an economist teaching at Stanford University, represents its more aggressive and doctrinaire wing. Baran's *The Political Economy of Growth* (1957) is indicative of this. The main thesis of the book may be briefly summarized: monopoly capital, controlling the destinies of imperialist countries, leads to stagnation at home and is hostile to economic development in underdeveloped countries. The ruling classes in the United States and other imperialist countries are bitterly opposed to industrialization of the colonial and semi-colonial world, where they back those strata who, for fear of losing their privileged positions, stand in the way of economic growth. Hence the main obstacle to growth in the underdeveloped countries is not a shortage of capital, but the squandering of the economic surplus by the parasitic upper classes combined with exploitation by the West. Therefore the only chance for the underdeveloped countries is to join the 'socialist world' which will give them economic assistance and will teach them how to operate the crash programmes of industrialization which have been successfully applied in Russia, China, and the 'people's democracies'. The book is considerably less sophisticated than Sweezy's work and consists in the main of a repetition of the familiar arguments of 'Marxist-Leninist' propaganda.

In the *Monthly Review* for October and November 1958, Professor Baran's discussion of the 'Crisis of Marxism?' turned out to be a strained attempt to vindicate Marxist orthodoxy in the face of facts that seem hardly to fit into the scheme. This involved him in a startling if amusing set of contradictions. He affirmed that 'none of Marx's conclusions have been vitiated, let alone refuted, by subsequent events', only to state a little later that 'the proletariat in the advanced countries has not developed in the way Marx anticipated. Bad as its condition has been, it was able to rise above the "inescapable, unvarnishable, imperative" misery which was observed by Marx, and which he expected would be accentuated with the passage of time.' Baran's position, though less modulated than that of Sweezy, does not really differ from his; the Western proletariat has missed the bus of history; Marxists in the West can only sit it out and wait till the triumphant growth of 'socialism' in the East finally vindicates them. Arthur K. Davis sums it up neatly in the November 1959 issue of *Monthly Review*:[12] 'Present indications suggest that the leadership of world civilization, held by Western nations during the

[12] *Ibid.*, p. 262.

M*

last two or three centuries, is returning to the East—where indeed it
has generally resided during most of history.'

The American Trotskyist movement has been split into a number of
groups and sects ever since its inception in the late 'twenties. It would
serve no purpose here to enumerate the great many groups—often
consisting of a mere handful of people—who at one time or another
claimed to be the true representatives of pure Trotskyism in the
United States.

The two main groups, since shortly before World War II, were
the Socialist Workers' Party, led by James P. Cannon, and the
Workers' Party (later Independent Socialist League), led by Max
Shachtman. Cannon and Shachtman had been important figures in
the early history of American Communism and in 1928 became the
leaders of the Trotskyist movement. They parted company in the
'great debate' on the character of the Soviet Union in the late 'thirties
and early 'forties. Cannon, backed by Leon Trotsky, maintained that
Russia was still a 'degenerate workers state', a workers' state because
the means of production were socialized, but a workers' state which
had fallen into the clutches of a bureaucracy which had perverted its
ends and subverted its means. Nevertheless, argued Cannon and his
co-thinkers, following an analogy first advanced by Leon Trotsky,
it is a state that must be defended by the international working class
just as a trade union, even if it has for the time being a reformist or
even counter-revolutionary leadership, is still a working-class institution and must be defended against its enemies. This position led the
Cannon group in due course to a defence of the Russian cause during
the Finnish war and throughout the subsequent course of World
War II. Subsequently they came quite logically to include the Russian
satellites as well as China among the historically progressive though
degenerated workers' states—the only concession they made was to
call them deformed rather than degenerate, since it would have been
hard to explain what these states had degenerated *from*.

In more recent years there have been other splits in the orthodox
Trotskyist movement, each group accusing the other of petty-
bourgeois deformation and abandonment of the only true class line.
But here again it would be tedious to follow developments in detail,
although it is perhaps worthy of note that Cannon's Socialist Workers' Party—pushing the pro-Soviet yet anti-Stalin orientation of
Trotsky to conclusions which the latter might well have abhorred—
has in recent years collaborated in a number of ways with the
American Communist Party, even running common electoral tickets
with communist fellow-travellers in New York. At a May Day
meeting in that city representatives of the party which claims to
represent the spirit of Trotsky shared a platform with representatives
of the party of Trotsky's assassins.

The theoretical contributions of this official wing of American Trotskyism have been nil in the period under consideration. Bourbons of the left, they forgot nothing and learnt nothing. Stale polemics in imitation of the style of Trotsky and Lenin alternate with standard analyses of the evils of American imperialism and monopoly capitalism and tedious reelings off of the beads of the Marxist rosary. The group is almost entirely divorced from the realities of American labour politics and is kept alive mainly by a combination of intellectual inertia and the fanatical devotion of its several hundred true believers. Its leader, James P. Cannon, now lives in semi-retirement in Los Angeles.

The history of the Shachtman wing of the Trotskyist movement is of considerably more interest. After the split with Cannon the Schahtman group counted among its members a number of first-rate writers, among them Dwight Macdonald and James Burnham (James Farrell, the novelist, became a sympathizer for a few years somewhat later). Though many left the group shortly after its foundation, it still enjoyed the allegiance of a number of intellectually alert younger people who were willing to depart from the straight path of orthodoxy when the situation seemed to require it. Having once had the courage to stand up to the towering authority of Trotsky, the founding father, they never again completely lost the habit of independent thought. This is not to say that their theoretical contributions in the 'forties and 'fifties carried much weight.

During World War II, Shachtman's Workers' Party took its stand on traditional left-wing socialist anti-war lines. It opposed the war aims of Russia and the West, denied that the war had a progressive character, and stood for a Third Camp opposed equally to the two warring camps. Though its spokesmen found it somewhat difficult to specify concretely who was meant to be in the Third Camp, the phrase was taken to mean a defence of the interests of the working classes and colonial nations. As to Russia, the Workers' Party considered it a basically anti-socialist society, a 'bureaucratic collectivism' equally removed from capitalism and socialism, a new type of social formation which lacked all progressive features.

In the post-war years the Workers' Party gradually began to question the Leninist form of party organization, the 'vanguard theory', and a number of other basic tenets of orthodox Trotskyism. In particular it stressed the need for democracy both inside the party and in society at large.

As one follows the development of the Shachtman group one notices over the years the gradual muting of all the major elements of Trotskyism-Leninism in its programme and orientation while orthodoxy is often still verbally affirmed. Shachtman, writing on socialist policy in a hypothetical Third World War, rejected such slogans as 'revolutionary defeatism' or 'transform the imperialist war into a civil war', advocating instead that 'socialist policy must be based on the idea of transforming the imperialist war into a democratic war'.[13] A master in the art of correct quotations, he quoted enough from Lenin to make this departure from Leninist orthodoxy palatable to the faithful, but when he explained that such a policy would provide for radical democratization of social and political life though it would *not yet* be socialism, he had in fact travelled a long way from the Leninist orthodoxy of earlier days.

On the domestic scene the Workers' Party—later the Independent Socialist League—considered the drift of the American economy towards a permanent war economy the outstanding post-war development. (See the articles by T. N. Vance in the six 1951 issues of the *New International*.) 'The dominant characteristic of the Permanent War Economy,' wrote Vance, 'is that war output becomes a legitimate end purpose of economic activity.' The basic characteristics of the Permanent War Economy, according to Vance, are the permanence of the high level of war outlays, which have become a legitimate expression of growing state intervention in the economy, and the high rates of capital accumulation and of production accompanied by insignificant levels of unemployment.

According to this theory, it would seem that capitalism has acquired a new lease of life, that a permanent war economy is an effective counter-measure to the tendency towards breakdown of the capitalist economy so often predicted by Marxist economists. But Vance argued, not altogether convincingly, that it is not a 'normal' capitalist operation since it must lead, for example, to declining standards of living and irresistible inflation. Hence, 'the major battles of the class struggle will arise over the question of who shall pay for the increase in war outlays and which class shall bear the major burden of inflation'. The Permanent War Economy, Vance argued, far from offering hopes of solving mankind's problems, represented a 'further stage on the road to barbarism'.

While the Shachtman group successively shed a good number of the old assumptions, it was still unable to discard the old orientations. Its followers had rejected belief in the progressive or socialist character of the Soviet Union; they had been led to recognize that economic trends in the United States, given the growing intervention of the state, could no longer be fitted into the classic Marxist framework; but they still advocated a political programme not basically at variance with the old model. Above all, they were not able to rid themselves of the belief in the inherently revolutionary character of the modern proletariat.[14] The working class remained for them the very mainstay and centre of socialism, the class struggle a regulative

[13] *The New International*, July-August 1951, p. 205.
[14] Cf. Shachtman in *Labor Action*, November 30, 1953.

idea from which they were not willing to depart. Having rejected the notion of the vanguard role of a revolutionary socialist organization, emphasizing as they did the need for a multi-party democracy, they now saw their role in the future as mainly that of a ginger group within a larger Labour Party. In fact, appeals for a Labour Party occurred with monotonous regularity in the publications of the group over the years. But the Labour Party which they so ardently desired has failed to appear. They cast envious glances at England, they hankered after a political situation in which they would become part of a larger movement as the militant, socialist, 'class struggle' wing, but no such movement has materialized. In the 'fifties their publications more and more came to exhibit a curious combination of nostalgia for the 'thirties, vicarious participation in British labour politics, and pious hopes for an American Labour Party of the future.

While the group around the *Monthly Review*, disappointed in the potentialities for revolution of the American working class, turned towards identification with the East, the Independent Socialist League, still maintaining its faith in the creative possibilities of the working class, in practice abandoned its Leninist theories and moved towards a position which became ever more indistinguishable from that of many 'reformists'. A resolution adopted in 1951 stated:

'The ISL declares that the program that it, as the socialist wing of the labor movement, puts forward for adoption by the labor movement, is not the rounded program for the socialist reorganization of society, but yet it is a program consistent with the fight to preserve and extend democracy and to protect the working class and its interests from the reactionary consequences of the permanent war economy and the war itself.'[15]

A modest aim indeed for a group which until a few years earlier had maintained its theoretical allegiance to Trotskyism.

The major activities of the ISL in the 'fifties consisted in a vigorous and consistent fight against Stalinism and for civil liberties. On both these counts it performed indeed an excellent educational task, not only for its own members but for wider circles. Yet it has become quite clear in the last few years that to perform such functions it was hardly necessary to maintain an independent organization. In 1958 the ISL was dissolved and its remnants joined Norman Thomas's non-Marxist Socialist Party.

One of the perennial themes in the American Marxist movement has been the need for 'Americanization'. This may seem somewhat strange to the European reader—one can hardly imagine a parallel concern in the British socialist movement; but it becomes more

[15] *New International*, July-August 1951, p. 216.

understandable if one realizes that Marxism in America was to a considerable degree anchored in immigrant groups existing in, but hardly a part of, American society. Appeals to 'Americanization' are a frequent theme in the early history of American socialism, and they recurred even in the communist movement. Here they often took the form of a theory of 'American exceptionalism'. The so-called Lovestone faction within the CPUSA claimed in the late 'twenties that Comintern statements about the decadence of world capitalism did not apply to America, that 'American capitalism is still on the upward grade, still in the ascendancy', and that it was therefore not even possible to speak of the stabilization of capitalism in America.[16] Given the exceptional conditions of American capitalism, they argued, the 'breakdown thesis' of the Comintern could not be applied mechanically in America and had to be modified in the light of American conditions; this heresy led, of course, to speedy expulsion.

The desire to Americanize their appeals, to take into account the exceptional circumstances of the American political and social scene, continued to be a main theme of discussion among Marxists of the 'forties and 'fifties. It led, for example, to the splitting off of a wing of the Trotskyists in 1953. This wing, under the leadership of Bert Cochran, proceeded to put out a magazine, *The American Socialist*. Though it did not make any significant theoretical contributions, it did at least attempt to adopt a mode of presentation more in tune with the current American scene than the pseudo-Leninese characteristic of the orthodox Trotskyist press; but Cochran's effort failed like so many preceding ones. (His magazine has now suspended publication.)

A number of former members of the American Communist Party, for example the former foreign editor of the *Daily Worker*, Joseph Starobin,[17] have recently also urged the need to attune Marxist analysis to the realities of American life.

Perhaps a more interesting effort to rethink the relationship between Marxism and the American scene was made in 1958 by Earl Browder, the one-time secretary of the American Communist Party, who was expelled in 1945 for 'right-wing deviationism'. Browder published a little book, *Marx and America, A Study of the Doctrine of Impoverishment*.[18] It is chiefly concerned with a discussion of Marx's doctrine that capitalism, in its development, increases the impoverishment of the working class; that, although there might be temporary fluctuations, the working class in the long run would never achieve

[16] Cf. Irving Howe and Lewis Coser, *The American Communist Party*, 1958, p. 165.
[17] *Monthly Review*, September 1959.
[18] New York, 1958.

wages higher than the minimum that would just cover the cost of the labourer's existence and reproduction. Browder attempts to show that Marx was well aware that real wages in America were considerably higher than in England or on the continent, and contends that Marx tried to explain away this awkward fact by asserting that it was no more than a temporary phenomenon which would disappear when America had evolved a fully capitalist economic system. Browder then shows that Marx, in a report to the First International in 1865, abandoned his earlier subsistence-wage theory in favour of a quite different theory according to which the value of labour is not fixed but variable, and is powerfully influenced by concrete social conditions in particular countries and by traditional standards of life. This new theory, however, was not published till thirty years later; while it appears alongside the earlier subsistence theory in *Capital*, no attempt was made to harmonize the two, since Marx does not seem to have realized their incompatibility.

His Marxian exegesis serves Browder as a means to explain America's exceptional social circumstances. He contends that most socialist and all communist propaganda and activities in America have been based on the subsistence-wage theory and that the non-recognition of the special conditions of America, which allowed for higher wage rates and improved standards, condemned such propaganda to sterility. American labour could not accept a theory which so obviously contradicted the facts, and thus rejected all socialist and communist theories. This, of course, raises more questions than it answers. In particular, if one accepts Browder's contentions that, contrary to orthodox Marxian theory, highly developed capitalist countries have a higher wage level, it would seem more plausible and economical to conclude that the high development of American capitalism with its concomitant high level of wages was a key factor in the isolation of the American Marxist movements from the great majority of American workers. The point would then seem not that a specific theory was wrong, but that the very conditions of the American working class made it indifferent to anti-capitalist appeals. Be this as it may, Browder's book is one of the very rare instances of an attempt to reformulate the American experience within the framework of neo-Marxist theory.

This essay does not purport to give an account of all Marxist political groups in the United States. The interested reader will still be able to find in certain specialized bookstores and news-stands the publications of a variety of political sects which in one way or another lay claim to the Marxist heritage. There are still followers of de Leon, staunch defenders of the proposition that concern with immediate issues and concrete political problems distracts from the main task of socialists—which is simply to propagandize for Socialism. There are Western Socialists, various Trotskyist splinter groups, and a variety of miscellaneous True Believers. But none of them, at least as far as this writer is concerned, can be said to have made any significant contribution to Marxist thought.

On the other hand there are of course a number of unaffiliated American radicals who can no longer be said to be, if they ever were, Marxists. In particular, the members of the American Socialist Party around Norman Thomas—surely the only major political figure that American socialism had produced since Eugene Debs—are by no means Marxist. Their advocacy of a mixed economy and their un-dogmatic approach to problems of contemporary socialism, make them more akin to the pragmatic non-Marxism of the British Labour Party or to the German SPD than to the tradition of Marxism.

Similarly the group of socialists and radicals, among them the present writer, who established and still publish the magazine *Dissent*, can hardly be said to constitute a Marxist tendency, though a few among them may still care to call themselves by that name. *Dissent* stated in its first issue (Winter 1954) that 'The accent of *Dissent* will be radical. Its tradition will be the tradition of democratic socialism. We shall try to reassert the libertarian values of the socialist ideal, and at the same time, to discuss freely and honestly what in the socialist tradition remains alive and what needs to be discarded and modified.' The magazine has become a gathering ground for non-sectarian, undogmatic radicals in America. It is perhaps a measure of its success that it would not be appropriate to discuss it in an essay on Marxism in the United States.

Marxian modes of analysis, certain strands of Marxist doctrine and of Marxist method, have become an enduring component of American radicalism, as well as of American social science. But Marxism as a political party and as an orthodox doctrine is all but dead in the United States.

XXVI. Japan: Divisions in Socialism

EDWARD SEIDENSTICKER

Two rather obvious points must be made at the outset. One is that Japanese Socialism is changing. It is a highly unstable movement, ridden by factional and ideological differences, and what is true at the moment of writing may not be true at the moment of publication. At this moment, there are two parties that call themselves Socialist: the Socialist Party and the Democratic Socialist Party (Minshu Shakaito). The latter, which split off from the Socialist Party in October 1959, is small enough to be coherent. It has recently suffered a severe electoral setback, however, and its future is dark. The Socialist Party, on the other hand, came out of the elections buoyant and optimistic, but continues to work with a badly articulated programme adopted in 1955.

The second point is still more obvious: that the Japanese Socialist movement is Japanese. Cliques and personalities are probably not as important as in conservative politics, but they are still important. A dispute that is ostensibly ideological, therefore, can also be a matter of old loyalties, old friendships and enmities, pre-war battles that no longer have any meaning. The deepest ideological division today is on the question of whether the Socialist movement should be Marxist or not, but the factions bear a marked resemblance to those that emerged when a burning question was debated in the late 'thirties, whether or not the Socialists should support the Japanese war on the continent. The question that is most warmly debated today, on the other hand, went relatively unnoticed before the war, when almost the whole of the Socialist movement—insofar as it was a movement, a matter of parties and not of isolated scholars—was Marxist. The issues change, the factions remain. This is said not to suggest that issues are of no importance, but rather to give warning that they are not as all-important as they would be in a Western context. A number of people who accept the programme of the Democratic Socialist Party are reluctant to support the party itself because of the personality and past of its leader.

No more will be made of either point in this essay, which will attempt to describe Japanese Socialism as it is at the moment and has been in the recent past, and will be timid about predicting the future of that unstable movement; and, having cautioned the reader that cliques exist, it will have none of the dull business of deciding who belongs to which and why, and measuring the warmth of the hatreds and affections.

The Socialist Party, organized late in 1945, got by at first with a platform that was little more than a slogan: the party would be democratic in politics, socialist in economics, pacifist in international affairs. People did, it is true, ask from time to time what this meant, but there was little open fighting until 1949, when a disastrous Socialist-Conservative coalition government, a huge bribery scandal, and an electoral setback forced the party to consider what it was and what it was doing. Was it a class party (*kaikyu seito*) or was it a 'popular party' (*kokumin seito*)? Was it a Marxist party, leading the proletariat to revolution, or was it a parliamentary party, prepared to accept the rules of the game, to advance and withdraw as its popular following rose and fell? A precarious compromise was reached: the Socialist Party was 'a mass party of a class nature' (*kaikyu-teki taishu seito*).

This compromise that pleased no one lasted until October 1951, when the party split. The occasion for the split was the San Francisco Treaty and its companion, the Japanese-American Security Treaty, which were signed that autumn and ratified the following spring. The disagreement was but one manifestation of the deeper disagreement over the nature of the party. The Marxists who believed in a class party were more reluctant to accept close treaty ties with the land of rampant capitalism than were the non-Marxist supporters of the mass or popular party. Conversely, the former insisted on a peace treaty with the Soviet Union, and the latter were prepared to let it wait awhile.

In October 1955, the party was reunited. More than a year earlier, the left wing (each wing of the split party had called itself the Socialist Party of Japan) had drawn up a platform announcing that it was a class party, but adding that the class it represented was now strong enough to make a 'peaceful revolution'. In preparation for the 1955 unity talks, the right wing replied with a draft platform which insisted upon parliamentary government as a matter of principle and not, as the left had implied, a matter of tactics. A disagreement is implicit throughout the two platforms on the question of whether the revolutionary process can be reversed by peaceful transfer of power.

They were somehow spliced together, and the reunited Socialist Party was once more what it had become in 1949, a 'mass party of a class nature'. Once more, the formula pleased no one.

Late in 1958, the fight began again. Professor Sakisaka Itsuro[1] of Kyushu University, an ideological leader of the left who had vociferously opposed the 1955 compromise, wrote an inflammatory

[1] Throughout this paper the Japanese name order is followed, with the surname first.

article demanding that the party return to its Marxist origins. This, although Professor Sakisaka denied it, was a call for a new split. (He described it rather as a call for 'purification'.) Almost simultaneously, Mr Nishio Suehiro, who now leads the Democratic Socialist Party, and who also opposed the 1955 unification, was cleared of a bribery charge that had hung over him since the days of that disastrous coalition government. His acquittal meant the return to the Socialist Party of a most determined and effective believer in a mass or popular party. As in 1949, however, it was an electoral setback—indeed a series of them—that brought the real battle. Three successive elections in the late spring and early summer of 1959 demonstrated that the steady growth of the party since the reverses of a decade before had come to an abrupt end. It was time, once more, to consider what it was and what it was about.

Here is the controversial plank of the 1955 platform: 'The stipulations regarding the duties of our party make clear its nature and structure. From the standpoint of the attainment of a Socialist revolution by democratic and peaceful means, the Socialist Party of Japan must inevitably be a mass party of a class nature. In other words, our party is an amalgamation of all the working classes, organizing a majority of the population, that majority being centred upon the labouring class and including farmers, fishermen, owners of medium and small commercial and manufacturing enterprises, and intellectuals.'

That this playing with words failed to solve the basic conflict is apparent from the rest of the document. The general nature of the Socialist revolution is made clear to some extent: there will be nationalization of basic industries, but private ownership and freedom to choose an occupation will survive. From there on, however, an unrepaired split is evident. On the one hand it is stated that democratic processes in the Western sense of the term will be respected after the revolution—there will be secret elections and civil rights and the rest. On the other hand, these assurances are dropped into a Marxist setting far from friendly to them.

Thus we learn of the increasing impoverishment of the masses, the contradictions of monopoly capitalism, and the imperialistic adventures of Japanese monopoly capitalism, now the servant of American monopoly capitalism. We learn, at the end of the sequence, that 'world capitalism has already accomplished its historical mission. Now it must give way to the new Socialism, the result of a peaceful democratic revolution.' This note—the inevitable process of history and the 'historical mission' of the Socialist Party—is sounded more than once before we reach the end.

One feels that something has been left undone, something has gone unexplained. One comes upon a statement like this, for instance: 'Through proper acts of the Diet and the influence and organized strength of the democratic masses who support those acts, we shall take adequate measures against anyone who attempts by illegal means to obstruct or to impose limiting conditions upon the policies of our [Socialist] government.'

To a strong believer in Marxist theories of the historical process, this could become an invitation to one-party government. Anything that went against the natural laws of history would be an intolerable evil, 'illegal' to say the least; and, as in a People's Democracy, the 'organized strength of the democratic masses' could always be counted upon. The question can be stated rather simply: in spite of the assurances about civil rights and free elections, how can a conservative party which has been informed that its historical role is over hope to be allowed to come back once a 'peaceful revolution' has voted it out of power?

The point is not that there is no answer to the question, or that the contradiction is irreconcilable. It is rather that there is no attempt at an answer. On the one hand there is the 'class party' with its belief in the historical mission of the class, and on the other hand there is the 'mass party' with its regard for the rights of the masses, and each has its way. They were allowed to write alternate planks of the 1955 party platform, so to speak.

Late in 1958 an organization called the Society for the Strengthening of the Socialist Party made its appearance. Its members included important labour leaders and members of the Socialist left, and its ideological spokesman was Professor Sakisaka. In December his controversial article, 'A Correct Platform and a Correct Machinery', appeared in the monthly publication *Socialism*. There were moves afoot, he began, to reorganize the Socialist Party, but the root of the problem was not organization but 'spirit'. Spirit could make do with an inadequate organization, but no organization, however well planned, could do anything without spirit. In a word, the Socialist Party had lost sight of its mission as a revolutionary party. It had not been united in 1955 at all, but rather spliced together, and the time had come for it to purge itself of discordant elements.

There had been a period, he continued, when a 'united front' was necessary and proper. That front had not had as its immediate aim revolution, but rather the building of the conditions under which a true revolutionary party could proceed to make a revolution. The conditions were now ripe. At home, the Labour movement was strong, and abroad two things were happening: the anti-colonial movement was on the rise, and the 'Socialist nations' (by this was meant the Soviet bloc) of Europe and Asia were growing in strength. What was needed, therefore, was a revolutionary party, which the Socialist Party had not been since 1955.

'I argued then that the "unification" of the Left-wing and Right-wing Socialist Parties was a mistake, and I think now that it was a mistake. . . . At a time like this, unsuited for a party of the united front, the reunited Socialist Party has a structure which makes it resemble such a party, and this fact has made its purification into the party of the Socialist revolution difficult, though not impossible. . . . As was pointed out in the platform of the old Left-wing Socialist Party, the coming Socialist revolution in our country may be a peaceful revolution. We must not forget, however, that it will be a revolution. It will therefore be the climax of the class struggle. In other words, it will be the fight whereby the political forces guided by the working class will effect a complete seizure of power from the political forces presently in power, centred upon the monopolist bourgeoisie. A peaceful revolution does not mean revolution by consultation and accord. . . . It is impossible to think of the fight by which power will finally and completely be taken from the ruling classes without thinking of a resort to some sort of force.'

As if to follow up this denial of the idea that power could ever be returned to a 'bourgeois party', Sohyo, the largest of the Japanese labour federations and the principal organized support for the Socialist Party, issued a strongly worded statement on New Year's Day, 1959. It said in part: 'We are opposed to the theory of two large parties each making concessions to the other, and to the theory that the Socialist Party should be a popular, national party (*kokumin seito*). . . . The so-called theory of two large parties argues for the establishment of common ground with the conservatives by bringing the Socialist Party to the Right, and for the smooth transfer of power between the two. There is an extreme cleavage between the impoverished life of the labourers, farmers, small businessmen, and unemployed masses who are the base of the Socialist Party, however . . . and the capitalist class which is the base of the Liberal Democratic Party, and the two parties can therefore never find common ground.' In addition to this stand against the possibility of returning power to the bourgeoisie, the Sohyo statement contains expressions of disbelief in the notion of majority rule.

Meanwhile, in November 1958, Mr Nishio had been acquitted by the Tokyo Superior Court. When the Public Prosecutor's Office announced its intention not to appeal, he was free to return to politics. He lost no time. Beginning with the congratulatory dinner on the occasion of the acquittal, he pushed away at his idea of a popular party. That the heart of the Socialist Party should be the labouring class, he said, was but natural; but it could not hope to gain power without support from the middle classes. He also insisted upon the need to make the party's devotion to parliamentary government quite clear. It must state unequivocally that it would allow itself to be voted out of office. Finally, he was critical of the party's foreign policies, which he found too sanguine about Communist China and too critical of the United States.

One feels that the position of the Socialist Party in foreign affairs had in fact departed from the 1955 platform, which was a brave attempt at neutrality. It had more to say about American mis-behaviour than about Soviet misbehaviour, to be sure, but to Japan the United States was a more conspicuous target. The fact that the Soviet bloc could also on occasion be a threat to world peace was duly recognized. By 1958, however, the foreign-policy pronounce-ments of the Socialist Party were indistinguishable from those of the Communists. It favoured a kind of disarmed 'neutrality' wholly to the advantage of the Sino-Soviet bloc. It favoured an immediate and, if necessary, unilateral termination of treaty relations with the United States, on grounds which ultimately came down to a belief that the presence of American troops in the Far East was a threat to a peace-loving China and therefore to peace in general. It held, on the other hand, that the Formosa question was not a proper one for inter-national discussion at all, but rather a Chinese domestic affair.

If anything, matters became worse in 1959. In March, Mr Asanuma Inejiro, Secretary-General of the party, made a remarkable statement in the course of a visit to Peking: 'American imperialism is the common enemy of Japan and China.' In the 1959 elections, the Socialist Party was in the curious position of defending China against the Japanese government.

There are a number of explanations for the shift to the left in international affairs: the impossibility of making theoretical conces-sions to a restive Socialist Left, and therefore the need to make practical concessions; the difficulty of finding electoral issues, since conservatives in Japan, as in other places, have a way of taking over Socialist planks; and the influence of Sohyo, the big labour federa-tion.

Whatever the explanation, Mr Nishio objected, and in effect called for a return to the foreign policy of 1955. Though neutrality was still the goal, it must be truly neutral—it must weaken neither of the two sides. Whereas the party was in favour of denouncing the Security Treaty with the United States, therefore, Mr Nishio was in favour of continued but loosened treaty relations.

The Left in its turn objected to his objections. Though not men-tioned by name, he was singled out for special attack in the Sohyo New Year statement: 'Sohyo strongly supports the foreign policy of the Socialist Party, which does not recognize the existence of two Chinas and which, adhering firmly to neutrality, calls for annulling the Security Treaty. . . . Within the party at the moment, however, there are splinter groups which, in defiance of its policies, call China an aggressor and publicly criticize the fight to annul the treaty.'

In January 1959, the chairman of the party, Mr Suzuki Mosaburo, made a statement which pleased the Nishio faction and surprised and angered the Left—surprise because Mr Suzuki, who was chairman of the Left-wing party before the 1955 unification, might have been expected to give the Left at least his tacit support. Instead he said that he saw no reason for revising the 1955 platform, and that he was disturbed by the tendency of the Left to belittle parliamentary processes and to emphasize 'the struggle outside the Diet'.

The Left nonetheless refrained from challenging Mr Suzuki to open battle. He has a way of making statements that offer comfort to the Left even when he seems to be drawing nearer the Right. Thus in the same month of January he made a strange declaration on the impossibility of 'playing see-saw' with the ruling Liberal Democratic Party, a declaration which, though later softened, seemed to be consistent with the views of Sohyo and Professor Sakisaka on the impossibility of relinquishing power to the conservatives. It was easier and safer for the Left to go on attacking the unequivocal Mr Nishio than for it to open fire on the ambiguous Mr Suzuki.

Besides, elections were coming up, and the Socialists stood to gain nothing from open bickering. A semblance of unity was maintained through two sets of local elections in the spring and elections for the Upper House of the Diet in June. All three were disappointing to the Socialists, but the last had to be recognized as a defeat of the first order. It took place in circumstances unusually favourable to them: the prestige of the governing party had been shaken during the winter by a badly timed attempt to strengthen the police, and all of the unpredictable elements, the weather and the like, happened to favour the Socialist chances. Yet nothing came of the advantage. The Socialist percentage of the total vote fell sharply from the previous Diet elections, although as a projection of a ten-year trend it had been expected to rise; and the Socialists polled well over four million votes fewer than the Liberal Democrats in a total of less than twenty million.

The party leaders openly recognized the defeat, and the debate broke out again. Why had it happened, and what was to be done? Most of the July issue of *Socialist Party*, a monthly published by the party, was given over to a symposium on 'How to Break through the One-third Wall', the 'wall' in question being the electoral barrier that had stopped the Socialists at a bare third of the seats in the Diet. There were twenty-four participants, and, as anyone who had been following the affairs of the party could have predicted, their views on how to accomplish the break-through fell into two groups. On the one hand, the party need not fear being associated, in practice or in the minds of the electorate, with the Communists, but should rather fear losing its radical, revolutionary colour and coming to look like the Liberal Democrats; and, on the other hand, it was frightening

away the floating vote by failing to distinguish itself from the Communists, and must try to win that vote from the Liberal Democrats
by making it clear beyond a doubt that fears about its authoritarian
tendencies were groundless.

In the course of the summer, each of the numerous party factions
came out with its programme for 'rebuilding the party'. As one
moved from Left to Right, a willingness to work with the Communists gave way to open hostility towards them. Only the very far
Left challenged the official formula, 'a mass party of a class nature',
but one side felt that it should be more class than mass, the other
that it should be more mass than class. In an attempt at compromise,
the faction that had led the old Right-wing party suggested that each
of the other factions subscribe to certain principles guaranteeing the
continuation of democratic parliamentary government, and, having
done so, call the party what it liked.

The strangest statement came from the dominant Suzuki faction.
It made a distinction between government 'under a Socialist system'
and government 'under the Socialist Party'. Unless wholly meaningless, the distinction was enough to revive fears that the parliamentary
system itself would be radically transformed 'under a Socialist
system'.

In mid-September the party convention had a crucial debate between Left and Right. A draft statement of current policy, drawn up
the preceding month, had answered none of the deeper questions—
indeed one felt that it had then vehemently seized on the Security
Treaty as an excuse for avoiding those questions. It was aptly called
'a pretty exercise in rhetoric'. Nothing was done to allay misgivings
about the extent to which the Socialist Party meant to respect the
parliamentary system.

The September convention promptly became a crucial debate
between Left and Right. A recess was called in the hope that something might be arranged to prevent an open split. Late in October it
reconvened, but no solution had been found in the intervening weeks.

The specific issue was whether or not certain statements by Mr
Nishio violated party discipline, and, if so, how he should be
punished. He had publicly indicated doubts about the Socialist policy
of opposing treaty relations with the United States when it was not
entirely clear how Japan was to survive without such relations, and
he had written an article for the hated Defence Agency[2] in which he
said that the principal world conflict was not between socialism and
capitalism but between totalitarianism and democracy.

Mr Nishio denied any intention of violating party doctrine, and
was able to find persuasive support for his views in the party scrip-

---

[2] Equivalent to a ministry. The Socialist Party opposes rearmament and considers the Defence Agency unconstitutional.

tures. It had become apparent that the Left meant to press the issue, however, and the Nishio faction boycotted the post-recess convention. Eventually it was decided that he should be reprimanded rather than expelled, but by that time the decision had no meaning. The Nishio faction had already bolted the party. At first calling itself the Socialist Club, it proclaimed itself the Democratic Socialist Party in January 1960. There have been a number of defectors from the parent Socialist Party since the October break, including the only Socialist who has been Prime Minister of Japan. The strength of the new party is now nearly a third that of the old in the Lower House of the Diet and about a quarter in the Upper. It does not, however, include the whole of the old Right-wing party. The leaders of that party have chosen to remain with the Socialist Party.

The platform of the Democratic Socialist Party, made public in January 1960, shows the influence of the new European Socialism. The word 'revolution' is not once used, a most revolutionary departure for a Socialist party in Japan. The mass nature of the party is emphasized, and its aims are described generally as the attainment of social justice and equal distribution of wealth and the protection of the individual from the machine and the organization. Public ownership has been demoted to but one of the possible ways of achieving those ends. The most telling criticism of the new platform is that it fails to give the party an unmistakable character of its own, as different from the Liberal Democratic Party as it is from the old Socialist Party.

In foreign affairs, the new party agrees with the parent party that the ultimate goal should be neutrality, but cautious against any move —specifically, the immediate abrogation of the treaty with the United States—that would upset the balance between the two camps. It urges disarmament with complete inspection, but recognizes the right of the Japanese to arm in their own defence until an accord has been reached on disarmament. China is 'one country with two governments'. Unlike the Socialist Party, the Democratic Socialist Party recognizes that the Formosa question is of an international character.

At the beginning of 1960, then, the question was whether Japanese Socialism could be led away from Marxist theory and a pro-Communist foreign policy by the growth of a new party. It cannot be said that the year gave an absolutely final answer to the question. It was a year of very great misfortune for the Democratic Socialist Party, however, and at the end of the year the larger question takes us back to 1958: can the same goal be accomplished by non-Marxists working from within the Socialist Party? The reverses suffered by the newer party would seem to support the view of its ideological sympathizers who stayed in the Socialist Party: that this second method of working change is the only possible one.

The rioting of May and June put the Democratic Socialists in an extremely difficult position. In theory they could not support the Socialist and Communist demonstrators, for an attempt to influence parliamentary procedures by force could not be condoned; but in practice the Democratic Socialist Party could not support the efforts of the ruling party to maintain orderly parliamentary operations, for it was by no means sure of being able to control its own membership. An impression of deviousness and ambiguity was therefore left on the mind of the electorate, and in the elections later in the year the party failed to create an image of itself as a distinct and useful entity. Even friendly papers sometimes found it a trifle chimerical.

As for the Socialists, the assassination of Mr Asanuma, who had earlier in the year become chairman of the party, gave them a splendid opportunity to stop talking about 'American imperialism'. Clearly Mr Asanuma's strong views on the subject were an embarrassment to the rest of the party leaders, who could see no electoral profit in them, and who set about convincing the electorate that neutralism meant hostility towards no one, no more towards the United States than towards the Soviet Union. Insofar as foreign policy influenced the November elections, the attempt would seem to have been a success. The Democratic Socialist Party, with its go-slow policy on neutralism and its belief that neutralism at this moment is necessarily un-neutral, was reduced to the status of a minor faction. The Socialists gained twenty-three seats in the Diet, and the Democratic Socialists lost the same number. The country thus seemed back almost precisely where it was before the Socialist split and the riots, the assassination, and the attempted assassinations of 1960. None of these events had been enough to make the electorate, or at least nine-tenths of it, change the party loyalties that had been registered two years before, at the last elections for the House of Representatives.

The Democratic Socialists polled three and a half million votes, to be sure, about three times the Communist vote. Yet their operations in the Diet will be severely limited, and they will henceforth have trouble finding money. Therefore the major question about the future of Japanese Socialism is whether or not moderates in the Socialist Party, who saw no future in working from without, can accomplish anything by working from within. This paper began with a refusal to make predictions. It cannot conclude, however, without reviewing some of the possibilities.

First, what is likely to be the result of the Socialist victory over the Democratic Socialists? It has already been noted that the Socialists were careful during the recent campaign to avoid postures of hostility towards the United States. That the policies of the party make certain fundamental assumptions rather insulting to the United States and sanguine towards the Soviet Union is not to be denied, but the party was noticeably less truculent during the campaign than it has been at any time in recent years, and the Asanuma line was quietly buried.

Evidently it was thought good election policy to move somewhat closer to the Democratic Socialists and avoid giving an impression of harshness and inflexibility. It may be feared that with the Democratic Socialist Party out of the way, at least for the time being, the move to the left will begin again; and, on the other hand, it may be thought possible that the new tactics have been judged a success and the notion of a 'mass party' will in practice emerge victorious over the notion of a 'class party'. In spite of the 1959 setback, the 'renovationist forces' now have a record of generally steady growth for a decade, and, with the upward curve theoretically leading to an electoral victory one day, the Socialist Party may not wish to frighten away undecided voters. In other words, the more reason it has to think itself not necessarily a perpetual minority, the better are the chances that doctrinaire notions of a class party will be allowed to fall into disuse. It is perhaps significant that the pre-election convention of the party adopted a policy statement (to be distinguished from the platform or constitution of 1955) which Professor Sakisaka thought dangerously near the error of meliorism. Although the statement was obscurity itself and will require much clarification in the months to come, one may be heartened by the fact that to Professor Sakisaka it seemed inadequately revolutionary.

Unfortunately, however, the Socialist Party cannot change of its own volition. It is completely dependent on Sohyo, the giant labour federation, for funds, and well over half of the Socialists elected in November are from Sohyo. As Sohyo dominates the Socialist Party, so Marxism dominates Sohyo. Yet there are possibilities for change. Sohyo may change, or it may see fit to loosen its grip on the Socialist Party.

About a year ago Sohyo began to let fall hints that political unionism had come to an impasse and that there must henceforth be more emphasis on economic problems. In the autumn of 1960 it went down to complete defeat in the bitterly fought Miike coal strike. The defeat hits at the heart of the Sohyo organization, the Coal Miners' Union having been considered among its strongest members; and a peculiar blindness on the part of the union leadership to the facts of the declining coal industry and the wishes of the miners may be largely blamed for the disaster. So perhaps we can expect a bout of self-reflection. An interesting detail of the recent elections was the failure of the Socialists to elect their man from the Miike district. He lost his seat to a Democratic Socialist who had the support of the dissident miners. And so perhaps the self-reflection will extend to the possibility of allowing the Socialist Party a little more freedom to run its own affairs. One cannot expect the Socialist Party to make a formal disavowal of Marxism, but it may be that, in true Japanese fashion, the fact will gradually depart from the codified form.

N

XXVII. India: Intellectuals and Rural Problems

SIBNARAYAN RAY

Modern Indian politics is the expression of a paradox. Here is a vast sub-continent where for centuries the overwhelming majority of the people have lived in virtually self-contained villages, their social organization effectively restricting all mobility, whether horizontal or vertical. It is a country of many languages and cultures, communities and religious sects, each with its own long history and with little traffic from one to the other. But the strongest aspiration of the new Indian elite is for the accomplishment of national unity. This is reflected in the Constitution, the Five-Year Plans, various measures of educational reform since independence, in the impatient cry for a national language and the insistent plea for what everyone from Prime Minister Nehru to the youngest local neophyte calls 'the emotional integration of India'. The stronger the divisive back-pull of past history, the more ardent is the demand for solidarity and unification.

The most startling illustration of this paradox is to be found in the emergence of socialism as the predominant ideology of contemporary political India. In many countries of the West, even more than a century after the industrial revolution, support for socialism is limited to a minority. The Indian economy is essentially agricultural; and yet here almost all political parties and movements are imbued with socialist ideas. The accent is not only on economic equality and social justice, but also on the superiority of organized collective effort to individual initiative, of public to private ownership. The three major political parties in India today—the Congress, the Praja Socialist, and the Communist—swear by socialism. Most of the minor parties and groups, themselves but splinters of the big three, are even more outspoken in their socialist professions. The Sarvodaya Movement with its spectacular land-gift programme is also oriented in the same direction. In recent years even some of the communal parties and organizations have veered round towards socialist programmes, under pressure from younger members and with a view to wider public support. The only notable exception is the Swatantra party. But it is very young and its organizational cohesion and popular following have yet to be put to some real test.

Of course, socialism in India, even more than socialism in the West, means all kinds of things to all kinds of people. But before we try to distinguish between the main trends of socialist thought in contemporary India, it is worthwhile to consider briefly the process which brought socialism as an ideology to such prominence in this country. This, I hope, will illumine some of the peculiar traits of Indian socialism and the nature of its deepseated ambivalence. It will also provide part of the historical context of the paradox of Indian politics.

Hindu society has for many centuries been hierarchically organized, the position of every individual inexorably pre-determined. He is born into his caste, marries within its fold, and his funeral is conducted according to his caste rites. For a short while the impact of Islam prompted several egalitarian reform movements which, however, ended by producing a few new sects. Islam in India soon lost its moral dynamism and was swamped by the far more powerful Hindu metaphysic of *Karma*. Again, the excessive preoccupation of the Hindu philosophers with the other world and *Moksha* (i.e. union with the Absolute) made them indifferent not only to material prosperity but also to social justice. This led, on the one hand, to the stunted growth of the natural sciences and the scarcity of technological inventions, and, on the other, to resigned acceptance of exploitation, tyranny, and every form of inequity. Belief in predeterminism combined with a general disregard for their physical circumstances bred in the Hindu mind a strong reluctance to engage in any activity which implied struggle and conflict. Moreover, the organization of the community in a network of virtually self-sufficient villages prevented the State from acquiring supreme importance in public life. The conception of fundamental rights or popular sovereignty was alien to Hindu thought, and consequently the people were by and large apolitical in their outlook. The rise and fall of dynasties hardly affected the villages where tradition and the authority of the Elders held complete sway.

It is obvious that a society of this type can hardly be expected to offer a favourable climate for the reception of socialism, at least in the sense in which it is generally understood in the West. Socialism advocates equality and believes in the supremacy of the 'general good'; it relies on science and technology for rapid improvement in the general standard of living which it considers to be the main purpose of social organization; it stresses the need for discontent with the established order and for struggle against vested interests; and it fully recognizes the crucial role of political power in social dynamics. There is little in Indian tradition to respond sympathetically to these ideas.

In the nineteenth century, however, India experienced a profound revolution. The British not only conquered this subcontinent; they also brought it for the first time under a stable and effective central administration. The omnipresence of the new political authority was felt even in the sleepy villages, thanks to the expanding network of roads, railways, and the postal and telegraphic services. These opened undreamt-of possibilities of physical movement and communication. Meanwhile, western education was bringing into existence a new middle-class intelligentsia eager to know and control their environment. The traditional antinomy between the material and the spiritual came to be disputed; the western-educated Indian middle class began to recognize that to pursue a richer spiritual life higher material standards were required. Interest began to shift from metaphysics to science and technology, from the comforts of intuitive omniscience to the painstaking disciplines of factual inquiry. At the same time, these new intellectuals were inspired by the examples and teachings of their Western mentors to ponder human destiny in terms of self-expression instead of self-effacement. Instead of being a marionette in the hands of fate, man now came to be conceived as the shaper of his own life, as free agent and creator.

At first, these intellectuals were very few in number and their attitude was largely apolitical and individualistic. Profoundly stirred by the liberating thoughts and ideals to which they had been recently introduced, they were very anxious to remove the many restrictions imposed by their own society and tradition. However, as their number increased and their aspirations became bolder and more insistent, they began to make the painful discovery that the restrictions were only partially indigenous. Their new pursuits were hampered on all sides by the omnipresence of an alien authority. The foreign rulers would not countenance freedom of thought and expression the moment it appeared to threaten their monopoly of power. Nor would they allow native enterprise in commerce or industry. In flagrant violation of the values preached by the West, the logic of colonialism pointed to perpetuation of economic backwardness and spiritual emasculation of the conquered people.

This discovery touched off a second revolution in the minds of the Indian intellectuals. They now realized that national independence was essential for the fulfilment of both their material and cultural aspirations. The traditional indifference to politics gave way to an obsession with political power. From the later part of the nineteenth century we therefore see increasing emphasis on the crucial role of the State in social reorganization and greater involvement of Indian intellectuals in political movements. Struggle and conflict were unavoidable means to the attainment of power. But the new aspirants to power were a small minority without access to key positions. Consequently, they stood no chance in their struggle against the highly organized and equipped foreign government unless they were able to mobilize the common people in their support. Social solidarity was essential for the achievement of political power, which in its turn was indispensable to the pursuit of material improvement and cultural growth.

Thus by the end of the nineteenth century a good section of educated Indians had already inclined towards socialism. The need for mass-support gave to Indian nationalism from the very beginning a strong socialist coloration. Bankim Chatterji, the first and most outstanding exponent of nationalism in this country, was also the author of the earliest systematic exposition of socialist doctrines in any Indian language (*Samya*, 1879). He conceived of the nation as an organic whole and demanded complete dedication of the individual to the collective good. The next most militant ideologist of nationalism, Swami Vivekananda, was even more outspoken in his advocacy of populist and egalitarian ideas.

But there was long way to travel between the intellectual recognition of the importance of social solidarity and its realization in practice. The greatest obstacles were 'that old, monumentally encompassing and deeply entrenched legacy from past history', the caste-system, and the outlook on life which sustained it. The overwhelming majority of the people, living in the villages, were completely trapped by this legacy. The new outlook and aspirations were, after all, essentially urban in character. Thus the intellectuals were confronted with a cruel dilemma. To be accomplished, their aims required support from the general community. But the very outlook which had given rise to those aims and aspirations tended to isolate them from the community. By remaining true to their lately acquired values and insights they could hardly hope to mobilize the rural population in their struggle for power. Solidarity was essential; yet to achieve it, they would have to make substantial compromises with the very forces which had for centuries impeded development and progress. Since, during the last sixty years, little fundamental change has taken place in the essentially agricultural character of Indian society, the dilemma remains unresolved, and it is the main source of the ambivalence of contemporary Indian socialism.

However insuperable the difficulties might have appeared to be, the need for solidarity was nonetheless felt to be very urgent. The intellectuals, therefore, turned to various sources for ideological sustenance and support. On the one hand, they tried to press into their service such trends and texts in the past history of India as had stressed equality and brotherhood in contradistinction to Brahmi-nical hierarchy—from Buddhism to the socio-religious reform movements of the later middle ages. Their novel aspirations would thus be provided with the halo of tradition, thereby making them appear less unfamiliar to the conservative rural community. The strategic wisdom of this approach has since then been more than amply demonstrated by the popular triumphs of Gandhi and Vinoba Bhave. But it had also certain very serious shortcomings. The Indian exponents of egalitarianism had been invariably opposed to material prosperity and conflict, and the movements they led had been altogether apolitical. The tradition they had to offer was, therefore, only in partial consonance with the aims and requirements of the urban intelligentsia. In fact, much of it was contrary to their way of thinking. Some, therefore, rejected it outright; others, recognizing its popular appeal, tried to maintain the traditionalist façade while pursuing under its cover their essentially heterodox programme. (This kind of double-think is today most startlingly illustrated by the Congress party with its ambitious five-year plans going hand in hand with the much advertised Buddha jayanti celebrations.)

The quest of the intellectuals for ideological moorings was, however, not limited to indigenous sources. Thanks to their English education, it was relatively easy for them to pick and choose from their Western mentors. During the later part of the nineteenth century and the early decades of the twentieth, we notice a growing interest among educated Indians in the social ideas of Rousseau, Comte, and Mazzini, of Ruskin, Tolstoy, and Kropotkin. They were studied in small groups, discussed in periodicals, and even translated into Indian languages. From the 'twenties of this century, however, two distinct streams of socialist thought began to pour in from the West, one emanating from the Fabians and the other from the Comintern. M. N. Roy, through the books, pamphlets, and periodicals sent by him clandestinely from Europe, introduced a section of discontented Indian intellectuals to the theory and practice of communism. Other Indians who went for advanced studies to various English Universities came back, many of them, as ardent admirers of British socialism. During the last few decades there has been a marked increase in the number of communists among educated Indians. It is, nevertheless, true that a sizeable section of Indian intellectuals is inclined towards a peaceful and constitutional variety of socialism, thanks partly to their respect for the indigenous tradition, but scarcely less to the influence of people like Bernard Shaw, Sidney and Beatrice Webb, R. H. Tawney, Harold Laski, G. D. H. Cole, and Lord Beveridge.

Socialism has thus infiltrated the minds of educated Indians, and to some extent it has helped to weaken the stranglehold of caste of the sects, and of parochialism in this country. But it has not yet succeeded in tackling the basic dilemma of contemporary India. India is now politically independent, but the problems of poverty, inequality, and social immobility continue to be as baffling as ever. To meet them effectively it is essential to mobilize public support behind a programme of radical reconstruction, but this implies acceptance of a philosophy of life which strikes at the root of the beliefs and institutions of an essentially rural society, and which, therefore, involves the danger of alienating the majority of the people who continue to live in the villages. This issue is central to every school of socialist thought in this country.

It should be clear then that socialism in India, in spite of its various trends, possesses certain common differential qualities. It has a strong nationalist orientation, both because of its long and close association with the struggle for independence, and because of its recognition of the supreme importance of national unity for socialist reconstruction. In the West, too, the socialist movement has suffered repeated disruption from chauvinistic sentiments and loyalties, but these are incomparably stronger in India, thanks to the bitter memory of colonial rule. Even the Communist Party, despite more than thirty years of organizational subservience to Moscow, finds it risky to flout these sentiments among its rank-and-file workers. Again, Indian socialism is extremely wary of criticizing popular beliefs and traditions. As a matter of fact, except for a very small group of radicals trained by M. N. Roy after his break with the Comintern, few socialists in India have expressed themselves in unambiguous terms against the rural conservatism of Hindu society and culture. Thirdly, the cadre of the socialist movement in the country is almost entirely drawn from the educated middle class. Lack of social mobility and educational opportunities has prevented the workers and the peasants from throwing up a leadership from within their own ranks.

But the most marked feature distinguishing Indian socialism from that of the highly industrialized West is that here it cannot present itself as the ideology of the urban proletariat. The industrial working class is numerically far too insignificant, and the Indian bourgeoisie has little capital and less enterprise. But if socialism has to promise not merely the levelling down of the rich few but also the levelling up of the poor many, then it must work out some feasible programme which would combine economic growth with equitable distribution. In India, however, a considerable part of the necessary savings and investment for economic growth has to come from the countryside. Fundamental changes in the economy and social organization of the village are therefore called for. What these changes are going to be and how they are to be brought about are, of course, controversial issues. But socialists of every persuasion in India are agreed that an agrarian revolution is the most urgent task of socialism in this country.

Recent developments in Indian socialism become meaningful in the above context. Four main trends are discernible, but they are not completely exclusive at one another. And all are haunted more or less by the common dilemma.

The first, which stems directly from Gandhi and has during the last fifteen years found powerful expression in the *Bhoodan* or land-gift movement of Vinoba Bhave and the writings of Jayaprakash Narayan, appears from the Indian point of view to be highly indigenous and suited to the temper of the rural population. Those who are acquainted with the chequered course of Western socialism would possibly find in this movement many anarchist echoes, but it is the anarchism not so much of Bakunin and Kropotkin as of Leo Tolstoy. Gandhi was not only opposed to the State but indifferent to material progress as well as to any change brought about by conflict or violence. He advocated *aparigraha* or the spirit of non-possession, and the elimination of vested interests and other forms of inequity through non-violence and *satyagraha*. Wealth, in his view, was not to be possessed but held in trust and used for the welfare of the entire community. Vinoba and Jayaprakash are trying to work out the fuller implications of these ideas, both in theory and in practice. The bhoodan movement was originally conceived as a counterblast to the appeal of militant communism to landless labourers. Vinoba set out to satisfy their land-hunger by persuading rich landowners to make voluntary gifts of their surplus lands, which were then to be redistributed to the needy. His targets are still very far from fulfilment, but the success of his appeal, at least in the first phase (about 2.4 million acres collected as free gifts in thirty months) was nothing short of miraculous. This encouraged him to call for other forms of gifts—*sampattidan*, *buddhidan*, *shramdan*, *gramdan*, and finally *jivandan* (i.e. gift of one's entire life)—and on their basis, to try to reconstruct villages in the pattern of an ideal family.

According to Vinoba, a good society should be *sasana-mukta* or free of government. There would be no political parties or elections. There would be only *gram-raj* or self-administering village communities where issues will be decided *unanimously* by a body of *sevaks* (or servants) who are themselves *unanimously* nominated (not elected) by the entire population of the village. Vinoba would not allow any majority—minority differences; until unanimity is achieved there would be no decision. All property will be held in common; the interest of the individual will be completely identified with the interest of the community. Voluntary limitation of wants would make it possible for the village to be economically self-sufficient. Money would be abolished and with it the entire paraphernalia of market economy. Production and distribution would be planned by the community with a view to meeting all the basic requirements of every one of its members. (Readers who know Hindi are referred to: *Sarvodaya Ki Adhar*; *Lok-niti*; *Sasan-mukta Samaj ki Aur*, etc.)

Vinoba's ideas are primarily addressed to the rural people; they are not widely known to, nor have they made any significant impact upon the urban educated. They have been propagated mostly through the spoken word; they are often couched in myths and parables; they sound somewhat naïvely oracular. His colleague, Jayaprakash, coming from an entirely different background, has been trying in recent years to present them in a more abstract, precise, coherent, and cautious manner, so that they may win the support of all those intellectuals who are already disillusioned with communism. Starting as an orthodox Marxist in the 'twenties, he had founded the Congress Socialist Party in 1934, and was its leader and principal spokesman for over a decade and a half. In the 'fifties, however, his views underwent profound transformation. He abandoned Marxism and went over completely to the *Sarvodaya* ideals of Gandhi and Vinoba. Basically his ideas are the same as Vinoba's, but there are important points of difference in their styles of thinking. Narayan's formulations are admittedly tentative; he has little of Vinoba's dogmatic assurance; he is anxious to learn from his critics; and, what is most important, he is at least aware of the serious problems which confront sarvodaya. He, too, is opposed to materialism and modern industrialism; he, too, advocates 'voluntary limitation of wants' and revitalization of village communities; he also desires the withering away of political parties and of the bureaucratic state. He is a thoroughgoing decentralist who believes that 'the local institution of people's self-government must rise from below and be susceptible not only to the thoughts, desires, and needs of the people, but also to their direct control'. But he also recognizes some of the dangers and difficulties of this approach, and is, therefore, anxious to provide such safeguards as would prevent the villages from degenerating into little tyrannies or stagnant communities. (For Jayaprakash's ideas, see his *Socialism to Sarvodaya*; *A Plea for Reconstruction of Indian Polity*; and the recent pamphlet, *Swaraj for the people*.)

In spite of Jayaprakash's efforts, however, the Sarvodaya version of socialism has not made much headway among the educated people in the cities. There are three main objections. In a poor country like India with its enormous and rapidly growing population, sarvodaya economy would only help to perpetuate the submarginal standard of living. The equality which it promises would at best mean equality in privation. Secondly, Jayaprakash's accent on 'the principle of an organically self-determining communal life' would lead to the submergence of the individual in the collectivity. Thirdly, it would break up the country into innumerable small units and thus destroy that unity and mobility, howsoever meagre and precarious, that had been achieved under foreign rule and in the course of the long and arduous struggle for independence. Besides, there is the usual, but not necessarily illegitimate, argument that the scheme is altogether impracticable in the context of our times.

The second main school of socialist thought stands in direct opposition to sarvodaya. It is, however, not necessary to discuss the communist approach in detail since it is essentially the same all over the world. Nevertheless, there are certain peculiarities of Indian communism which should not pass unnoticed. Although subservient to Moscow, the Indian Communist Party, except for a few years during the later part of the Second World War, has generally tried to maintain a nationalist camouflage. At the moment it is faced with a serious crisis, due to the Chinese aggression on Indian territory. But this crisis has also revealed that the majority of its leaders as well as the rank and file are unwilling to give up their nationalist professions. Secondly, Indian communism, in spite of its programme of rapid industrialization, has preferred from tactical considerations to soft-pedal its attack on tradition and religious faith. In this respect it has been very different from European communism; it has often deliberately watered down its materialistic philosophy to avoid openly alienating the general community. Thirdly, Indian communists have found it more realistic and advantageous to think of the socialist movement in India in terms of a multi-class leadership instead of the more orthodox conception of the dictatorship of the proletariat. In fact, every time it has been forced to the more orthodox line by the dictates from Moscow, the consequences have been disastrous for the party. Fourthly, and possibly most significant of all, in recent years the party has officially declared itself in favour of the constitutional method of coming to power through elections. The reasons are, of course, strategic; but the relative success of this approach (illustrated for the first time in the formation of a Communist Cabinet in one of the states of the Indian Union) may eventually lead to some fundamental revision in the ideology of Indian communism.

In its economic programme, the CPI advocates nationalization of all key industries, and phased elimination of every form of private ownership. In respect of agriculture, although its ultimate aim is complete collectivization, as an immediate step it presses for abolition of absentee landlordism without compensation, and redistribution of lands with fixed ceilings and direct tenancy under the state. It demands mobilization of all idle savings, if necessary through confiscation, and rapid industrialization on state initiative.

The appeal of communism in India is limited primarily to the educated lower middle class, which constitutes the most dissatisfied and voluble section of the population. It has also some following among the organized workers and landless peasants. Its main appeal lies in its promise of rapid economic development, but at the same time its greatest handicap is its failure to provide itself with strong indigenous moorings. To what extent it will be able to expand its influence in the coming years depends very much on the success or failure of its principal rival in India today—the third main stream of socialism represented jointly by the Indian National Congress and the Praja Socialist Party.

These two parties, although apparently ranged against one another, in reality have very little in their ideology and programme which they do not share in common. They both pay lip-service to Ghandism and are anxious to give to their ideas a distinctly national outlook. But they both recognize the vital importance of modern technology and of assistance from the more advanced industrial countries of the West in promoting the economic development of India. The 'socialist pattern of society' to which the Congress has been officially committed since 1955 is in no essential respect different from the programme of the PSP. Both subscribe to the political philosophy of democratic socialism, and although they do not usually admit it, their approach to social reconstruction has been deeply influenced by the writings of the British neo-Fabians. Unlike the Sarvodaya school, they appreciate that government is not only indispensable to civilized society, but can also be the principal instrument for reducing social inequality and for achieving better standards of living. They are not, however, altogether unaware of the dangers of statism; in fact, their common aim is to reconcile planning on a national scale with devolution of authority. In contradistinction to the communists, they are both unambiguously opposed to totalitarianism and dictatorship. Both believe that social equality can be reconciled with individual freedom and better living conditions for all, and that these objectives can be best realized by a democratic state.

The Congress, however, does not possess any outstanding theories to provide it with a systematic social philosophy. In recent years a small group (called Socialist Forum) under Nehru's inspiration has been trying to explore the basic assumptions of the political and economic programme of the party, but it has not yet produced anything of significance. For an understanding of the Congress approach to socialism, one has, therefore, to rely primarily on the speeches of the Indian Prime Minister. However, a more concrete and pragmatic formulation of these ideas is to be found in the *Outlines* of the three Five-Year Plans. The following excerpts from the statement of objectives in the *Draft Outline of the Third Five-Year Plan* clearly express the Congress conception of socialism. '. . . the objective of planned development is not only to increase production and attain higher levels of living, but also to secure a social and economic order based on the values of freedom and democracy in which justice, social, economic, and political, shall inform all the institutions of the national life. . . . In reconstructing social and economic institutions, a large responsibility rests with the State on behalf of the entire community. The State has to plan its own investments and to influence and regulate economic activity within the private sector so as to ensure the co-ordinated development of all the available resources. . . . A socialist pattern of society has to be based on increased production through the use of modern science and technology and on equitable distribution of income and wealth. . . . The socialist pattern places special emphasis on the needs of the small producers and envisages a rapidly growing co-operative sector, in particular in respect of agriculture, medium and small scale industry, trade and distribution, and many fields of social services. . . . In the short run, there may sometimes be a conflict between the economic and social objectives of developmental planning. The claims of economic and social equality and those of increased employment may have to be reconciled with the requirements of production. Experience of the working of the first two plans suggests that on the whole the most satisfactory results are likely to be achieved by a balanced advance in all directions. . . .'

The approach indicated above is also shared by the PSP. In fact, the most elaborate exposition of this conception of socialism is offered not by the leaders of the Congress but by the few theoreticians of the PSP, in particular by Asoka Mehta. In various books and pamphlets like *Politics of Planned Economy*, *Socialism and Peasantry*, *Studies in Asian Socialism*, etc., Mehta has tried to explore the significance of democratic socialism in the peculiar Indian context. His arguments are often laboured, and sometimes vague and inconclusive, but his theory of 'the compulsions of a backward economy' clearly suggests that 'the areas of agreement' between the Congress and the PSP are much wider than the areas of disagreement. The only difference would seem to be that the Congress, being in power, has to be more cautious and compromising in its handling of both vested interests and public opinion, whereas the PSP, being in opposition, can press for greater speed and consistency between profession and practice.

At the moment this third school of socialism seems to enjoy the largest following in India. But this is rather deceptive, because within the Congress many accept this conception of socialism not from any genuine appreciation of its merits but from blind faith in Nehru, and because in the ranks of the PSP, the insidious spell of neither Vinoba nor Marx is altogether broken. More serious still, both these parties suffer from a lamentable paucity of thinkers, writers, and exponents, who can completely develop, express, or spread their ideas. The Congress relies heavily on its past prestige and present power; but the former is already worn thin, and the latter is not as secure as the Congress leaders complacently assume it to be. The PSP is very much a divided house, and its influence on the younger generation seems to be on the wane.

The fourth school of socialism may yet have something to contribute to the revitalization of the Congress and the PSP. This school, which draws its inspiration mainly from the later writings of M. N. Roy (after his disillusionment with Marxism), is not organized as a political party but works primarily as an intellectual and educational movement. The Radical Humanists are numerically a small group, but many of their ideas have already found their way into the thinking of the leaders of other political parties and social movements. Historically, the Radicals were among the first in this country to adumbrate the theory of grass-roots democracy, and to explain how this would require not rejection but reorientation of modern technology to suit the needs of a highly diversified system of small and medium-sized industries in the countryside. Both the Congress and the PSP leaders have been influenced by their ideas, and even Jayaprakash has publicly acknowledged his indebtedness to the later writings of M. N. Roy. But the Radicals would have no truck with the Tolstoyan ethic of Sarvodaya. They maintain that the aim of a good society is to help to release and unfold the many creative potentialities of all its individual members, and that this requires abundance, increasing ranges of choice, greater social and physical mobility, and more respect for individual differences. They recognize the constructive role of the State, but give far more importance than either the Congress or the PSP to the growth of the co-operative sector in the national economy and to devolution of powers and functions to local and professional bodies.

But the most significant respect in which the Radicals differ from all the other schools of socialism in India is in the priority they give to what they call the 'cultural renaissance' of the Indian people. The urgent need, they admit, is the modernization of Indian agriculture, but this cannot be accomplished while the people in the villages continue to be dominated by tradition. They have to be educated in scientific outlook and libertarian values, to develop intellectual curiosity and strong aspirations for a richer and fuller life, to have faith in their power to reshape their lives, and to take full responsibility for their own action. Neither an effective grass-roots democracy nor an expanding co-operative economy can grow without the dissemination of a scientific humanist outlook among the people. Education on these lines, however difficult in the beginning, is the main task of socialist intellectuals in India. (For details, see M. N. Roy, *New Orientation, New Humanism*, and *Parties, Politics and Power*.)

Radicals have taken upon themselves this rather thankless task; it is not surprising that their movement is restricted to small groups of intellectuals, mainly in the cities and university towns of India. What influence they have had so far is certainly not due to numbers or to organizational cohesion; it comes from the relative clarity and cogency of their ideas, and the intellectual integrity and competence of some of the spokesmen of this movement. However, they are no more immune than the other groups to the dilemma of the Indian situation, although they do not seem to share their ambivalence. There is real danger that this movement may disintegrate because of its failure to expand in an alien milieu. On the other hand, there is also the brighter possibility that the Radicals may help to strengthen both the Congress and the PSP with ideas and exponents, and thus not only revitalize those organizations but also make their socialism more oriented towards the scientific humanist outlook.

These then are the main trends of socialism in contemporary India. Socialism here is clearly not a working-class movement. It had its origin in the need of the urban middle-class intellectuals for solidarity with the rural agricultural population. That search for solidarity still continues.

INDEX OF NAMES

SUBJECT INDEX

CONTRIBUTORS

RENÉ AHLBERG, whose book on Deborin and Soviet philosophy was published in 1960, teaches at the Free University, Berlin.

G. L. ARNOLD is a former editor of *Twentieth Century* and the author of *Pattern of World Conflict* (Allen & Unwin).

SAMUEL BARON, Professor of Modern History at Grinnel College, Iowa, is working on a book on the life and thought of Plekhanov.

DANIEL BELL is Professor of Sociology at Columbia University, and the author of *The End of Ideology* (Free Press, Glencoe, Ill.).

FRANCIS L. CARSTEN, Masaryk Professor of Central European History at London University, is the author of *The Origins of Prussia* and *Princes and Parliaments in Germany*.

LEWIS COSER is Professor of Sociology at Brandeis University and joint editor of *Dissent*; author of *The Functions of Social Conflict* (1956) and joint author of *The American Communist Party* (1958), and *Sociological Theory*.

MELVIN CROAN, of the Department of Government at Harvard University, is preparing a study of the SED regime and East German Society.

JEAN DUVIGNAUD, formerly one of the editors of *Arguments*, formerly Professor of Philosophy at the University of Paris, is now Director of Centre d'Etudes des Sciences Sociales at the University of Tunis.

IRING FETSCHER, of the University of Tübingen, is the Editor of *Marxismus-Studien*.

GIORGIO GALLI, who studied Jurisprudence, is the author of *Storia del Partito Communista Italiana* (1958) and *La Sinistra Italiana nel Dopoguerra*. Contributor to *Critica Sociale*, *Il Mulino*, and *Il Ponte*.

CHRISTIAN GNEUSS, who studied history and the history of art, works for the North German Radio and has contributed to *Marxismus-Studien*.

WILLIAM E. GRIFFITH, a lecturer in Political Science and a Research Associate of the Centre for International Studies of the Massachusetts Institute of Technology, is engaged on a book on Eastern Europe, 1953–56.

SIDNEY HEITMAN, Assistant Professor at Colorado State University, is the author of an annotated bibliography of N. I. Bukharin and his forthcoming biography.

ROBERT C. NORTH, Professor of History at Stanford University, is the author of *Moscow and Chinese Communism* and joint author of *The Soviet Union and the East 1920–27.*

SIBNARAYAN RAY, Head of the Department of English, SIES College, Bombay, is the author of several works in English and Bengali, among them *Radicalism, In Man's own Image* (jointly with Mrs Ellen Roy), *Explorations.*

KARL REYMAN, who was a journalist in East Europe before 1948, has written articles on Soviet and East European developments for various American and Asian publications.

JÜRGEN RÜHLE is the author of *Das Gefesselte Theatre* (1957) and *Literatur und Revolution* (1960).

HEINZ SCHURER is the chief librarian of the School of Slavonic Studies in the University of London.

EDWARD SEIDENSTICKER is an American writer who has spent many years in Japan and written several studies of Japanese life and letters. He has translated a number of books from the Japanese.

ALFRED SHERMAN, at one time special *Observer* correspondent in Belgrade, is the author of several studies on the Middle East, Israel, and Eastern Europe.

HERMAN SINGER, formerly editor of the *Socialist Call*, has contributed to a number of American periodicals, including the *New Republic* and *Dissent.*

S. V. UTECHIN, Senior Research Officer in Soviet Studies at the London School of Economics and Political Science, is the editor of *Everyman's Encyclopedia on Russia.*

MORRIS WATNICK, formerly at the Russian Research Centre of Harvard University, is now teaching at the Department of Political Science, Brandeis University. He is the author of several studies on the intelligentsia in the under-developed countries, on the problem of class-consciousness, and has recently translated R. Hilferding's *Das Finanzkapital.*

ALFRED ZAUBERMAN works at the London School of Economics and Political Science on the Eastern and Central European economies. He is the author of *Economic Imperialism, Industrial Development in Czechoslovakia, East Germany, Poland, 1937–56,* and *The Soviet Debate on the Law of Value and Price* (in *Value and Plan* edited by G. Grossman).

Z. A. B. ZEMAN, formerly Research Fellow of St Antony's College, Oxford, and a member of the staff of *The Economist,* London. He is the editor of *Germany and Revolution in Russia, 1915–18* (Oxford University Press, 1958), and author of *The Break-up of the Habsburg Empire, 1914–18: A Study in National and Social Revolution* (Oxford University Press, 1961). Presently working on a biography of Parvus.